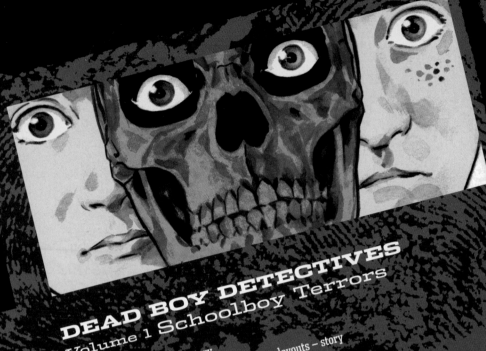

DEAD BOY DETECTIVES
Volume 1 Schoolboy Terrors

Toby Litt Writer – story

Mark Buckingham Penciller – layouts – story

Gary Erskine Andrew Pepoy Inkers

Russ Braun Victor Santos Finishers

Lee Loughridge Colorist

Todd Klein Letterer

Mark Buckingham (with thanks to D'Israeli) Cover Artist

Dead Boy Detectives
created by Neil Gaiman

Shelly Bond Executive Editor – Vertigo and Editor – Original Series
Gregory Lockard Associate Editor – Original Series
Sara Miller Assistant Editor – Original Series
Peter Hamboussi Editor
Robbin Brosterman Design Director – Books
Louis Prandi Publication Design
Hank Kanalz Senior VP – Vertigo & Integrated Publishing
Diane Nelson President
Dan DiDio and Jim Lee Co-Publishers
Geoff Johns Chief Creative Officer
Amit Desai Senior VP – Marketing & Franchise Management
Amy Genkins Senior VP – Business & Legal Affairs
Nairi Gardiner Senior VP – Finance

Jeff Boison VP – Publishing Planning
Mark Chiarello VP – Art Direction & Design
John Cunningham VP – Marketing
Terri Cunningham VP – Editorial Administration
Larry Ganem VP – Talent Relations & Services
Alison Gill Senior VP – Manufacturing & Operations
Jay Kogan VP – Business & Legal Affairs, Publishing
Jack Mahan VP – Business Affairs, Talent
Nick Napolitano VP – Manufacturing Administration
Sue Pohja VP – Book Sales
Fred Ruiz VP – Manufacturing Operations
Courtney Simmons Senior VP – Publicity
Bob Wayne Senior VP – Sales

DEAD BOY DETECTIVES
VOLUME 1: SCHOOL BOY TERRORS
Published by DC Comics. Copyright © 2014
DC Comics. All Rights Reserved.

Originally published in single magazine form in DEAD BOY DETECTIVES 1-6, TIME WARP 1, THE
WITCHING HOUR 1 and GHOSTS 1 © 2013, 2014 DC Comics. All Rights Reserved. All characters, their
distinctive likenesses and related elements featured in this publication are trademarks of DC Comics.
Vertigo is a trademark of DC Comics. The stories, characters and incidents featured in this publication
are entirely fictional. DC Comics does not read or accept unsolicited ideas, stories or artwork.
DC Comics, 1700 Broadway, New York, NY 10019
A Warner Bros. Entertainment Company.
Printed in the USA. First Printing.
ISBN: 978-1-4012-4889-5

Library of Congress Cataloging-in-Publication Data is Available.

SUSTAINABLE
FORESTRY
INITIATIVE

Certified Chain of Custody
20% Certified Forest Content,
80% Certified Sourcing
www.sfiprogram.org
SFI-01042
APPLIES TO TEXT STOCK ONLY

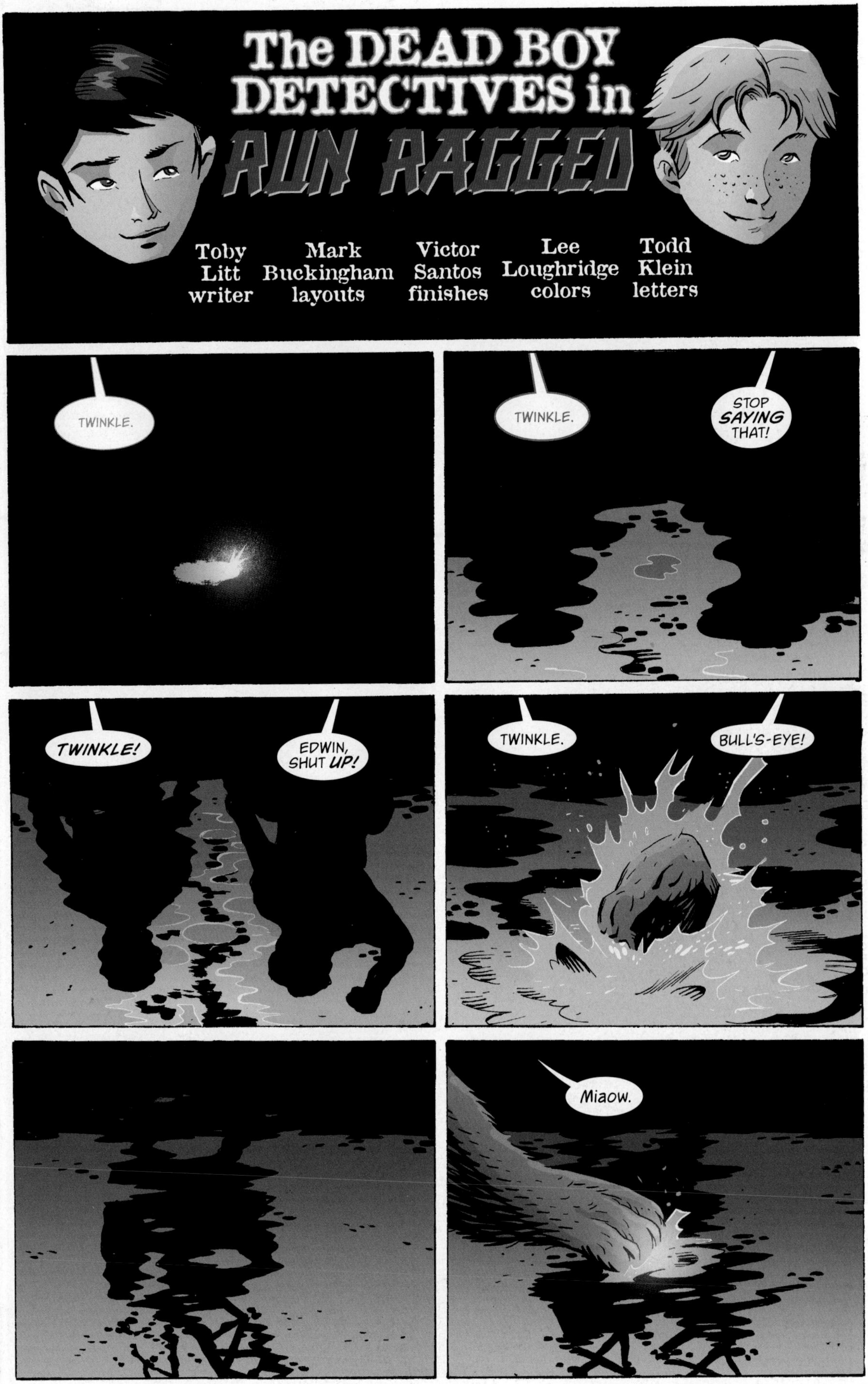
The DEAD BOY DETECTIVES in
RUN RAGGED
Toby Litt writer
Mark Buckingham layouts
Victor Santos finishes
Lee Loughridge colors
Todd Klein letters
TWINKLE.
TWINKLE.
STOP SAYING THAT!
TWINKLE!
EDWIN, SHUT UP!
TWINKLE.
BULL'S-EYE!
Miaow.

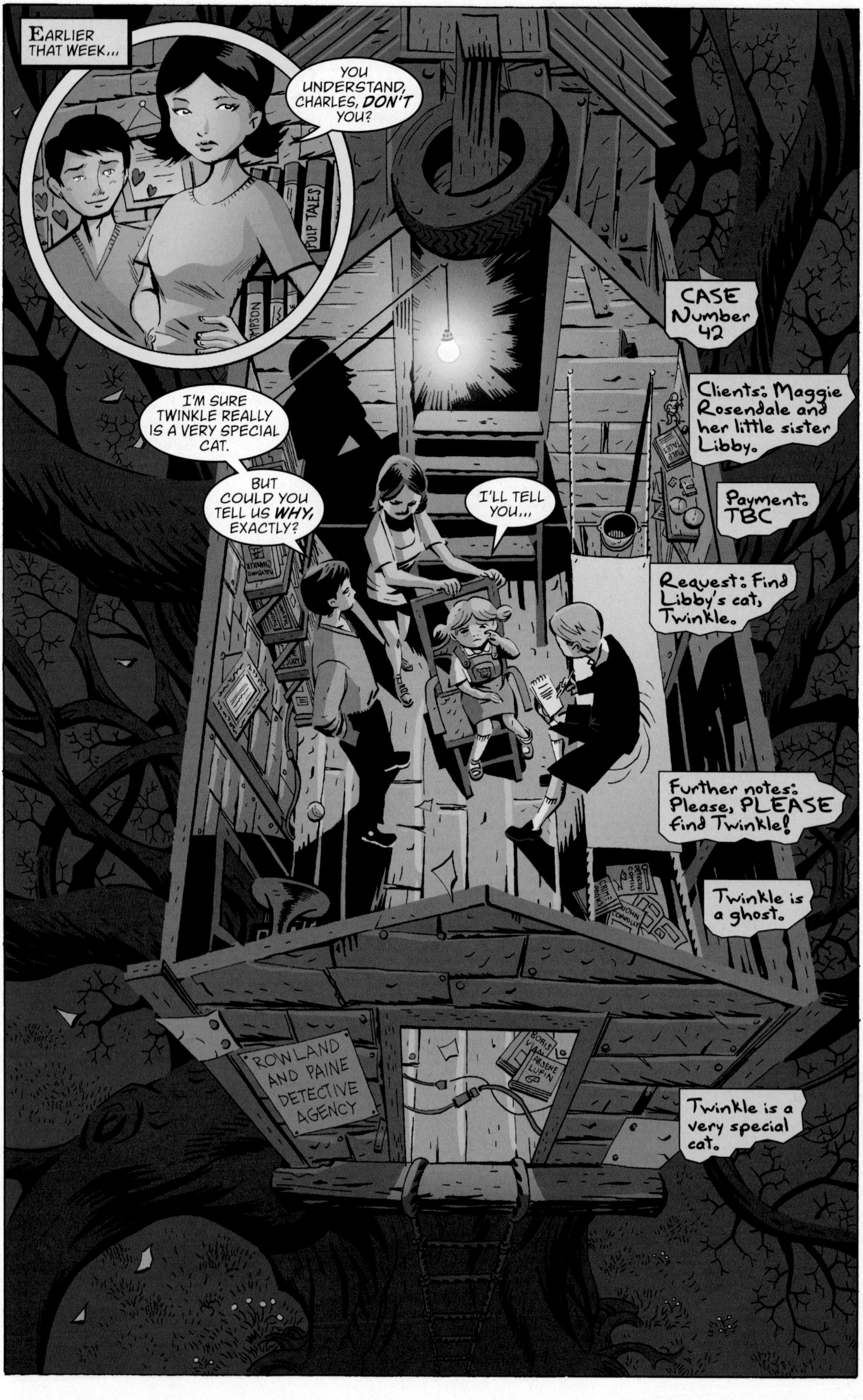
EARLIER THAT WEEK...
YOU UNDERSTAND, CHARLES, DON'T YOU?
PULP TALES
I'M SURE TWINKLE REALLY IS A VERY SPECIAL CAT.
BUT COULD YOU TELL US WHY, EXACTLY?
I'LL TELL YOU...
CASE Number 42
Clients: Maggie Rosendale and her little sister Libby.
Payment: TBC
Request: Find Libby's cat, Twinkle.
Further notes: Please, PLEASE find Twinkle!
Twinkle is a ghost.
ROWLAND AND PAINE DETECTIVE AGENCY
BORIS VIAN
ARSENE LUPIN
Twinkle is a very special cat.

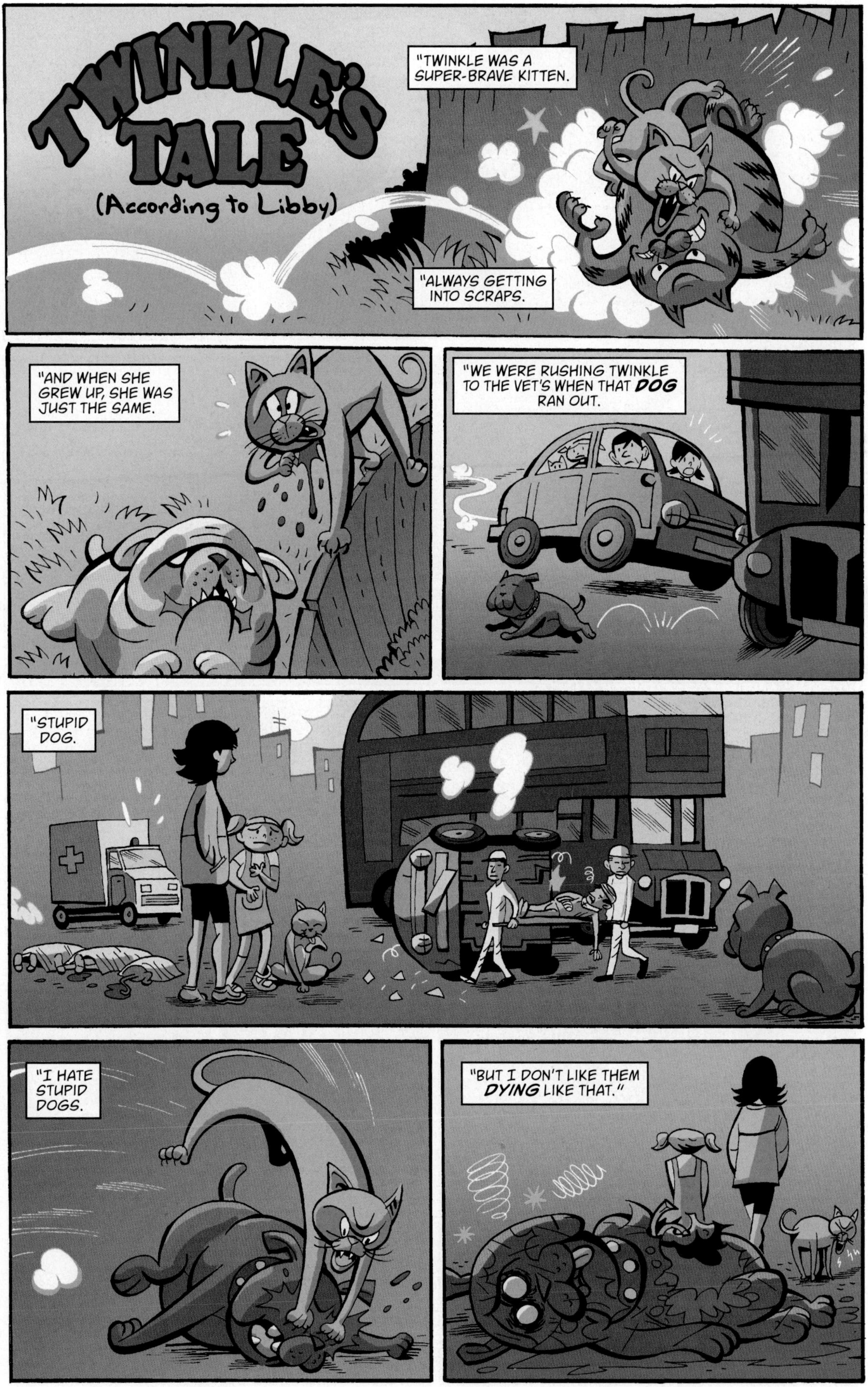
TWINKLE'S TALE
(According to Libby)
"TWINKLE WAS A SUPER-BRAVE KITTEN.
"ALWAYS GETTING INTO SCRAPS.
"AND WHEN SHE GREW UP, SHE WAS JUST THE SAME.
"WE WERE RUSHING TWINKLE TO THE VET'S WHEN THAT DOG RAN OUT.
"STUPID DOG.
"I HATE STUPID DOGS.
"BUT I DON'T LIKE THEM DYING LIKE THAT."

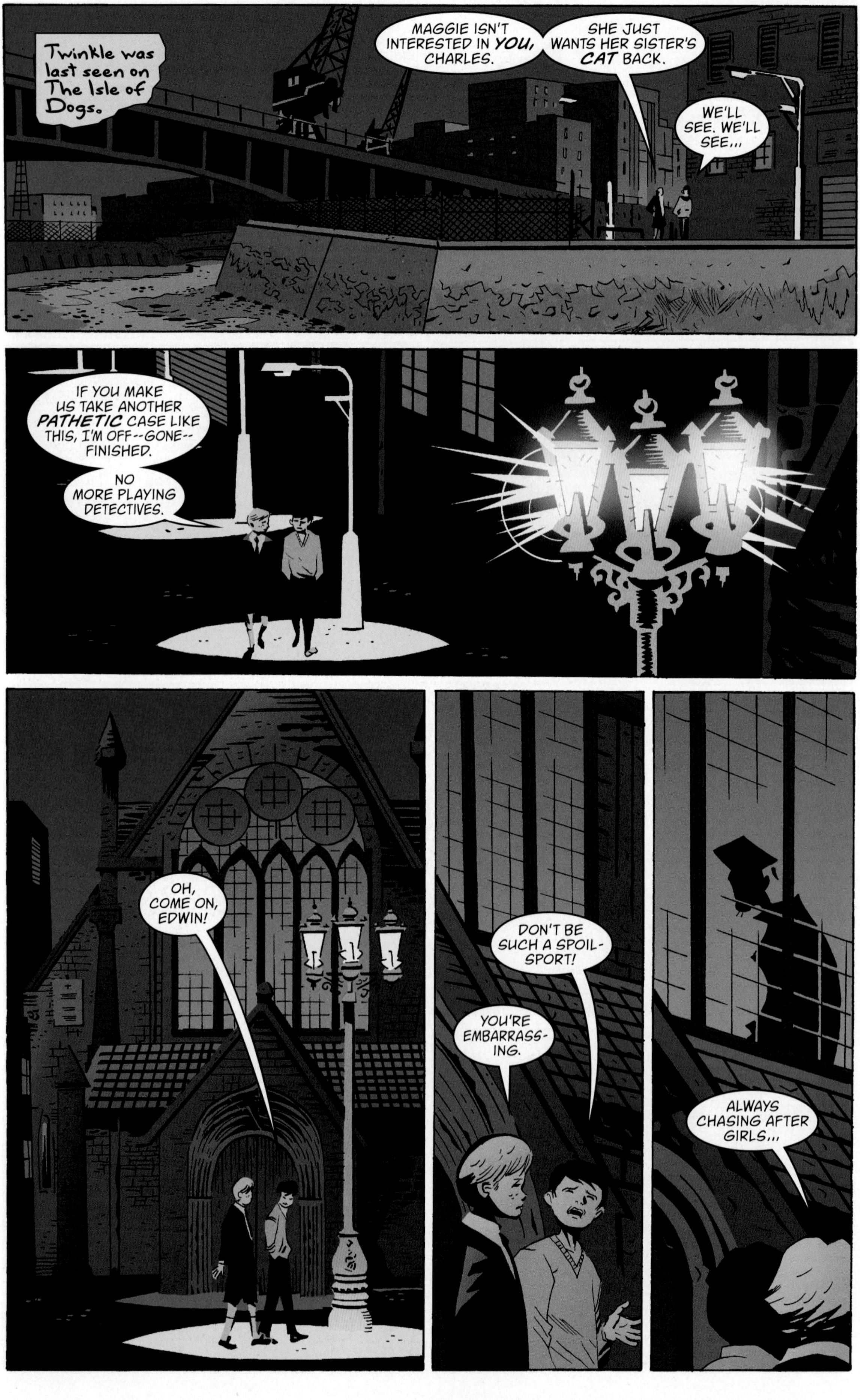
Twinkle was last seen on The Isle of Dogs.
MAGGIE ISN'T INTERESTED IN YOU, CHARLES.
SHE JUST WANTS HER SISTER'S CAT BACK.
WE'LL SEE. WE'LL SEE...
IF YOU MAKE US TAKE ANOTHER PATHETIC CASE LIKE THIS, I'M OFF--GONE--FINISHED.
NO MORE PLAYING DETECTIVES.
OH, COME ON, EDWIN!
DON'T BE SUCH A SPOIL-SPORT!
YOU'RE EMBARRASS-ING.
ALWAYS CHASING AFTER GIRLS...

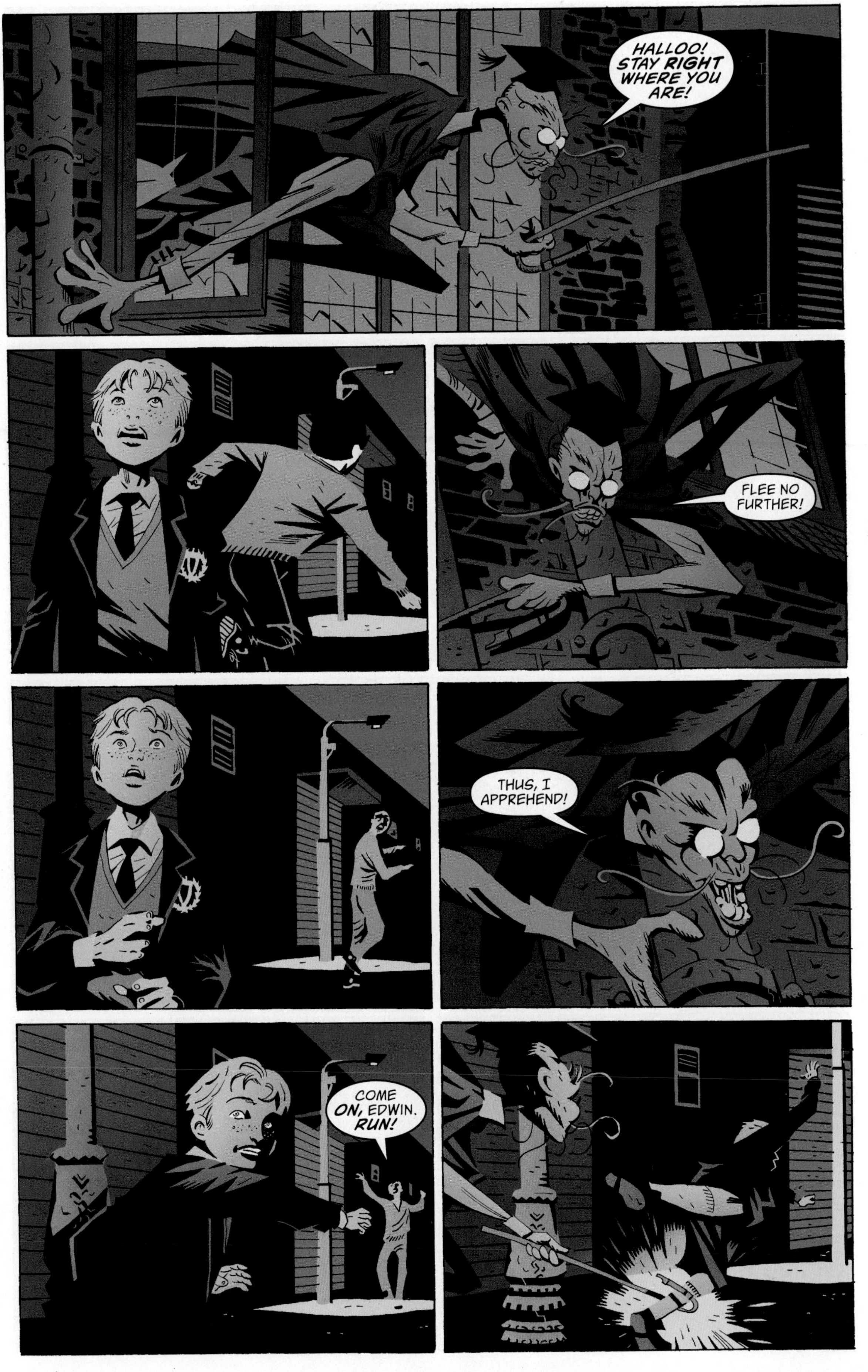
HALLOO! STAY RIGHT WHERE YOU ARE!
FLEE NO FURTHER!
THUS, I APPREHEND!
COME ON, EDWIN. RUN!

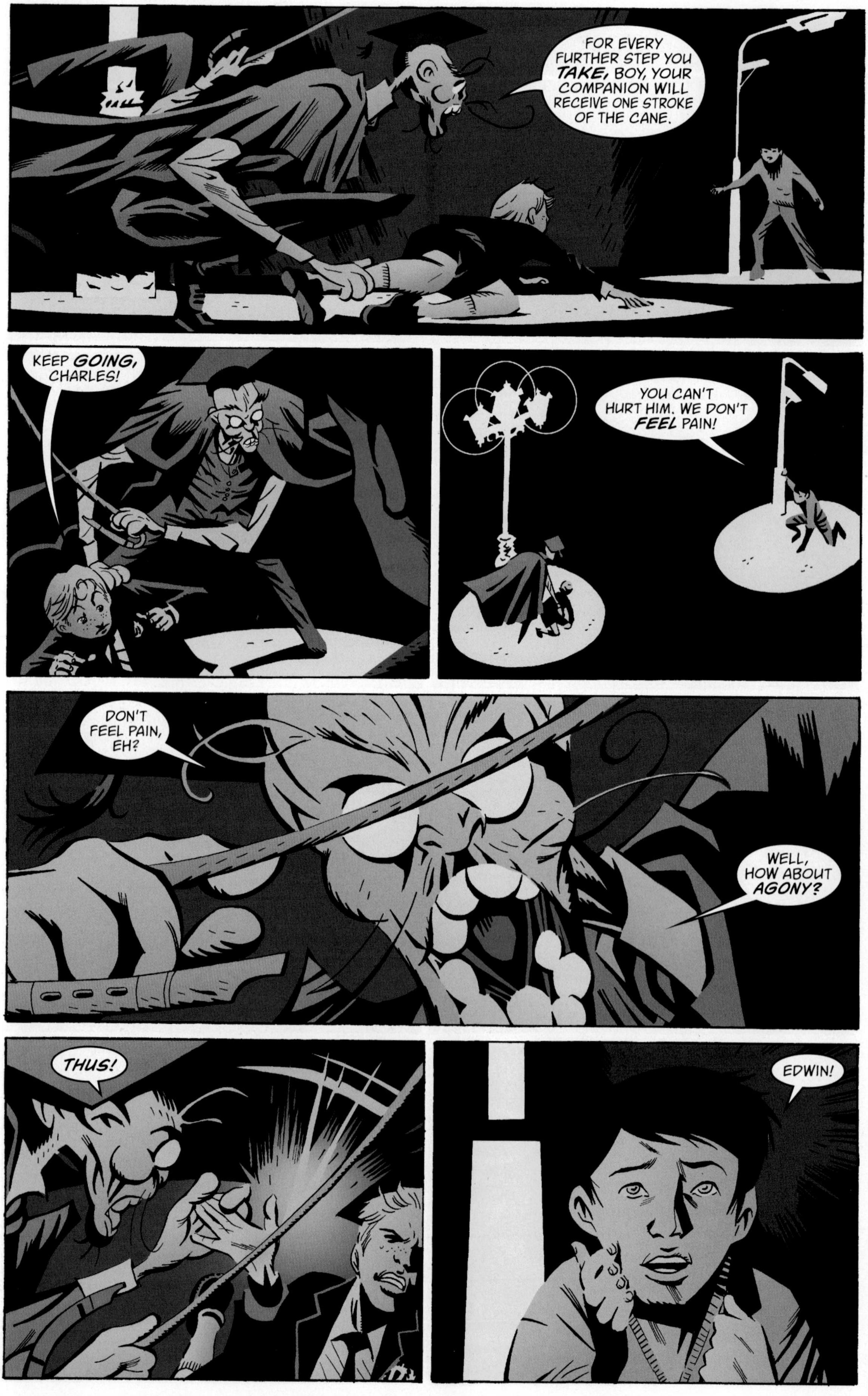
FOR EVERY FURTHER STEP YOU TAKE, BOY, YOUR COMPANION WILL RECEIVE ONE STROKE OF THE CANE.
KEEP GOING, CHARLES!
YOU CAN'T HURT HIM. WE DON'T FEEL PAIN!
DON'T FEEL PAIN, EH?
WELL, HOW ABOUT AGONY?
THUS!
EDWIN!

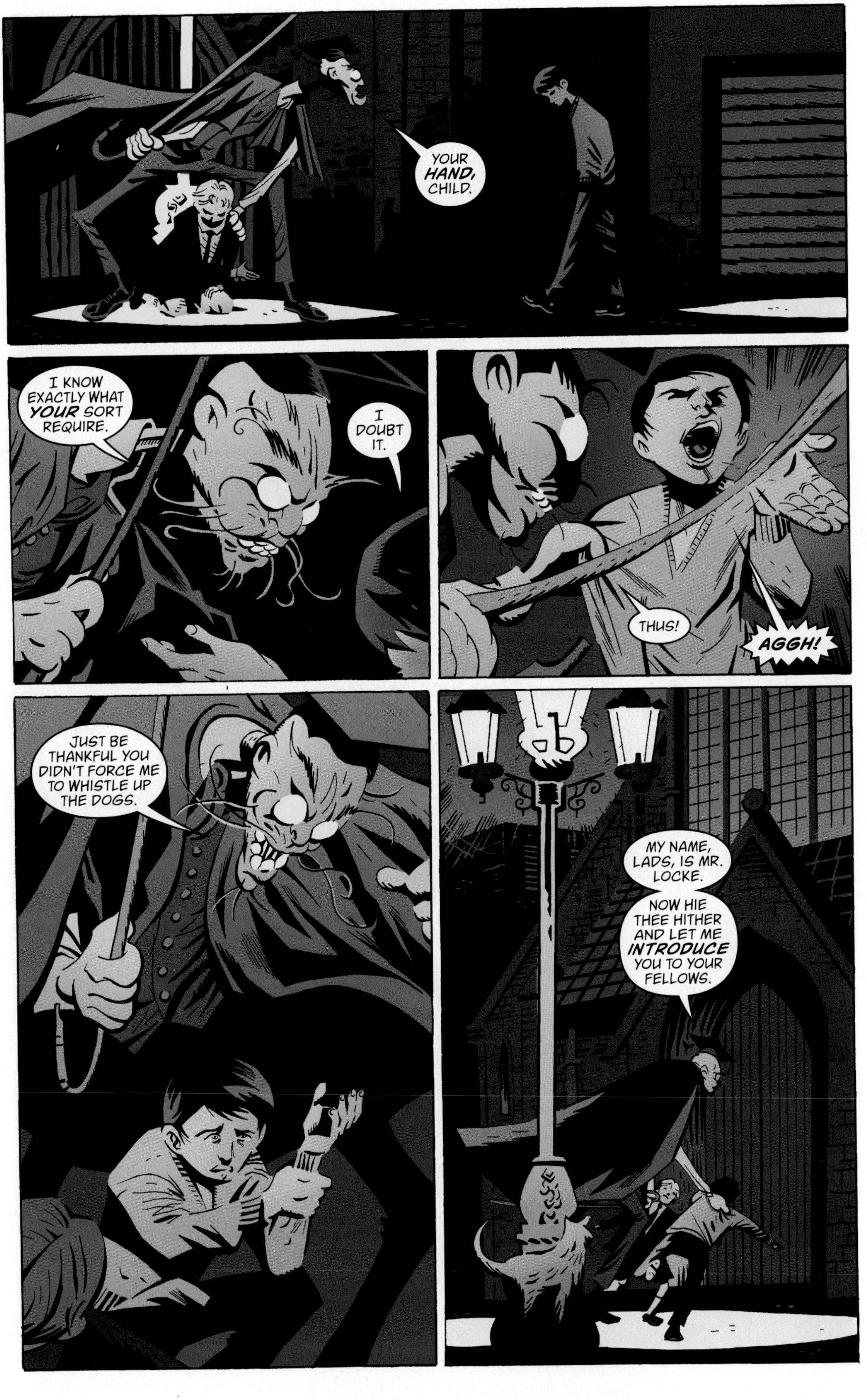
YOUR HAND, CHILD.
I KNOW EXACTLY WHAT YOUR SORT REQUIRE.
I DOUBT IT.
THUS!
AGGH!
JUST BE THANKFUL YOU DIDN'T FORCE ME TO WHISTLE UP THE DOGS.
MY NAME, LADS, IS MR. LOCKE.
NOW HIE THEE HITHER AND LET ME INTRODUCE YOU TO YOUR FELLOWS.

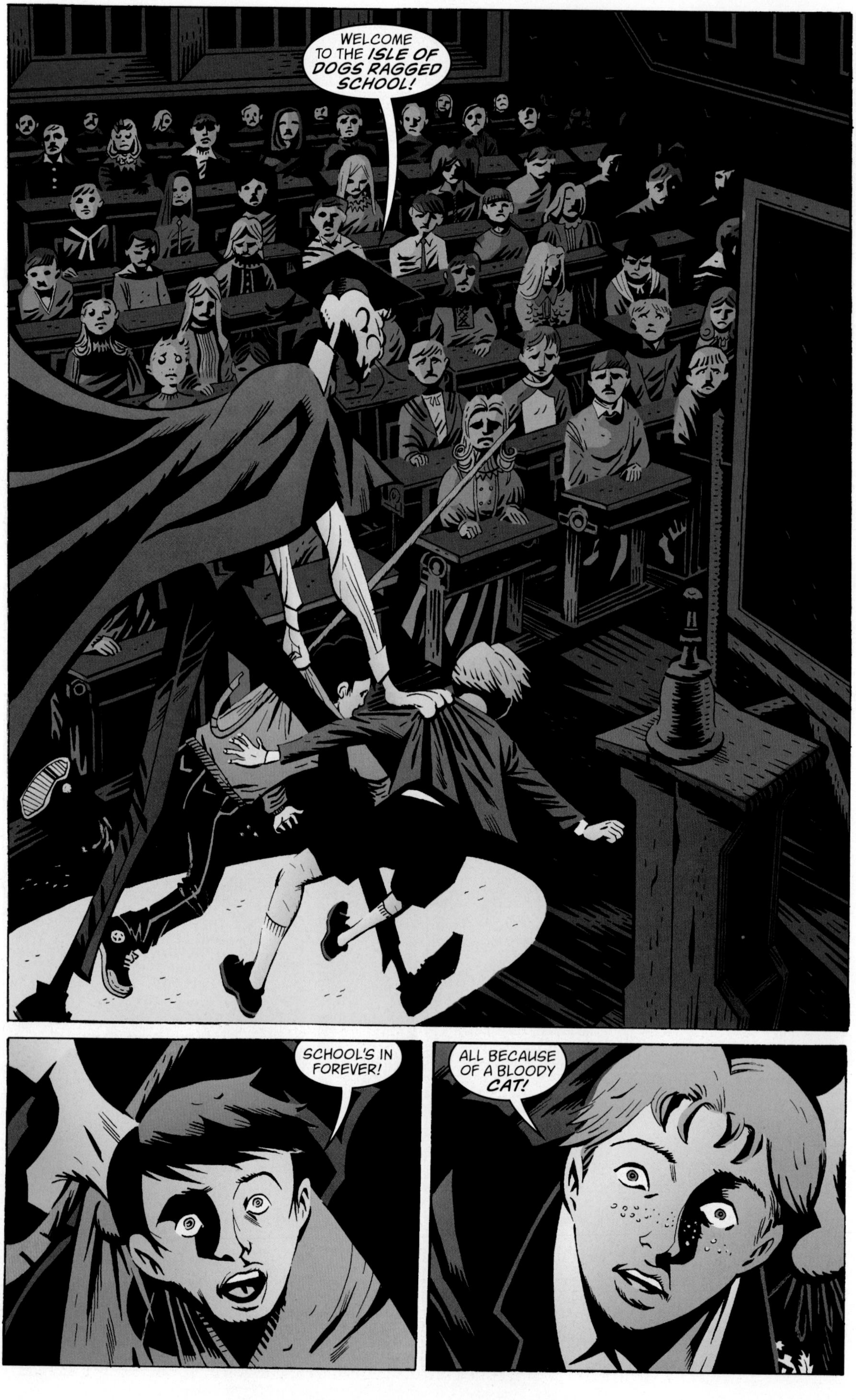
WELCOME TO THE ISLE OF DOGS RAGGED SCHOOL!
SCHOOL'S IN FOREVER!
ALL BECAUSE OF A BLOODY CAT!

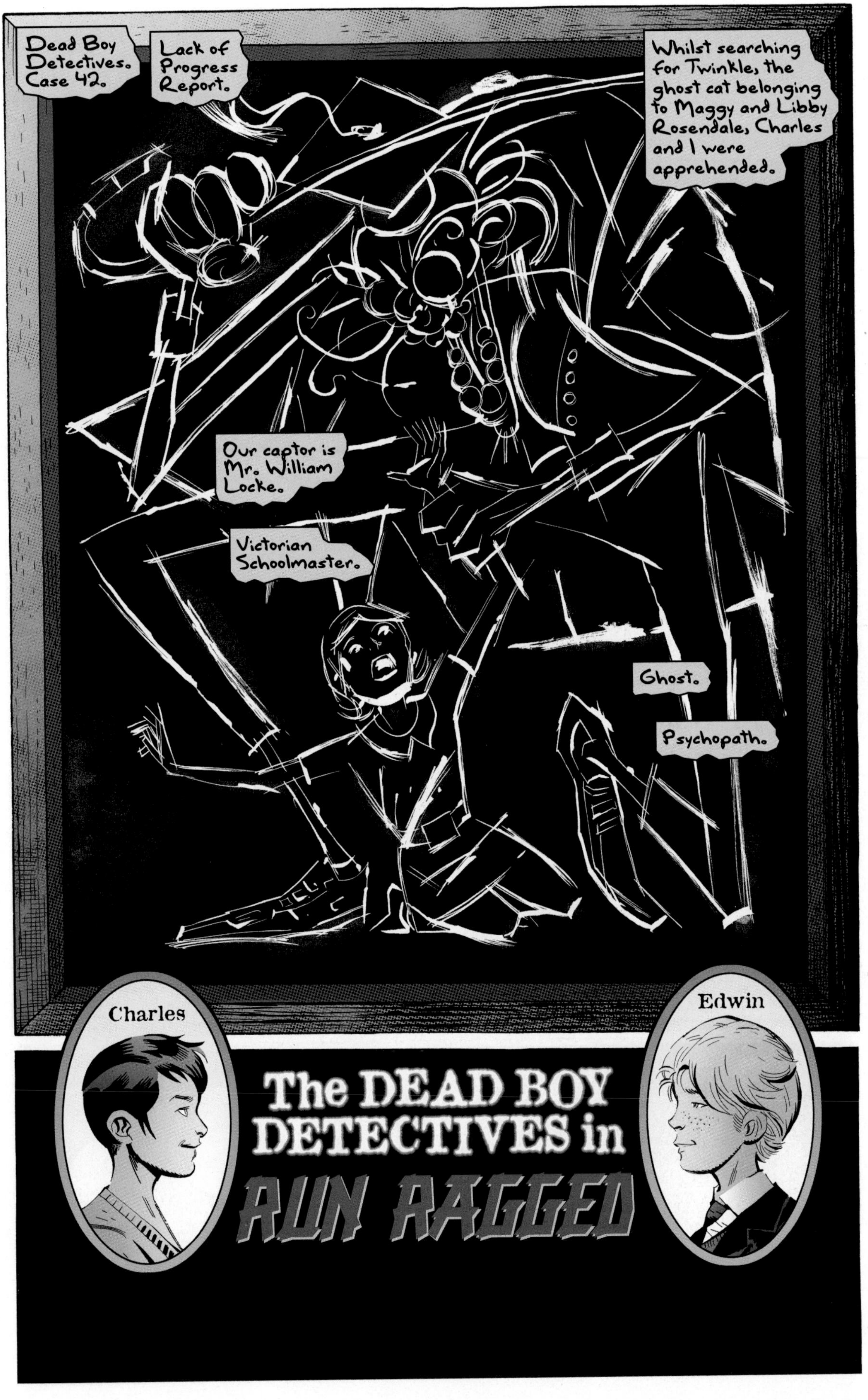
Dead Boy Detectives. Case 42.
Lack of Progress Report.
Whilst searching for Twinkle, the ghost cat belonging to Maggy and Libby Rosendale, Charles and I were apprehended.
Our captor is Mr. William Locke.
Victorian Schoolmaster.
Ghost.
Psychopath.
Charles
Edwin
The DEAD BOY DETECTIVES in
RUN RAGGED

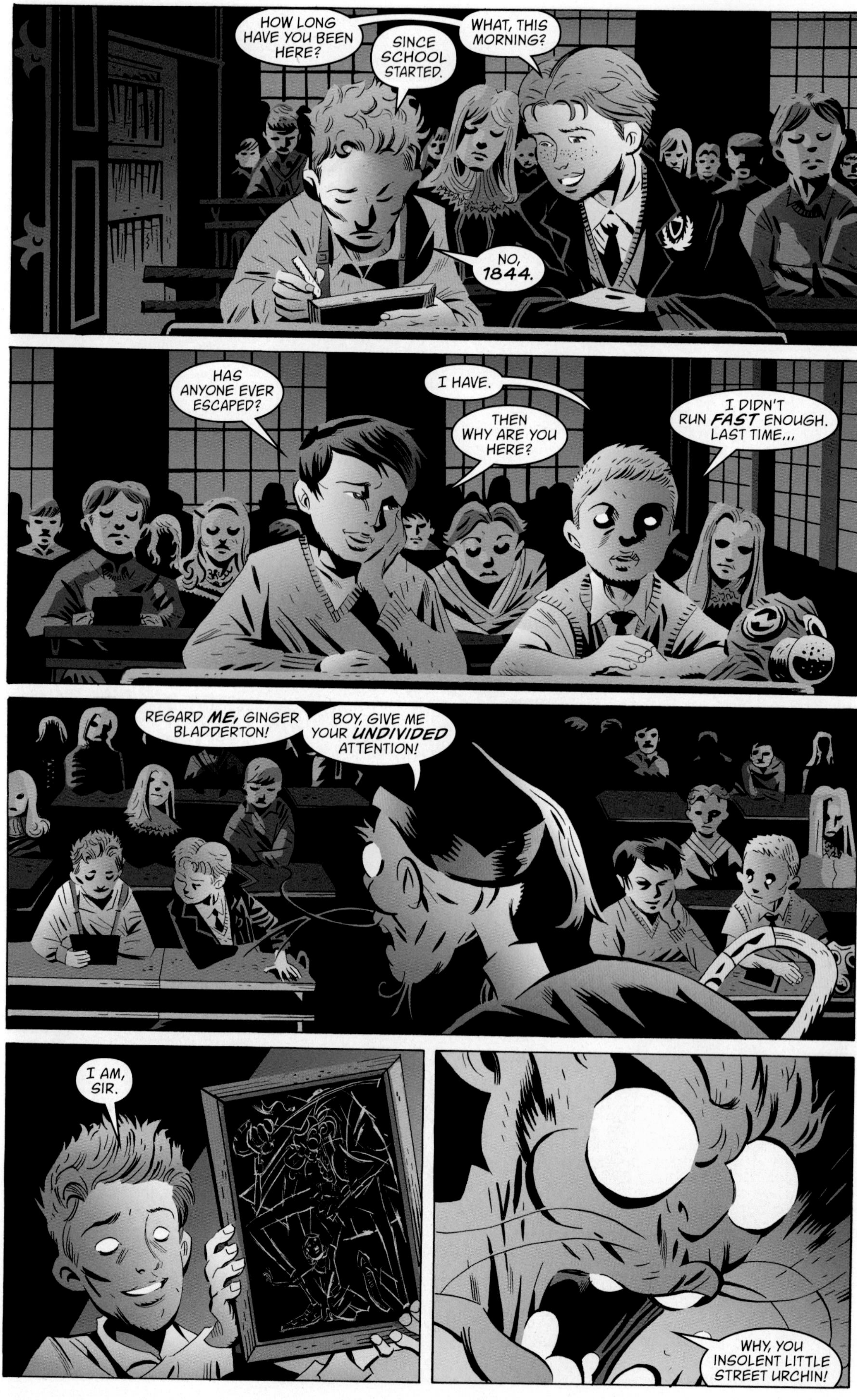
HOW LONG HAVE YOU BEEN HERE?
WHAT, THIS MORNING?
SINCE SCHOOL STARTED.
NO, 1844.
HAS ANYONE EVER ESCAPED?
I HAVE.
THEN WHY ARE YOU HERE?
I DIDN'T RUN FAST ENOUGH. LAST TIME...
REGARD ME, GINGER BLADDERTON!
BOY, GIVE ME YOUR UNDIVIDED ATTENTION!
I AM, SIR.
WHY, YOU INSOLENT LITTLE STREET URCHIN!

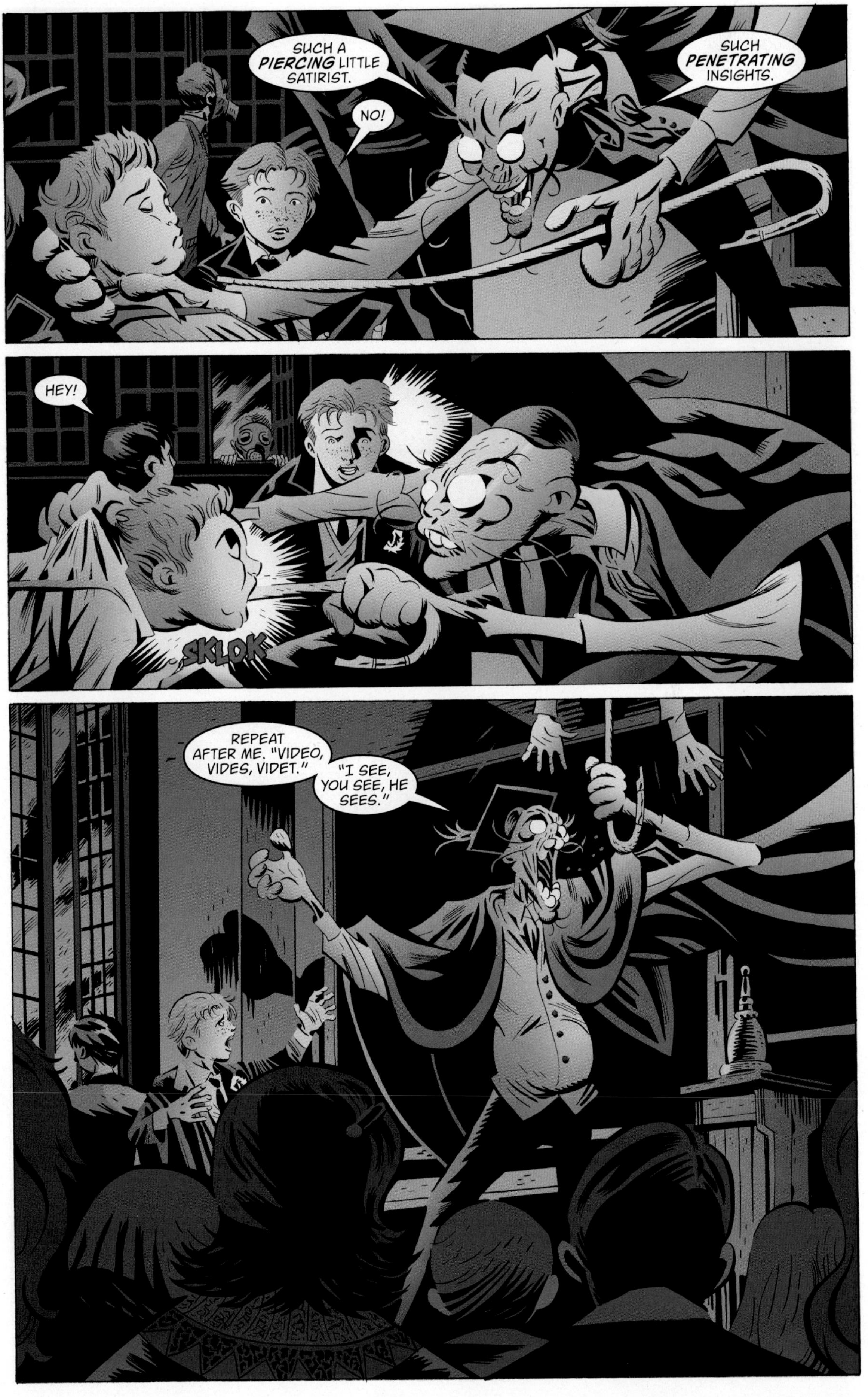
SUCH A PIERCING LITTLE SATIRIST.
SUCH PENETRATING INSIGHTS.
NO!
HEY!
SKLOK
REPEAT AFTER ME. "VIDEO, VIDES, VIDET."
"I SEE, YOU SEE, HE SEES."

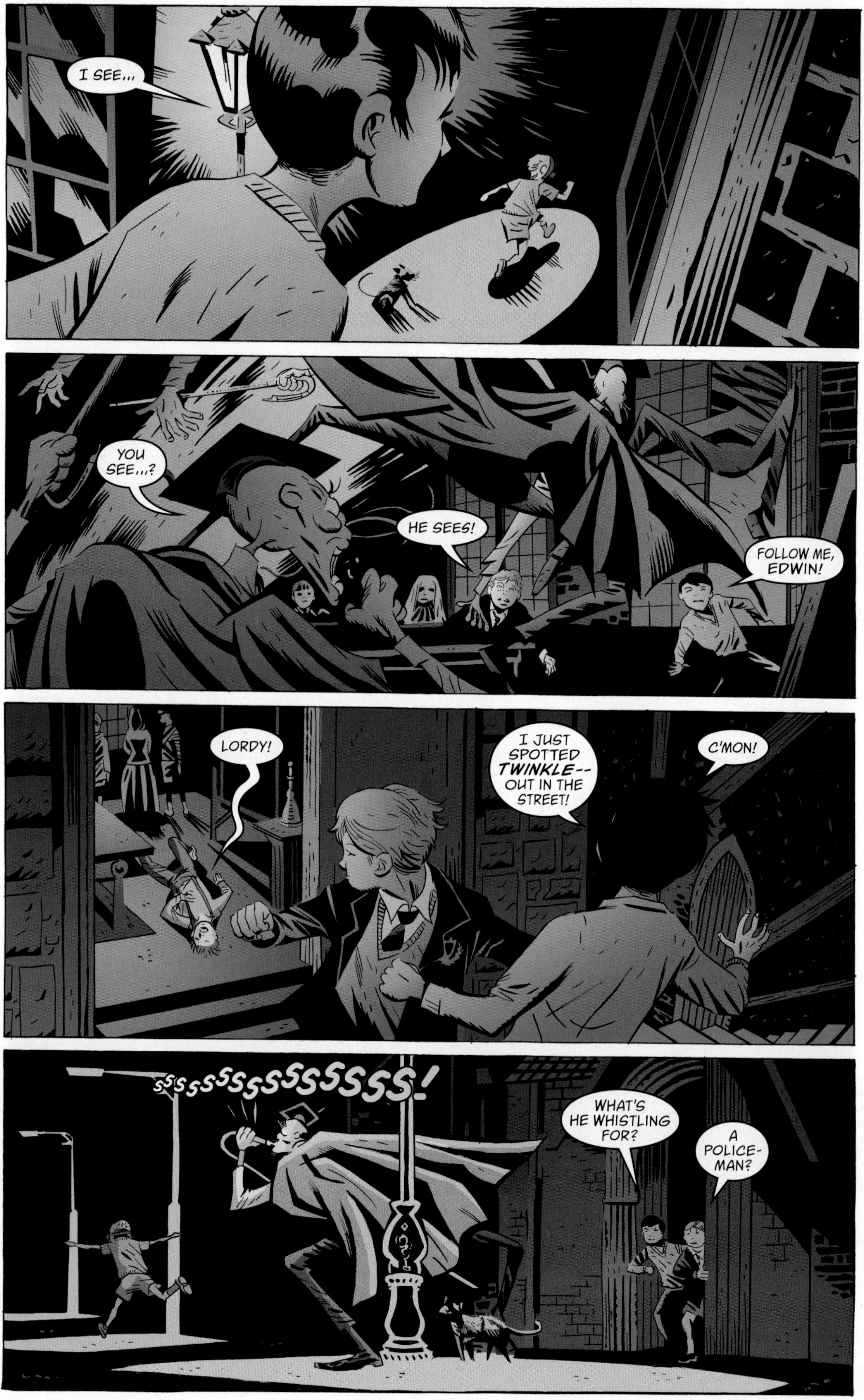
I SEE...
YOU SEE...?
HE SEES!
FOLLOW ME, EDWIN!
LORDY!
I JUST SPOTTED TWINKLE-- OUT IN THE STREET!
C'MON!
SSSSSSSSSSSSSSS!
WHAT'S HE WHISTLING FOR?
A POLICE-MAN?

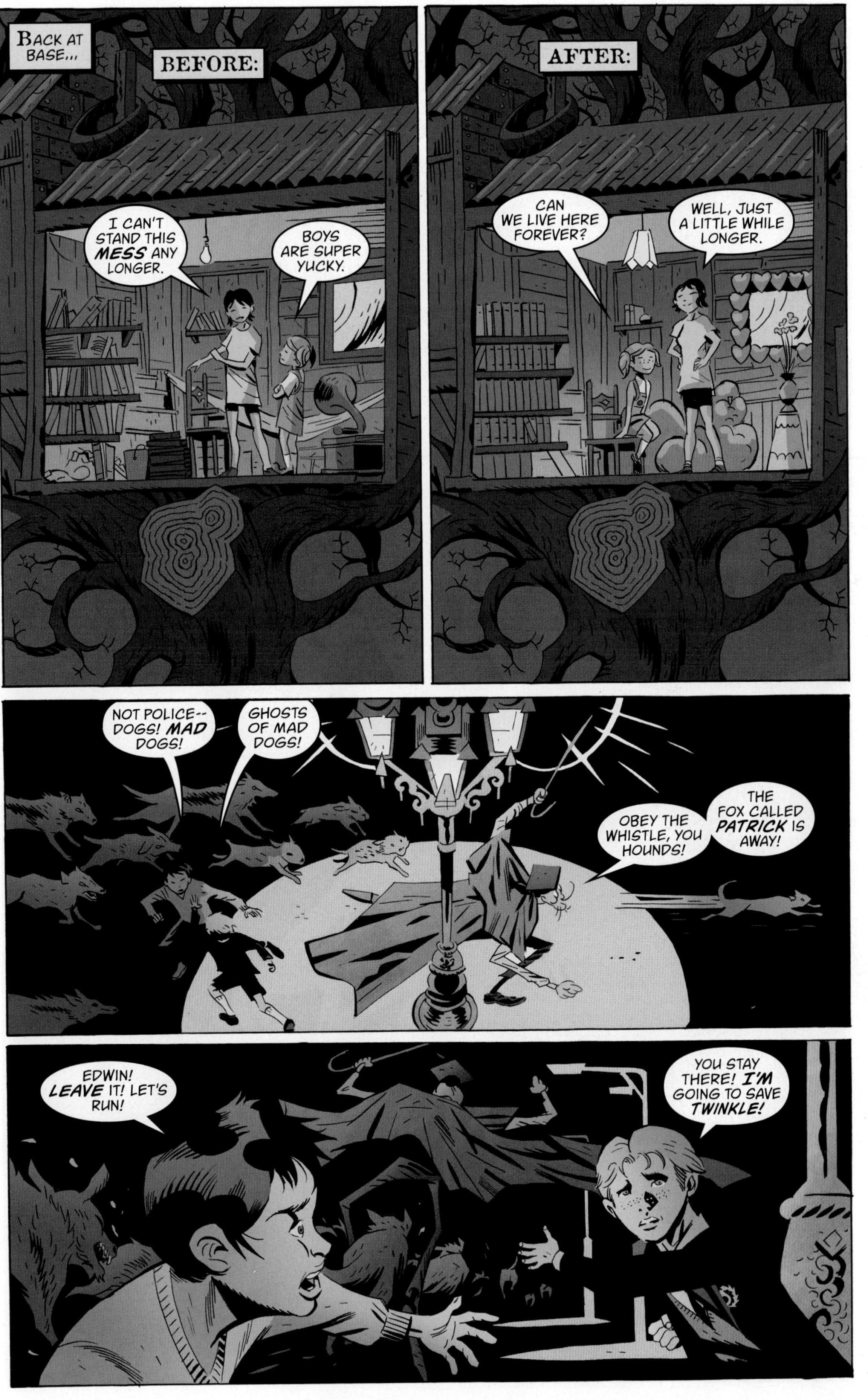
BACK AT BASE...
BEFORE:
I CAN'T STAND THIS MESS ANY LONGER.
BOYS ARE SUPER YUCKY.
AFTER:
CAN WE LIVE HERE FOREVER?
WELL, JUST A LITTLE WHILE LONGER.
NOT POLICE-- DOGS! MAD DOGS!
GHOSTS OF MAD DOGS!
OBEY THE WHISTLE, YOU HOUNDS!
THE FOX CALLED PATRICK IS AWAY!
EDWIN! LEAVE IT! LET'S RUN!
YOU STAY THERE! I'M GOING TO SAVE TWINKLE!

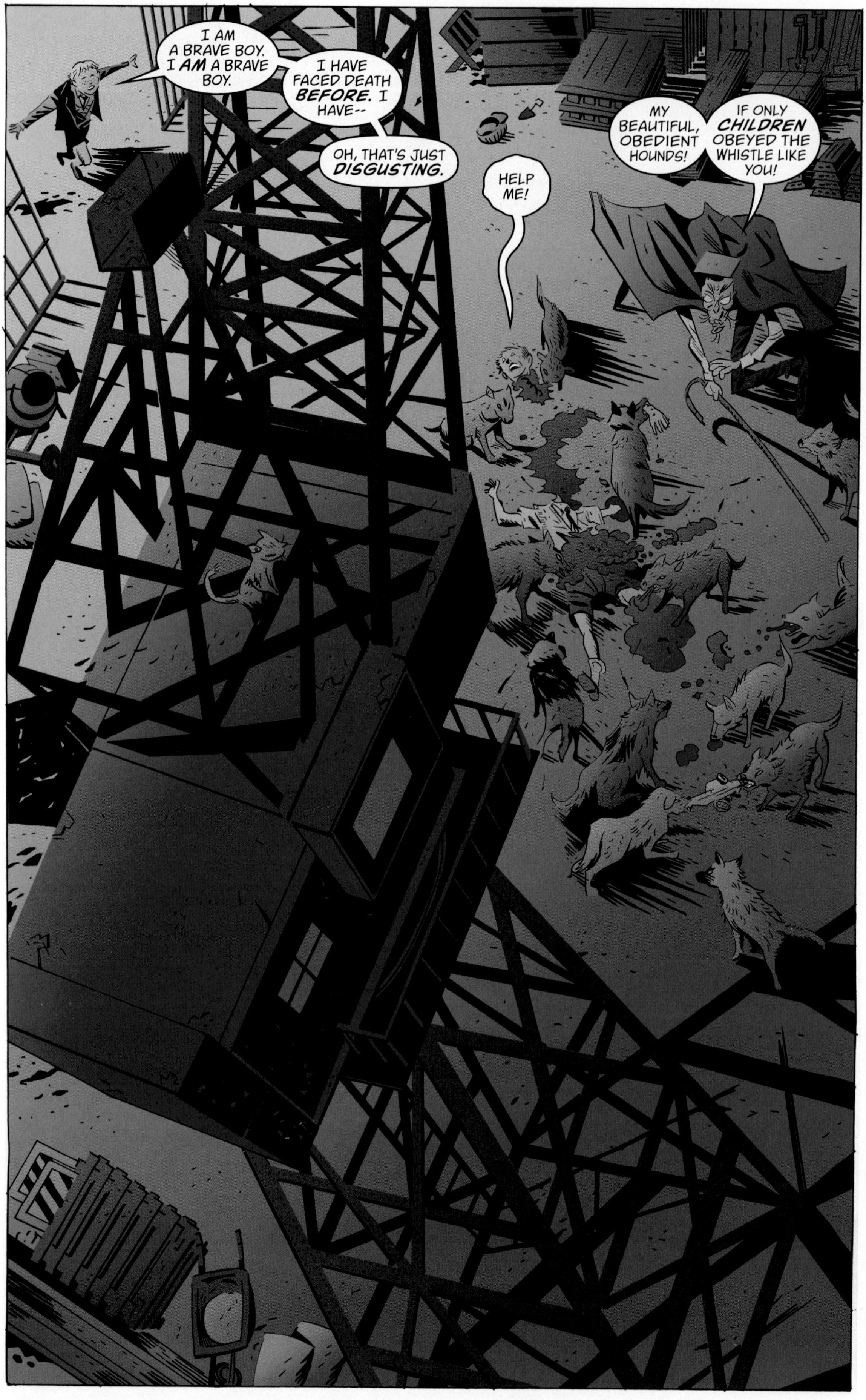
I AM A BRAVE BOY. I AM A BRAVE BOY.
I HAVE FACED DEATH BEFORE. I HAVE--
OH, THAT'S JUST DISGUSTING.
HELP ME!
MY BEAUTIFUL, OBEDIENT HOUNDS!
IF ONLY CHILDREN OBEYED THE WHISTLE LIKE YOU!

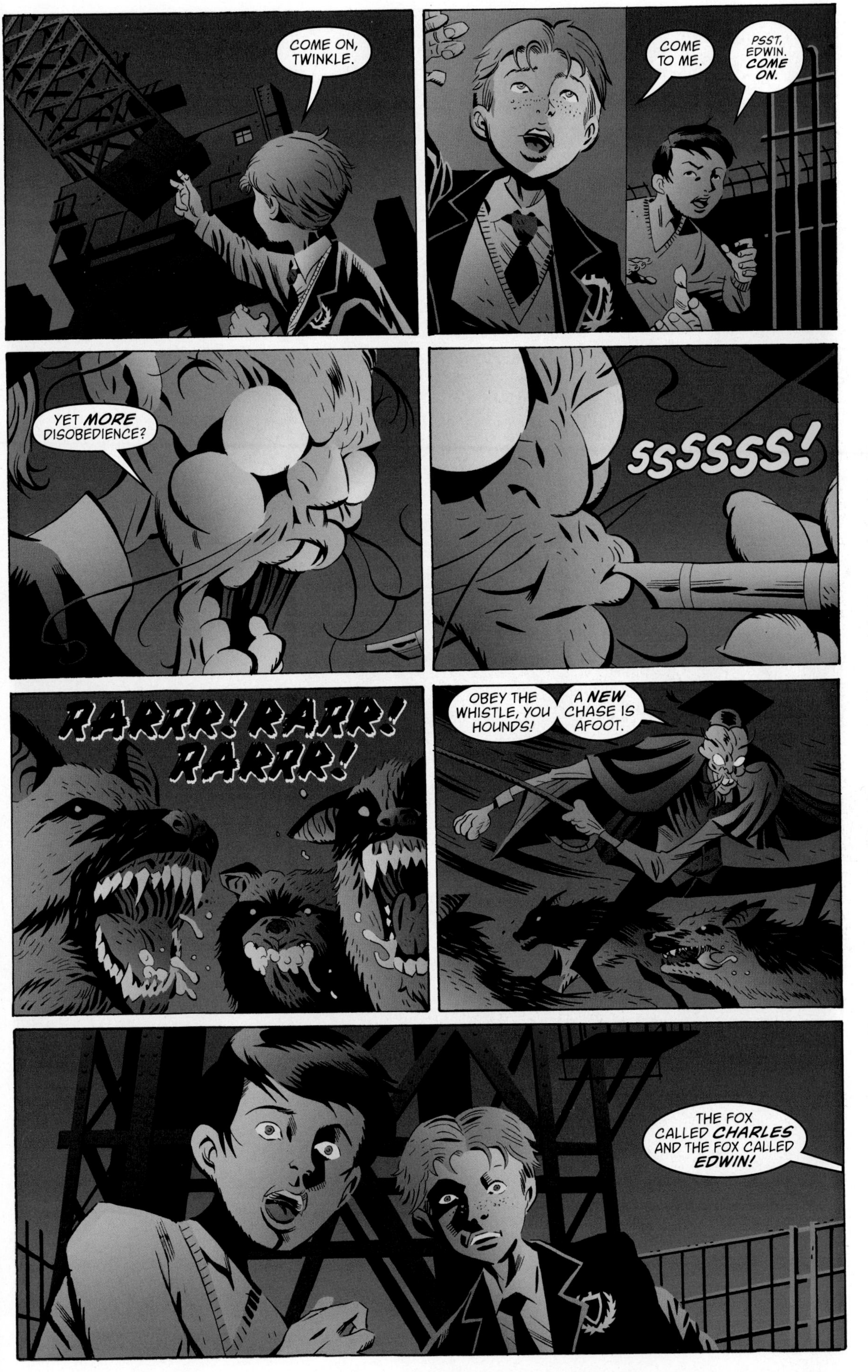
COME ON, TWINKLE.
COME TO ME.
PSST, EDWIN. **COME ON.**
YET **MORE** DISOBEDIENCE?
SSSSSS!
RARRR! RARR! RARRR!
OBEY THE WHISTLE, YOU HOUNDS!
A **NEW** CHASE IS AFOOT.
THE FOX CALLED **CHARLES** AND THE FOX CALLED **EDWIN!**

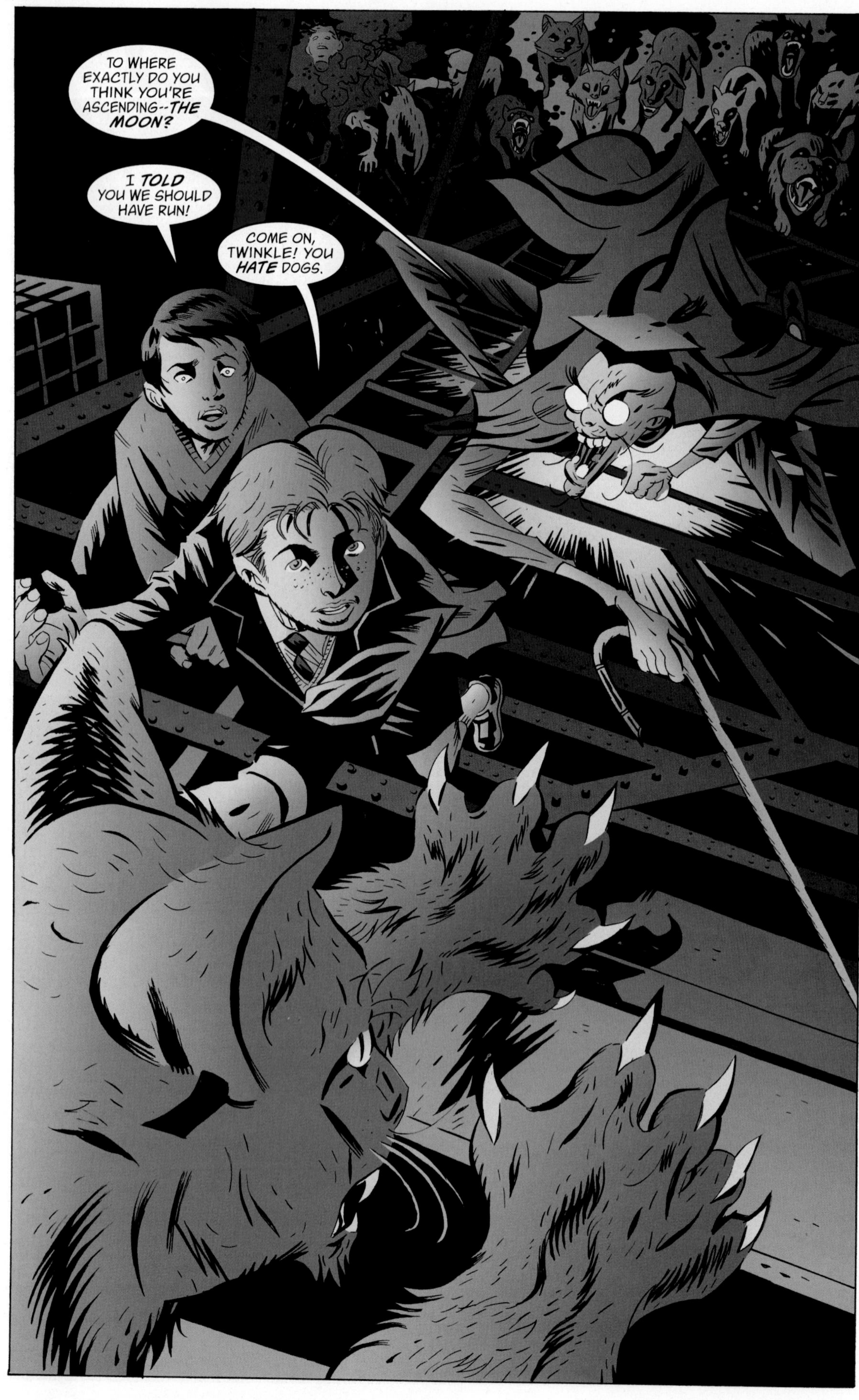
TO WHERE EXACTLY DO YOU THINK YOU'RE ASCENDING--THE MOON?
I TOLD YOU WE SHOULD HAVE RUN!
COME ON, TWINKLE! YOU HATE DOGS.

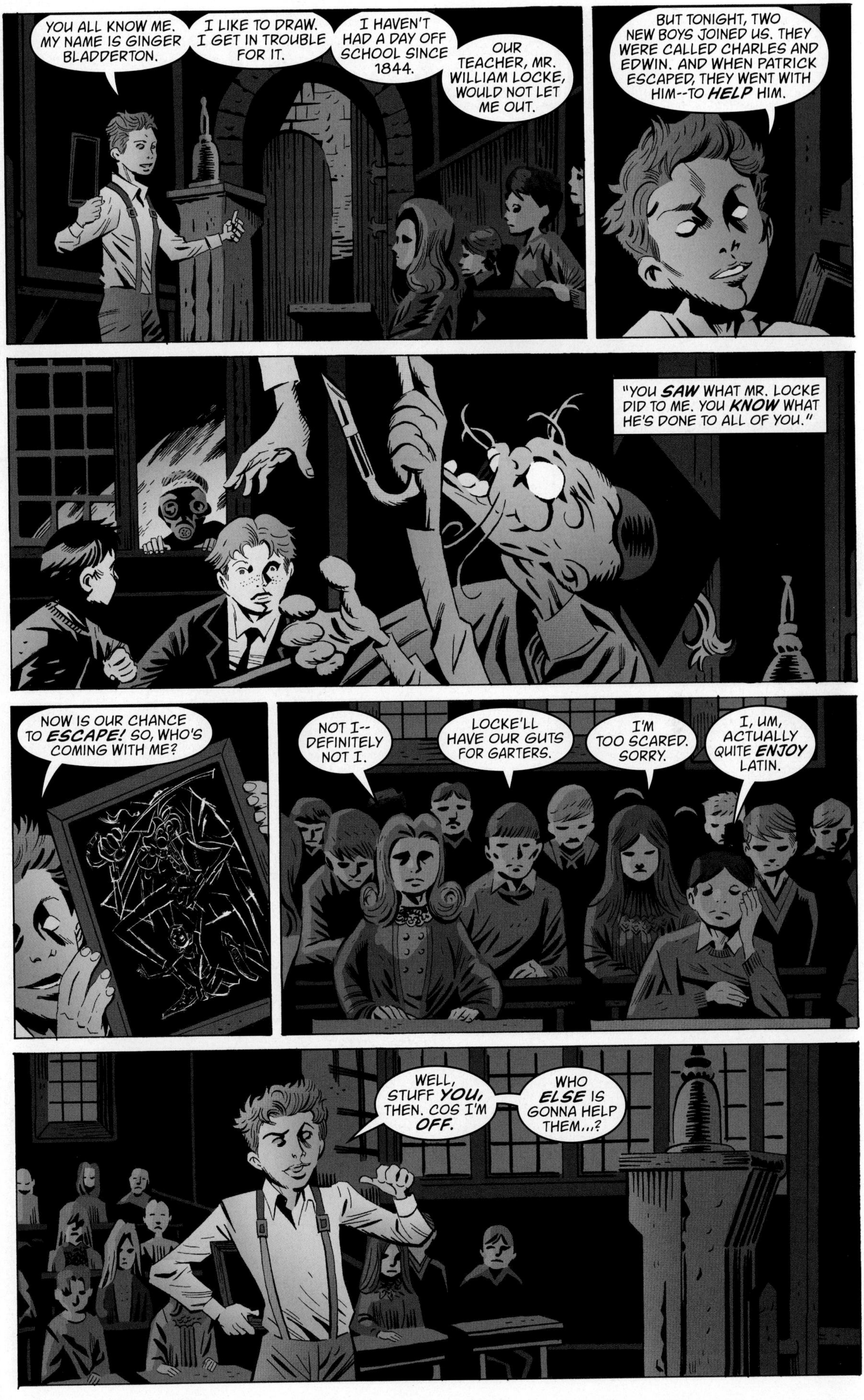

YOU ALL KNOW ME. MY NAME IS GINGER BLADDERTON.
I LIKE TO DRAW. I GET IN TROUBLE FOR IT.
I HAVEN'T HAD A DAY OFF SCHOOL SINCE 1844.
OUR TEACHER, MR. WILLIAM LOCKE, WOULD NOT LET ME OUT.
BUT TONIGHT, TWO NEW BOYS JOINED US. THEY WERE CALLED CHARLES AND EDWIN. AND WHEN PATRICK ESCAPED, THEY WENT WITH HIM--TO HELP HIM.
"YOU SAW WHAT MR. LOCKE DID TO ME. YOU KNOW WHAT HE'S DONE TO ALL OF YOU."
NOW IS OUR CHANCE TO ESCAPE! SO, WHO'S COMING WITH ME?
NOT I-- DEFINITELY NOT I.
LOCKE'LL HAVE OUR GUTS FOR GARTERS.
I'M TOO SCARED. SORRY.
I, UM, ACTUALLY QUITE ENJOY LATIN.
WELL, STUFF YOU, THEN. COS I'M OFF.
WHO ELSE IS GONNA HELP THEM...?

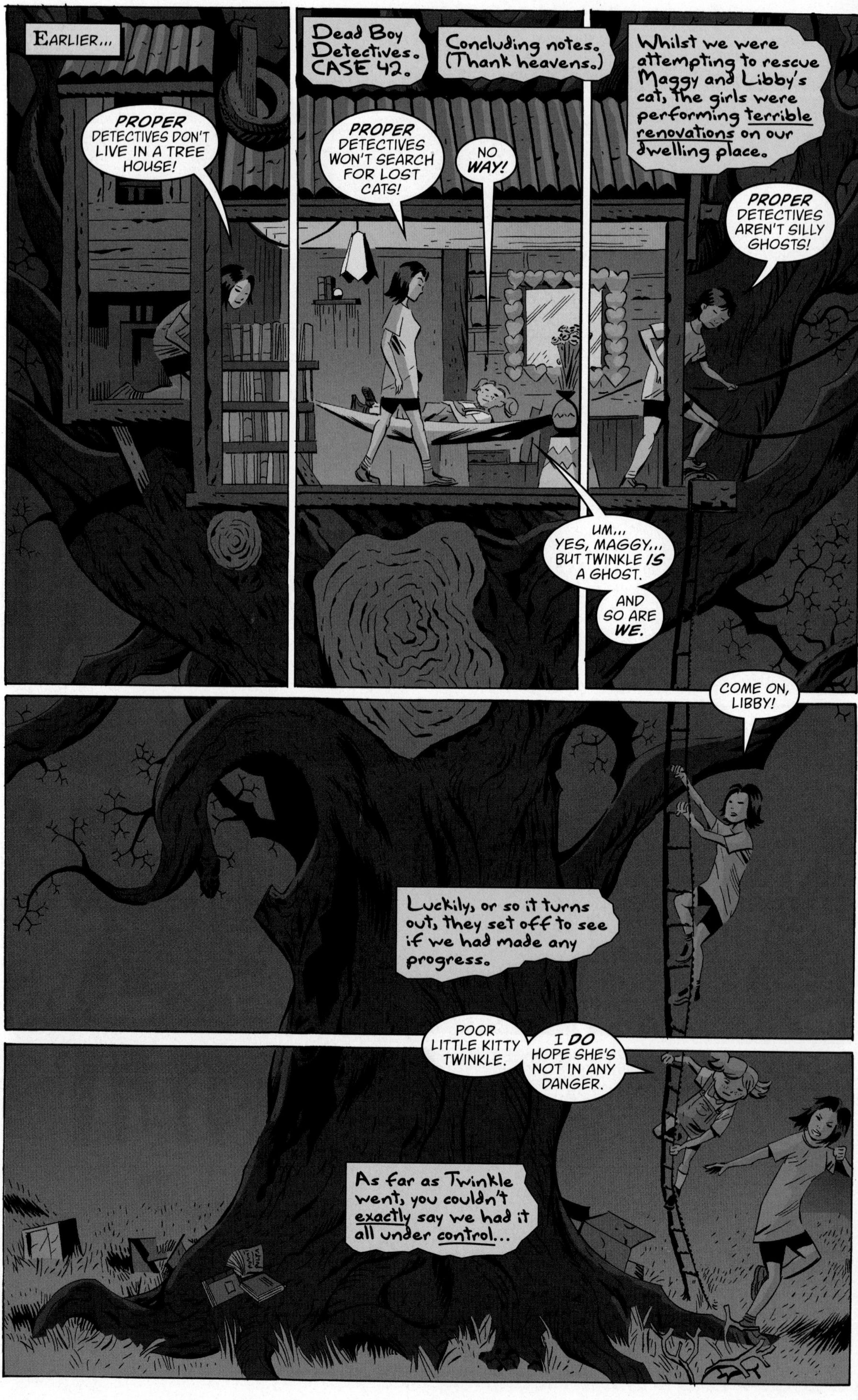
EARLIER...
PROPER DETECTIVES DON'T LIVE IN A TREE HOUSE!
Dead Boy Detectives. CASE 42.
PROPER DETECTIVES WON'T SEARCH FOR LOST CATS!
NO WAY!
Concluding notes. (Thank heavens.)
Whilst we were attempting to rescue Maggy and Libby's cat, the girls were performing terrible renovations on our dwelling place.
PROPER DETECTIVES AREN'T SILLY GHOSTS!
UM... YES, MAGGY... BUT TWINKLE IS A GHOST.
AND SO ARE WE.
COME ON, LIBBY!
Luckily, or so it turns out, they set off to see if we had made any progress.
POOR LITTLE KITTY TWINKLE.
I DO HOPE SHE'S NOT IN ANY DANGER.
As far as Twinkle went, you couldn't exactly say we had it all under control...

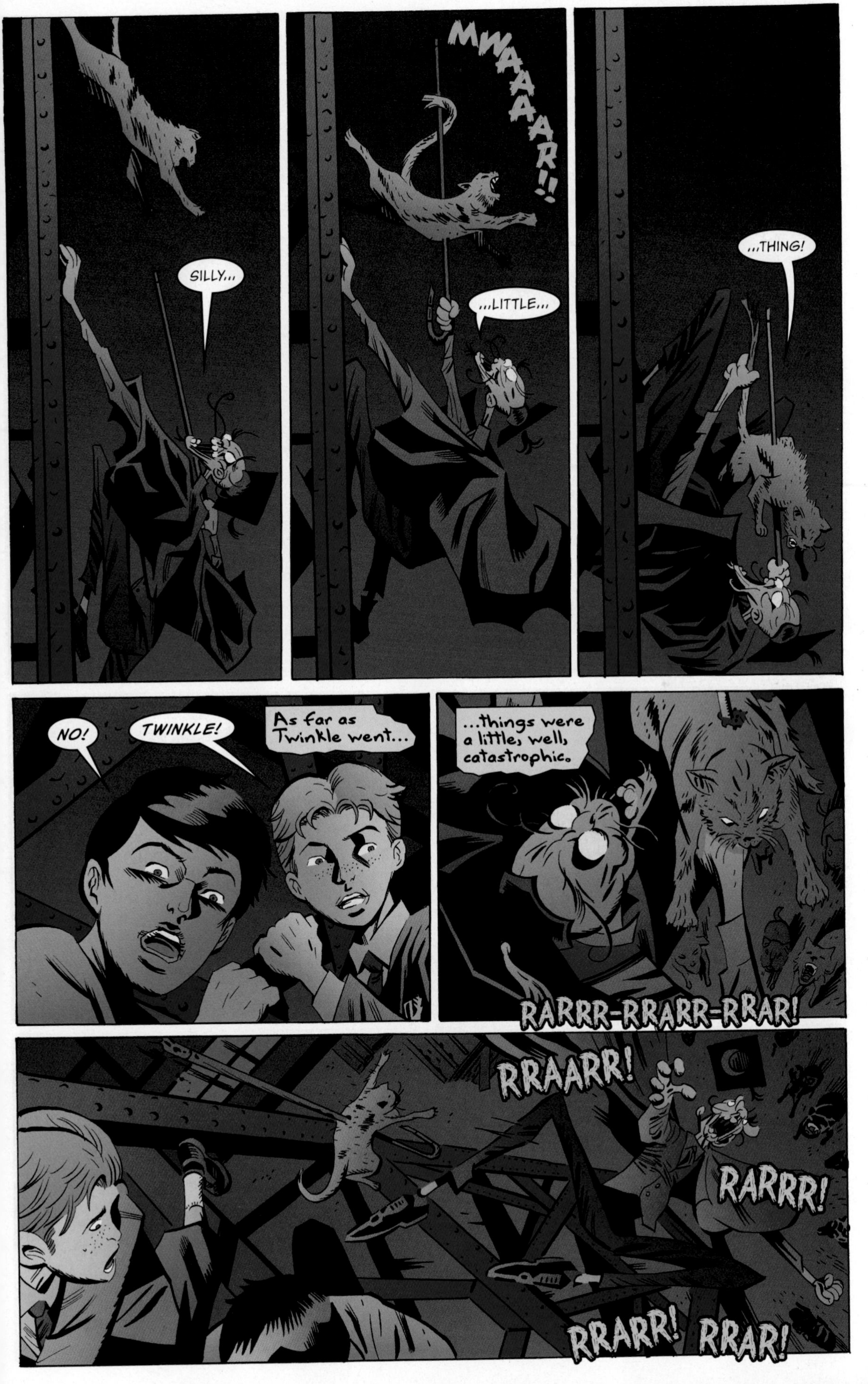

SILLY...
MWAAAAAR!!
...LITTLE...
...THING!
NO!
TWINKLE!
As far as Twinkle went...
...things were a little, well, catastrophic.
RARRR-RRARR-RRAR!
RRAARR!
RARRR!
RRARR! RRAR!

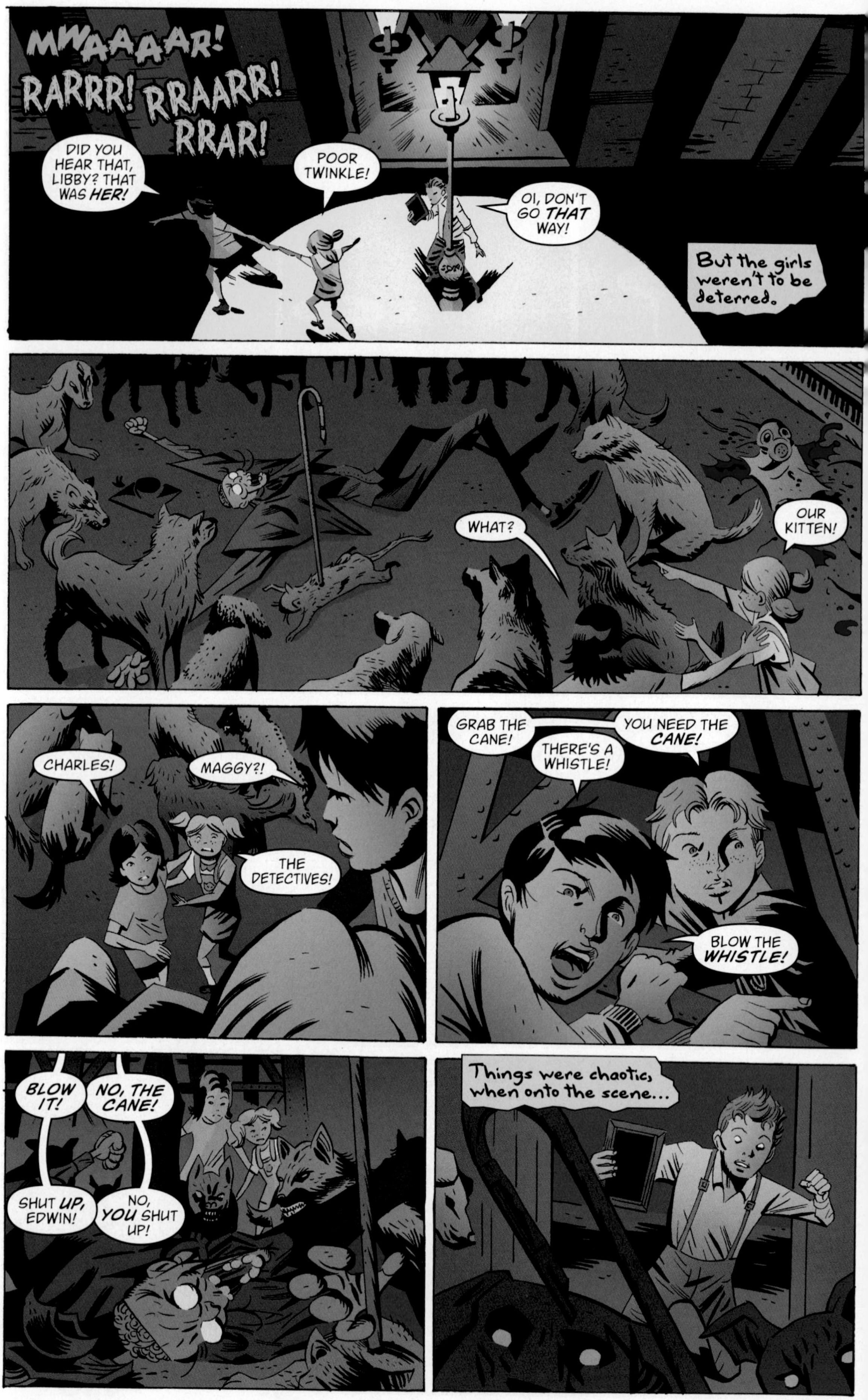
MWAAAAR!
RARRR! RRAARR! RRAR!
DID YOU HEAR THAT, LIBBY? THAT WAS HER!
POOR TWINKLE!
OI, DON'T GO THAT WAY!
But the girls weren't to be deterred.
WHAT?
OUR KITTEN!
CHARLES!
MAGGY?!
THE DETECTIVES!
GRAB THE CANE!
YOU NEED THE CANE!
THERE'S A WHISTLE!
BLOW THE WHISTLE!
BLOW IT!
NO, THE CANE!
SHUT UP, EDWIN!
NO, YOU SHUT UP!
Things were chaotic, when onto the scene...

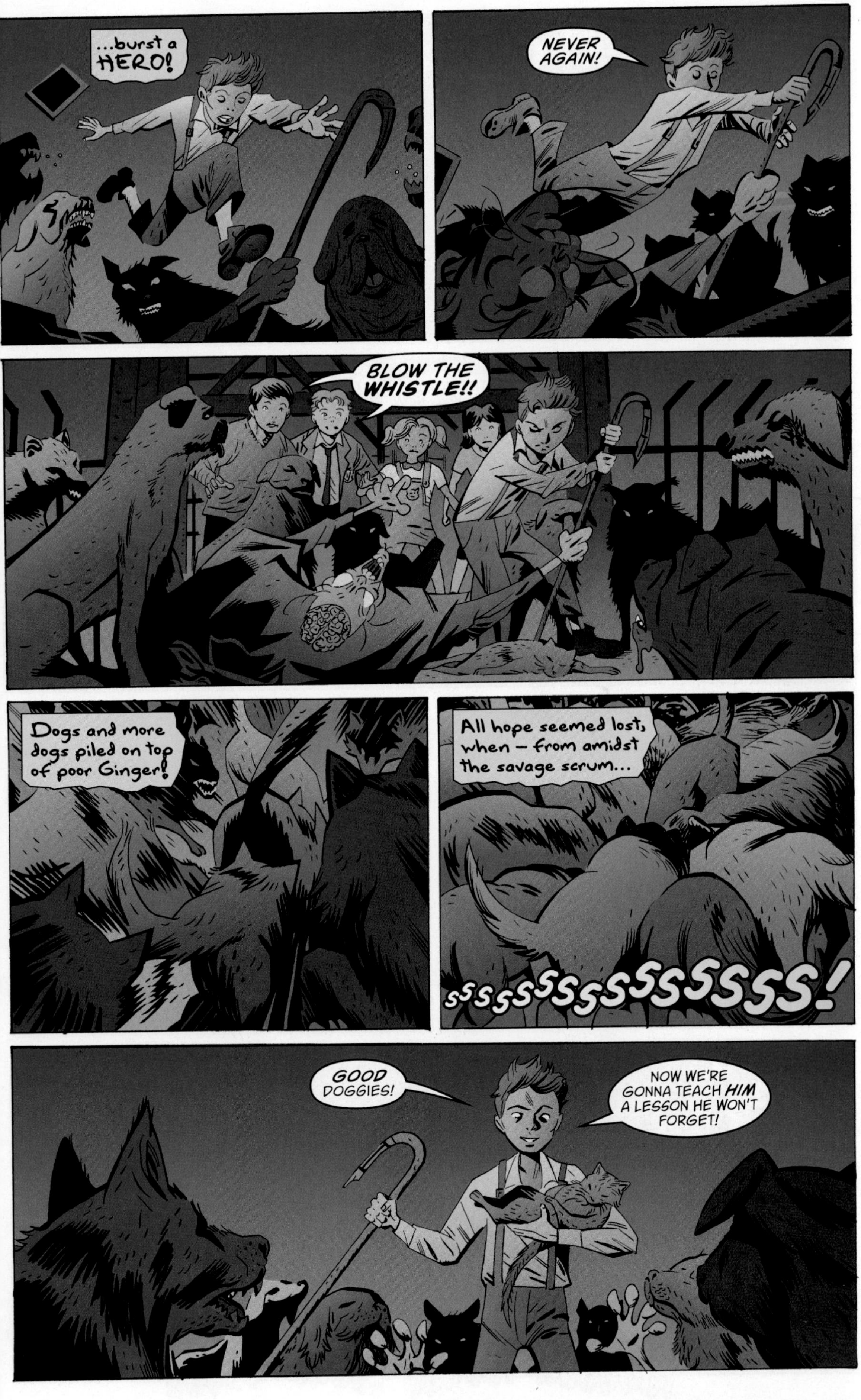

...burst a HERO!
NEVER AGAIN!
BLOW THE WHISTLE!!
Dogs and more dogs piled on top of poor Ginger!
All hope seemed lost, when – from amidst the savage scrum...
SSSSSSSSSSSSSS!
GOOD DOGGIES!
NOW WE'RE GONNA TEACH HIM A LESSON HE WON'T FORGET!

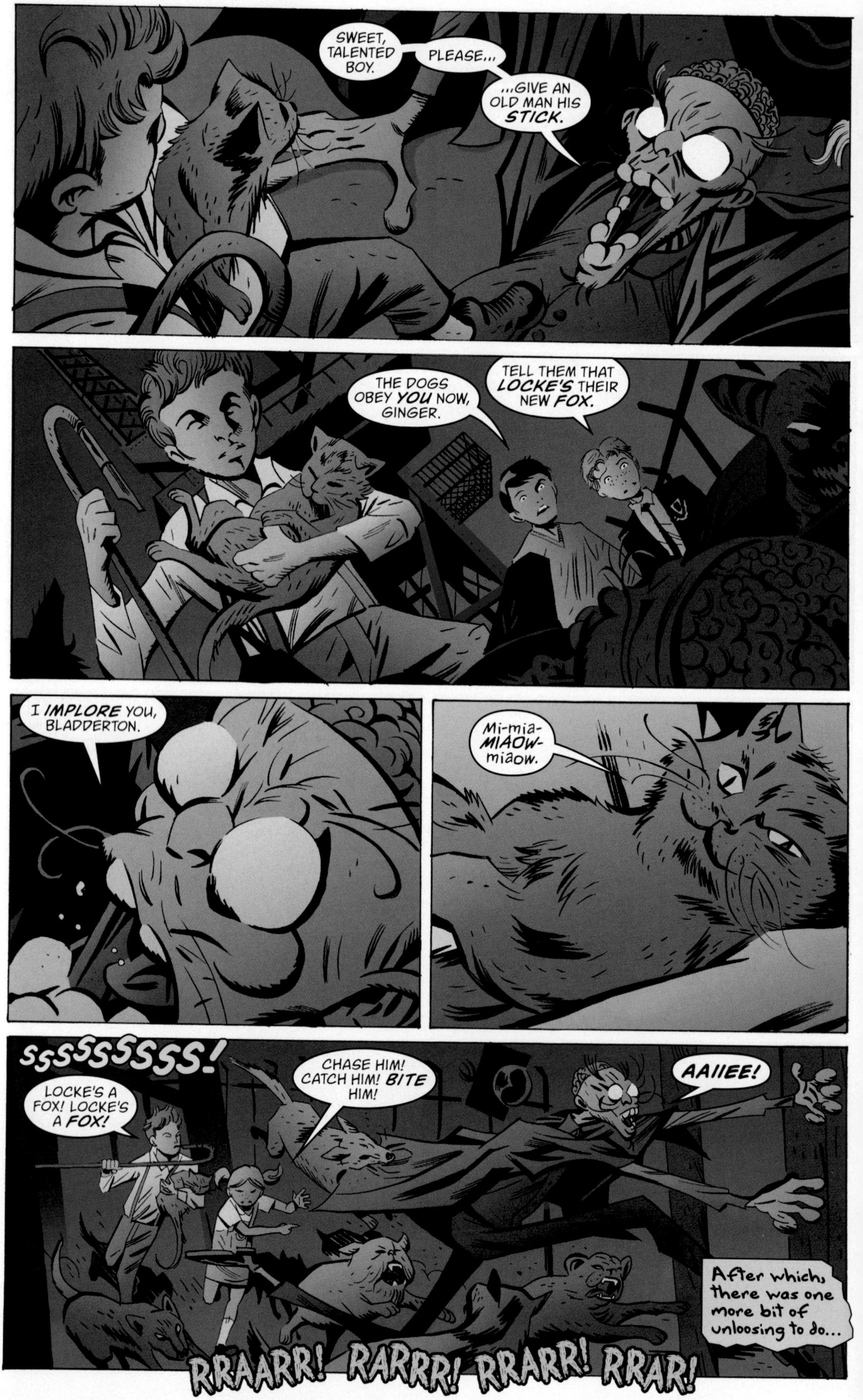
SWEET, TALENTED BOY.
PLEASE...
...GIVE AN OLD MAN HIS STICK.
THE DOGS OBEY YOU NOW, GINGER.
TELL THEM THAT LOCKE'S THEIR NEW FOX.
I IMPLORE YOU, BLADDERTON.
Mi-mia-MIAOW-miaow.
SSSSSSSSS!
LOCKE'S A FOX! LOCKE'S A FOX!
CHASE HIM! CATCH HIM! BITE HIM!
AAIIEE!
After which, there was one more bit of unloosing to do...
RRAARR! RARRR! RRARR! RRAR!

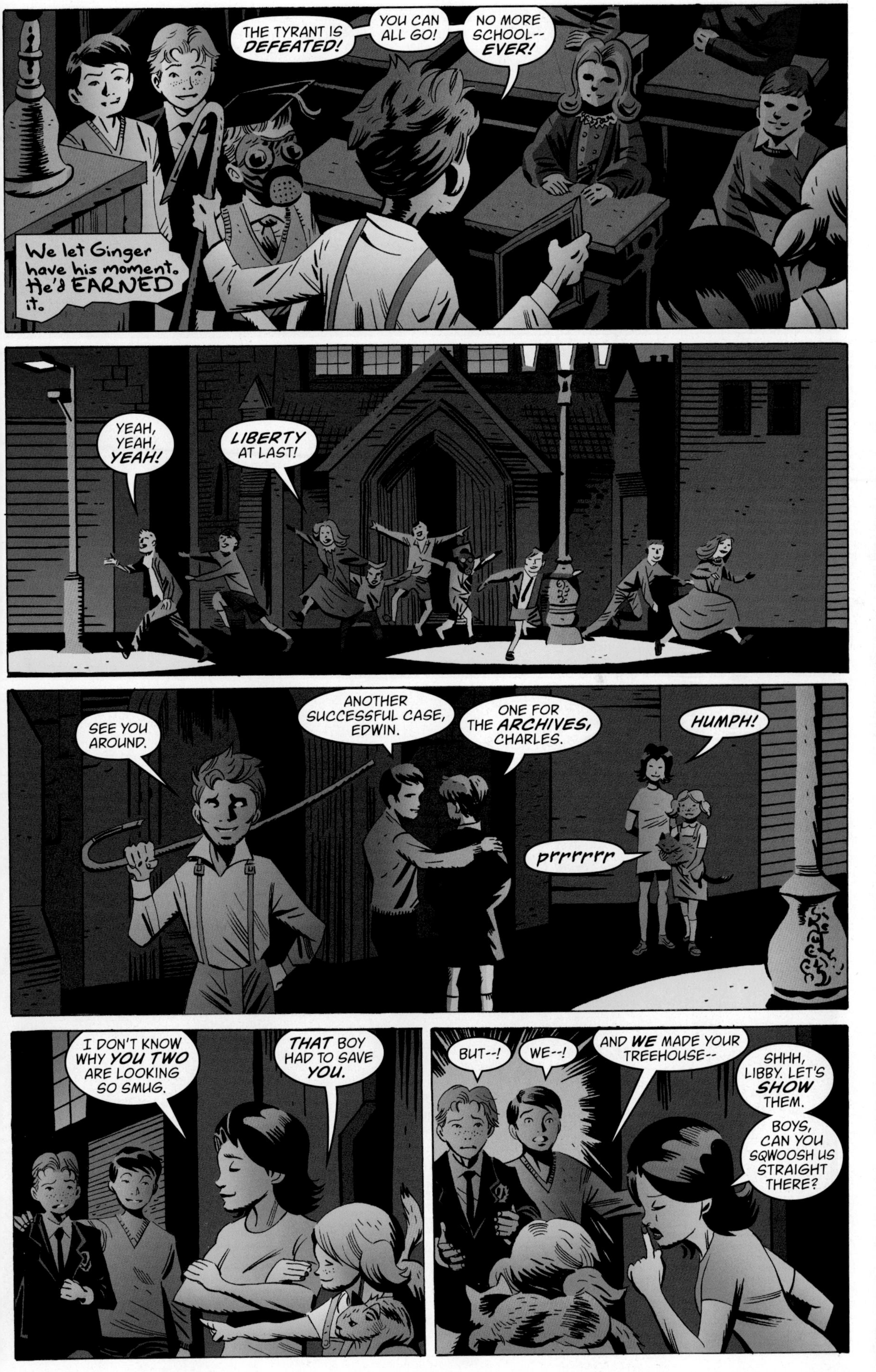

THE TYRANT IS DEFEATED!
YOU CAN ALL GO!
NO MORE SCHOOL-- EVER!
We let Ginger have his moment. He'd EARNED it.
YEAH, YEAH, YEAH!
LIBERTY AT LAST!
SEE YOU AROUND.
ANOTHER SUCCESSFUL CASE, EDWIN.
ONE FOR THE ARCHIVES, CHARLES.
HUMPH!
prrrrrr
I DON'T KNOW WHY YOU TWO ARE LOOKING SO SMUG.
THAT BOY HAD TO SAVE YOU.
BUT--!
WE--!
AND WE MADE YOUR TREEHOUSE--
SHHH, LIBBY. LET'S SHOW THEM.
BOYS, CAN YOU SQWOOSH US STRAIGHT THERE?

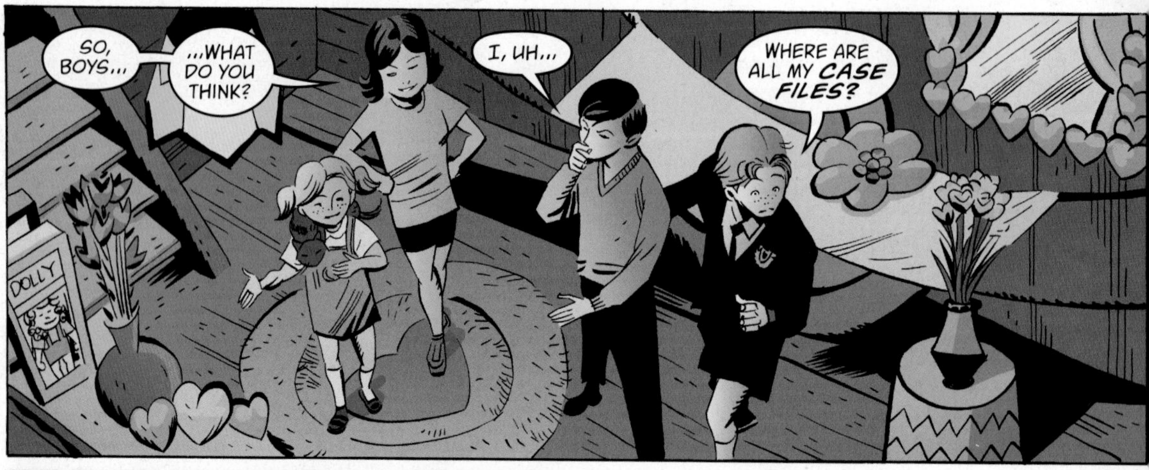
SO, BOYS...
...WHAT DO YOU THINK?
I, UH...
WHERE ARE ALL MY CASE FILES?
DOLLY

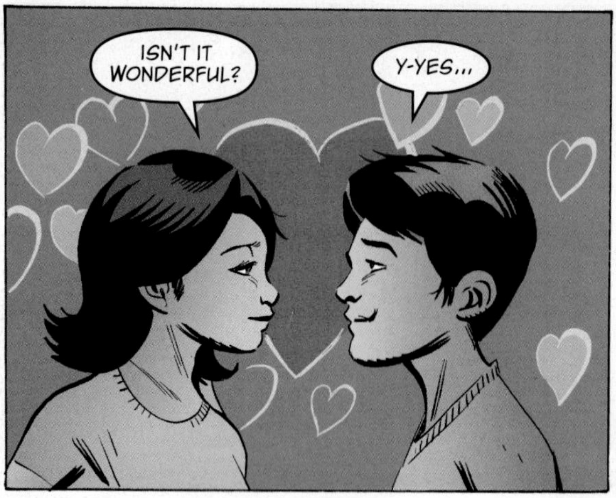
ISN'T IT WONDERFUL?
Y-YES...

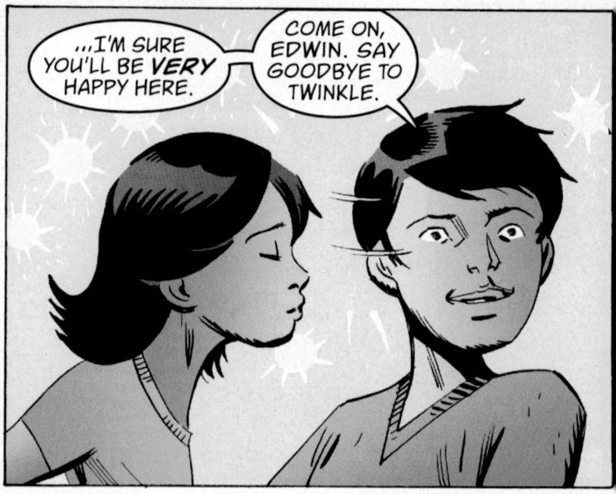
...I'M SURE YOU'LL BE VERY HAPPY HERE.
COME ON, EDWIN. SAY GOODBYE TO TWINKLE.

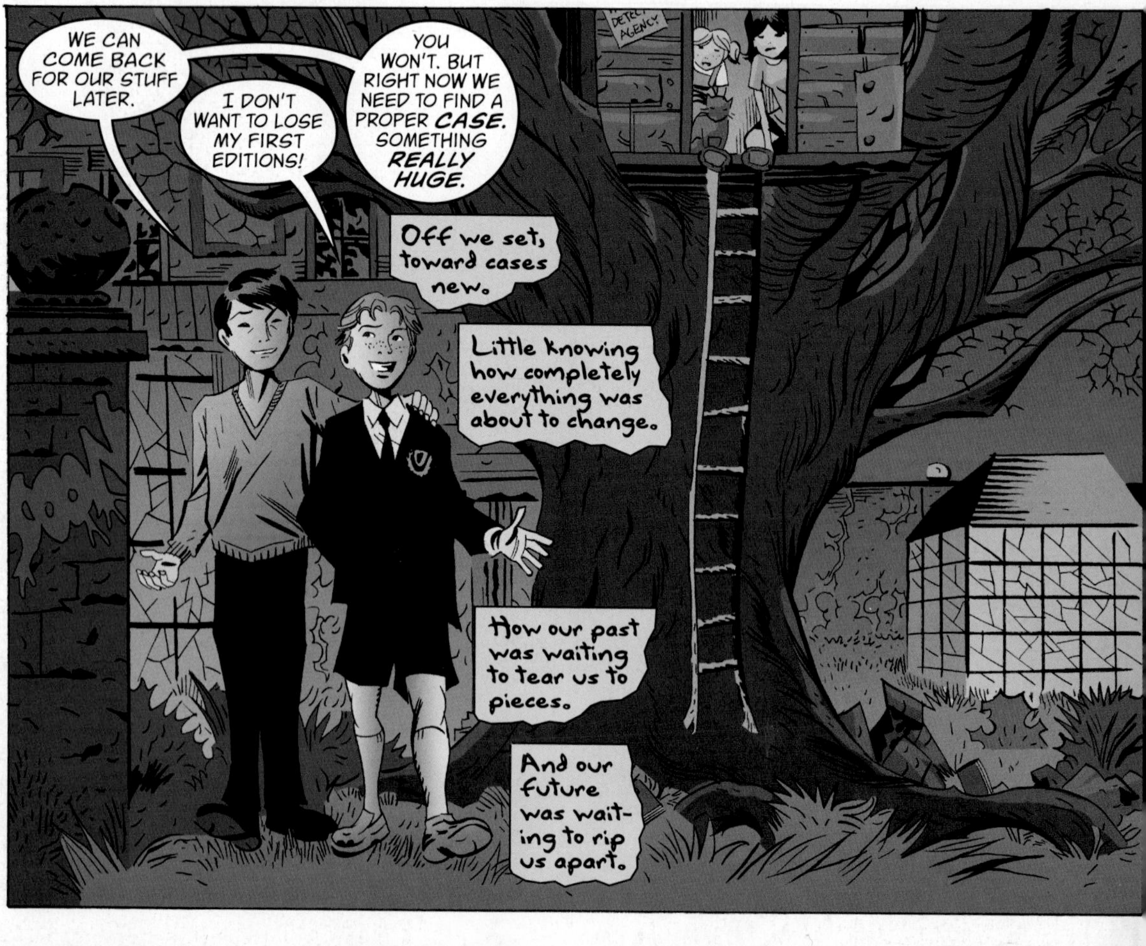
WE CAN COME BACK FOR OUR STUFF LATER.
I DON'T WANT TO LOSE MY FIRST EDITIONS!
YOU WON'T. BUT RIGHT NOW WE NEED TO FIND A PROPER CASE. SOMETHING REALLY HUGE.
Off we set, toward cases new.
Little knowing how completely everything was about to change.
How our past was waiting to tear us to pieces.
And our future was waiting to rip us apart.

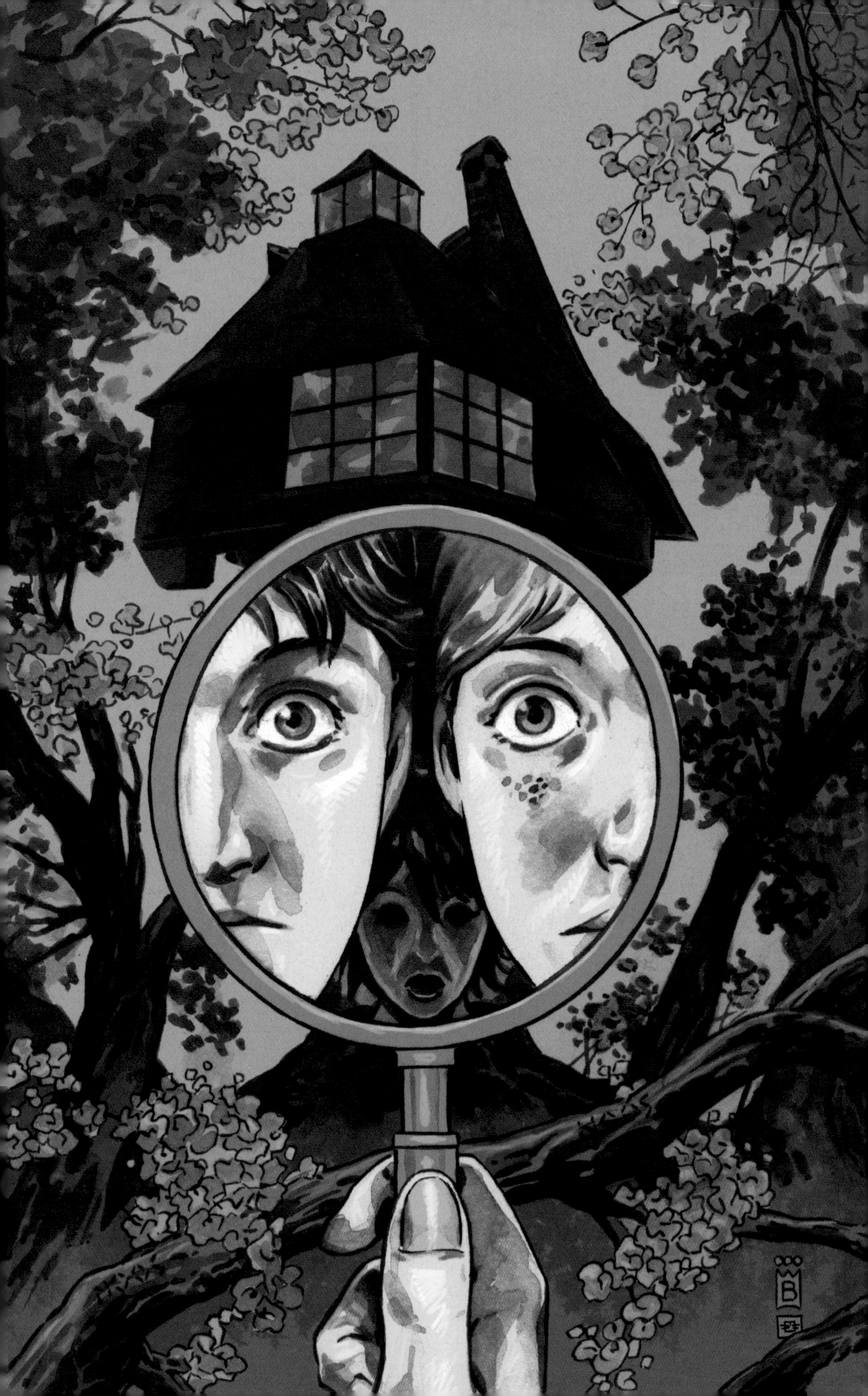

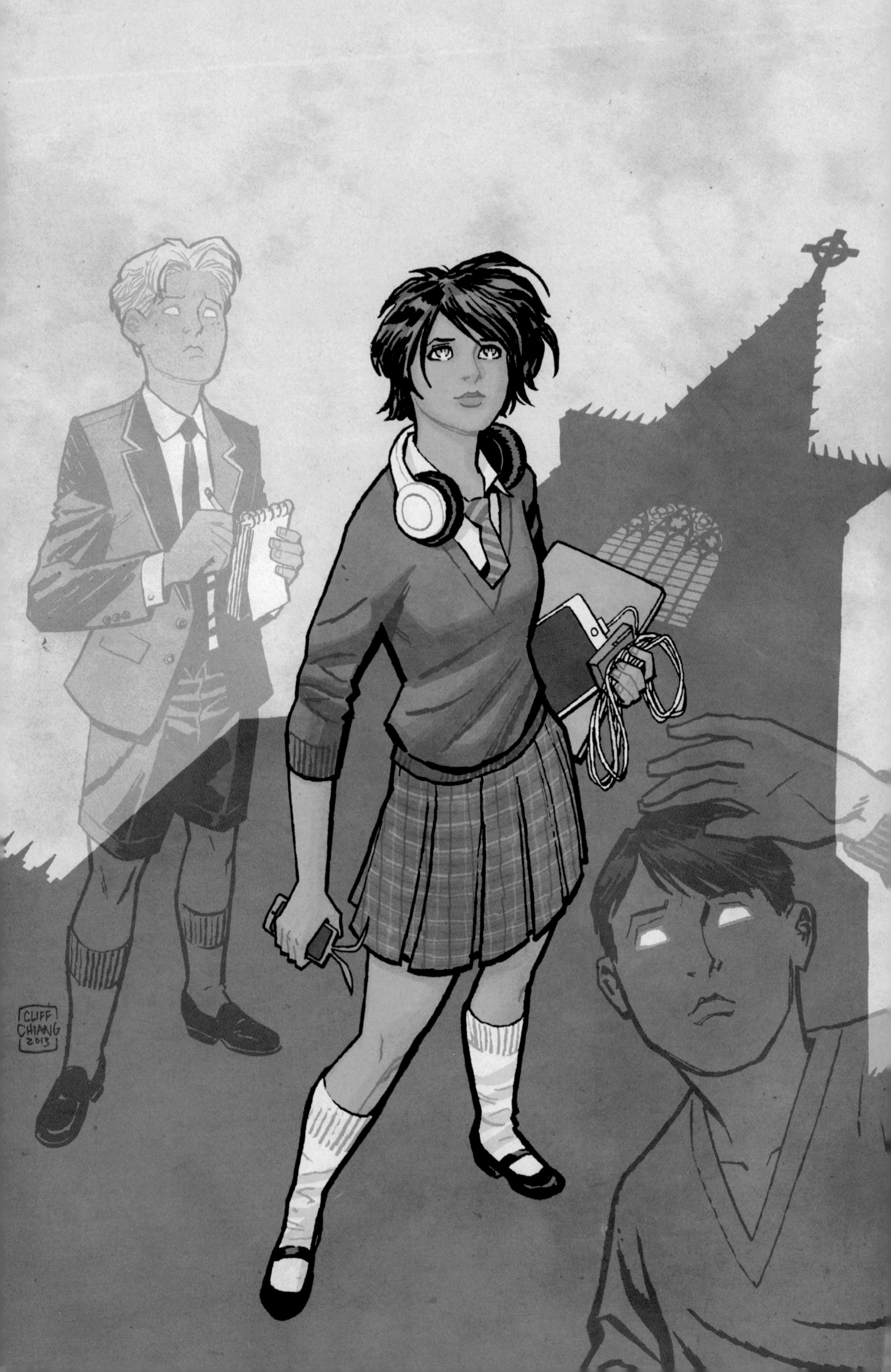

DEAD BOY DETECTIVES #1 variant cover
Art by Cliff Chiang

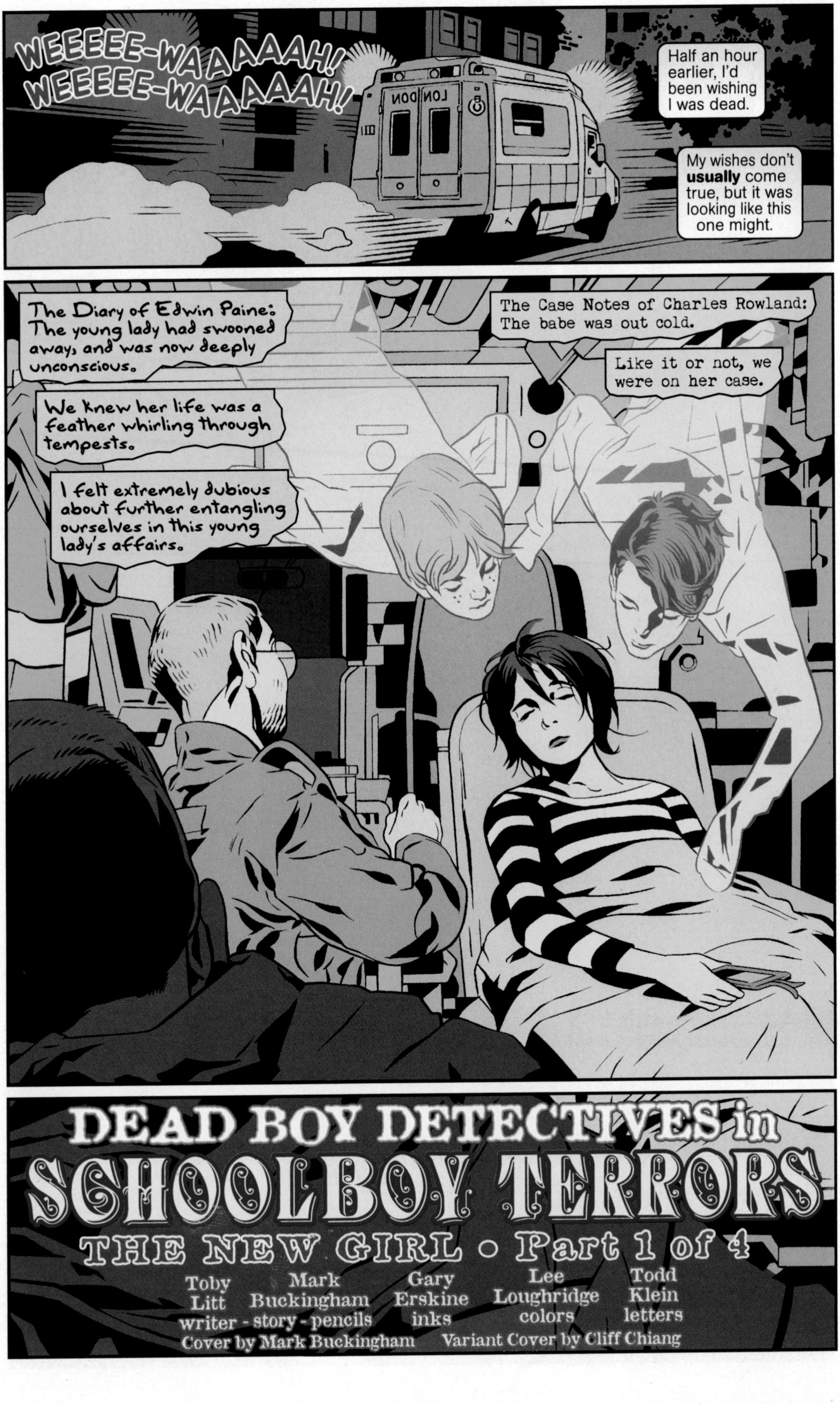
WEEEEE-WAAAAAH! WEEEEE-WAAAAAH!
Half an hour earlier, I'd been wishing I was dead.
My wishes don't **usually** come true, but it was looking like this one might.
The Diary of Edwin Paine: The young lady had swooned away, and was now deeply unconscious.
We knew her life was a feather whirling through tempests.
I felt extremely dubious about further entangling ourselves in this young lady's affairs.
The Case Notes of Charles Rowland: The babe was out cold.
Like it or not, we were on her case.
DEAD BOY DETECTIVES in
SCHOOLBOY TERRORS
THE NEW GIRL • Part 1 of 4
Toby Litt writer - Mark Buckingham story - pencils
Gary Erskine inks
Lee Loughridge colors
Todd Klein letters
Cover by Mark Buckingham
Variant Cover by Cliff Chiang

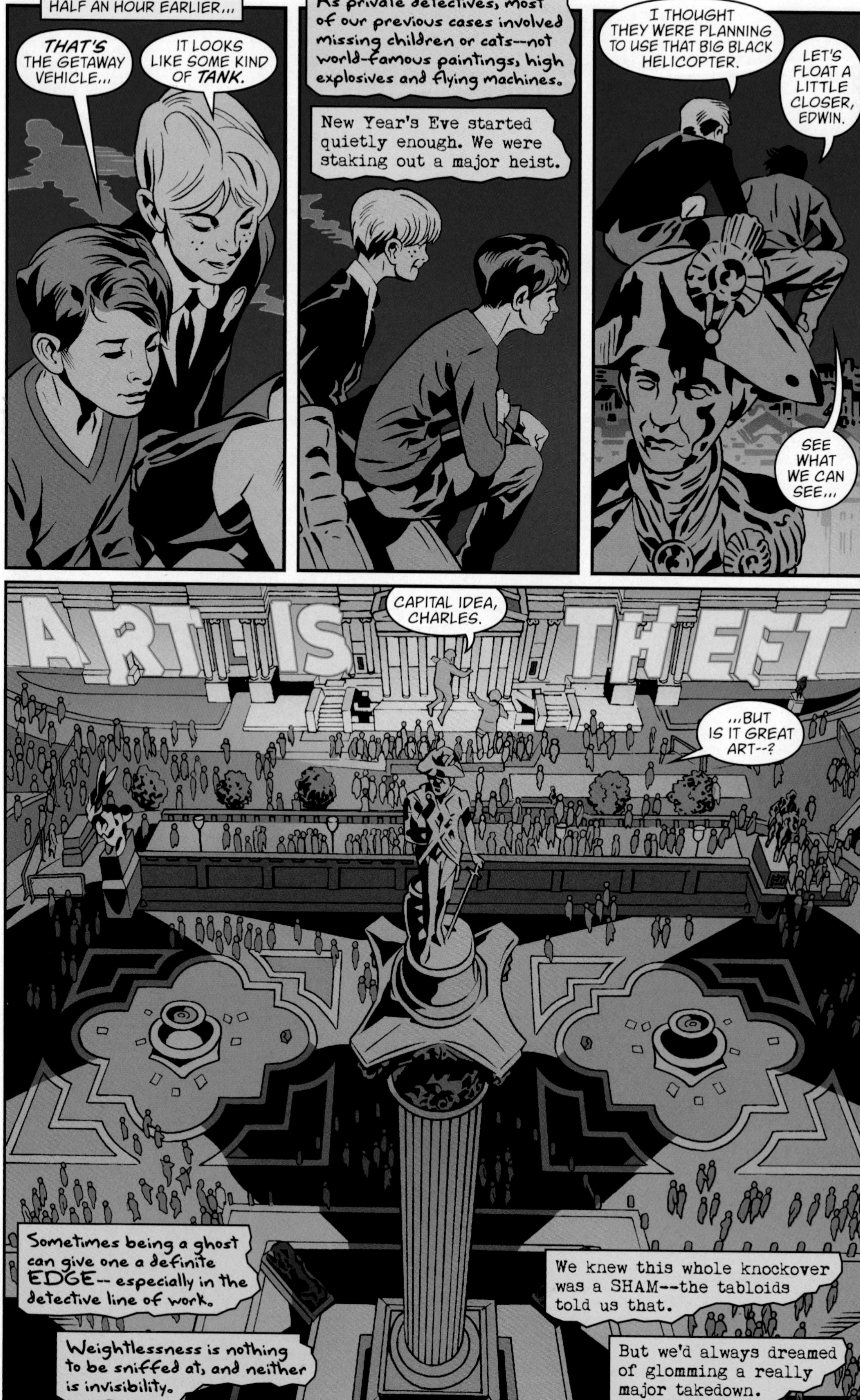

HALF AN HOUR EARLIER...
THAT'S THE GETAWAY VEHICLE...
IT LOOKS LIKE SOME KIND OF TANK.
As private detectives, most of our previous cases involved missing children or cats--not world-famous paintings, high explosives and flying machines.
New Year's Eve started quietly enough. We were staking out a major heist.
I THOUGHT THEY WERE PLANNING TO USE THAT BIG BLACK HELICOPTER.
LET'S FLOAT A LITTLE CLOSER, EDWIN.
SEE WHAT WE CAN SEE...
ART IS THEFT
CAPITAL IDEA, CHARLES.
...BUT IS IT GREAT ART--?
Sometimes being a ghost can give one a definite EDGE-- especially in the detective line of work.
Weightlessness is nothing to be sniffed at, and neither is invisibility.
We knew this whole knockover was a SHAM--the tabloids told us that.
But we'd always dreamed of glomming a really major takedown.

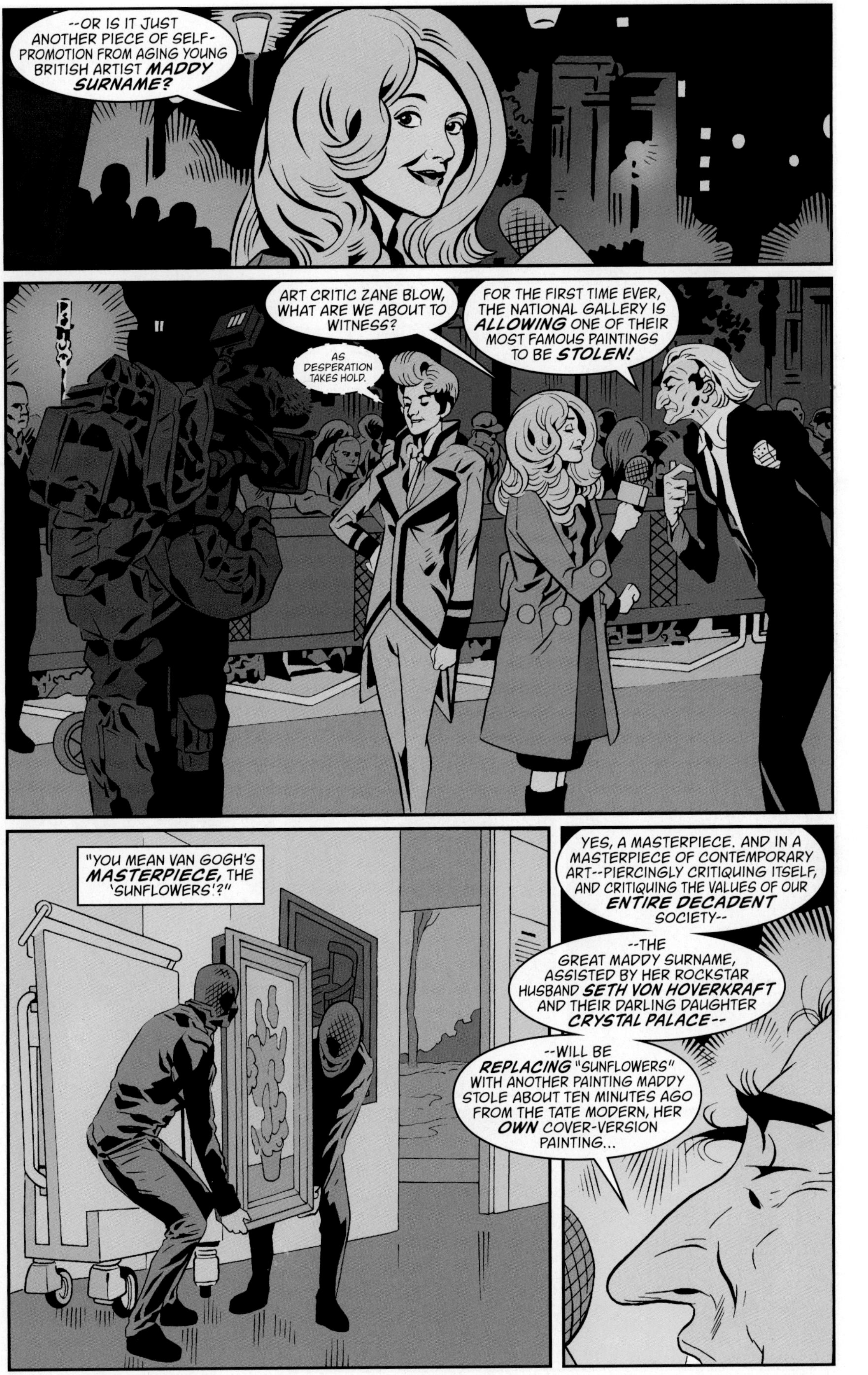
--OR IS IT JUST ANOTHER PIECE OF SELF-PROMOTION FROM AGING YOUNG BRITISH ARTIST MADDY SURNAME?
ART CRITIC ZANE BLOW, WHAT ARE WE ABOUT TO WITNESS?
AS DESPERATION TAKES HOLD.
FOR THE FIRST TIME EVER, THE NATIONAL GALLERY IS ALLOWING ONE OF THEIR MOST FAMOUS PAINTINGS TO BE STOLEN!
"YOU MEAN VAN GOGH'S MASTERPIECE, THE 'SUNFLOWERS'?"
YES, A MASTERPIECE. AND IN A MASTERPIECE OF CONTEMPORARY ART--PIERCINGLY CRITIQUING ITSELF, AND CRITIQUING THE VALUES OF OUR ENTIRE DECADENT SOCIETY--
--THE GREAT MADDY SURNAME, ASSISTED BY HER ROCKSTAR HUSBAND SETH VON HOVERKRAFT AND THEIR DARLING DAUGHTER CRYSTAL PALACE--
--WILL BE REPLACING "SUNFLOWERS" WITH ANOTHER PAINTING MADDY STOLE ABOUT TEN MINUTES AGO FROM THE TATE MODERN, HER OWN COVER-VERSION PAINTING...

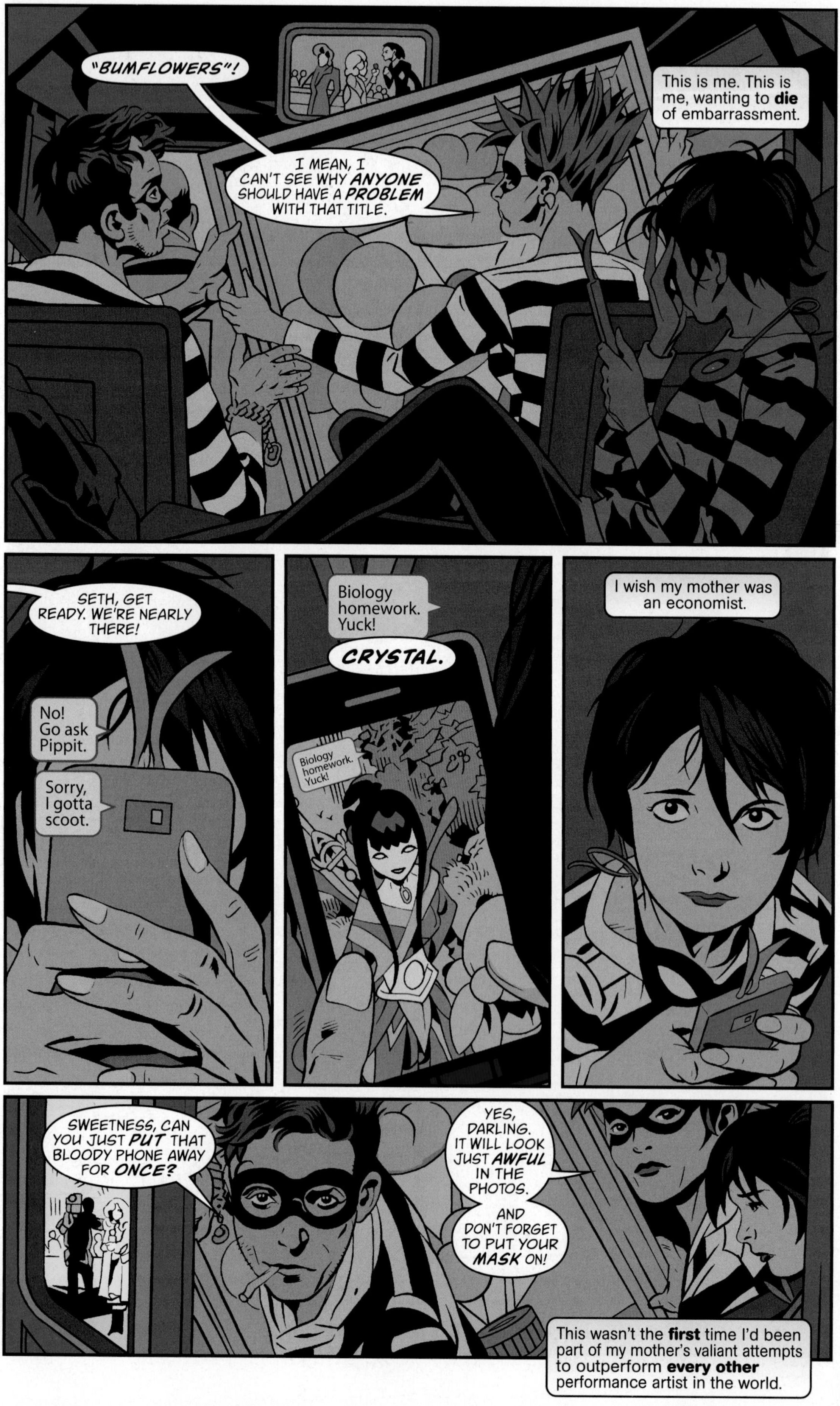
"BUMFLOWERS"!
I MEAN, I CAN'T SEE WHY ANYONE SHOULD HAVE A PROBLEM WITH THAT TITLE.
This is me. This is me, wanting to die of embarrassment.
SETH, GET READY. WE'RE NEARLY THERE!
No! Go ask Pippit.
Sorry, I gotta scoot.
Biology homework. Yuck!
CRYSTAL.
Biology homework. Yuck!
I wish my mother was an economist.
SWEETNESS, CAN YOU JUST PUT THAT BLOODY PHONE AWAY FOR ONCE?
YES, DARLING. IT WILL LOOK JUST AWFUL IN THE PHOTOS.
AND DON'T FORGET TO PUT YOUR MASK ON!
This wasn't the first time I'd been part of my mother's valiant attempts to outperform every other performance artist in the world.

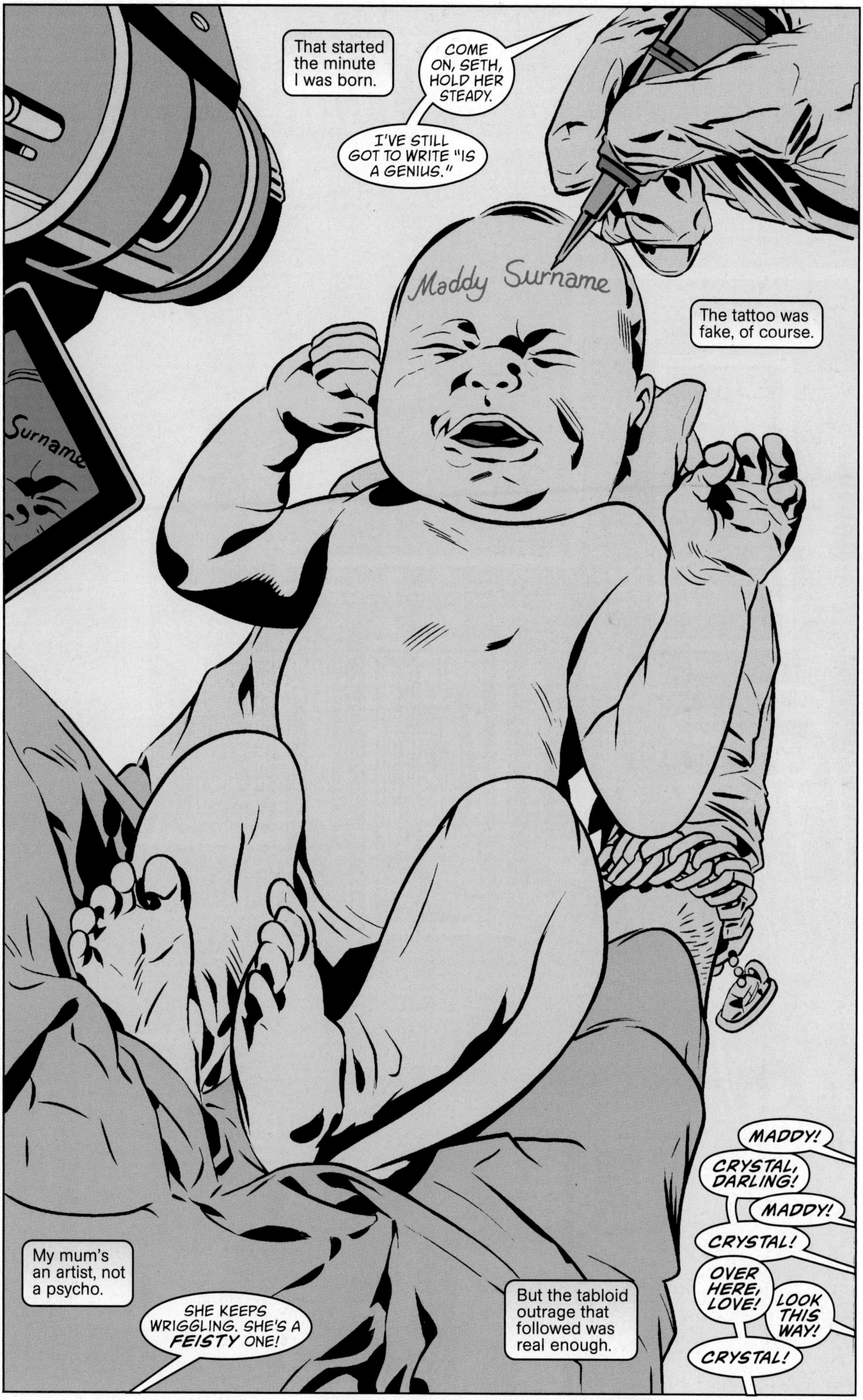
That started the minute I was born.
COME ON, SETH, HOLD HER STEADY.
I'VE STILL GOT TO WRITE "IS A GENIUS."
Maddy Surname
Surname
The tattoo was fake, of course.
MADDY!
CRYSTAL, DARLING!
MADDY!
CRYSTAL!
OVER HERE, LOVE!
LOOK THIS WAY!
CRYSTAL!
My mum's an artist, not a psycho.
SHE KEEPS WRIGGLING. SHE'S A FEISTY ONE!
But the tabloid outrage that followed was real enough.

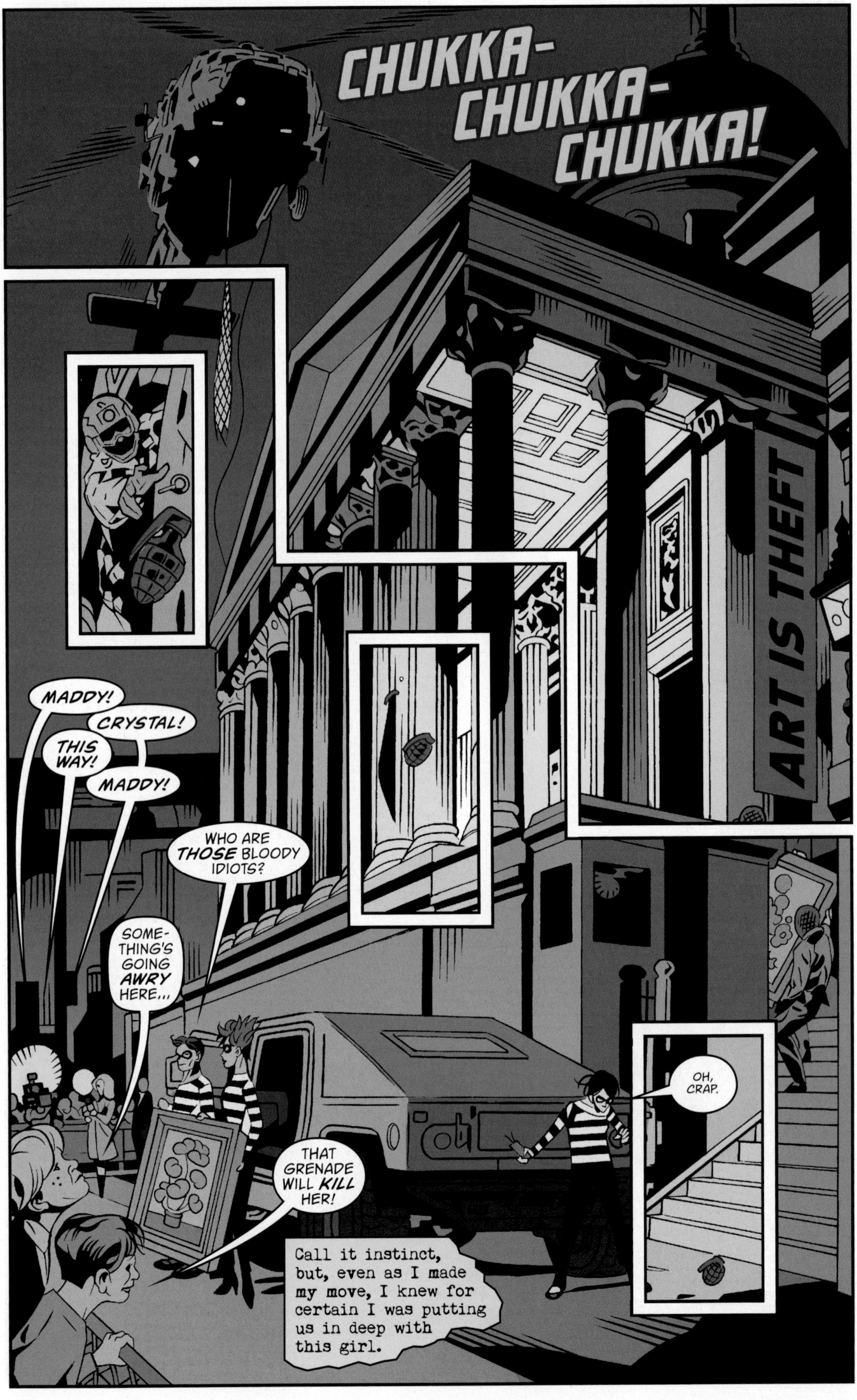
CHUKKA-
CHUKKA-
CHUKKA!
ART IS THEFT
MADDY!
CRYSTAL!
THIS WAY!
MADDY!
WHO ARE THOSE BLOODY IDIOTS?
SOME-THING'S GOING AWRY HERE...
OH, CRAP.
THAT GRENADE WILL KILL HER!
Call it instinct, but, even as I made my move, I knew for certain I was putting us in deep with this girl.

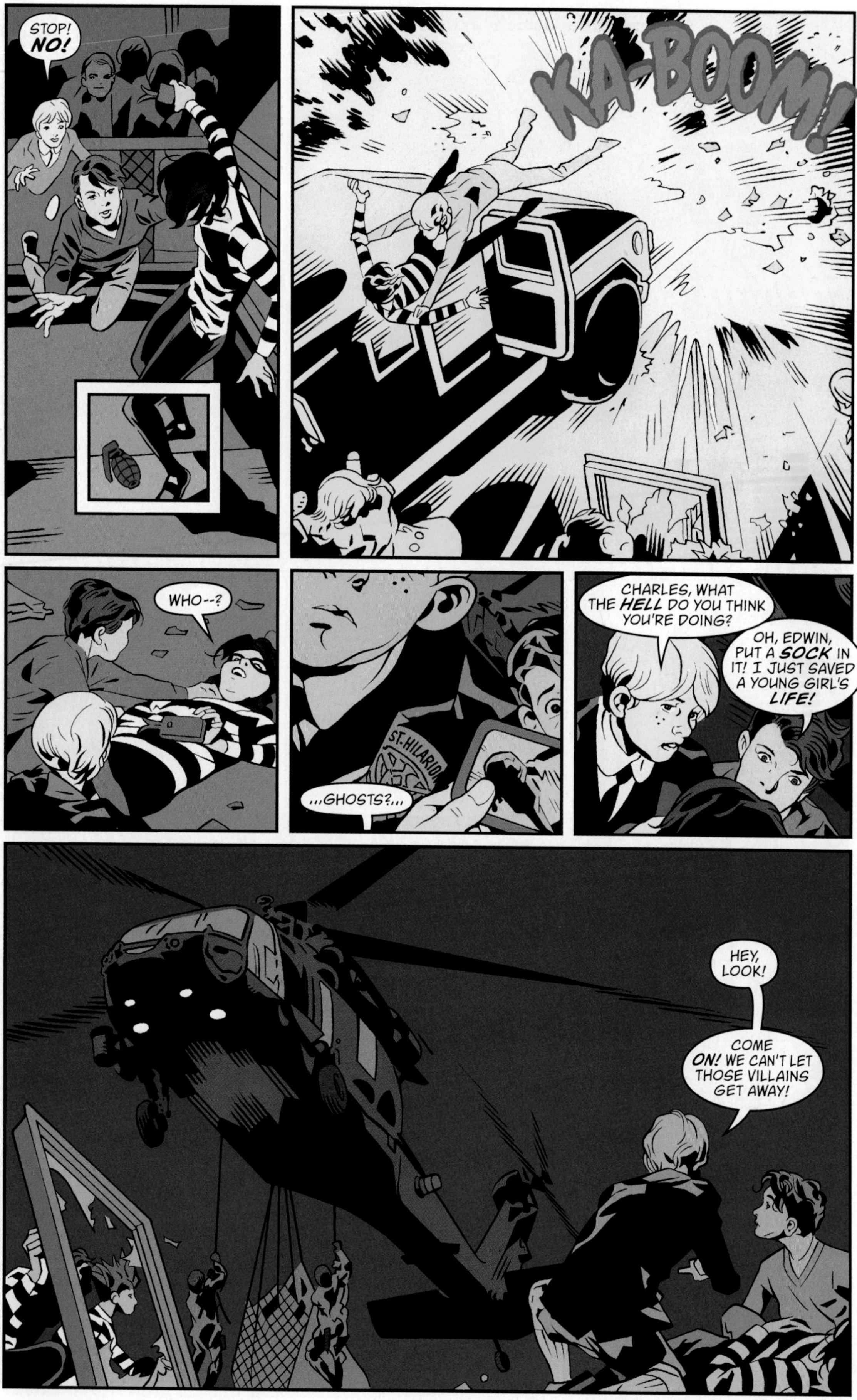
STOP! NO!
KA-BOOM!
WHO--?
...GHOSTS?...
ST. HILARION
CHARLES, WHAT THE HELL DO YOU THINK YOU'RE DOING?
OH, EDWIN, PUT A SOCK IN IT! I JUST SAVED A YOUNG GIRL'S LIFE!
HEY, LOOK!
COME ON! WE CAN'T LET THOSE VILLAINS GET AWAY!

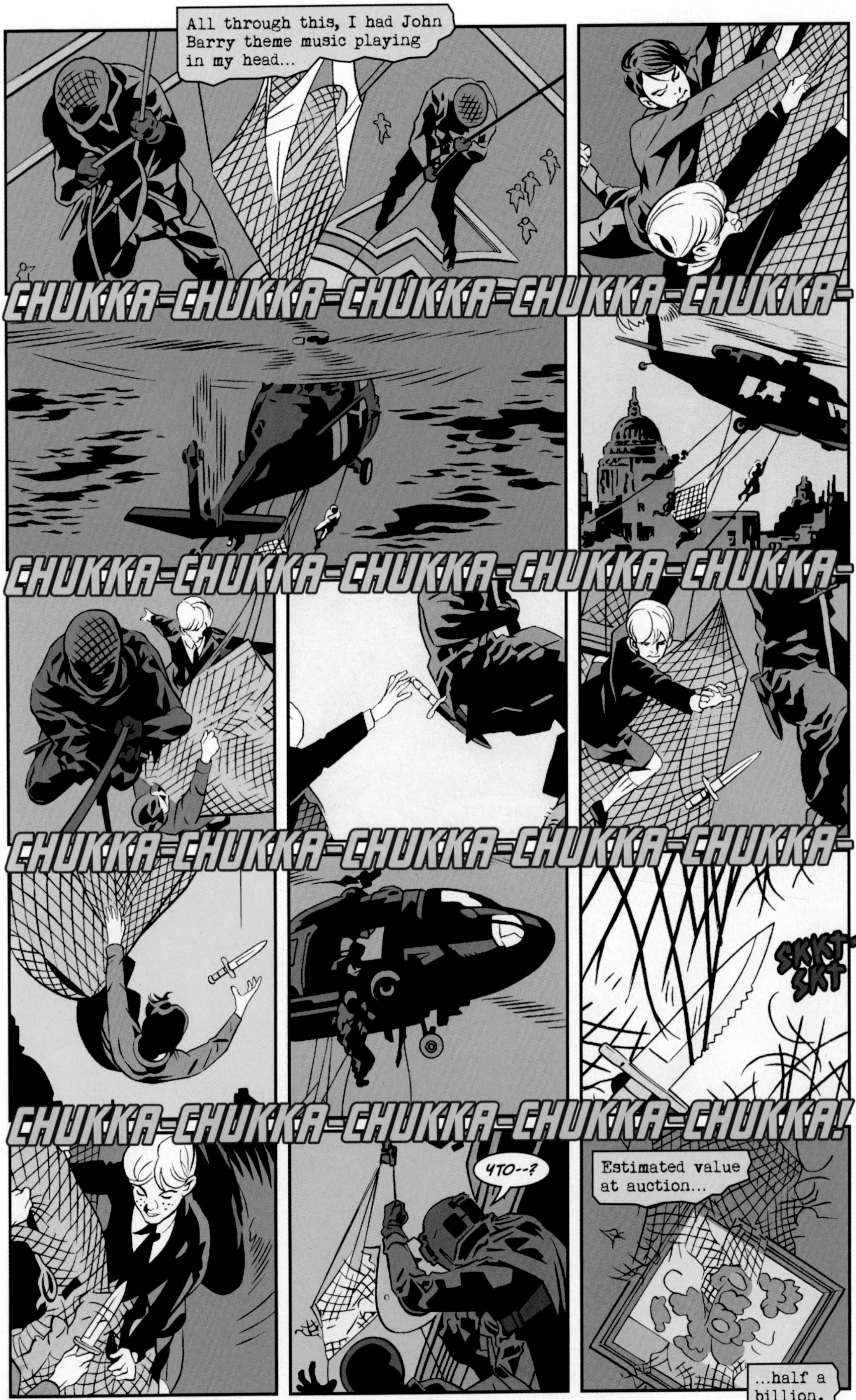
All through this, I had John Barry theme music playing in my head...
CHUKKA-CHUKKA-CHUKKA-CHUKKA-CHUKKA-
CHUKKA-CHUKKA-CHUKKA-CHUKKA-CHUKKA-
CHUKKA-CHUKKA-CHUKKA-CHUKKA-CHUKKA-
SKKT-SKT
CHUKKA-CHUKKA-CHUKKA-CHUKKA-CHUKKA!
ЧТО--?
Estimated value at auction...
...half a billion.

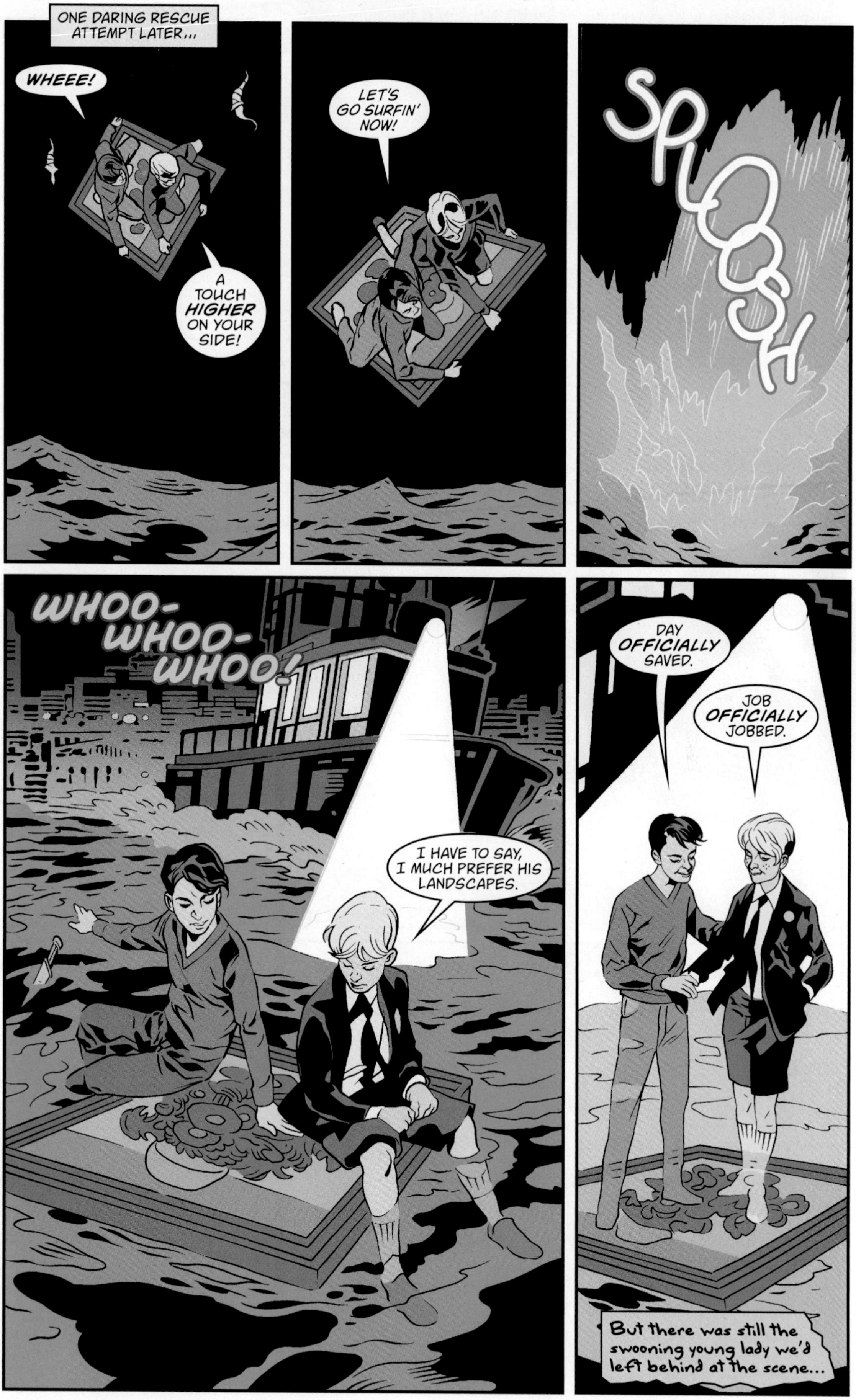
ONE DARING RESCUE ATTEMPT LATER...
WHEEE!
A TOUCH HIGHER ON YOUR SIDE!
LET'S GO SURFIN' NOW!
SPLOOSH
WHOO-WHOO-WHOO!
I HAVE TO SAY, I MUCH PREFER HIS LANDSCAPES.
DAY OFFICIALLY SAVED.
JOB OFFICIALLY JOBBED.
But there was still the swooning young lady we'd left behind at the scene...

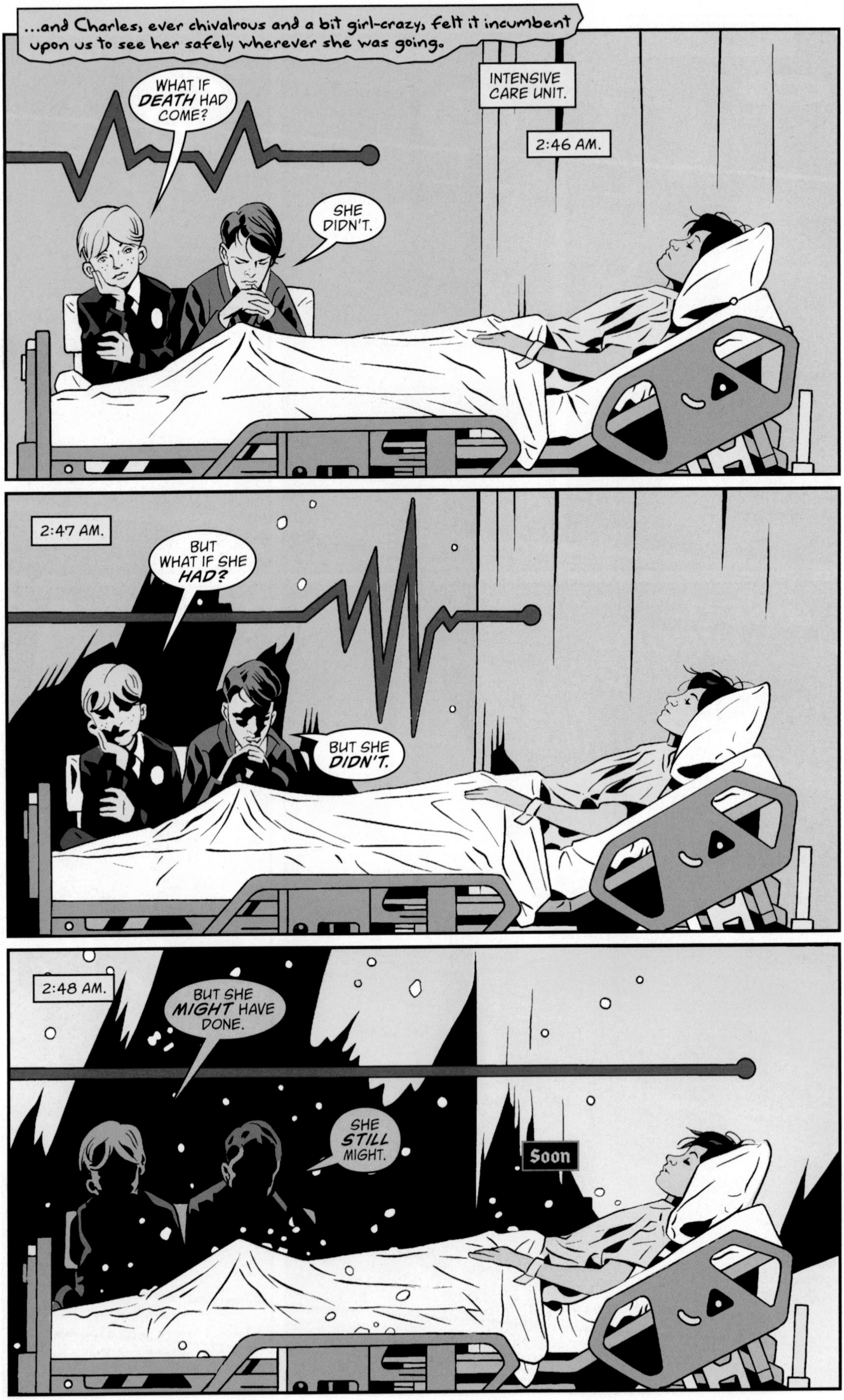
...and Charles, ever chivalrous and a bit girl-crazy, felt it incumbent upon us to see her safely wherever she was going.
INTENSIVE CARE UNIT.
2:46 AM.
WHAT IF DEATH HAD COME?
SHE DIDN'T.
2:47 AM.
BUT WHAT IF SHE HAD?
BUT SHE DIDN'T.
2:48 AM.
BUT SHE MIGHT HAVE DONE.
SHE STILL MIGHT.
Soon

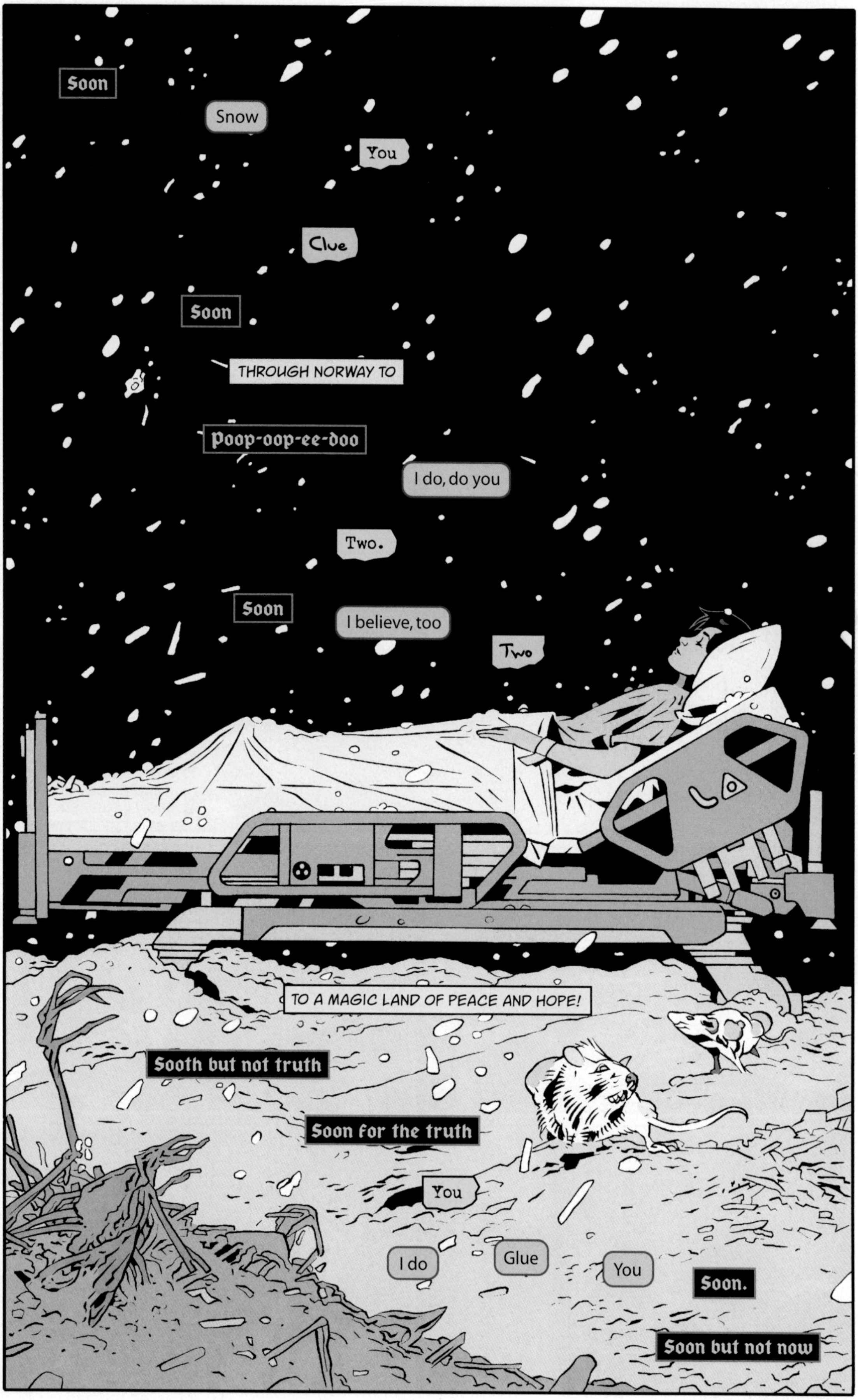
Soon
Snow
You
Clue
Soon
THROUGH NORWAY TO
Poop-oop-ee-doo
I do, do you
Two.
Soon
I believe, too
Two
TO A MAGIC LAND OF PEACE AND HOPE!
Sooth but not truth
Soon for the truth
You
I do
Glue
You
Soon.
Soon but not now

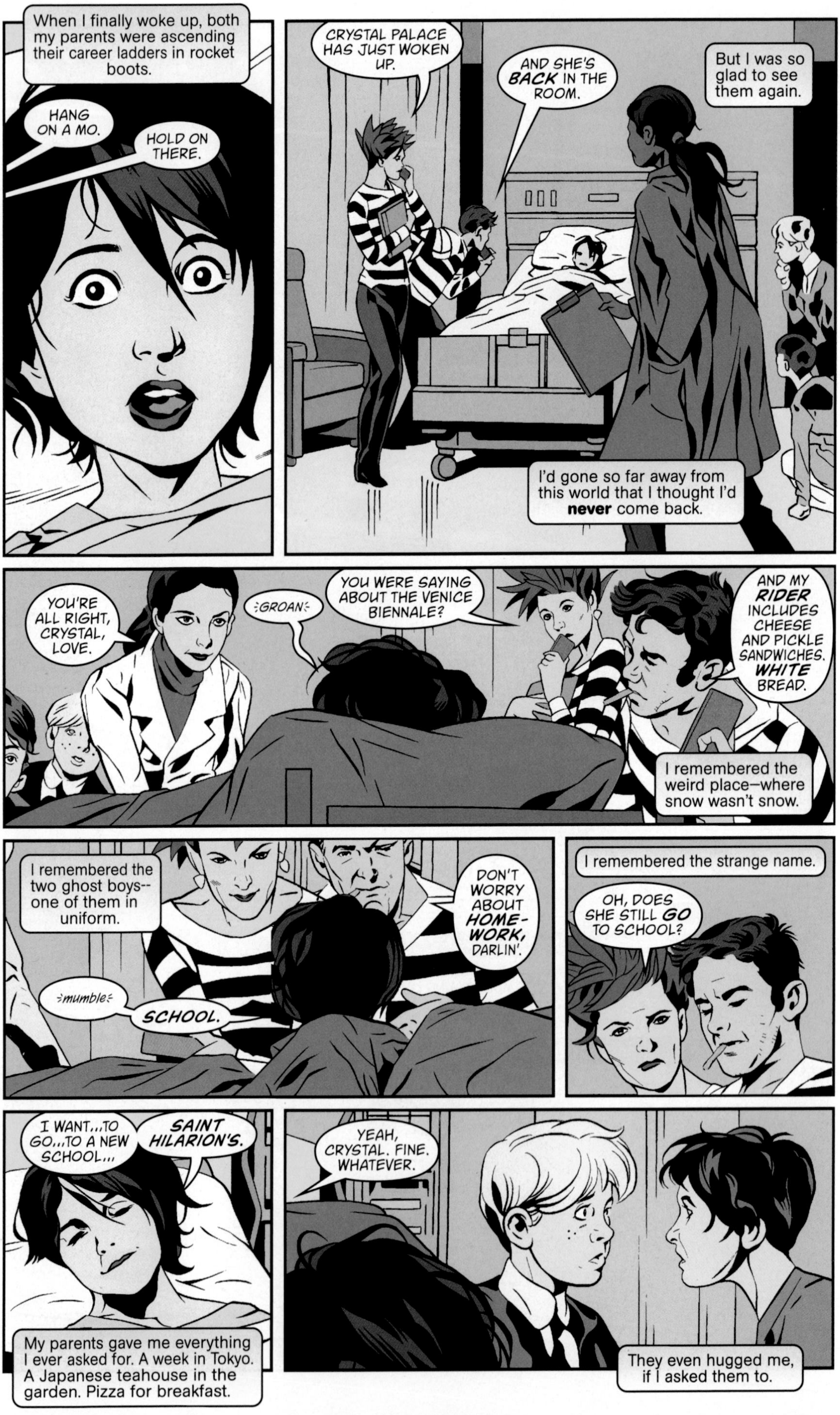

When I finally woke up, both my parents were ascending their career ladders in rocket boots.
HANG ON A MO.
HOLD ON THERE.
CRYSTAL PALACE HAS JUST WOKEN UP.
AND SHE'S BACK IN THE ROOM.
But I was so glad to see them again.
I'd gone so far away from this world that I thought I'd never come back.
YOU'RE ALL RIGHT, CRYSTAL, LOVE.
GROAN
YOU WERE SAYING ABOUT THE VENICE BIENNALE?
AND MY RIDER INCLUDES CHEESE AND PICKLE SANDWICHES. WHITE BREAD.
I remembered the weird place—where snow wasn't snow.
I remembered the two ghost boys-- one of them in uniform.
DON'T WORRY ABOUT HOME-WORK, DARLIN'.
mumble
SCHOOL.
I remembered the strange name.
OH, DOES SHE STILL GO TO SCHOOL?
I WANT...TO GO...TO A NEW SCHOOL...
SAINT HILARION'S.
My parents gave me everything I ever asked for. A week in Tokyo. A Japanese teahouse in the garden. Pizza for breakfast.
YEAH, CRYSTAL. FINE. WHATEVER.
They even hugged me, if I asked them to.

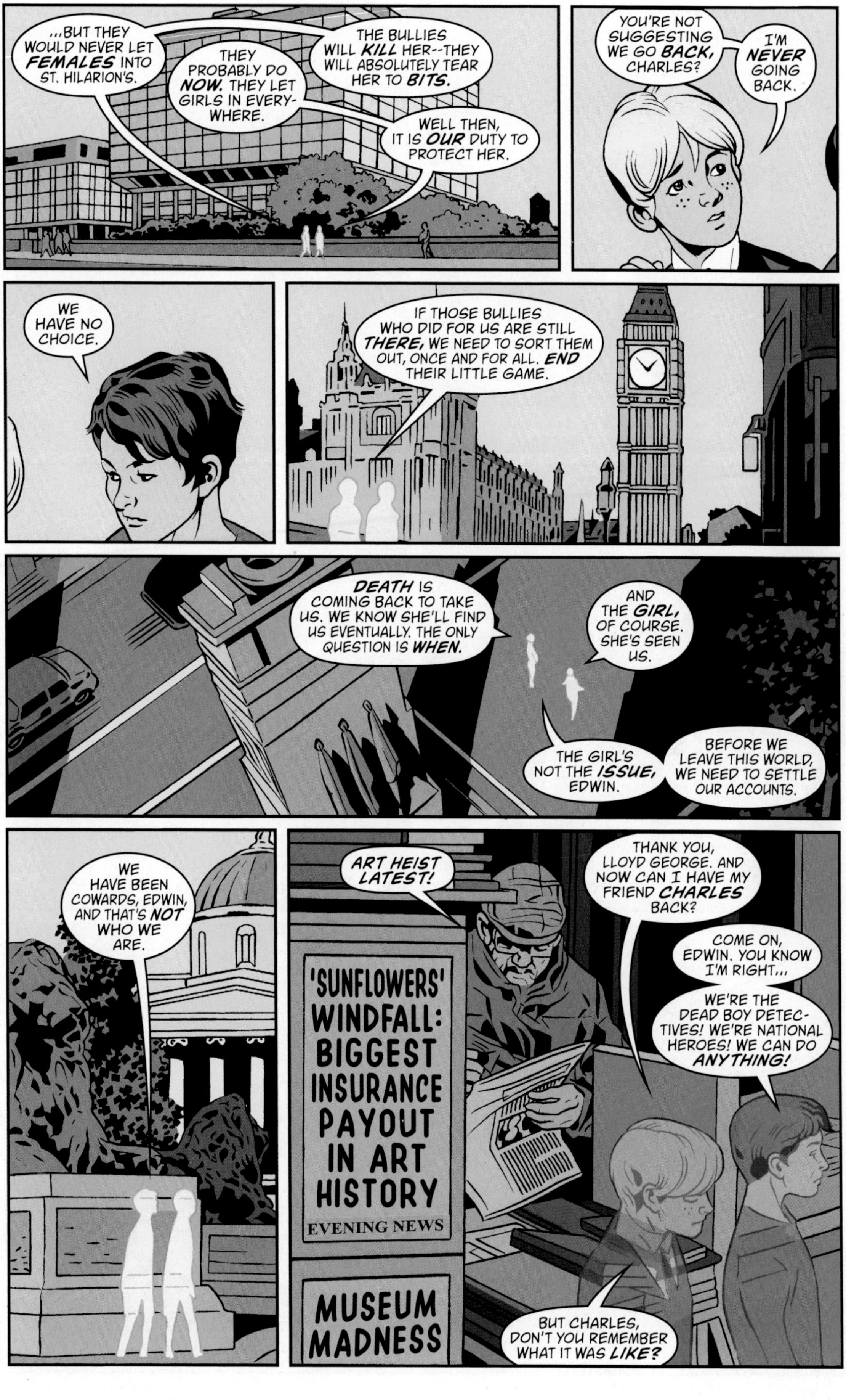

...BUT THEY WOULD NEVER LET FEMALES INTO ST. HILARION'S.
THEY PROBABLY DO NOW. THEY LET GIRLS IN EVERYWHERE.
THE BULLIES WILL KILL HER--THEY WILL ABSOLUTELY TEAR HER TO BITS.
WELL THEN, IT IS OUR DUTY TO PROTECT HER.
YOU'RE NOT SUGGESTING WE GO BACK, CHARLES?
I'M NEVER GOING BACK.
WE HAVE NO CHOICE.
IF THOSE BULLIES WHO DID FOR US ARE STILL THERE, WE NEED TO SORT THEM OUT, ONCE AND FOR ALL. END THEIR LITTLE GAME.
DEATH IS COMING BACK TO TAKE US. WE KNOW SHE'LL FIND US EVENTUALLY. THE ONLY QUESTION IS WHEN.
AND THE GIRL, OF COURSE. SHE'S SEEN US.
THE GIRL'S NOT THE ISSUE, EDWIN.
BEFORE WE LEAVE THIS WORLD, WE NEED TO SETTLE OUR ACCOUNTS.
WE HAVE BEEN COWARDS, EDWIN, AND THAT'S NOT WHO WE ARE.
ART HEIST LATEST!
'SUNFLOWERS' WINDFALL: BIGGEST INSURANCE PAYOUT IN ART HISTORY
EVENING NEWS
MUSEUM MADNESS
THANK YOU, LLOYD GEORGE. AND NOW CAN I HAVE MY FRIEND CHARLES BACK?
COME ON, EDWIN. YOU KNOW I'M RIGHT...
WE'RE THE DEAD BOY DETECTIVES! WE'RE NATIONAL HEROES! WE CAN DO ANYTHING!
BUT CHARLES, DON'T YOU REMEMBER WHAT IT WAS LIKE?

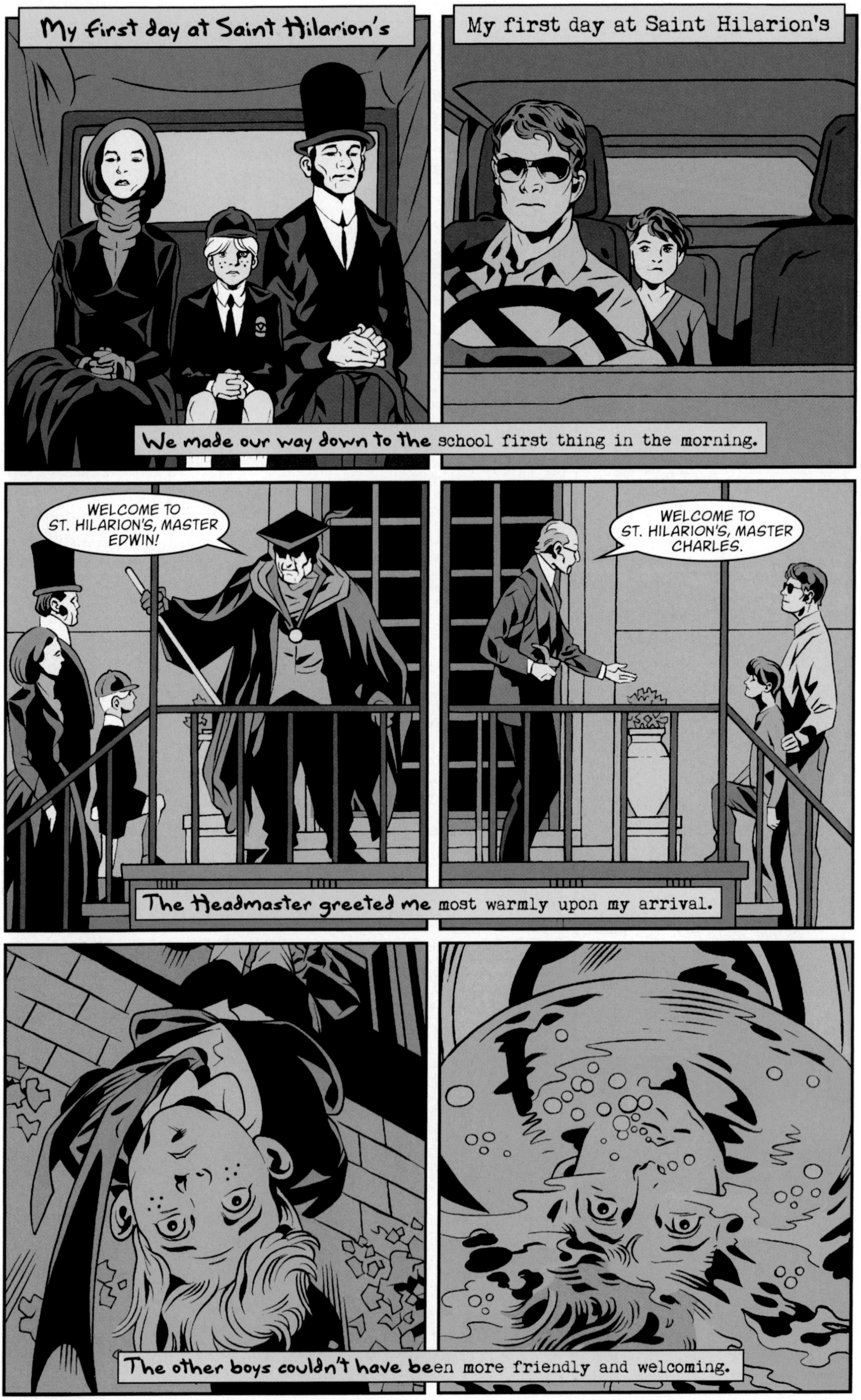
My first day at Saint Hilarion's
My first day at Saint Hilarion's
We made our way down to the school first thing in the morning.
WELCOME TO ST. HILARION'S, MASTER EDWIN!
WELCOME TO ST. HILARION'S, MASTER CHARLES.
The Headmaster greeted me most warmly upon my arrival.
The other boys couldn't have been more friendly and welcoming.

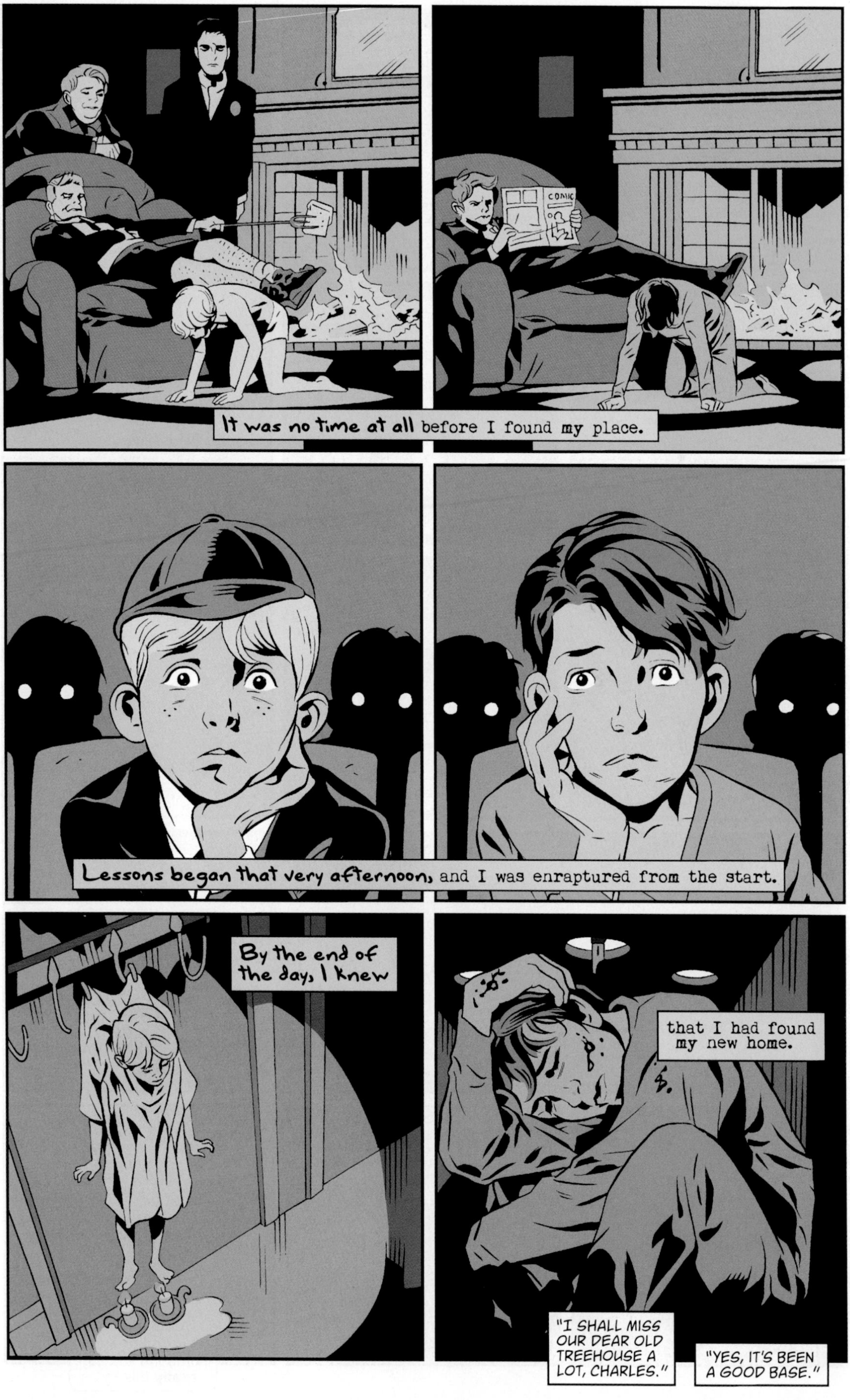
COMIC
It was no time at all before I found my place.
Lessons began that very afternoon, and I was enraptured from the start.
By the end of the day, I knew
that I had found my new home.
"I SHALL MISS OUR DEAR OLD TREEHOUSE A LOT, CHARLES."
"YES, IT'S BEEN A GOOD BASE."

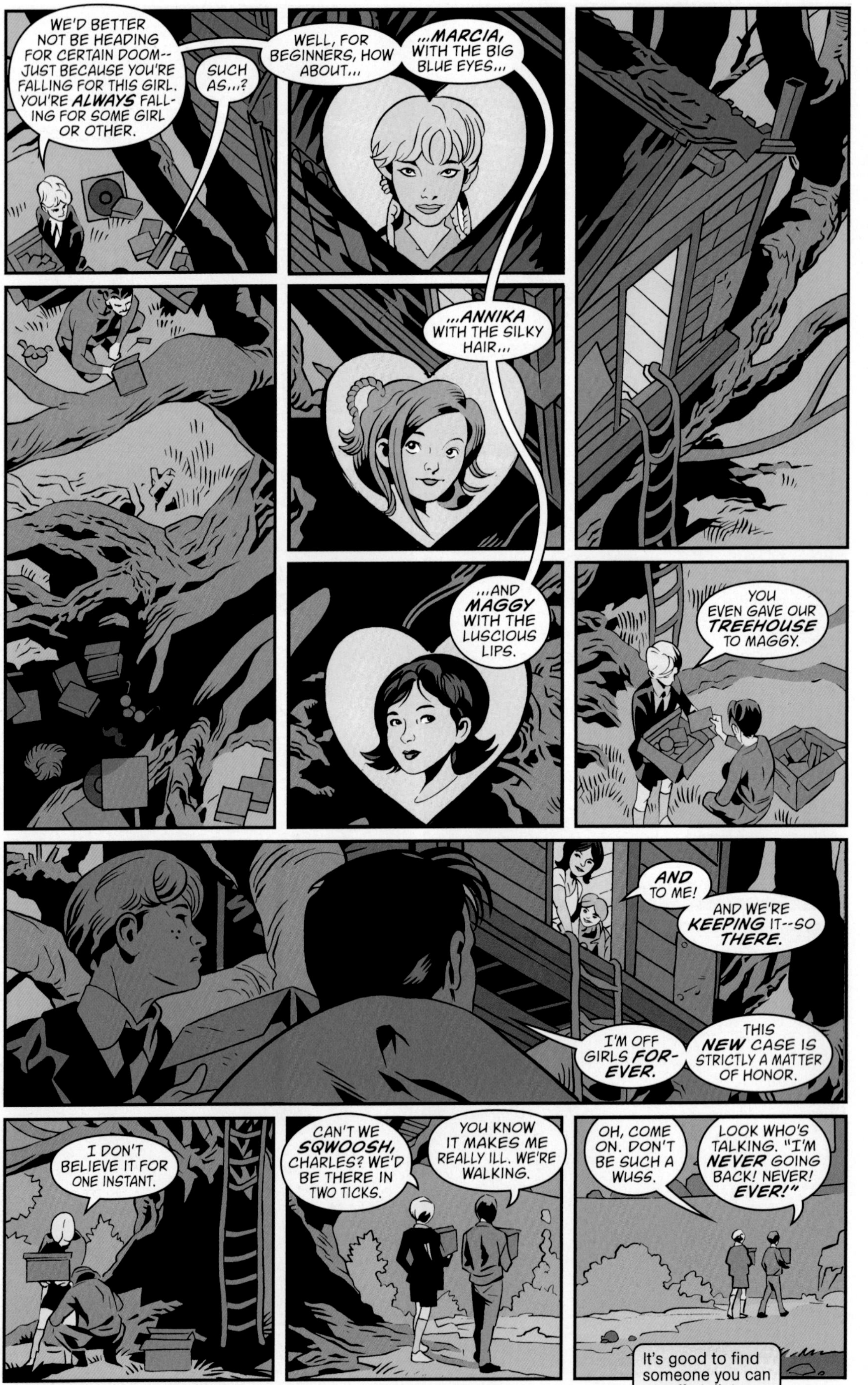
WE'D BETTER NOT BE HEADING FOR CERTAIN DOOM--JUST BECAUSE YOU'RE FALLING FOR THIS GIRL. YOU'RE ALWAYS FALLING FOR SOME GIRL OR OTHER.
SUCH AS...?
WELL, FOR BEGINNERS, HOW ABOUT...
...MARCIA, WITH THE BIG BLUE EYES...
...ANNIKA WITH THE SILKY HAIR...
...AND MAGGY WITH THE LUSCIOUS LIPS.
YOU EVEN GAVE OUR TREEHOUSE TO MAGGY.
AND TO ME!
AND WE'RE KEEPING IT--SO THERE.
I'M OFF GIRLS FOR-EVER.
THIS NEW CASE IS STRICTLY A MATTER OF HONOR.
I DON'T BELIEVE IT FOR ONE INSTANT.
CAN'T WE SQWOOSH, CHARLES? WE'D BE THERE IN TWO TICKS.
YOU KNOW IT MAKES ME REALLY ILL. WE'RE WALKING.
OH, COME ON. DON'T BE SUCH A WUSS.
LOOK WHO'S TALKING. "I'M NEVER GOING BACK! NEVER! EVER!"
It's good to find someone you can really talk to.

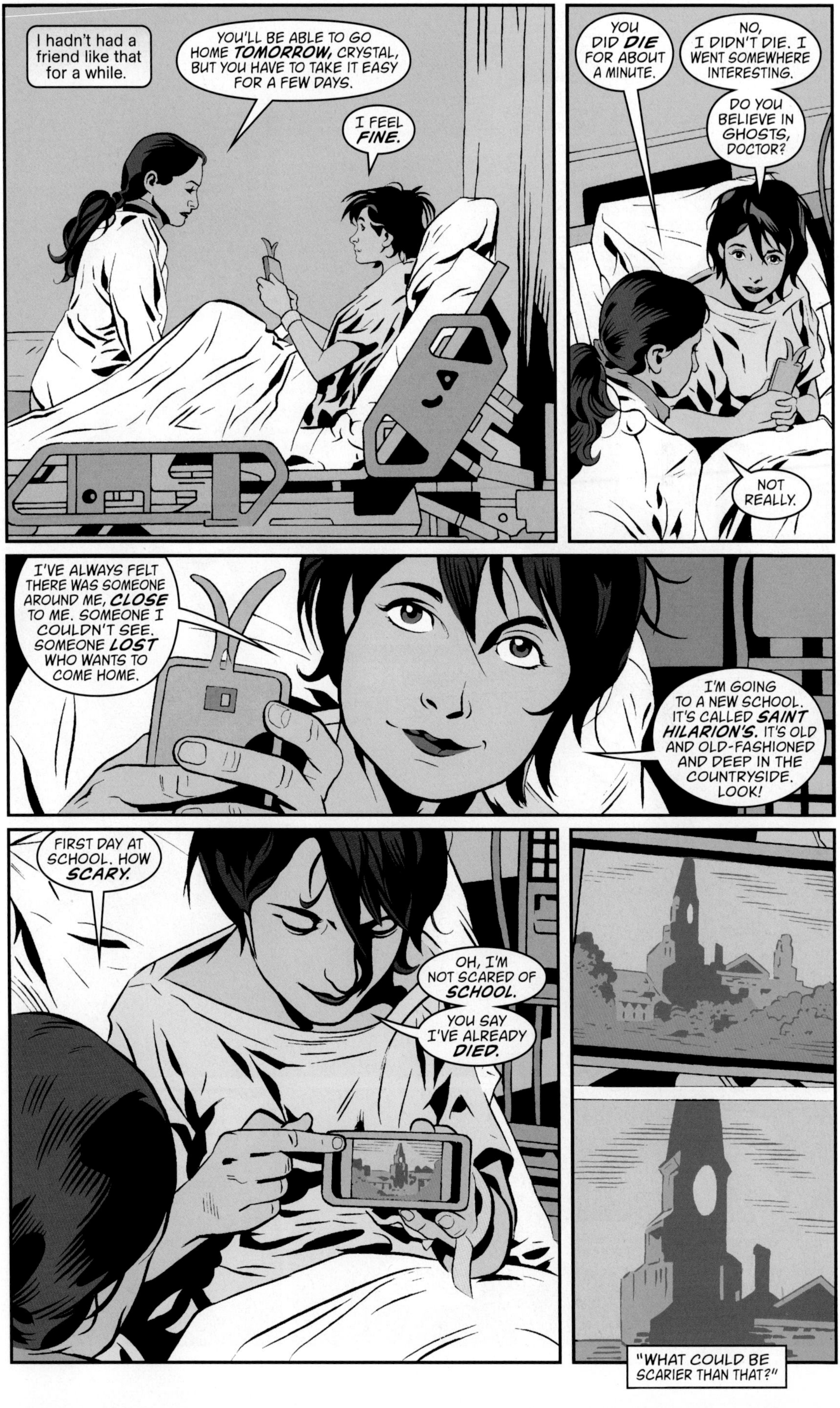

I hadn't had a friend like that for a while.
YOU'LL BE ABLE TO GO HOME TOMORROW, CRYSTAL, BUT YOU HAVE TO TAKE IT EASY FOR A FEW DAYS.
I FEEL FINE.
YOU DID DIE FOR ABOUT A MINUTE.
NO, I DIDN'T DIE. I WENT SOMEWHERE INTERESTING.
DO YOU BELIEVE IN GHOSTS, DOCTOR?
NOT REALLY.
I'VE ALWAYS FELT THERE WAS SOMEONE AROUND ME, CLOSE TO ME. SOMEONE I COULDN'T SEE. SOMEONE LOST WHO WANTS TO COME HOME.
I'M GOING TO A NEW SCHOOL. IT'S CALLED SAINT HILARION'S. IT'S OLD AND OLD-FASHIONED AND DEEP IN THE COUNTRYSIDE. LOOK!
FIRST DAY AT SCHOOL. HOW SCARY.
OH, I'M NOT SCARED OF SCHOOL.
YOU SAY I'VE ALREADY DIED.
"WHAT COULD BE SCARIER THAN THAT?"

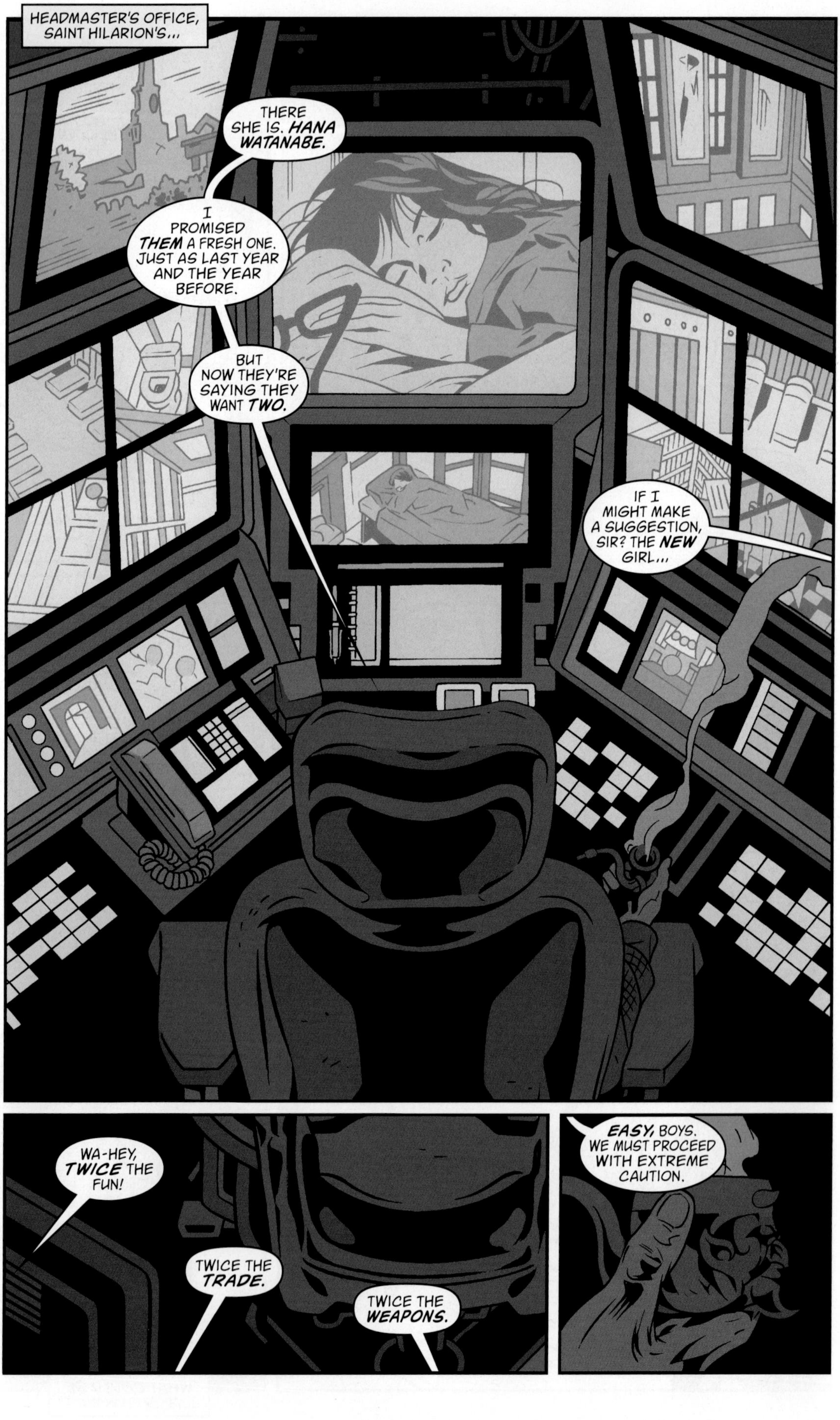
HEADMASTER'S OFFICE, SAINT HILARION'S...
THERE SHE IS. HANA WATANABE.
I PROMISED THEM A FRESH ONE. JUST AS LAST YEAR AND THE YEAR BEFORE.
BUT NOW THEY'RE SAYING THEY WANT TWO.
IF I MIGHT MAKE A SUGGESTION, SIR? THE NEW GIRL...
WA-HEY, TWICE THE FUN!
TWICE THE TRADE.
TWICE THE WEAPONS.
EASY, BOYS. WE MUST PROCEED WITH EXTREME CAUTION.

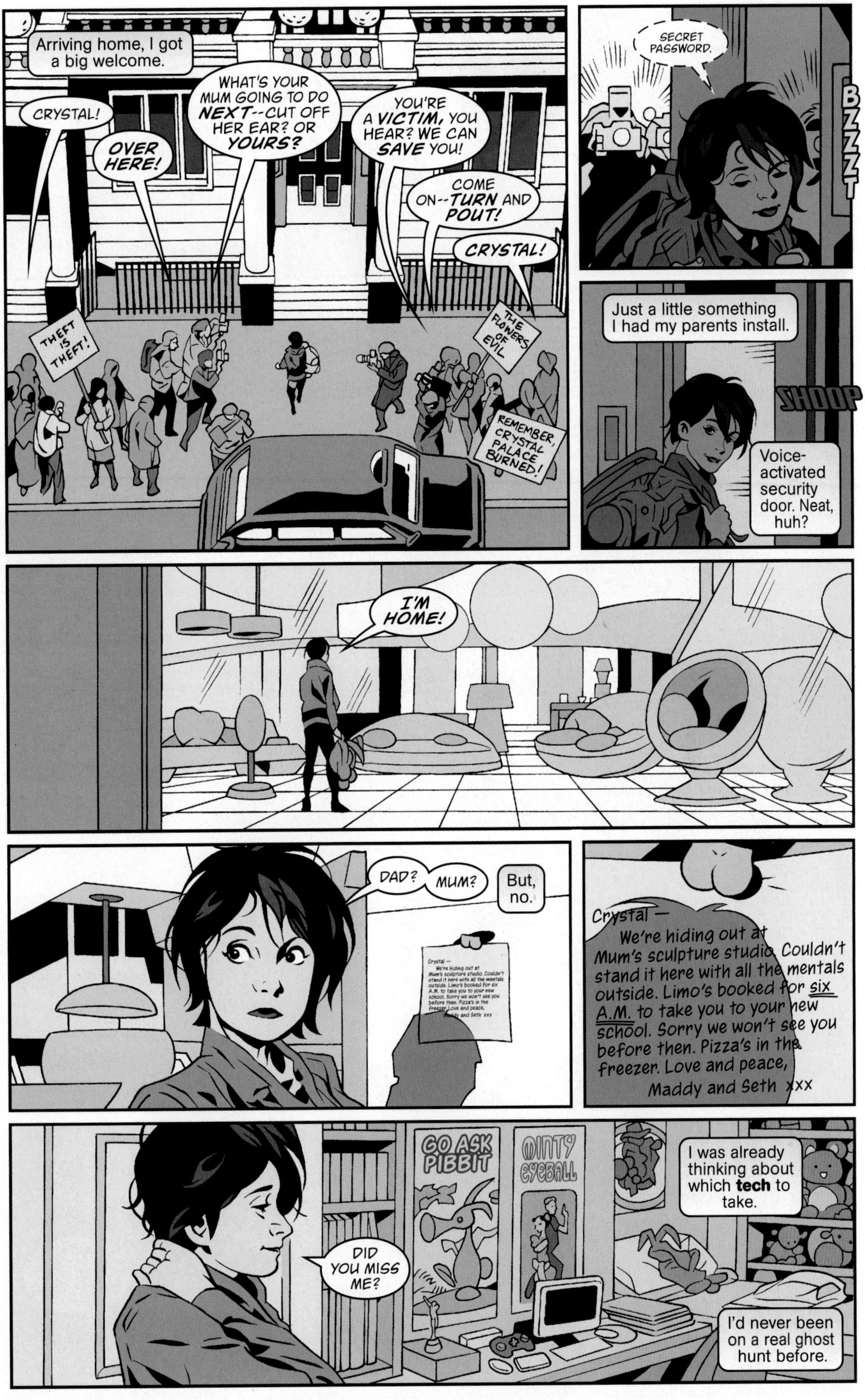

Arriving home, I got a big welcome.
CRYSTAL!
OVER HERE!
WHAT'S YOUR MUM GOING TO DO NEXT--CUT OFF HER EAR? OR YOURS?
YOU'RE A VICTIM, YOU HEAR? WE CAN SAVE YOU!
COME ON--TURN AND POUT!
CRYSTAL!
THEFT IS THEFT!
THE FLOWERS OF EVIL
REMEMBER, CRYSTAL PALACE BURNED!
SECRET PASSWORD.
BZZZT
Just a little something I had my parents install.
SHOOP
Voice-activated security door. Neat, huh?
I'M HOME!
DAD?
MUM?
But, no.
Crystal — We're hiding out at Mum's sculpture studio. Couldn't stand it here with all the mentals outside. Limo's booked for six A.M. to take you to your new school. Sorry we won't see you before then. Pizza's in the freezer. Love and peace, Maddy and Seth xxx
GO ASK PIBBIT
MINTY EYEBALL
I was already thinking about which tech to take.
DID YOU MISS ME?
I'd never been on a real ghost hunt before.

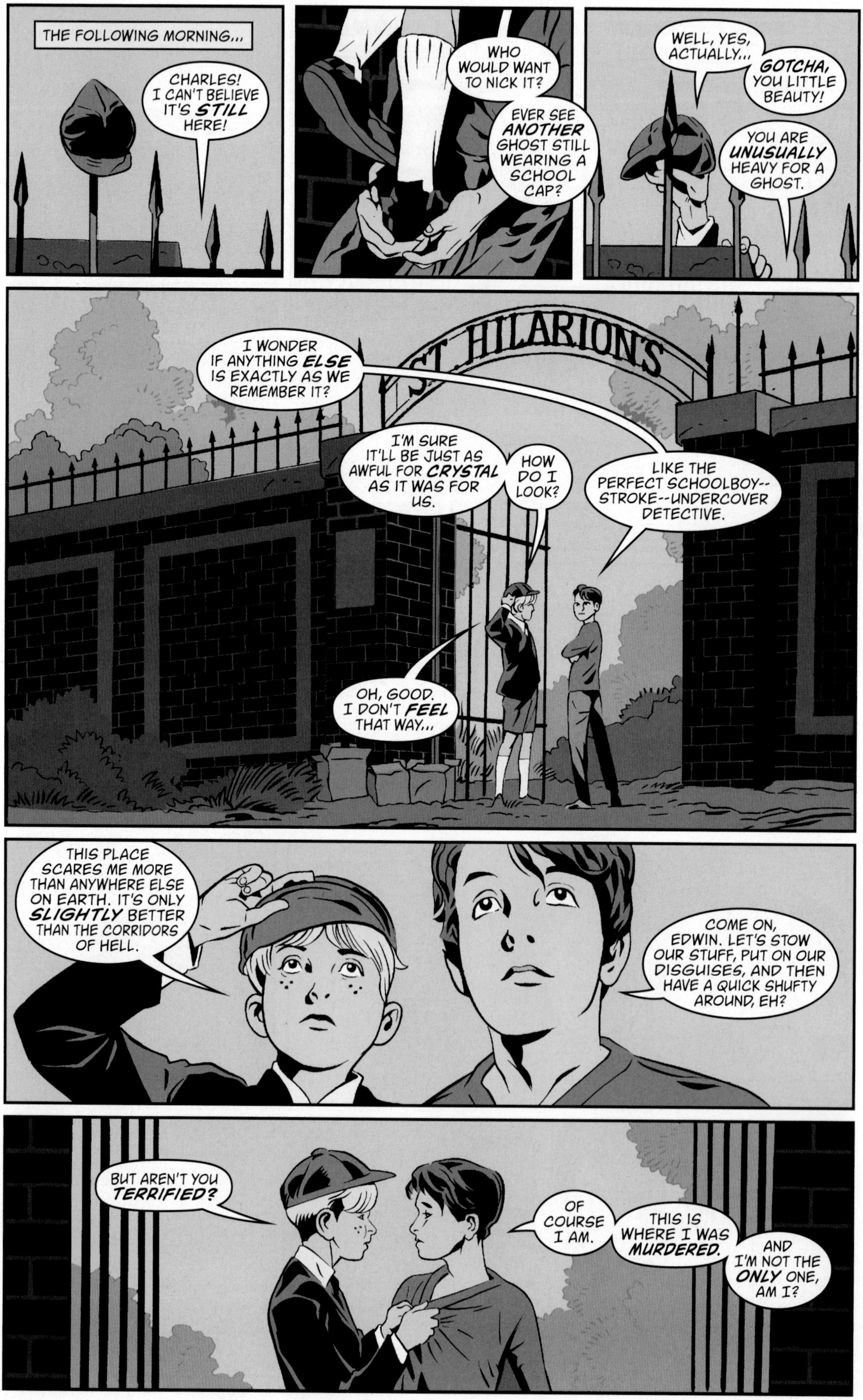
THE FOLLOWING MORNING...
CHARLES! I CAN'T BELIEVE IT'S STILL HERE!
WHO WOULD WANT TO NICK IT?
EVER SEE ANOTHER GHOST STILL WEARING A SCHOOL CAP?
WELL, YES, ACTUALLY... GOTCHA, YOU LITTLE BEAUTY!
YOU ARE UNUSUALLY HEAVY FOR A GHOST.
ST. HILARION'S
I WONDER IF ANYTHING ELSE IS EXACTLY AS WE REMEMBER IT?
I'M SURE IT'LL BE JUST AS AWFUL FOR CRYSTAL AS IT WAS FOR US.
HOW DO I LOOK?
LIKE THE PERFECT SCHOOLBOY--STROKE--UNDERCOVER DETECTIVE.
OH, GOOD. I DON'T FEEL THAT WAY...
THIS PLACE SCARES ME MORE THAN ANYWHERE ELSE ON EARTH. IT'S ONLY SLIGHTLY BETTER THAN THE CORRIDORS OF HELL.
COME ON, EDWIN. LET'S STOW OUR STUFF, PUT ON OUR DISGUISES, AND THEN HAVE A QUICK SHUFTY AROUND, EH?
BUT AREN'T YOU TERRIFIED?
OF COURSE I AM.
THIS IS WHERE I WAS MURDERED.
AND I'M NOT THE ONLY ONE, AM I?

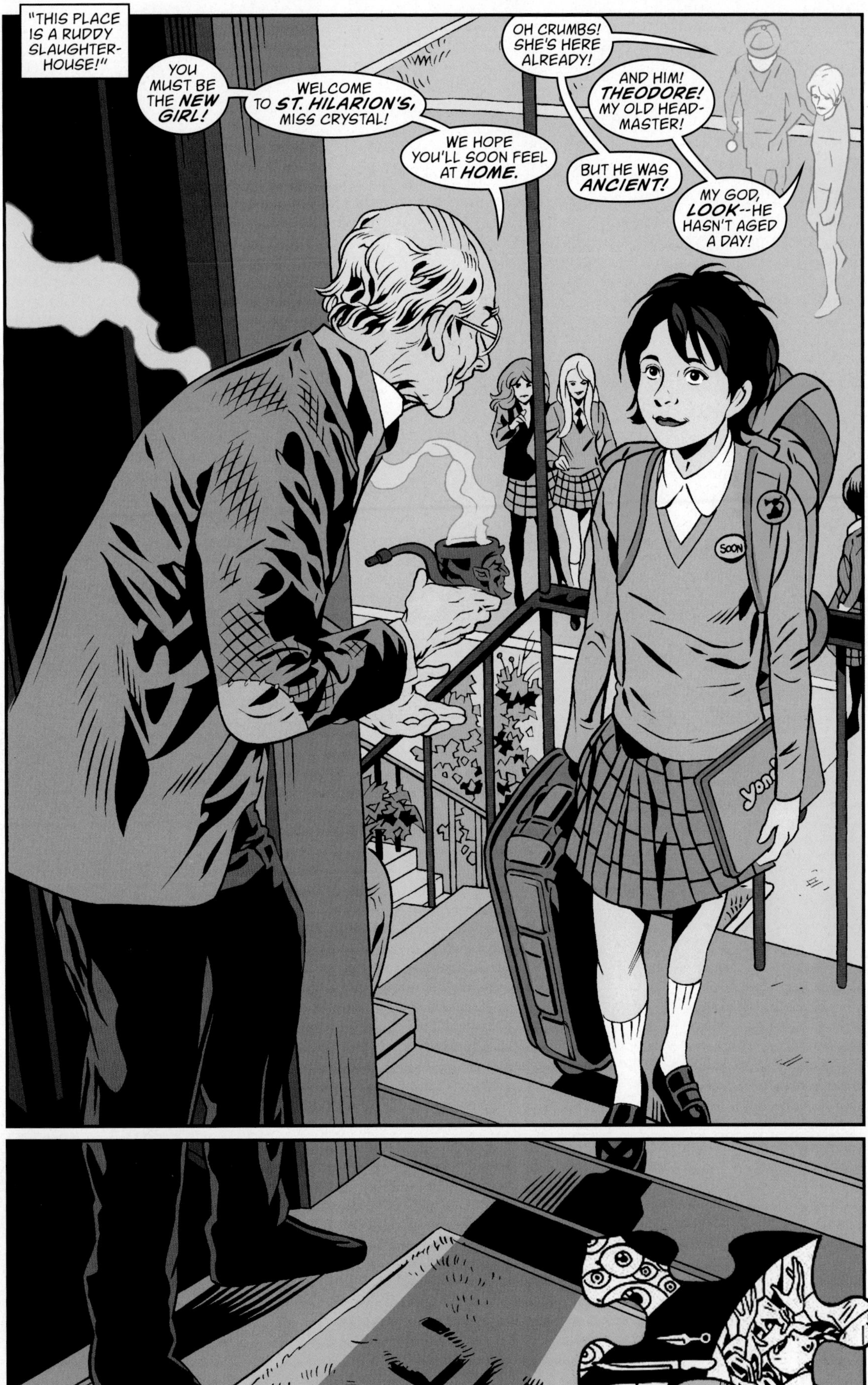
"THIS PLACE IS A RUDDY SLAUGHTER-HOUSE!"
YOU MUST BE THE **NEW GIRL!**
WELCOME TO **ST. HILARION'S,** MISS CRYSTAL!
WE HOPE YOU'LL SOON FEEL AT **HOME.**
OH CRUMBS! SHE'S HERE ALREADY!
BUT HE WAS **ANCIENT!**
AND HIM! **THEODORE!** MY OLD HEAD-MASTER!
MY GOD, **LOOK**--HE HASN'T AGED A DAY!
SOON

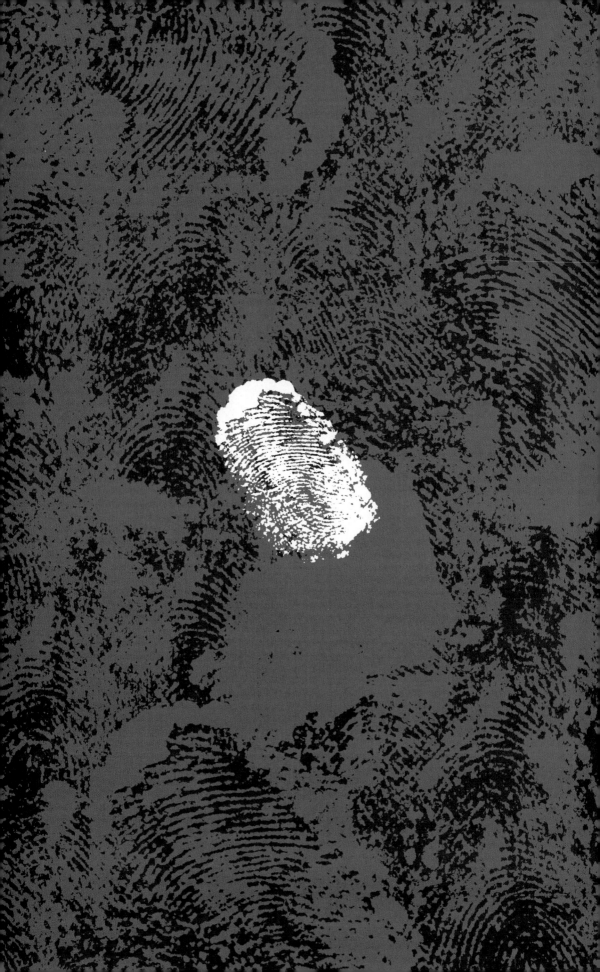

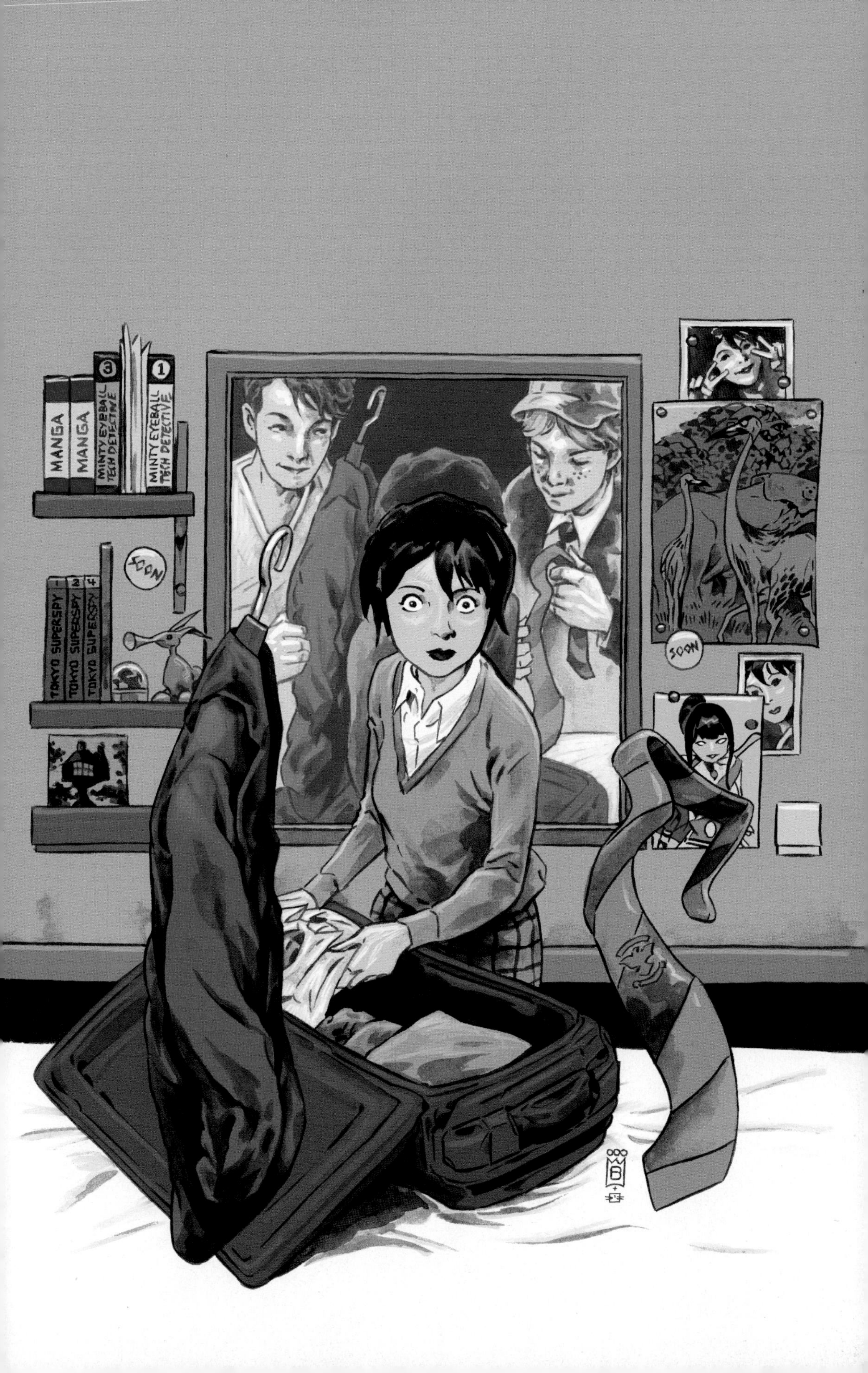
MANGA
MANGA
3
MINTY EYEBALL TECH DETECTIVE
1
MINTY EYEBALL TECH DETECTIVE
SOON
TOKYO SUPERSPY
TOKYO SUPERSPY
TOKYO SUPERSPY
SOON

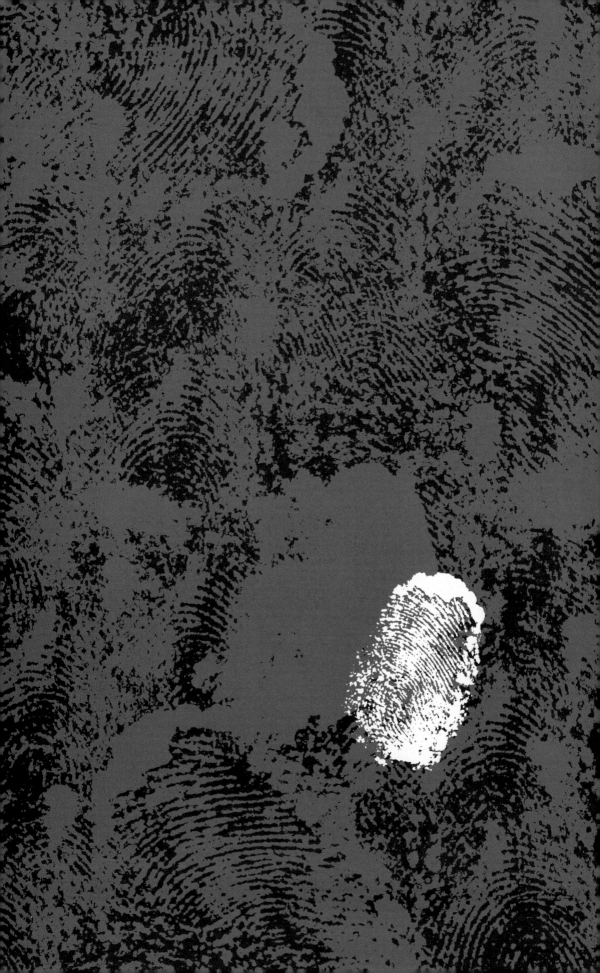

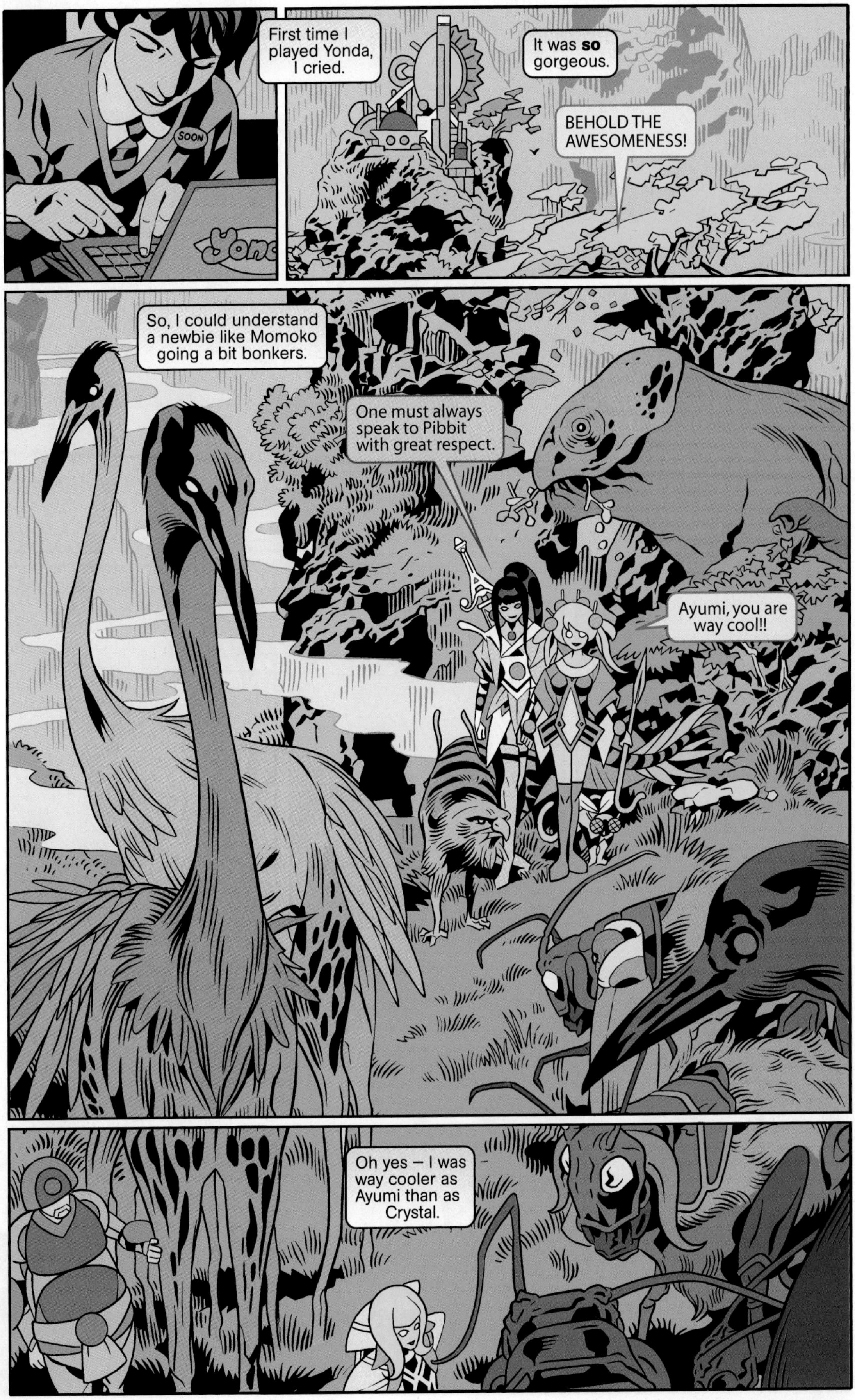

Yonc
SOON
First time I played Yonda, I cried.
It was **so** gorgeous.
BEHOLD THE AWESOMENESS!
So, I could understand a newbie like Momoko going a bit bonkers.
One must always speak to Pibbit with great respect.
Ayumi, you are way cool!!
Oh yes — I was way cooler as Ayumi than as Crystal.

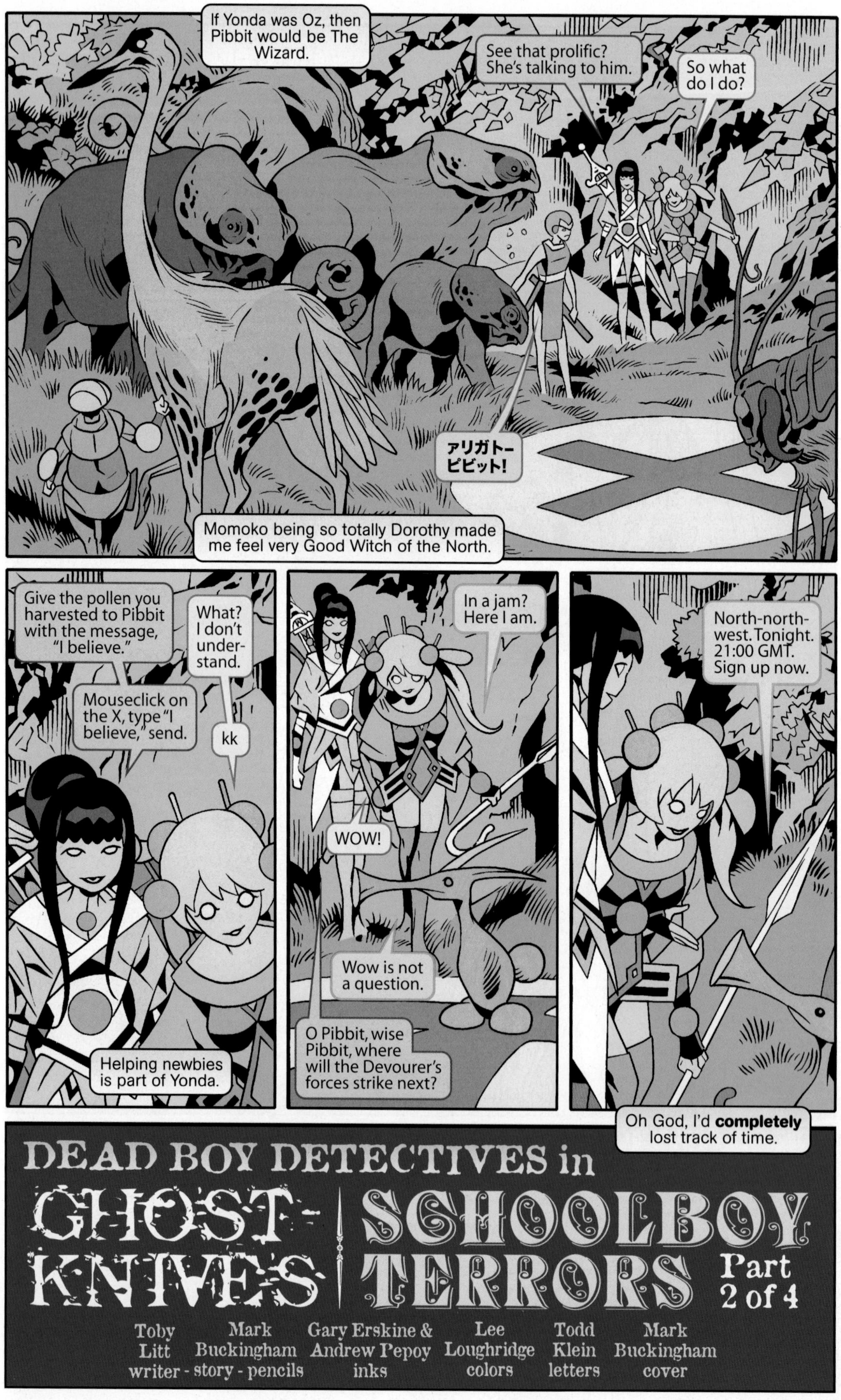
If Yonda was Oz, then Pibbit would be The Wizard.
See that prolific? She's talking to him.
So what do I do?
アリガトー ピビット!
Momoko being so totally Dorothy made me feel very Good Witch of the North.
Give the pollen you harvested to Pibbit with the message, "I believe."
What? I don't under-stand.
Mouseclick on the X, type "I believe," send.
kk
Helping newbies is part of Yonda.
In a jam? Here I am.
WOW!
Wow is not a question.
O Pibbit, wise Pibbit, where will the Devourer's forces strike next?
North-north-west. Tonight. 21:00 GMT. Sign up now.
Oh God, I'd **completely** lost track of time.

DEAD BOY DETECTIVES in

GHOST-KNIVES | SCHOOLBOY TERRORS Part 2 of 4

Toby Litt writer - Mark Buckingham story - pencils
Gary Erskine & Andrew Pepoy inks
Lee Loughridge colors
Todd Klein letters
Mark Buckingham cover

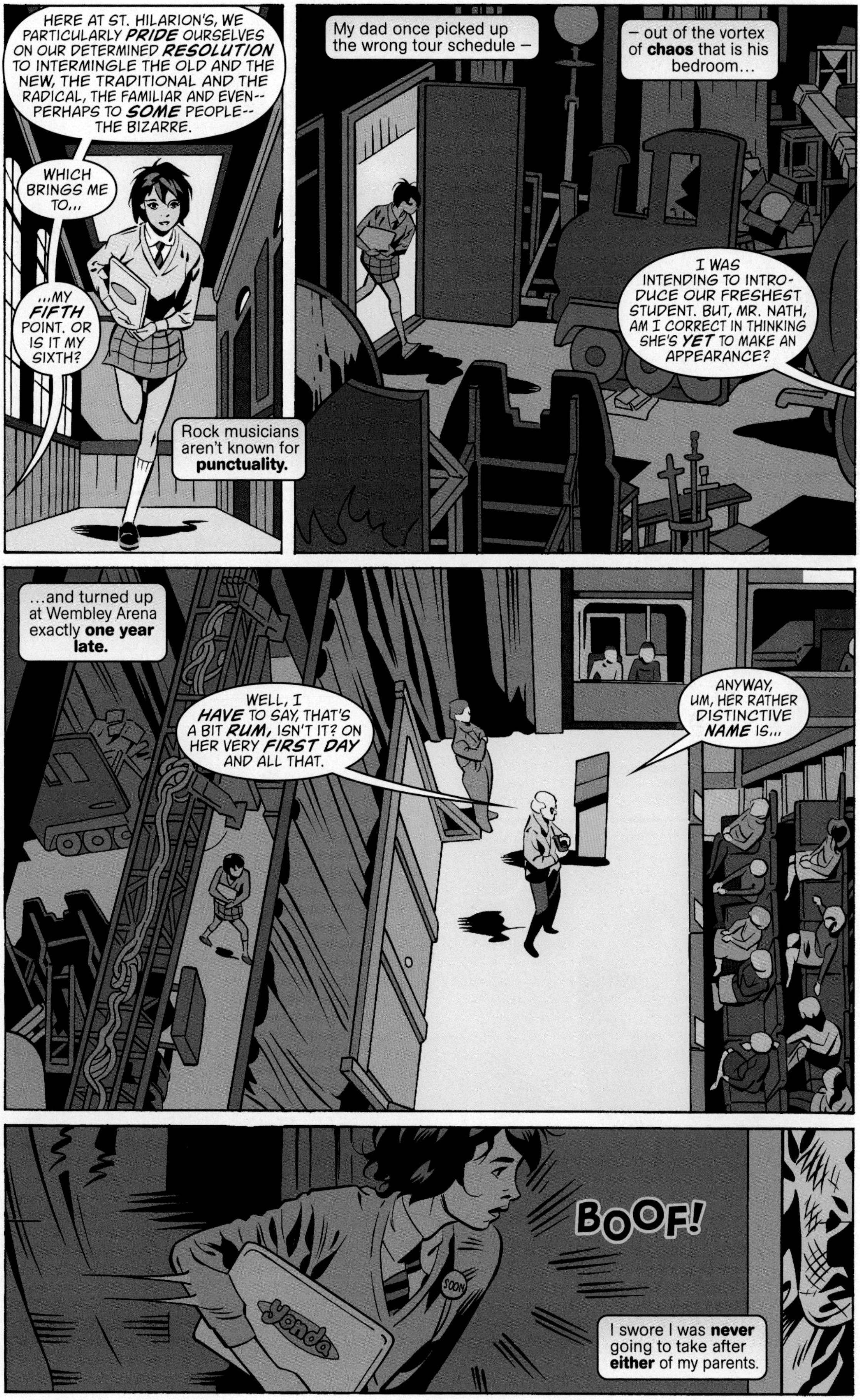
HERE AT ST. HILARION'S, WE PARTICULARLY PRIDE OURSELVES ON OUR DETERMINED RESOLUTION TO INTERMINGLE THE OLD AND THE NEW, THE TRADITIONAL AND THE RADICAL, THE FAMILIAR AND EVEN-- PERHAPS TO SOME PEOPLE-- THE BIZARRE.
WHICH BRINGS ME TO...
...MY FIFTH POINT. OR IS IT MY SIXTH?
Rock musicians aren't known for punctuality.
My dad once picked up the wrong tour schedule –
– out of the vortex of chaos that is his bedroom...
I WAS INTENDING TO INTRODUCE OUR FRESHEST STUDENT. BUT, MR. NATH, AM I CORRECT IN THINKING SHE'S YET TO MAKE AN APPEARANCE?
...and turned up at Wembley Arena exactly one year late.
WELL, I HAVE TO SAY, THAT'S A BIT RUM, ISN'T IT? ON HER VERY FIRST DAY AND ALL THAT.
ANYWAY, UM, HER RATHER DISTINCTIVE NAME IS...
BOOF!
SOON
Yonda
I swore I was never going to take after either of my parents.

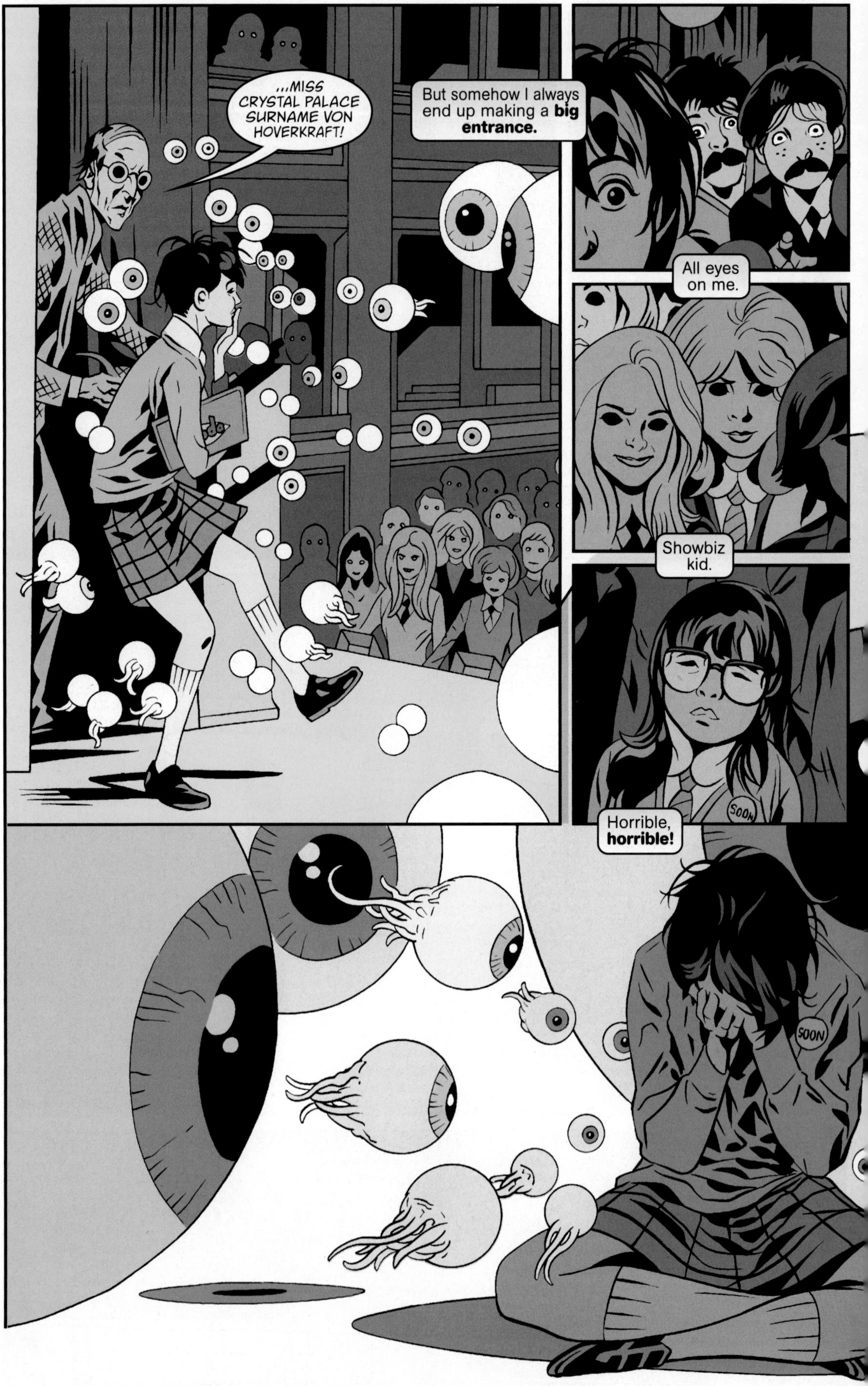
...MISS CRYSTAL PALACE SURNAME VON HOVERKRAFT!
But somehow I always end up making a **big entrance.**
All eyes on me.
Showbiz kid.
SOON
Horrible, **horrible!**
SOON

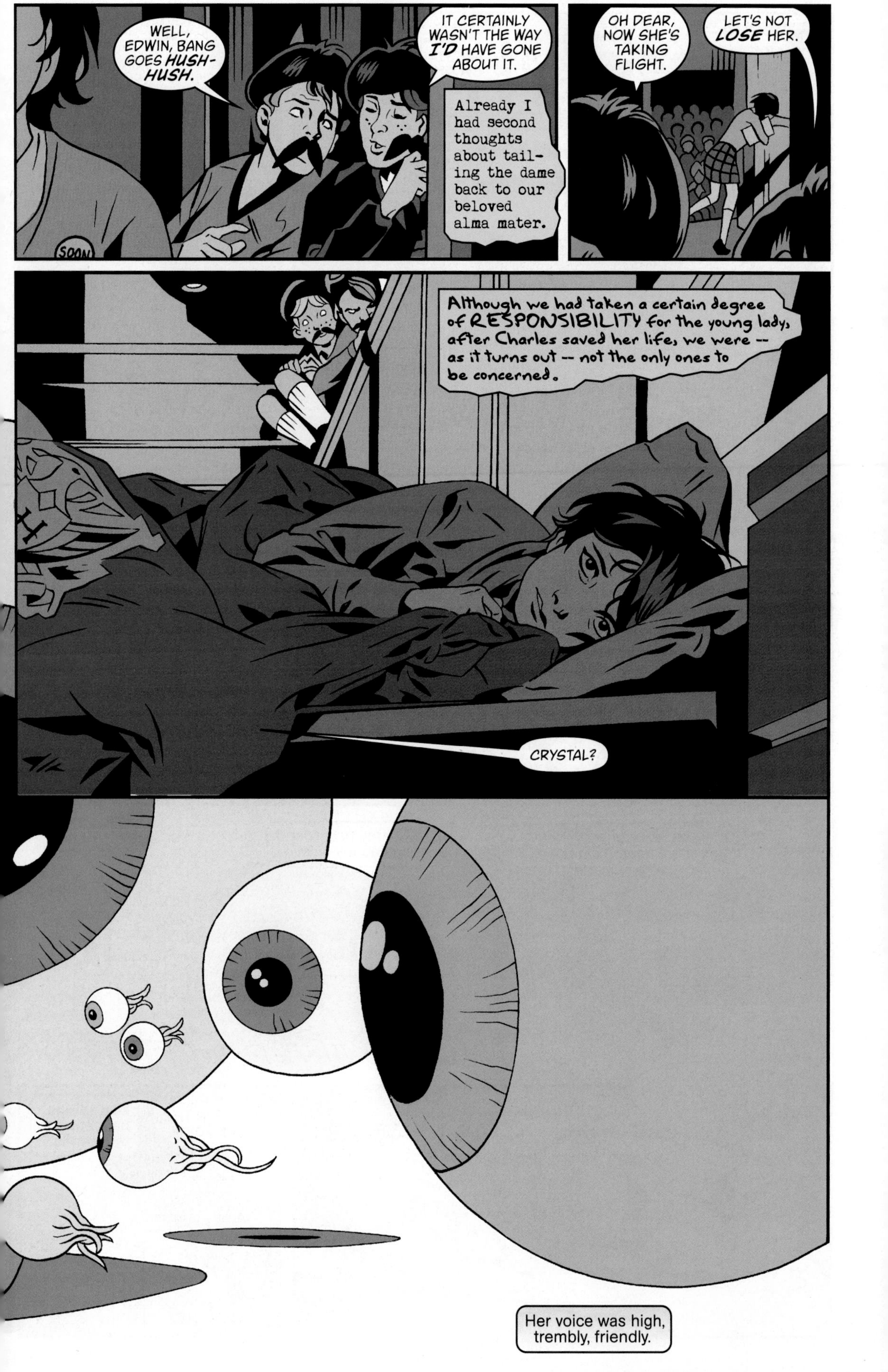
WELL, EDWIN, BANG GOES HUSH-HUSH.
IT CERTAINLY WASN'T THE WAY I'D HAVE GONE ABOUT IT.
Already I had second thoughts about tailing the dame back to our beloved alma mater.
OH DEAR, NOW SHE'S TAKING FLIGHT.
LET'S NOT LOSE HER.
SOON
Although we had taken a certain degree of RESPONSIBILITY for the young lady, after Charles saved her life, we were -- as it turns out -- not the only ones to be concerned.
CRYSTAL?
Her voice was high, trembly, friendly.

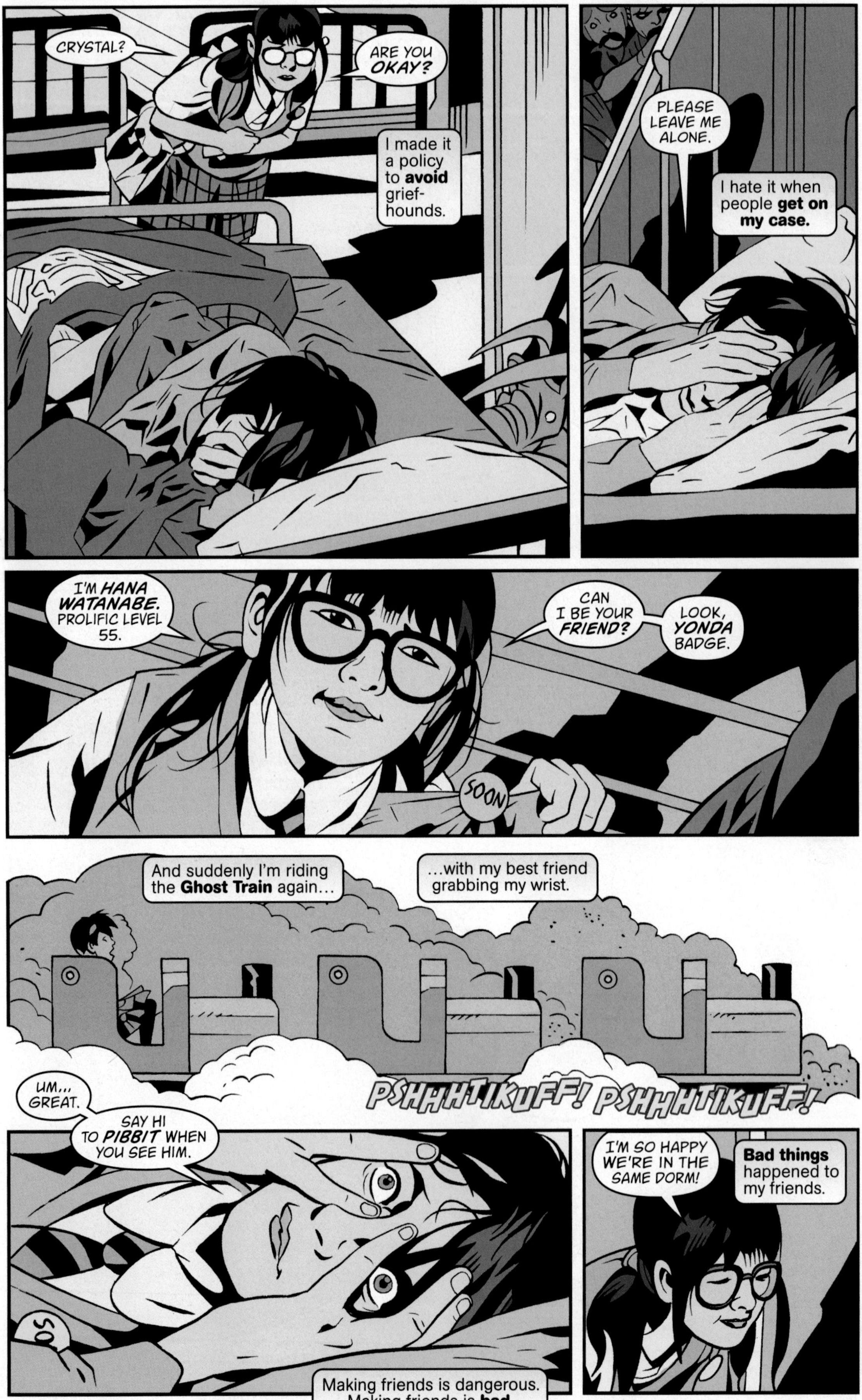
CRYSTAL?
ARE YOU OKAY?
I made it a policy to **avoid** grief-hounds.
PLEASE LEAVE ME ALONE.
I hate it when people **get on my case.**
I'M HANA WATANABE. PROLIFIC LEVEL 55.
CAN I BE YOUR FRIEND?
LOOK, YONDA BADGE.
SOON
And suddenly I'm riding the **Ghost Train** again...
...with my best friend grabbing my wrist.
PSHHHTIKUFF! PSHHHTIKUFF!
UM... GREAT.
SAY HI TO PIBBIT WHEN YOU SEE HIM.
I'M SO HAPPY WE'RE IN THE SAME DORM!
Bad things happened to my friends.
Making friends is dangerous. Making friends is **bad.**

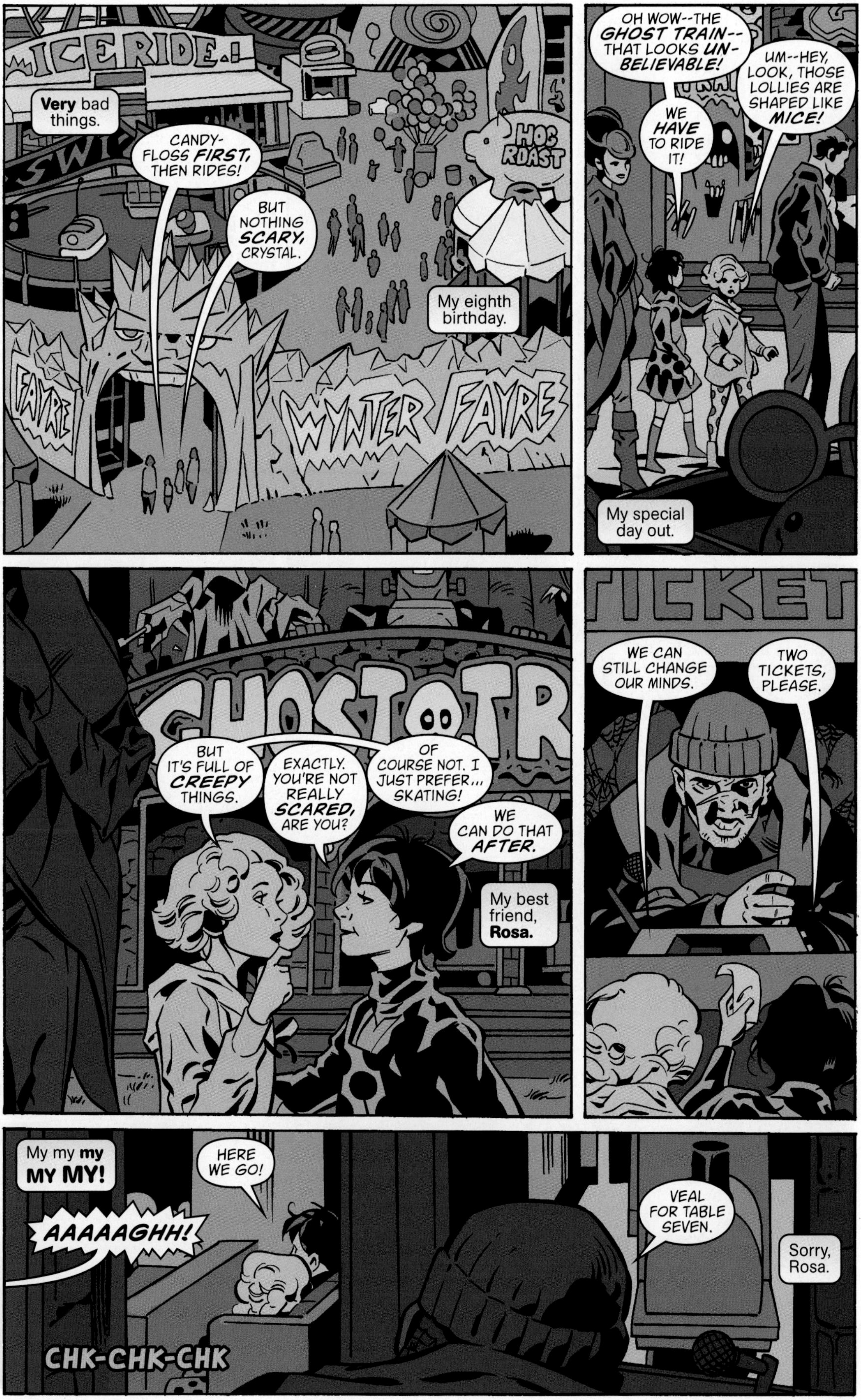
ICERIDE
Very bad things.
CANDY-FLOSS FIRST, THEN RIDES!
BUT NOTHING SCARY, CRYSTAL.
HOG ROAST
My eighth birthday.
WYNTER FAYRE
FAYRE
OH WOW--THE GHOST TRAIN--THAT LOOKS UN-BELIEVABLE!
WE HAVE TO RIDE IT!
UM--HEY, LOOK, THOSE LOLLIES ARE SHAPED LIKE MICE!
My special day out.
BUT IT'S FULL OF CREEPY THINGS.
EXACTLY. YOU'RE NOT REALLY SCARED, ARE YOU?
OF COURSE NOT. I JUST PREFER... SKATING!
WE CAN DO THAT AFTER.
My best friend, Rosa.
TICKET
WE CAN STILL CHANGE OUR MINDS.
TWO TICKETS, PLEASE.
My my my MY MY!
AAAAAGHH!
HERE WE GO!
VEAL FOR TABLE SEVEN.
Sorry, Rosa.
CHK-CHK-CHK

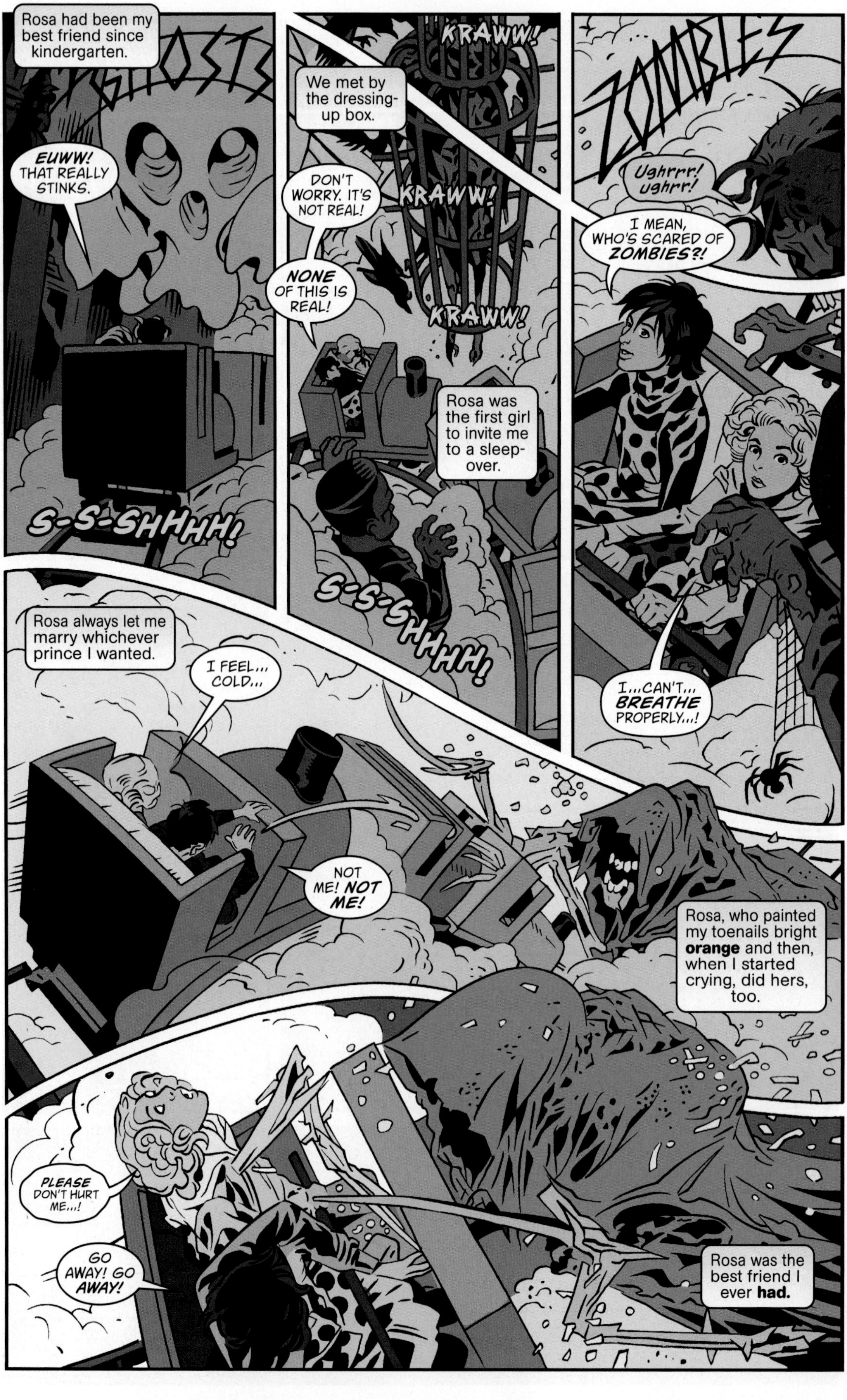

Rosa had been my best friend since kindergarten.
GHOSTS
EUWW! THAT REALLY STINKS.
S-S-SHHHH!
KRAWW!
We met by the dressing-up box.
DON'T WORRY. IT'S NOT REAL!
KRAWW!
NONE OF THIS IS REAL!
KRAWW!
Rosa was the first girl to invite me to a sleep-over.
S-S-SHHHH!
ZOMBIES
Ughrrr! ughrr!
I MEAN, WHO'S SCARED OF ZOMBIES?!
I...CAN'T... BREATHE PROPERLY...!
Rosa always let me marry whichever prince I wanted.
I FEEL... COLD...
NOT ME! NOT ME!
Rosa, who painted my toenails bright orange and then, when I started crying, did hers, too.
PLEASE DON'T HURT ME...!
GO AWAY! GO AWAY!
Rosa was the best friend I ever had.

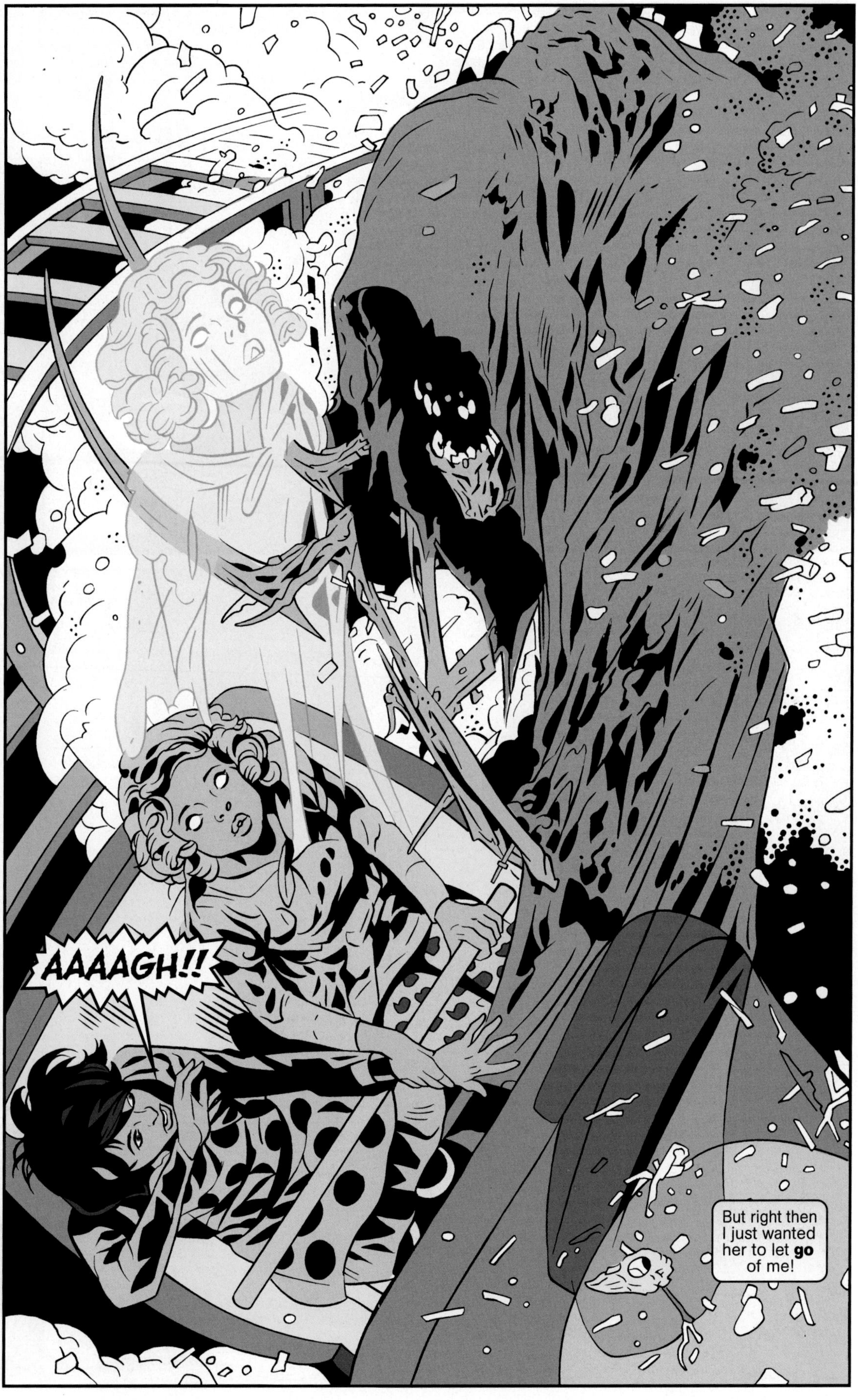
AAAAGH!!
But right then I just wanted her to let **go** of me!

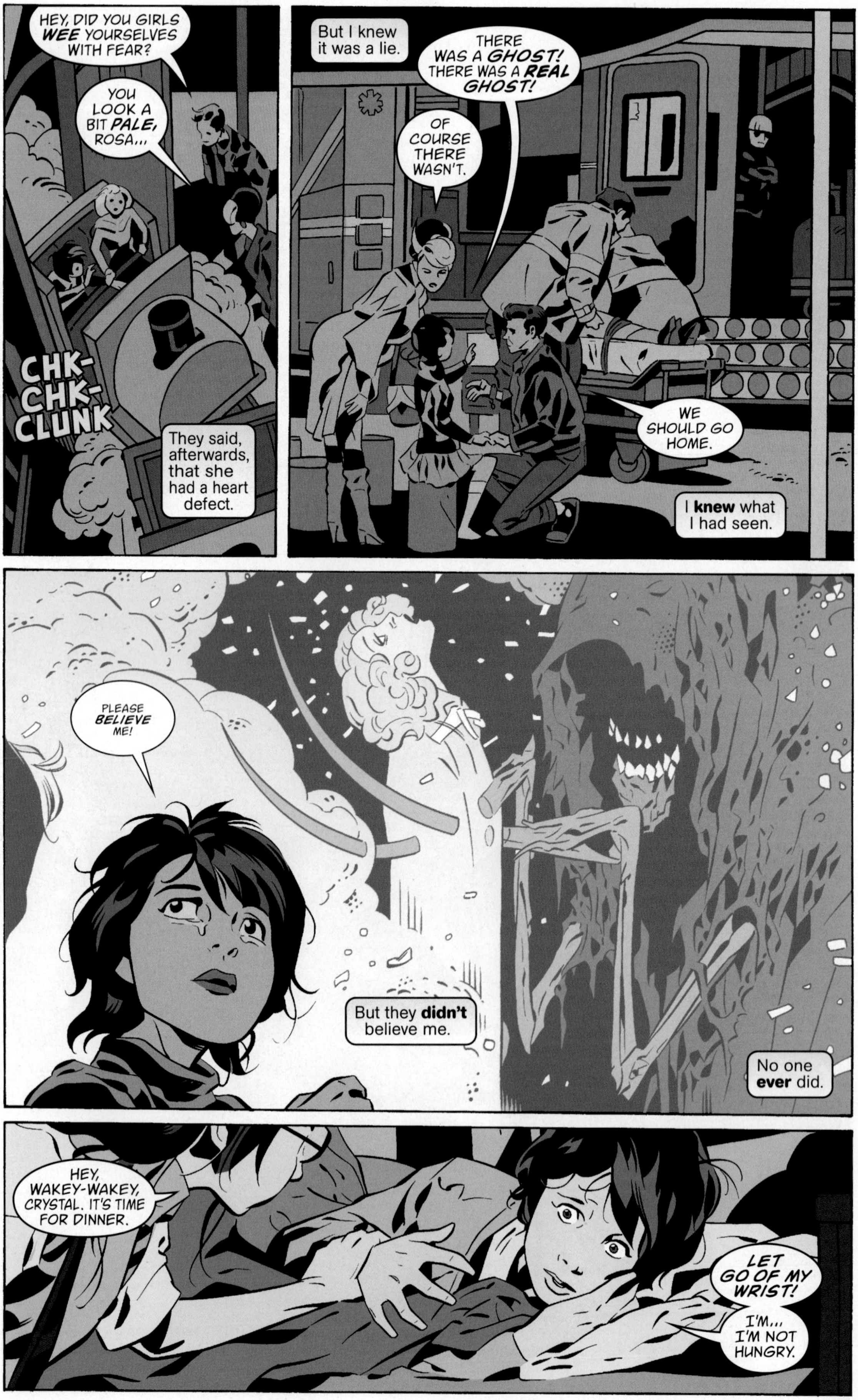
HEY, DID YOU GIRLS WEE YOURSELVES WITH FEAR?
YOU LOOK A BIT PALE, ROSA...
CHK-CHK-CLUNK
They said, afterwards, that she had a heart defect.
But I knew it was a lie.
THERE WAS A GHOST! THERE WAS A REAL GHOST!
OF COURSE THERE WASN'T.
WE SHOULD GO HOME.
I knew what I had seen.
PLEASE BELIEVE ME!
But they didn't believe me.
No one ever did.
HEY, WAKEY-WAKEY, CRYSTAL. IT'S TIME FOR DINNER.
LET GO OF MY WRIST!
I'M... I'M NOT HUNGRY.

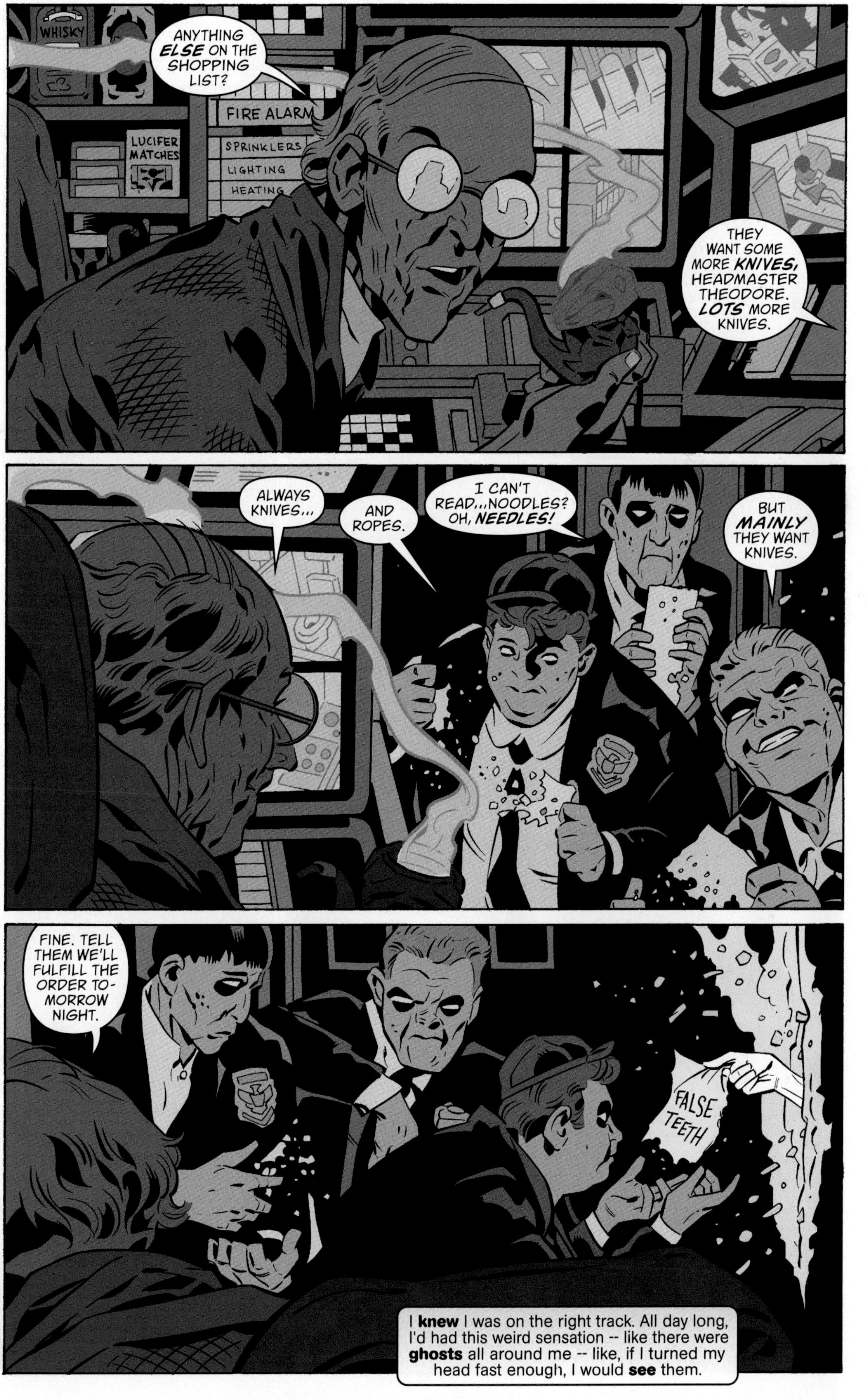
WHISKY
ANYTHING ELSE ON THE SHOPPING LIST?
FIRE ALARM
LUCIFER MATCHES
SPRINKLERS
LIGHTING
HEATING
THEY WANT SOME MORE KNIVES, HEADMASTER THEODORE. LOTS MORE KNIVES.
ALWAYS KNIVES...
AND ROPES.
I CAN'T READ...NOODLES? OH, NEEDLES!
BUT MAINLY THEY WANT KNIVES.
FINE. TELL THEM WE'LL FULFILL THE ORDER TO-MORROW NIGHT.
FALSE TEETH
I knew I was on the right track. All day long, I'd had this weird sensation -- like there were ghosts all around me -- like, if I turned my head fast enough, I would see them.

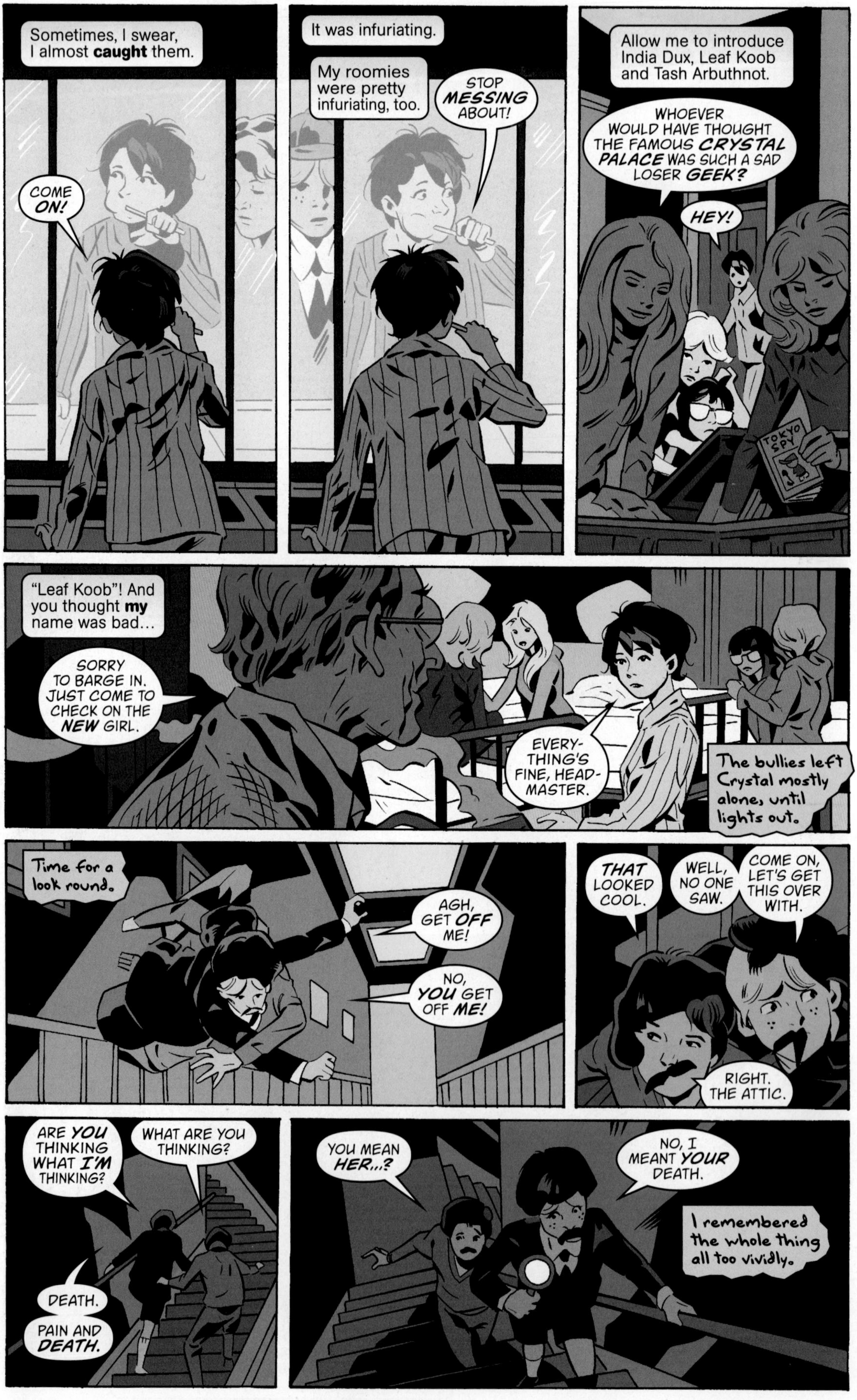
Sometimes, I swear, I almost **caught** them.
COME ON!
It was infuriating.
My roomies were pretty infuriating, too.
STOP MESSING ABOUT!
Allow me to introduce India Dux, Leaf Koob and Tash Arbuthnot.
WHOEVER WOULD HAVE THOUGHT THE FAMOUS CRYSTAL PALACE WAS SUCH A SAD LOSER GEEK?
HEY!
TOKYO SPY
"Leaf Koob"! And you thought **my** name was bad...
SORRY TO BARGE IN. JUST COME TO CHECK ON THE NEW GIRL.
EVERY-THING'S FINE, HEAD-MASTER.
The bullies left Crystal mostly alone, until lights out.
Time for a look round.
AGH, GET OFF ME!
NO, YOU GET OFF ME!
THAT LOOKED COOL.
WELL, NO ONE SAW.
COME ON, LET'S GET THIS OVER WITH.
RIGHT. THE ATTIC.
ARE YOU THINKING WHAT I'M THINKING?
WHAT ARE YOU THINKING?
DEATH.
PAIN AND DEATH.
YOU MEAN HER...?
NO, I MEANT YOUR DEATH.
I remembered the whole thing all too vividly.

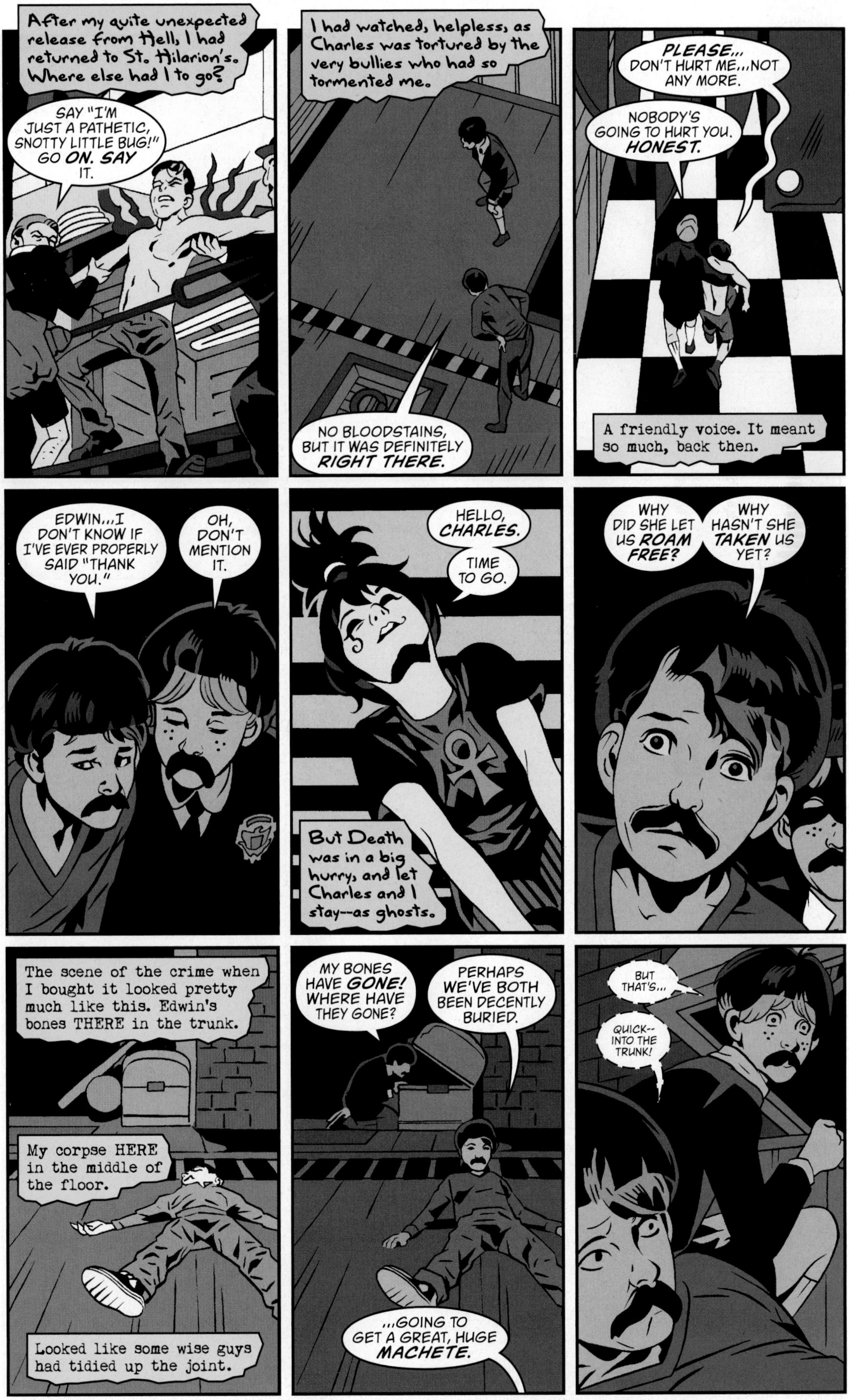
After my quite unexpected release from Hell, I had returned to St. Hilarion's. Where else had I to go?
SAY "I'M JUST A PATHETIC, SNOTTY LITTLE BUG!" GO ON. SAY IT.
I had watched, helpless, as Charles was tortured by the very bullies who had so tormented me.
NO BLOODSTAINS, BUT IT WAS DEFINITELY RIGHT THERE.
PLEASE... DON'T HURT ME...NOT ANY MORE.
NOBODY'S GOING TO HURT YOU. HONEST.
A friendly voice. It meant so much, back then.
EDWIN...I DON'T KNOW IF I'VE EVER PROPERLY SAID "THANK YOU."
OH, DON'T MENTION IT.
HELLO, CHARLES.
TIME TO GO.
But Death was in a big hurry, and let Charles and I stay--as ghosts.
WHY DID SHE LET US ROAM FREE?
WHY HASN'T SHE TAKEN US YET?
The scene of the crime when I bought it looked pretty much like this. Edwin's bones THERE in the trunk.
My corpse HERE in the middle of the floor.
Looked like some wise guys had tidied up the joint.
MY BONES HAVE GONE! WHERE HAVE THEY GONE?
PERHAPS WE'VE BOTH BEEN DECENTLY BURIED.
...GOING TO GET A GREAT, HUGE MACHETE.
BUT THAT'S...
QUICK--INTO THE TRUNK!

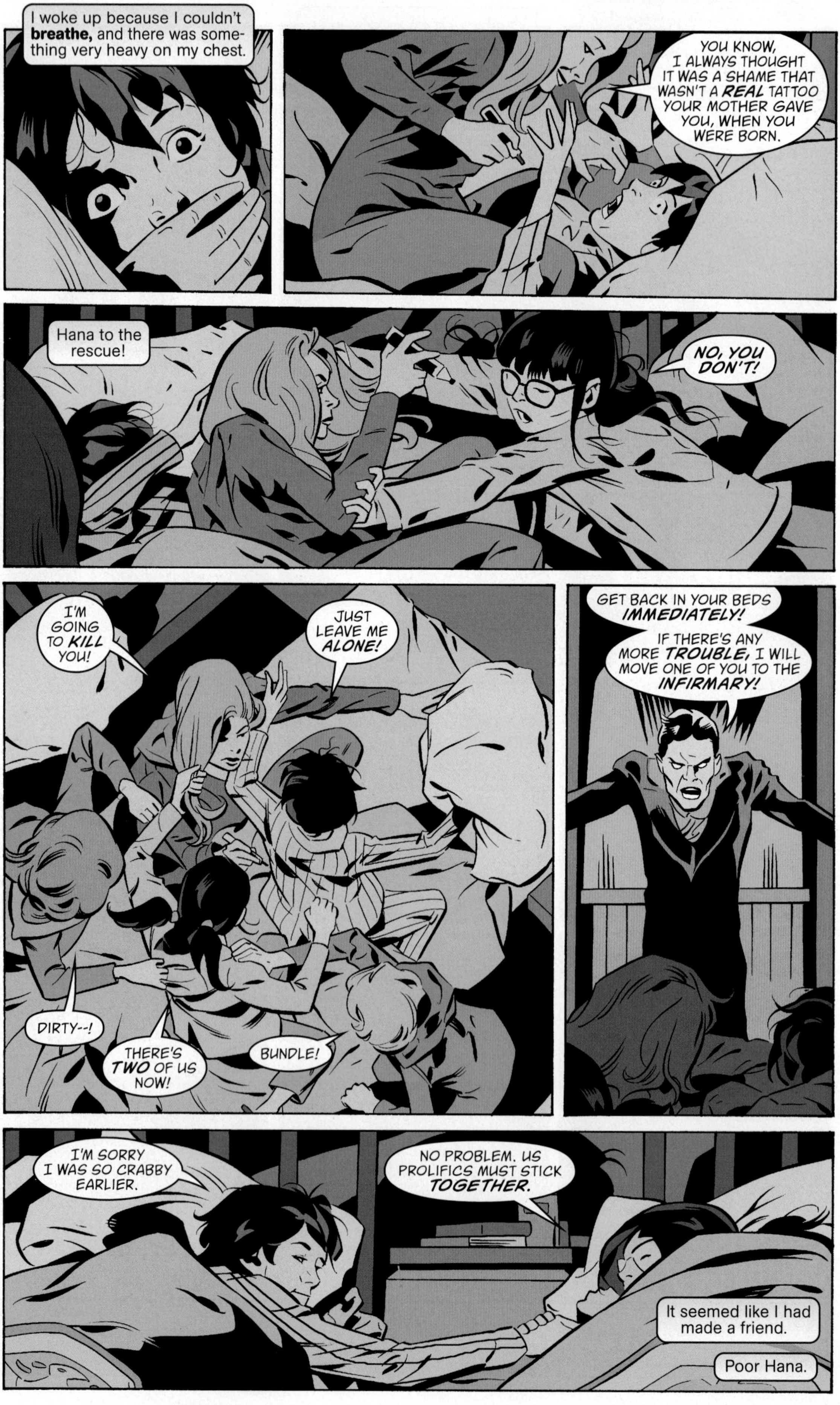
I woke up because I couldn't **breathe,** and there was something very heavy on my chest.
YOU KNOW, I ALWAYS THOUGHT IT WAS A SHAME THAT WASN'T A *REAL* TATTOO YOUR MOTHER GAVE YOU, WHEN YOU WERE BORN.
Hana to the rescue!
NO, YOU DON'T!
I'M GOING TO *KILL* YOU!
JUST LEAVE ME *ALONE!*
DIRTY--!
THERE'S *TWO* OF US NOW!
BUNDLE!
GET BACK IN YOUR BEDS *IMMEDIATELY!*
IF THERE'S ANY MORE *TROUBLE,* I WILL MOVE ONE OF YOU TO THE *INFIRMARY!*
I'M SORRY I WAS SO CRABBY EARLIER.
NO PROBLEM. US PROLIFICS MUST STICK *TOGETHER.*
It seemed like I had made a friend.
Poor Hana.

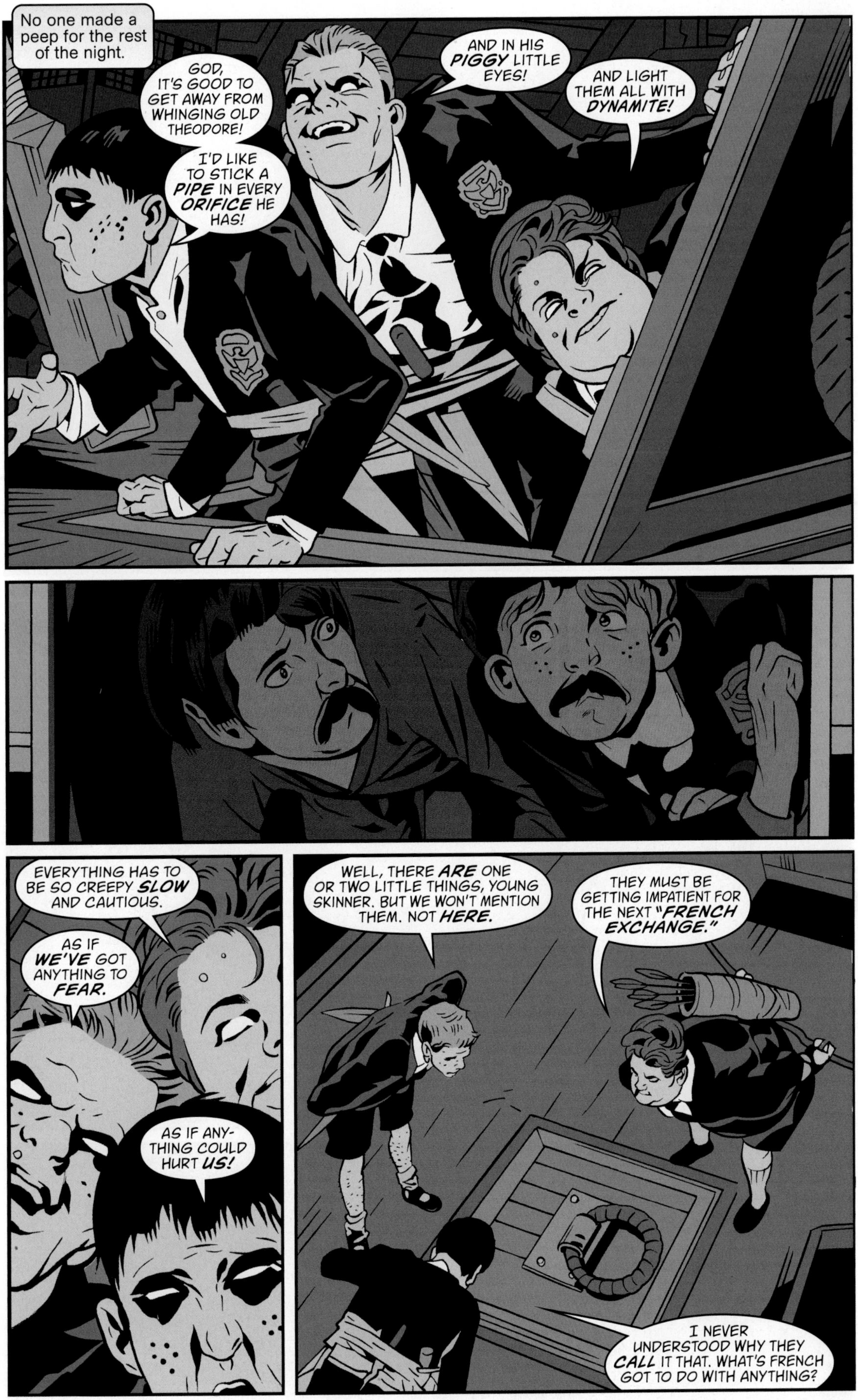
No one made a peep for the rest of the night.
GOD, IT'S GOOD TO GET AWAY FROM WHINGING OLD THEODORE!
I'D LIKE TO STICK A PIPE IN EVERY ORIFICE HE HAS!
AND IN HIS PIGGY LITTLE EYES!
AND LIGHT THEM ALL WITH DYNAMITE!
EVERYTHING HAS TO BE SO CREEPY SLOW AND CAUTIOUS.
AS IF WE'VE GOT ANYTHING TO FEAR.
AS IF ANYTHING COULD HURT US!
WELL, THERE ARE ONE OR TWO LITTLE THINGS, YOUNG SKINNER. BUT WE WON'T MENTION THEM. NOT HERE.
THEY MUST BE GETTING IMPATIENT FOR THE NEXT "FRENCH EXCHANGE."
I NEVER UNDERSTOOD WHY THEY CALL IT THAT. WHAT'S FRENCH GOT TO DO WITH ANYTHING?

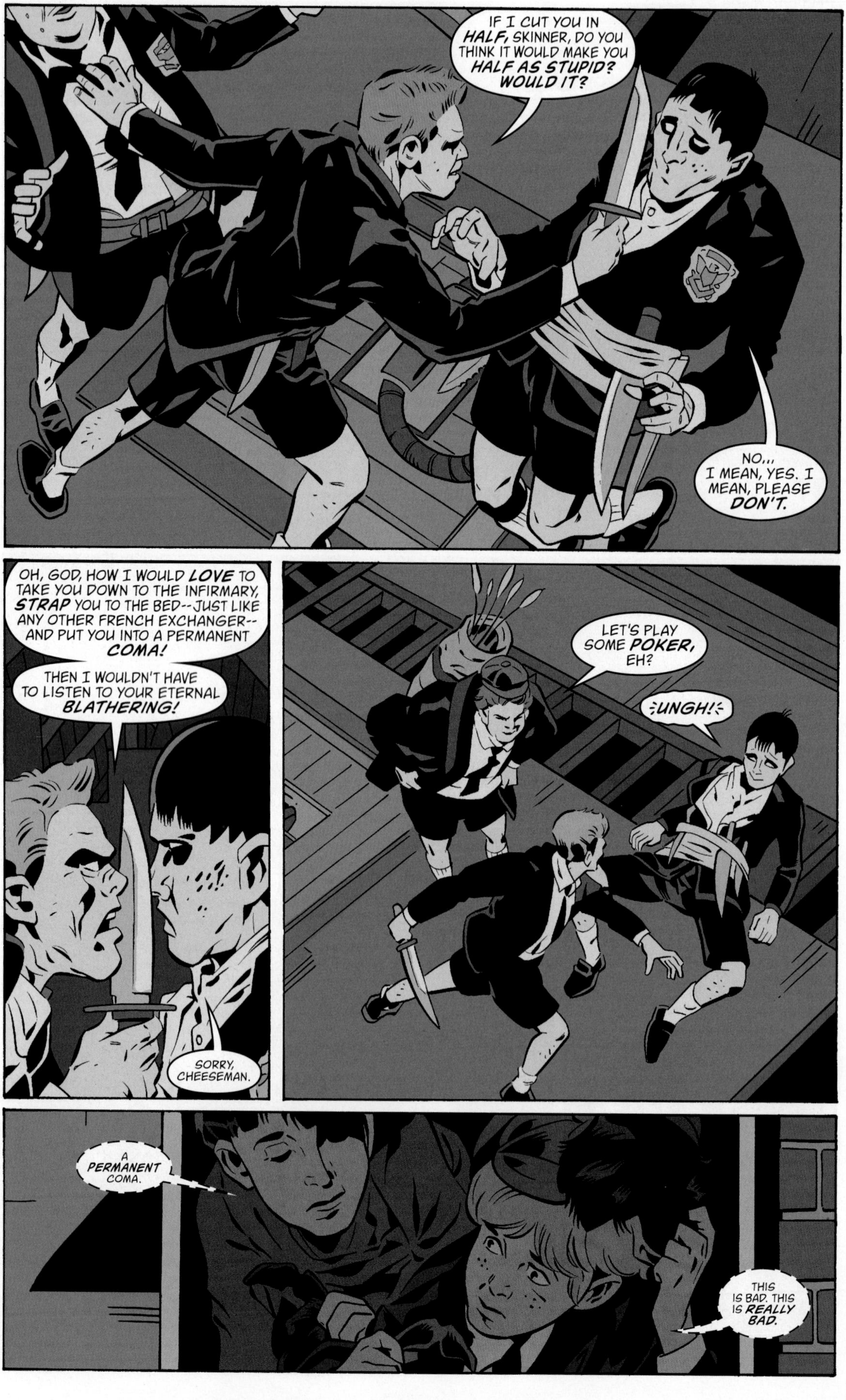
IF I CUT YOU IN HALF, SKINNER, DO YOU THINK IT WOULD MAKE YOU HALF AS STUPID? WOULD IT?
NO... I MEAN, YES. I MEAN, PLEASE DON'T.
OH, GOD, HOW I WOULD LOVE TO TAKE YOU DOWN TO THE INFIRMARY, STRAP YOU TO THE BED--JUST LIKE ANY OTHER FRENCH EXCHANGER--AND PUT YOU INTO A PERMANENT COMA!
THEN I WOULDN'T HAVE TO LISTEN TO YOUR ETERNAL BLATHERING!
SORRY, CHEESEMAN.
LET'S PLAY SOME POKER, EH?
UNGH!
A PERMANENT COMA.
THIS IS BAD. THIS IS REALLY BAD.

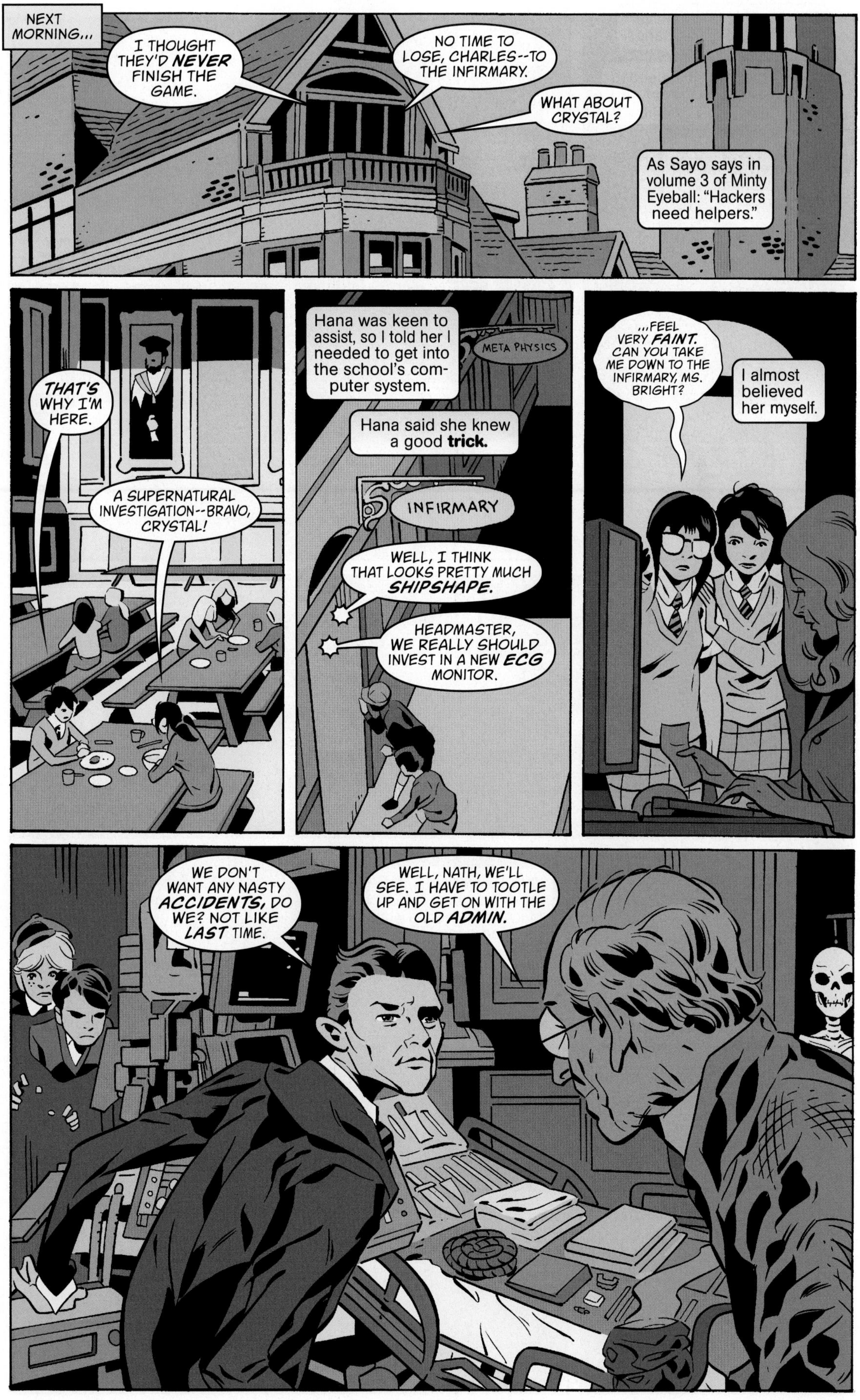
NEXT MORNING...
I THOUGHT THEY'D NEVER FINISH THE GAME.
NO TIME TO LOSE, CHARLES--TO THE INFIRMARY.
WHAT ABOUT CRYSTAL?
As Sayo says in volume 3 of Minty Eyeball: "Hackers need helpers."
THAT'S WHY I'M HERE.
A SUPERNATURAL INVESTIGATION--BRAVO, CRYSTAL!
Hana was keen to assist, so I told her I needed to get into the school's computer system.
META PHYSICS
Hana said she knew a good trick.
INFIRMARY
WELL, I THINK THAT LOOKS PRETTY MUCH SHIPSHAPE.
HEADMASTER, WE REALLY SHOULD INVEST IN A NEW ECG MONITOR.
...FEEL VERY FAINT. CAN YOU TAKE ME DOWN TO THE INFIRMARY, MS. BRIGHT?
I almost believed her myself.
WE DON'T WANT ANY NASTY ACCIDENTS, DO WE? NOT LIKE LAST TIME.
WELL, NATH, WE'LL SEE. I HAVE TO TOOTLE UP AND GET ON WITH THE OLD ADMIN.

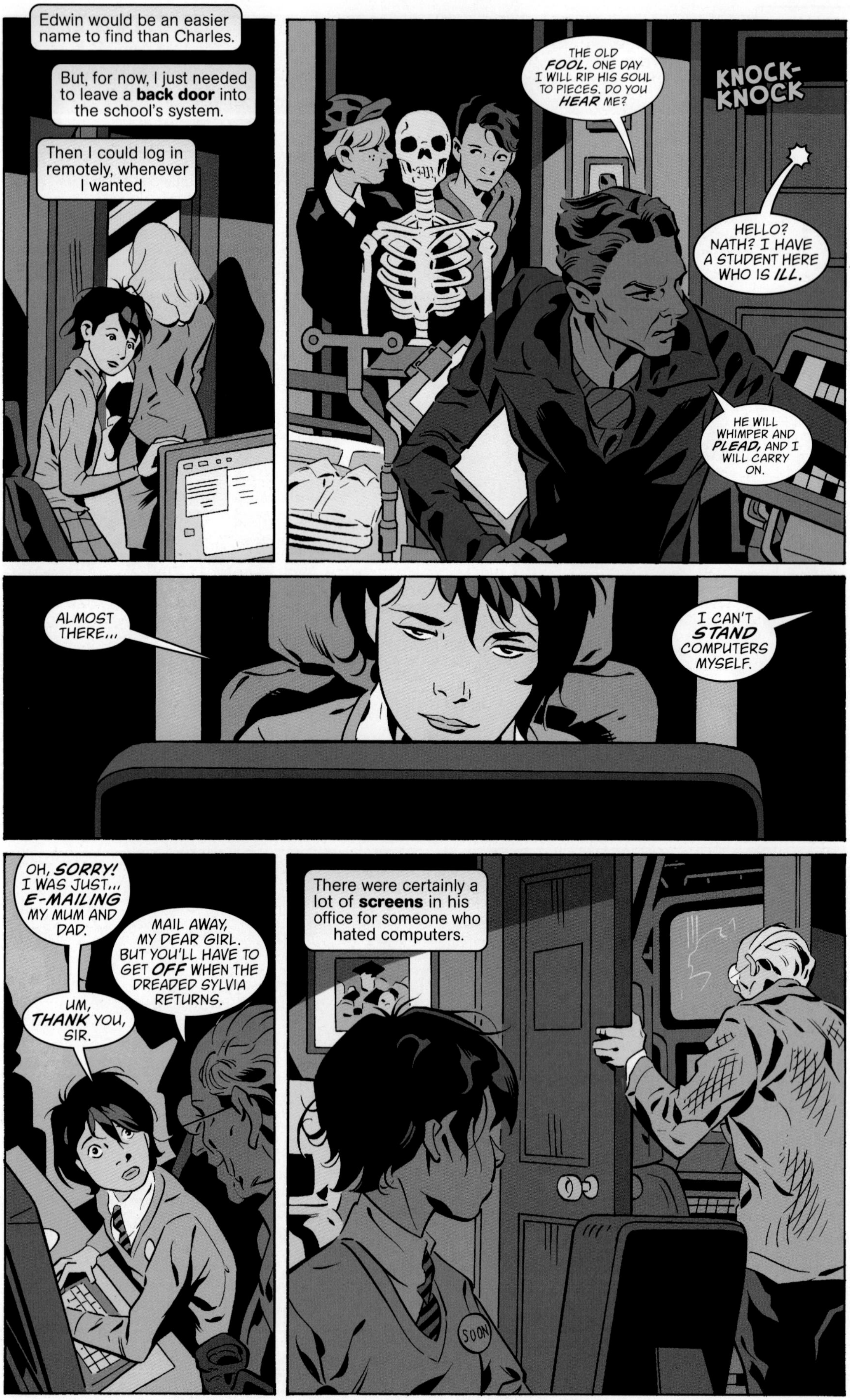

Edwin would be an easier name to find than Charles.
But, for now, I just needed to leave a **back door** into the school's system.
Then I could log in remotely, whenever I wanted.
THE OLD FOOL. ONE DAY I WILL RIP HIS SOUL TO PIECES. DO YOU HEAR ME?
KNOCK-KNOCK
HELLO? NATH? I HAVE A STUDENT HERE WHO IS ILL.
HE WILL WHIMPER AND PLEAD, AND I WILL CARRY ON.
ALMOST THERE...
I CAN'T STAND COMPUTERS MYSELF.
OH, SORRY! I WAS JUST... E-MAILING MY MUM AND DAD.
MAIL AWAY, MY DEAR GIRL. BUT YOU'LL HAVE TO GET OFF WHEN THE DREADED SYLVIA RETURNS.
UM, THANK YOU, SIR.
There were certainly a lot of **screens** in his office for someone who hated computers.
SOON

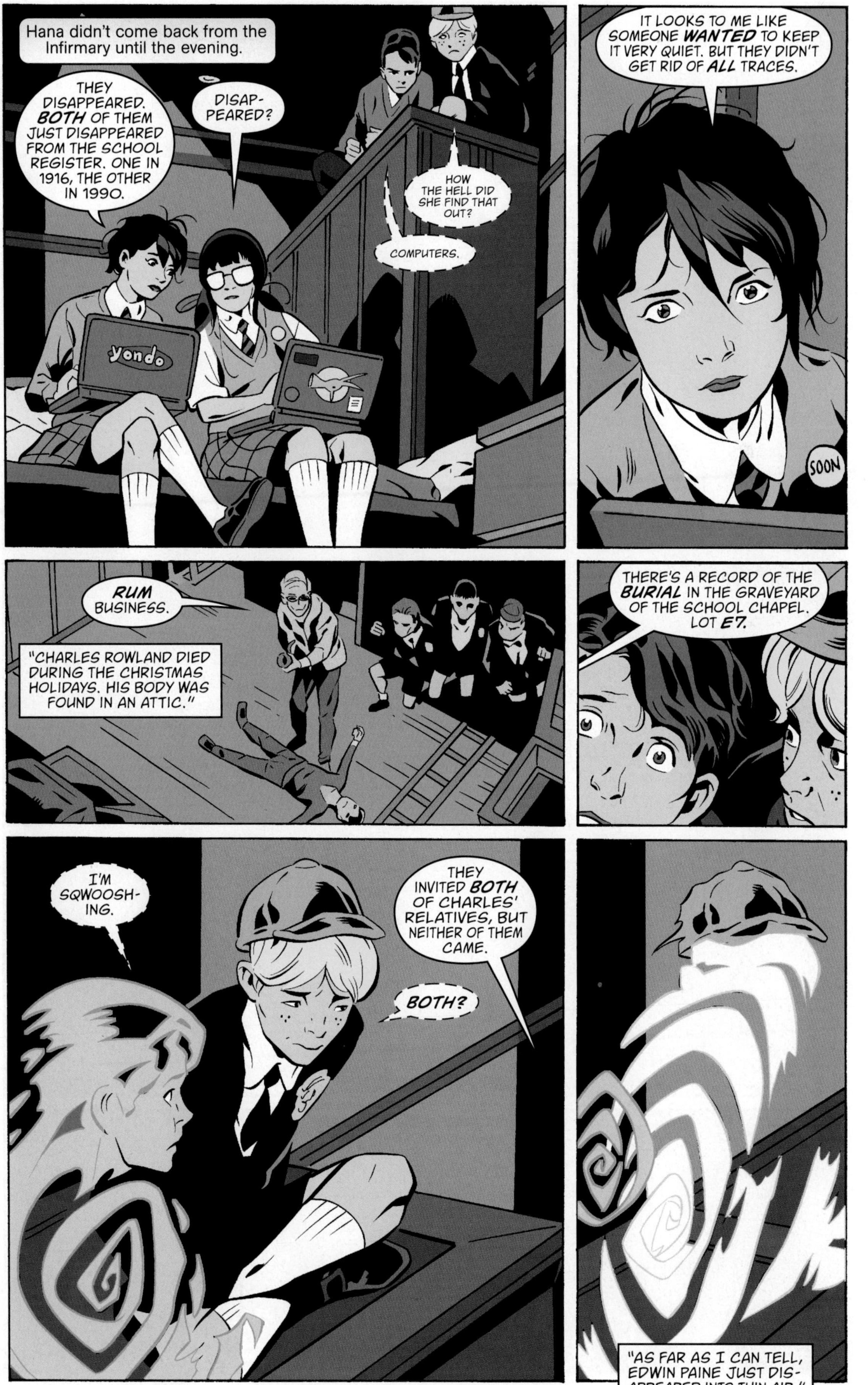

Hana didn't come back from the Infirmary until the evening.
THEY DISAPPEARED. BOTH OF THEM JUST DISAPPEARED FROM THE SCHOOL REGISTER. ONE IN 1916, THE OTHER IN 1990.
DISAP-PEARED?
HOW THE HELL DID SHE FIND THAT OUT?
COMPUTERS.
yondo
IT LOOKS TO ME LIKE SOMEONE WANTED TO KEEP IT VERY QUIET. BUT THEY DIDN'T GET RID OF ALL TRACES.
SOON
RUM BUSINESS.
"CHARLES ROWLAND DIED DURING THE CHRISTMAS HOLIDAYS. HIS BODY WAS FOUND IN AN ATTIC."
THERE'S A RECORD OF THE BURIAL IN THE GRAVEYARD OF THE SCHOOL CHAPEL. LOT E7.
I'M SQWOOSH-ING.
THEY INVITED BOTH OF CHARLES' RELATIVES, BUT NEITHER OF THEM CAME.
BOTH?
"AS FAR AS I CAN TELL, EDWIN PAINE JUST DIS-APPEARED INTO THIN AIR."

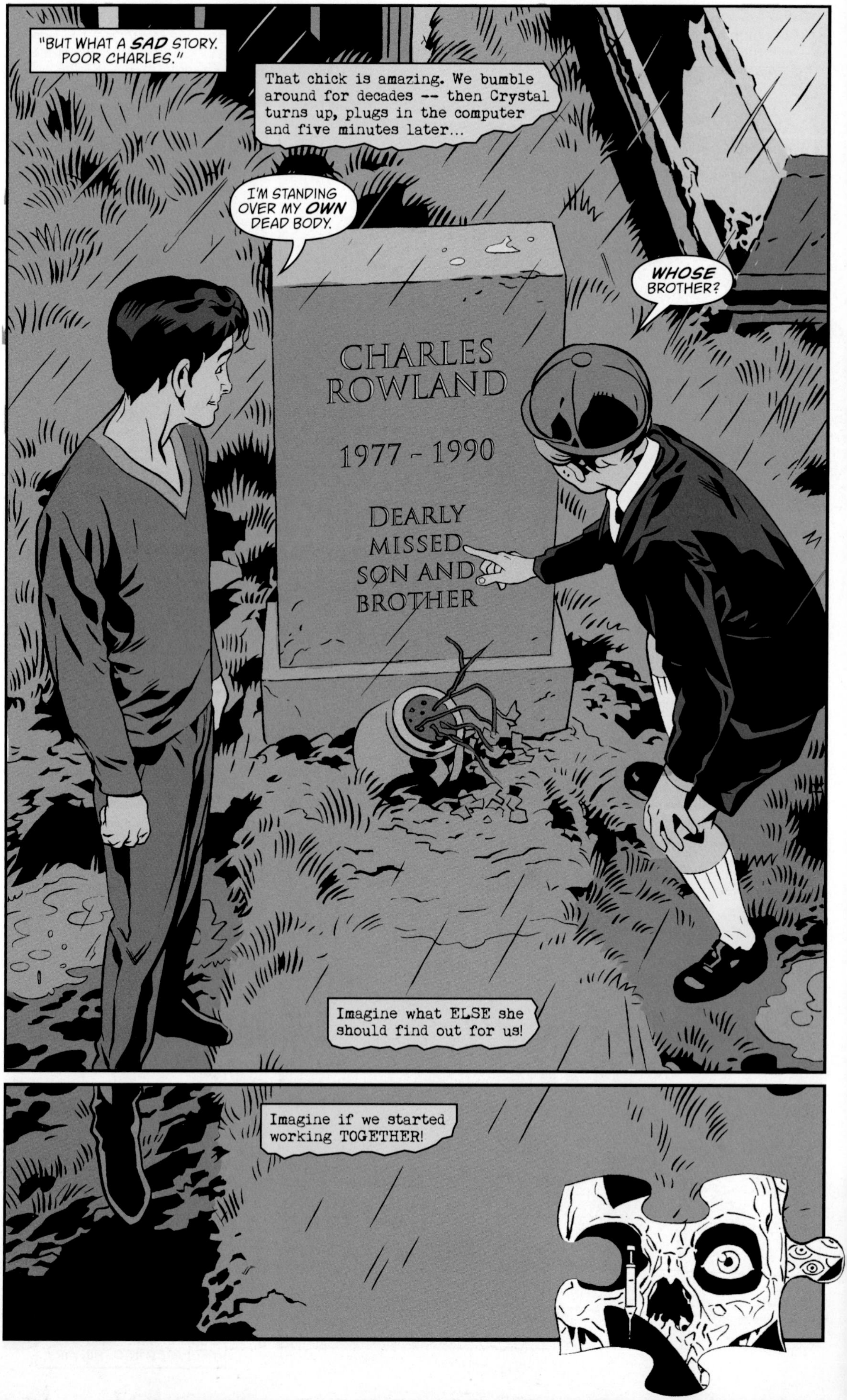
"BUT WHAT A SAD STORY. POOR CHARLES."
That chick is amazing. We bumble around for decades -- then Crystal turns up, plugs in the computer and five minutes later...
I'M STANDING OVER MY OWN DEAD BODY.
WHOSE BROTHER?
CHARLES ROWLAND
1977 - 1990
DEARLY MISSED SON AND BROTHER
Imagine what ELSE she should find out for us!
Imagine if we started working TOGETHER!

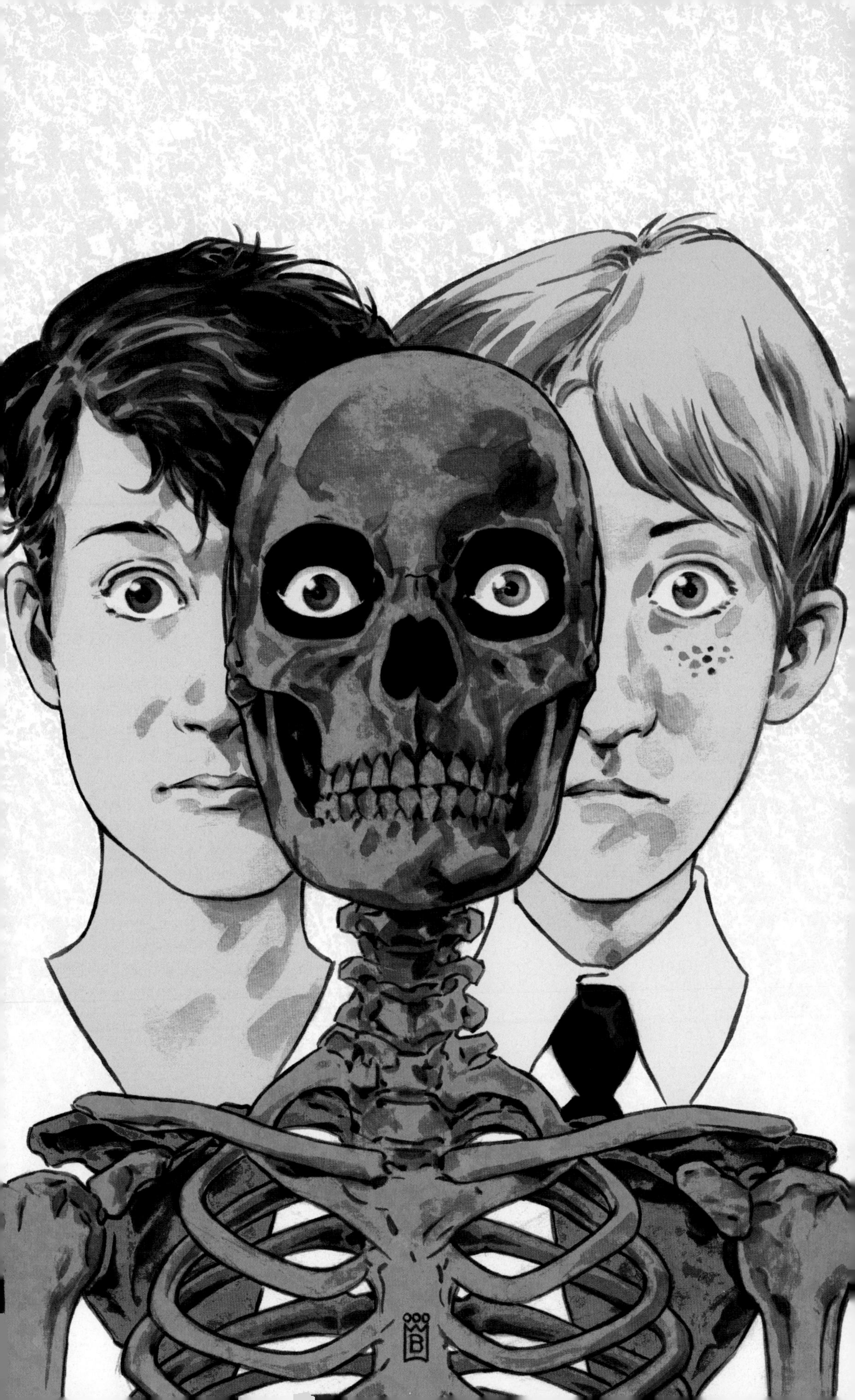

Happening all of a sudden upon your own gravestone... I suppose it would have a powerful effect upon anyone.

CHARLES
ROWLAND

1977 - 1990

DEARLY
MISSED
SON AND
BROTHER

I HAVE A BROTHER...

...OR A SISTER!

For one terrible moment, I thought that dear old Charles had decided to give it all up— sublunary existence, the detective agency, my friendship...

CHARLES! STOP THAT!

WHAT ON EARTH DO YOU THINK YOU'RE DOING?!

INVESTIGATING!

I should have known him better than that.

But I didn't envy the old blighter, going down there...

DEAD BOY DETECTIVES in

SOUL-STRIPPED | SCHOOLBOY TERRORS Part 3 of 4

Toby Litt	Mark Buckingham	Gary Erskine	Lee Loughridge	Todd Klein	Mark Buckingham
writer - story - pencils		inks	colors	letters	cover

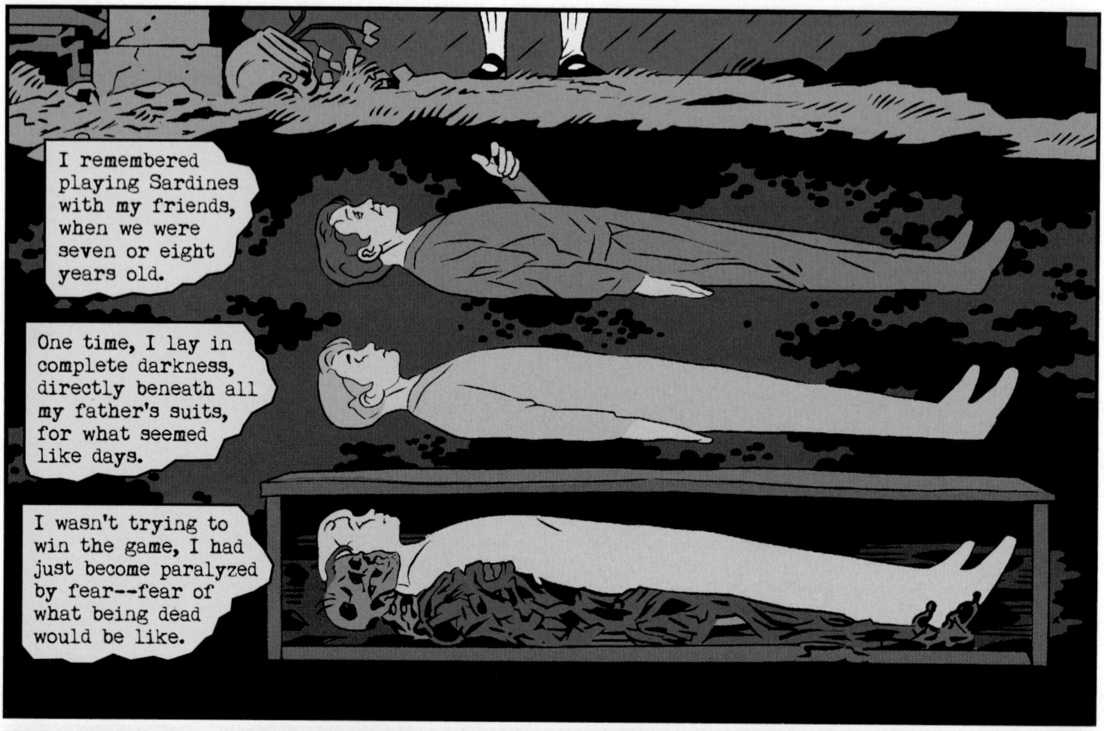
I remembered playing Sardines with my friends, when we were seven or eight years old.
One time, I lay in complete darkness, directly beneath all my father's suits, for what seemed like days.
I wasn't trying to win the game, I had just become paralyzed by fear--fear of what being dead would be like.

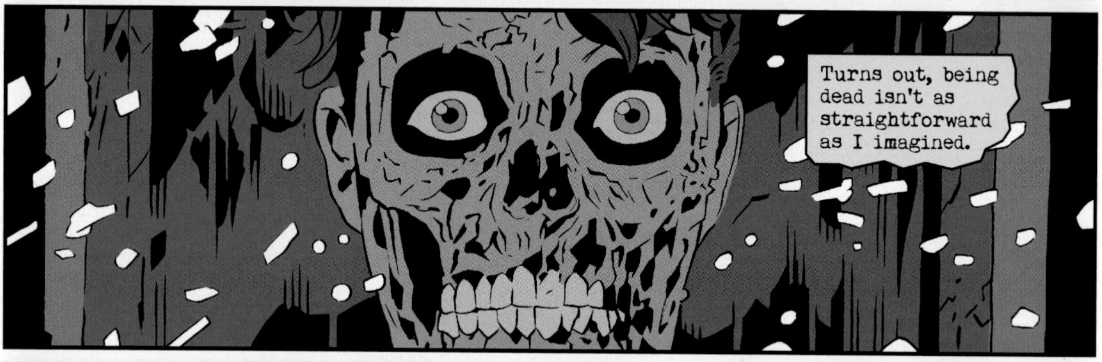
Turns out, being dead isn't as straightforward as I imagined.

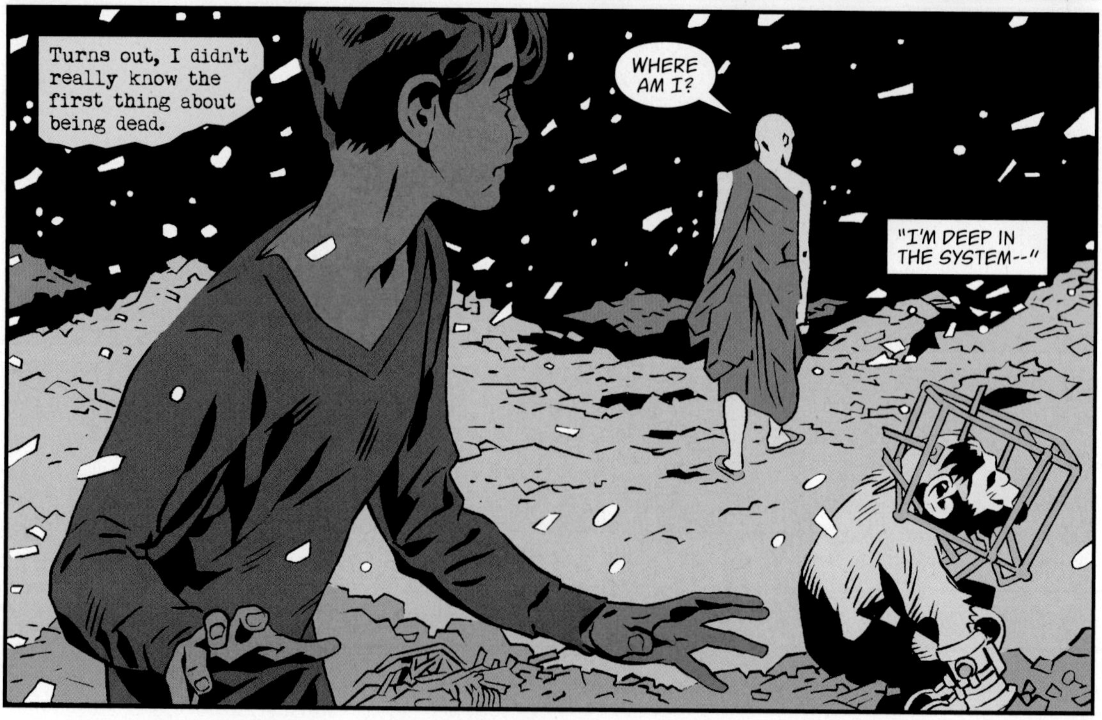
Turns out, I didn't really know the first thing about being dead.
WHERE AM I?
"I'M DEEP IN THE SYSTEM--"

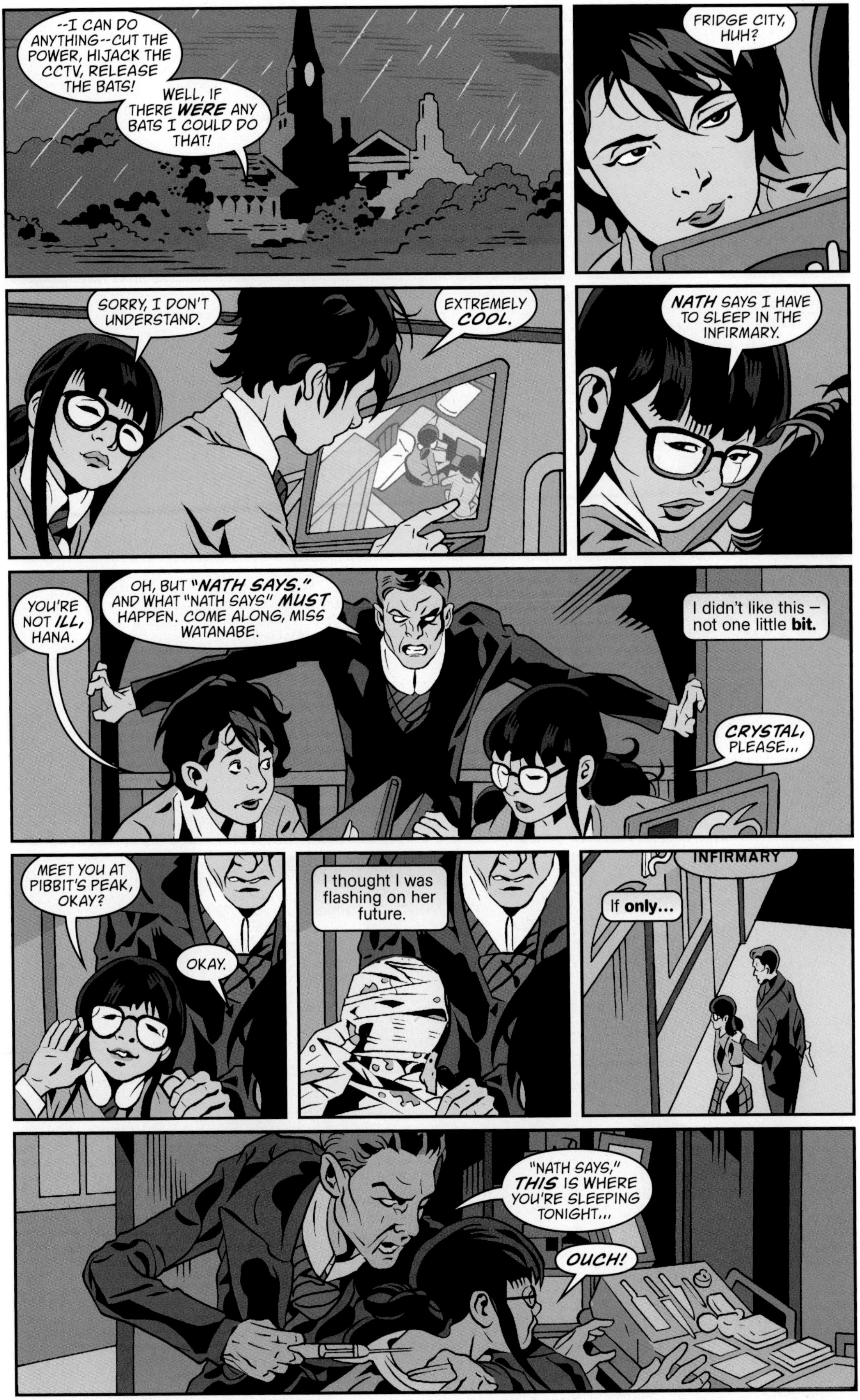
--I CAN DO ANYTHING--CUT THE POWER, HIJACK THE CCTV, RELEASE THE BATS!
WELL, IF THERE WERE ANY BATS I COULD DO THAT!
FRIDGE CITY, HUH?
SORRY, I DON'T UNDERSTAND.
EXTREMELY COOL.
NATH SAYS I HAVE TO SLEEP IN THE INFIRMARY.
YOU'RE NOT ILL, HANA.
OH, BUT "NATH SAYS." AND WHAT "NATH SAYS" MUST HAPPEN. COME ALONG, MISS WATANABE.
I didn't like this – not one little bit.
CRYSTAL, PLEASE...
MEET YOU AT PIBBIT'S PEAK, OKAY?
OKAY.
I thought I was flashing on her future.
INFIRMARY
If only...
"NATH SAYS," THIS IS WHERE YOU'RE SLEEPING TONIGHT...
OUCH!

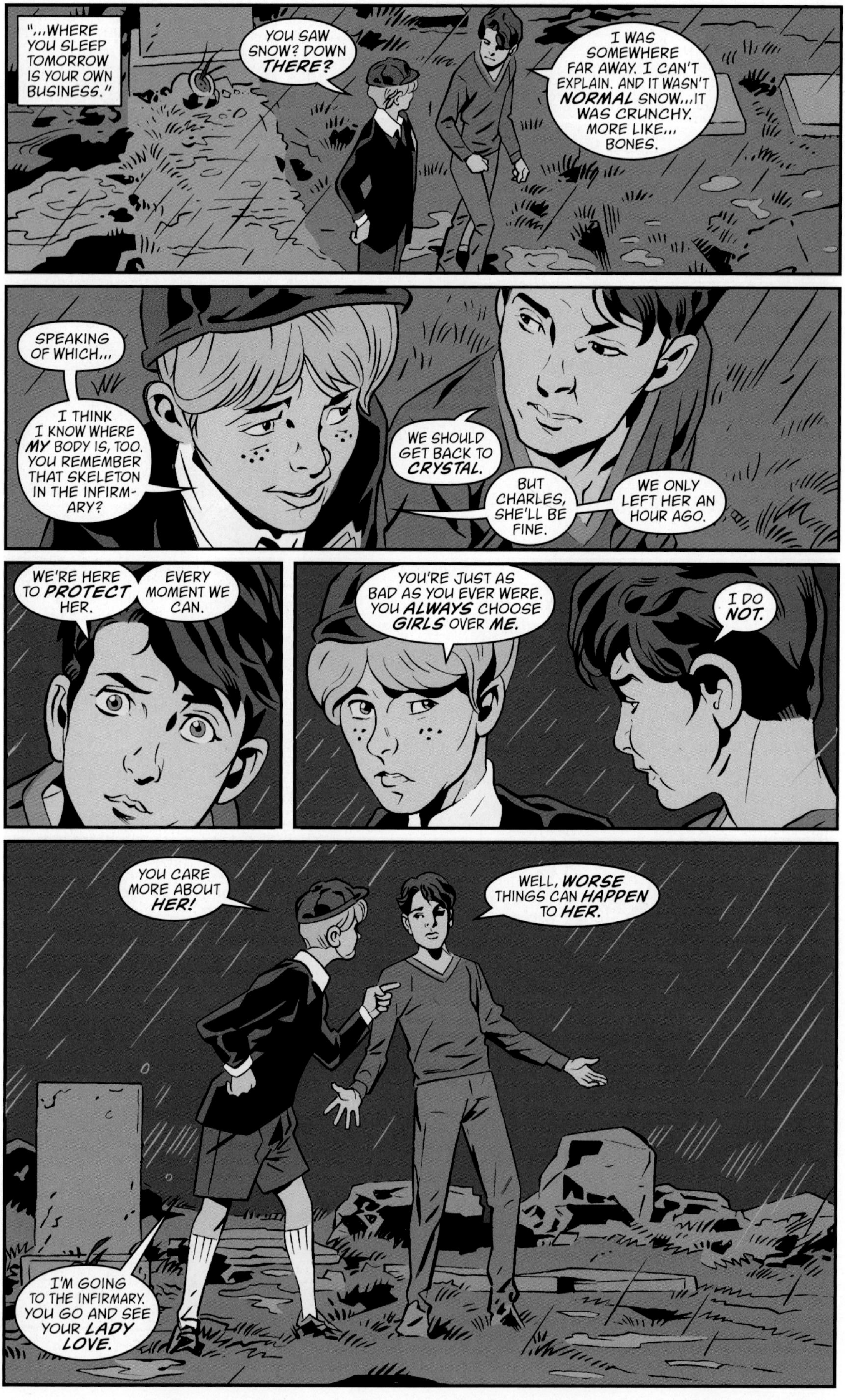
"...WHERE YOU SLEEP TOMORROW IS YOUR OWN BUSINESS."
YOU SAW SNOW? DOWN THERE?
I WAS SOMEWHERE FAR AWAY. I CAN'T EXPLAIN. AND IT WASN'T NORMAL SNOW...IT WAS CRUNCHY. MORE LIKE... BONES.
SPEAKING OF WHICH...
I THINK I KNOW WHERE MY BODY IS, TOO. YOU REMEMBER THAT SKELETON IN THE INFIRM- ARY?
WE SHOULD GET BACK TO CRYSTAL.
BUT CHARLES, SHE'LL BE FINE.
WE ONLY LEFT HER AN HOUR AGO.
WE'RE HERE TO PROTECT HER.
EVERY MOMENT WE CAN.
YOU'RE JUST AS BAD AS YOU EVER WERE. YOU ALWAYS CHOOSE GIRLS OVER ME.
I DO NOT.
YOU CARE MORE ABOUT HER!
WELL, WORSE THINGS CAN HAPPEN TO HER.
I'M GOING TO THE INFIRMARY. YOU GO AND SEE YOUR LADY LOVE.

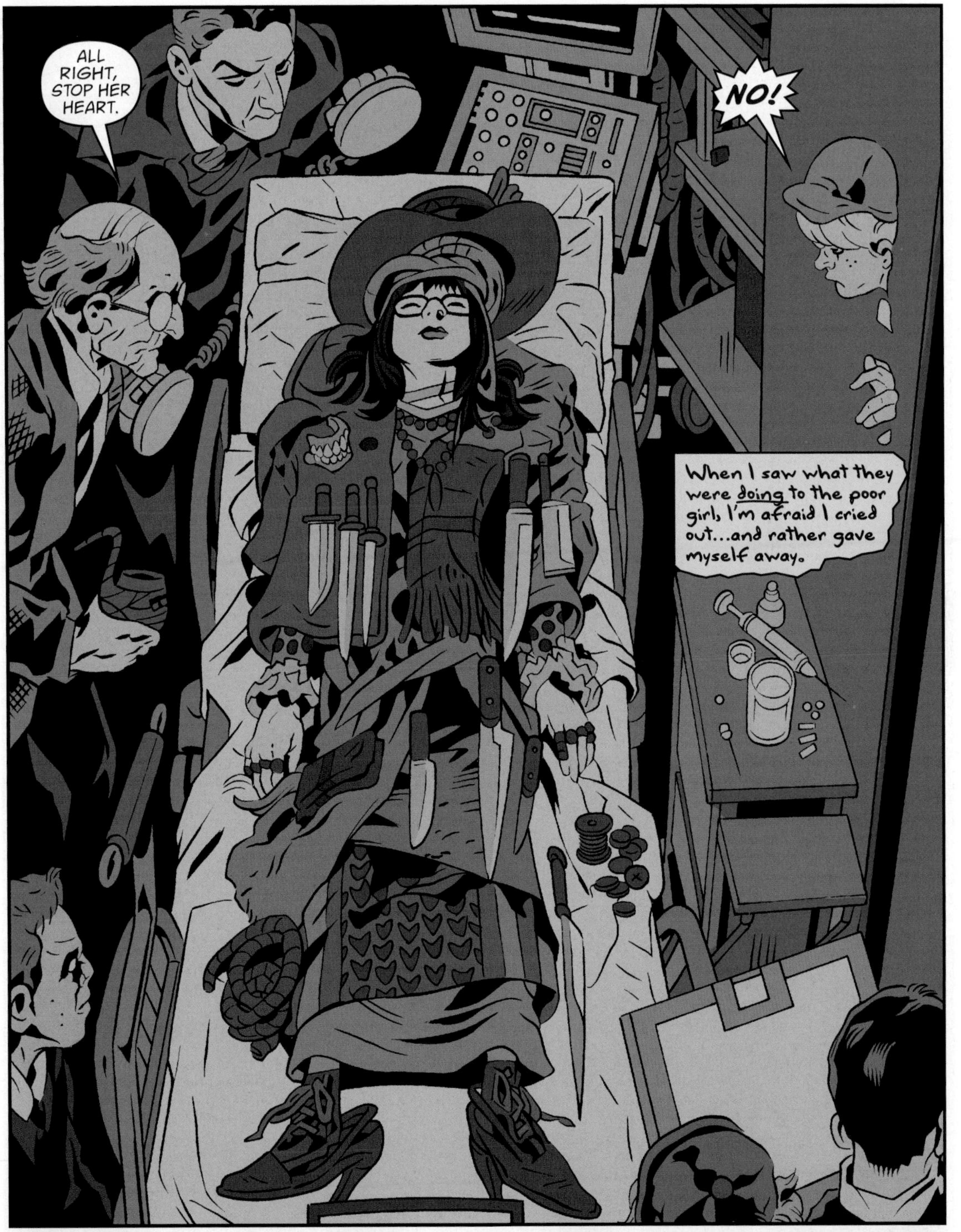
ALL RIGHT, STOP HER HEART.
NO!
When I saw what they were doing to the poor girl, I'm afraid I cried out...and rather gave myself away.

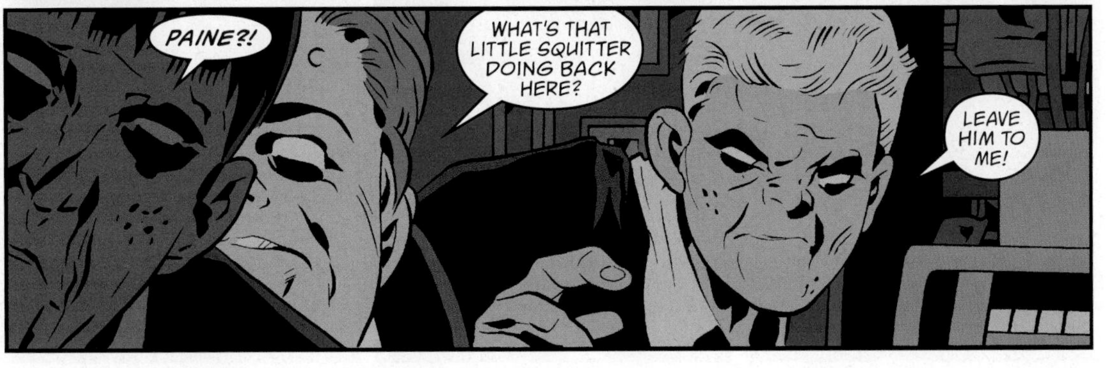
PAINE?!
WHAT'S THAT LITTLE SQUITTER DOING BACK HERE?
LEAVE HIM TO ME!

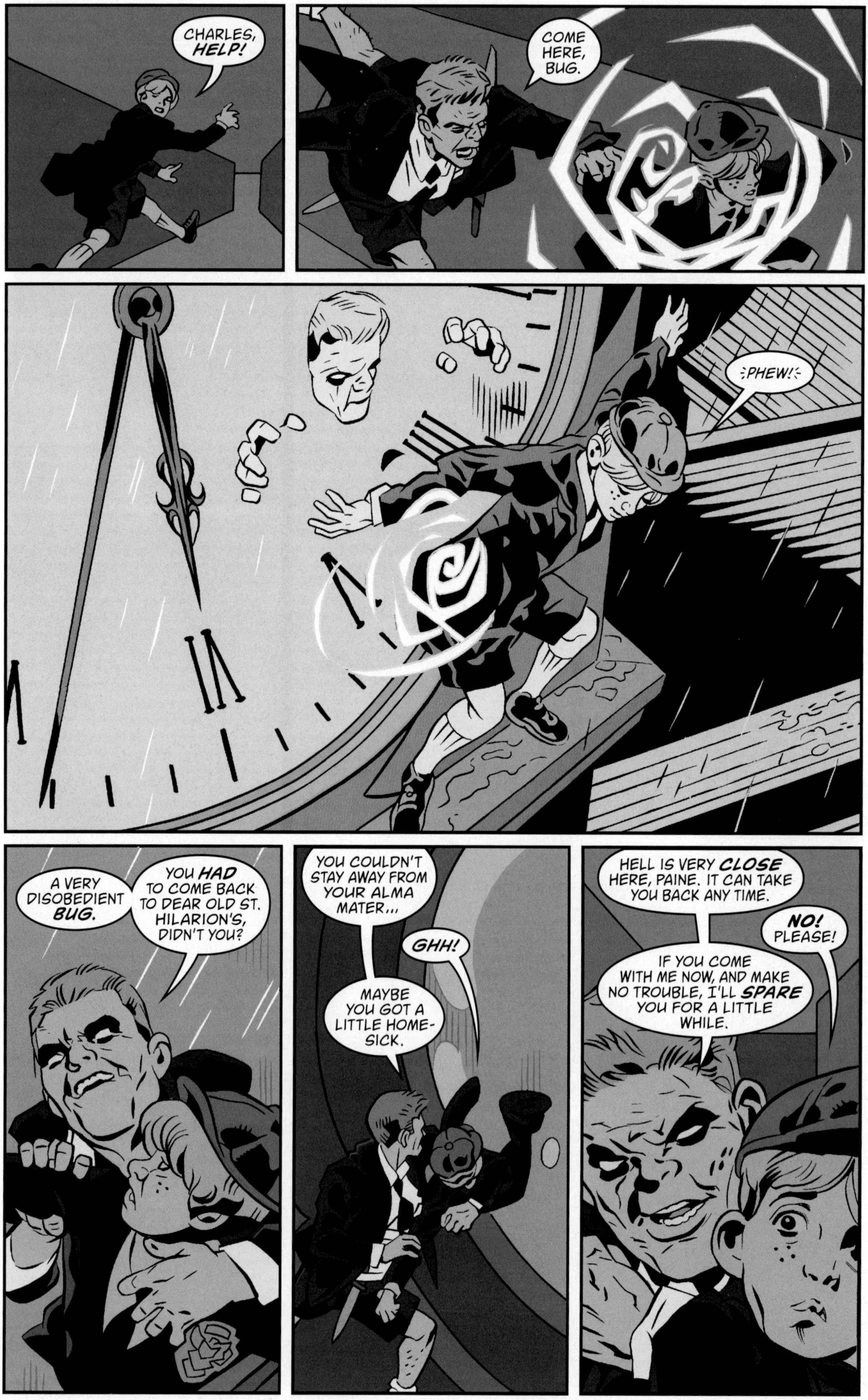
CHARLES, HELP!
COME HERE, BUG.
PHEW!
A VERY DISOBEDIENT BUG.
YOU HAD TO COME BACK TO DEAR OLD ST. HILARION'S, DIDN'T YOU?
YOU COULDN'T STAY AWAY FROM YOUR ALMA MATER...
GHH!
MAYBE YOU GOT A LITTLE HOME-SICK.
HELL IS VERY CLOSE HERE, PAINE. IT CAN TAKE YOU BACK ANY TIME.
NO! PLEASE!
IF YOU COME WITH ME NOW, AND MAKE NO TROUBLE, I'LL SPARE YOU FOR A LITTLE WHILE.

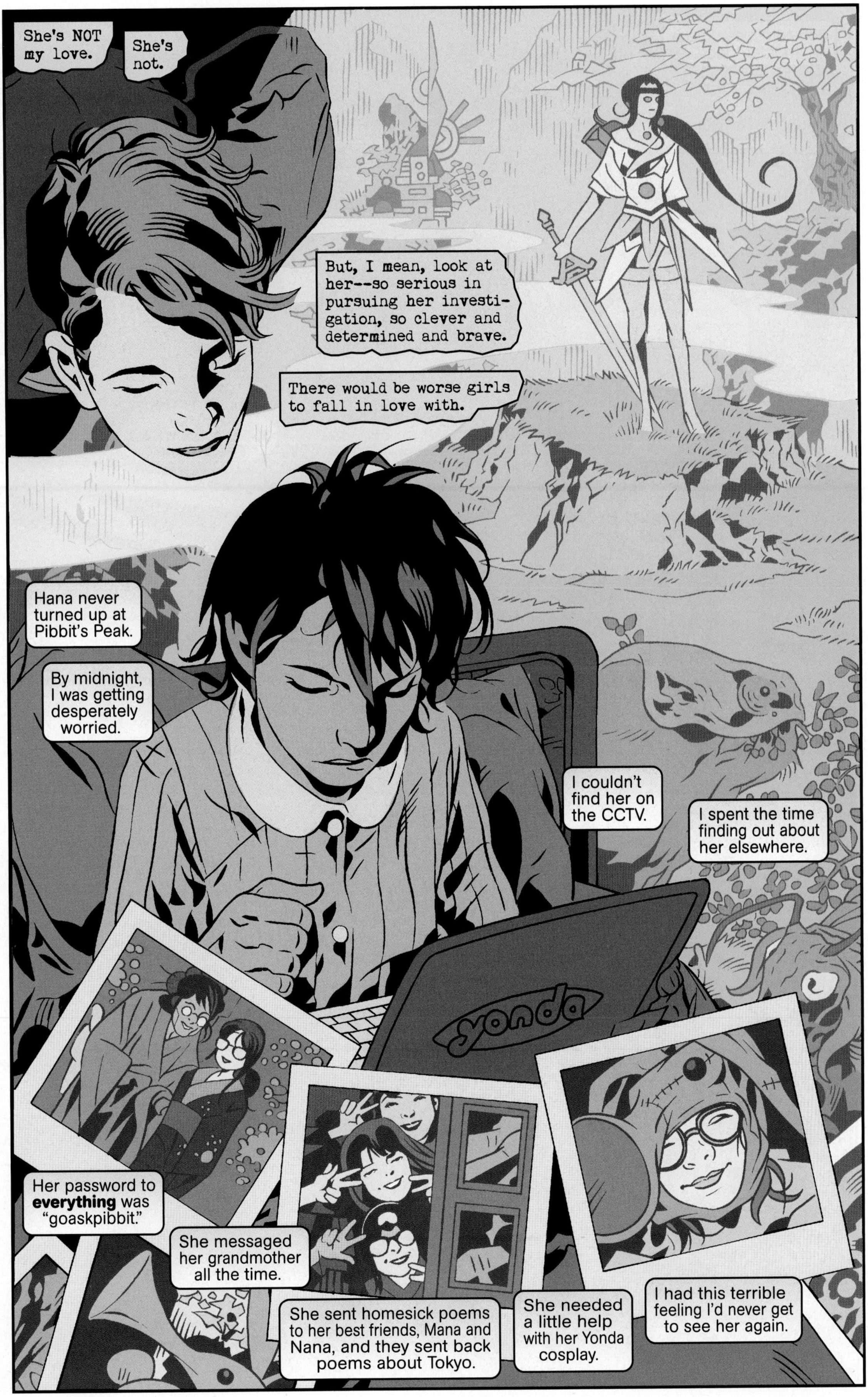
She's NOT my love.
She's not.
But, I mean, look at her--so serious in pursuing her investigation, so clever and determined and brave.
There would be worse girls to fall in love with.
Hana never turned up at Pibbit's Peak.
By midnight, I was getting desperately worried.
I couldn't find her on the CCTV.
I spent the time finding out about her elsewhere.
yonda
Her password to **everything** was "goaskpibbit."
She messaged her grandmother all the time.
She sent homesick poems to her best friends, Mana and Nana, and they sent back poems about Tokyo.
She needed a little help with her Yonda cosplay.
I had this terrible feeling I'd never get to see her again.

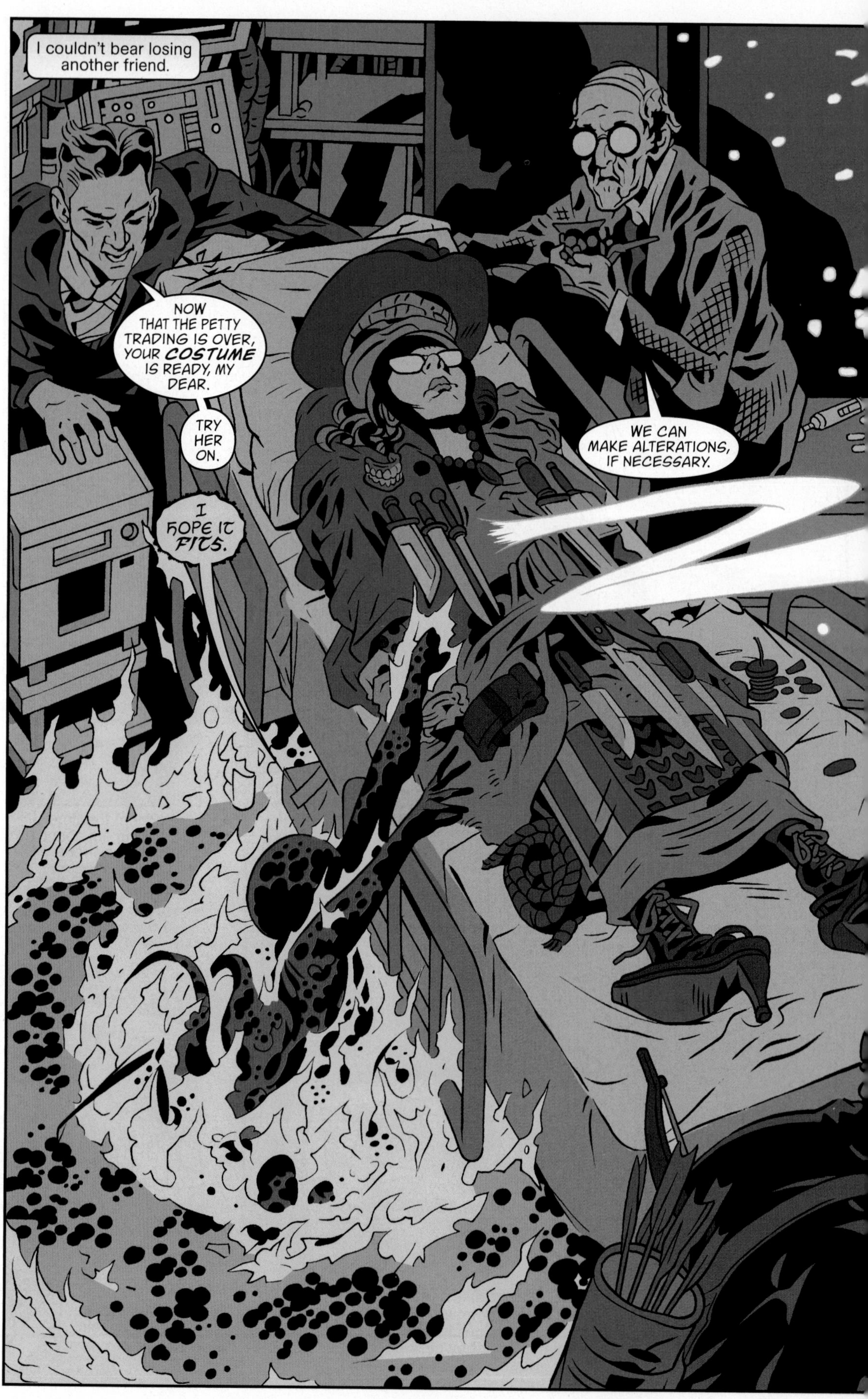

I couldn't bear losing another friend.
NOW THAT THE PETTY TRADING IS OVER, YOUR COSTUME IS READY, MY DEAR.
TRY HER ON.
WE CAN MAKE ALTERATIONS, IF NECESSARY.
I HOPE IT FITS.

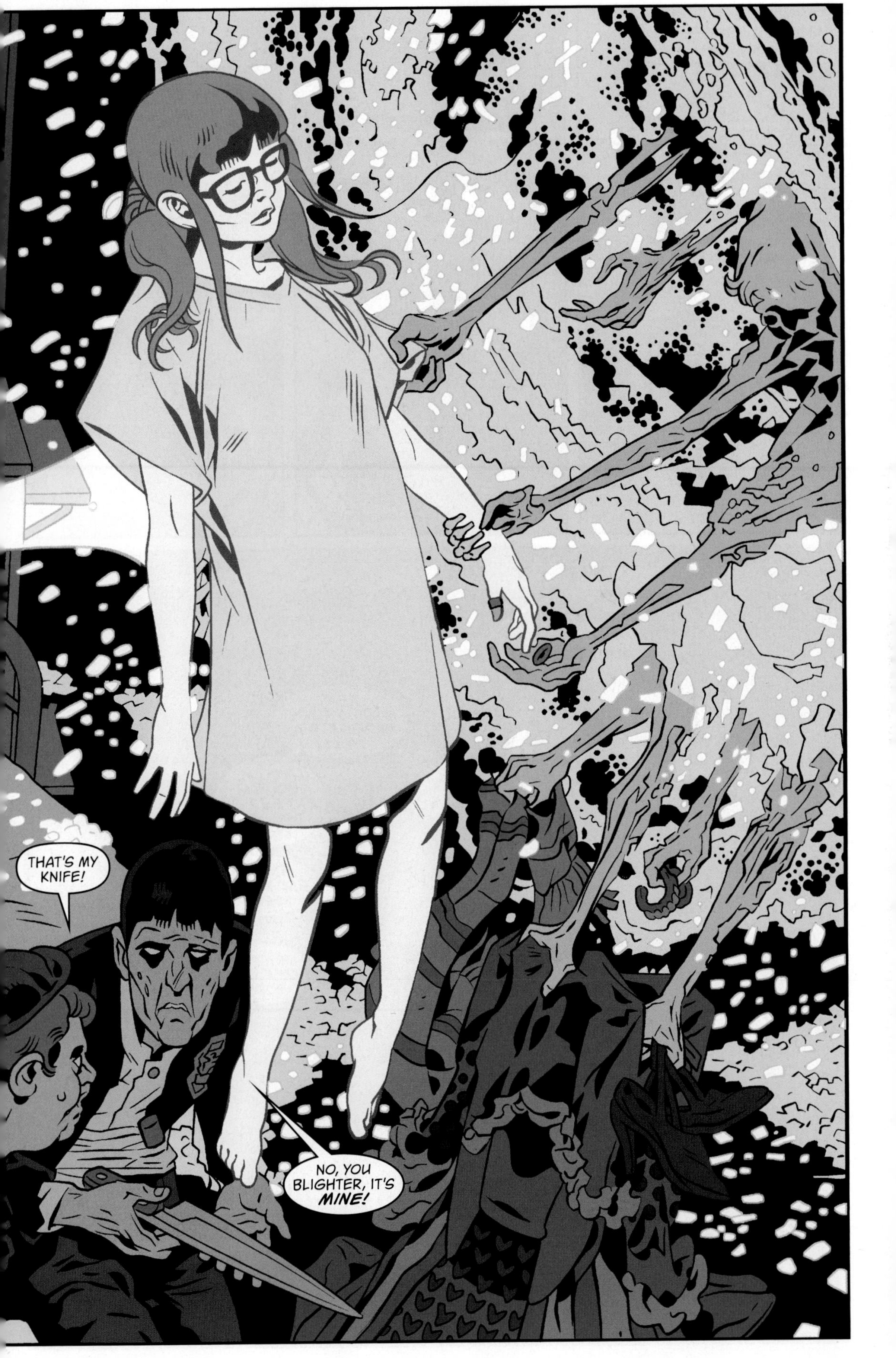
THAT'S MY KNIFE!
NO, YOU BLIGHTER, IT'S MINE!

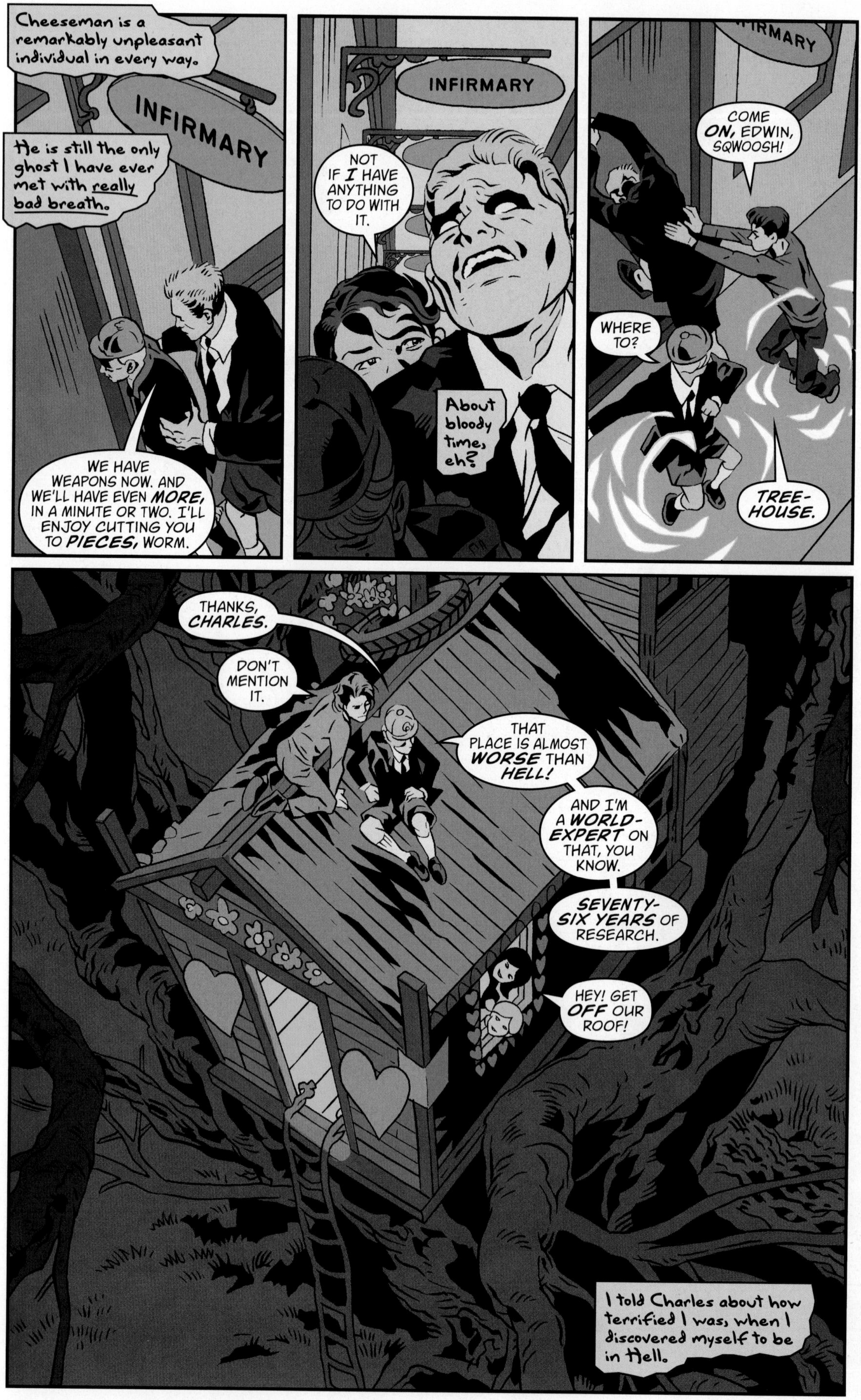

Cheeseman is a remarkably unpleasant individual in every way.
INFIRMARY
He is still the only ghost I have ever met with really bad breath.
WE HAVE WEAPONS NOW. AND WE'LL HAVE EVEN MORE, IN A MINUTE OR TWO. I'LL ENJOY CUTTING YOU TO PIECES, WORM.
INFIRMARY
NOT IF I HAVE ANYTHING TO DO WITH IT.
About bloody time, eh?
IRMARY
COME ON, EDWIN, SQWOOSH!
WHERE TO?
TREE-HOUSE.
THANKS, CHARLES.
DON'T MENTION IT.
THAT PLACE IS ALMOST WORSE THAN HELL!
AND I'M A WORLD-EXPERT ON THAT, YOU KNOW.
SEVENTY-SIX YEARS OF RESEARCH.
HEY! GET OFF OUR ROOF!
I told Charles about how terrified I was, when I discovered myself to be in Hell.

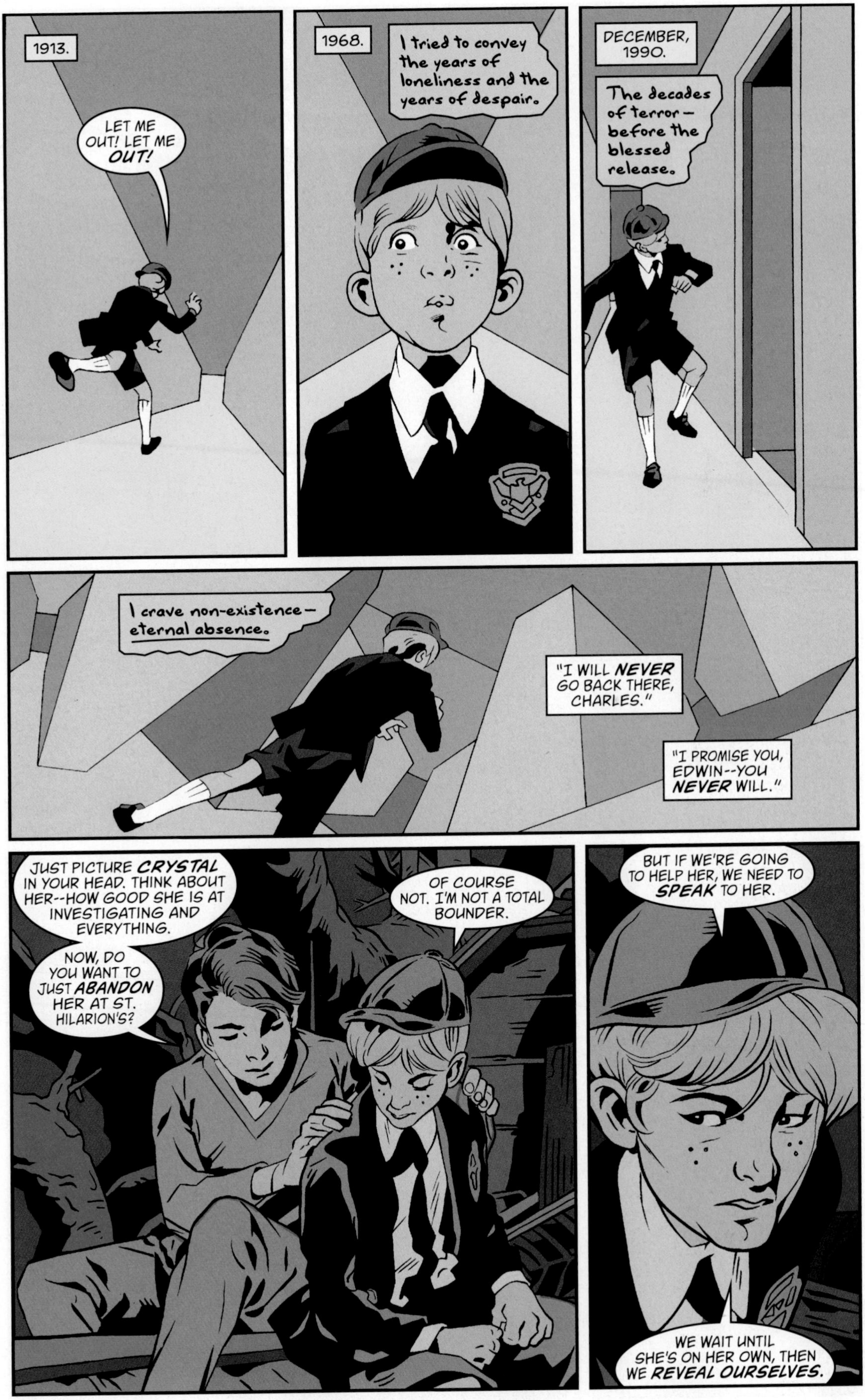
1913.
LET ME OUT! LET ME OUT!
1968.
I tried to convey the years of loneliness and the years of despair.
DECEMBER, 1990.
The decades of terror—before the blessed release.
I crave non-existence—eternal absence.
"I WILL NEVER GO BACK THERE, CHARLES."
"I PROMISE YOU, EDWIN--YOU NEVER WILL."
JUST PICTURE CRYSTAL IN YOUR HEAD. THINK ABOUT HER--HOW GOOD SHE IS AT INVESTIGATING AND EVERYTHING.
NOW, DO YOU WANT TO JUST ABANDON HER AT ST. HILARION'S?
OF COURSE NOT. I'M NOT A TOTAL BOUNDER.
BUT IF WE'RE GOING TO HELP HER, WE NEED TO SPEAK TO HER.
WE WAIT UNTIL SHE'S ON HER OWN, THEN WE REVEAL OURSELVES.

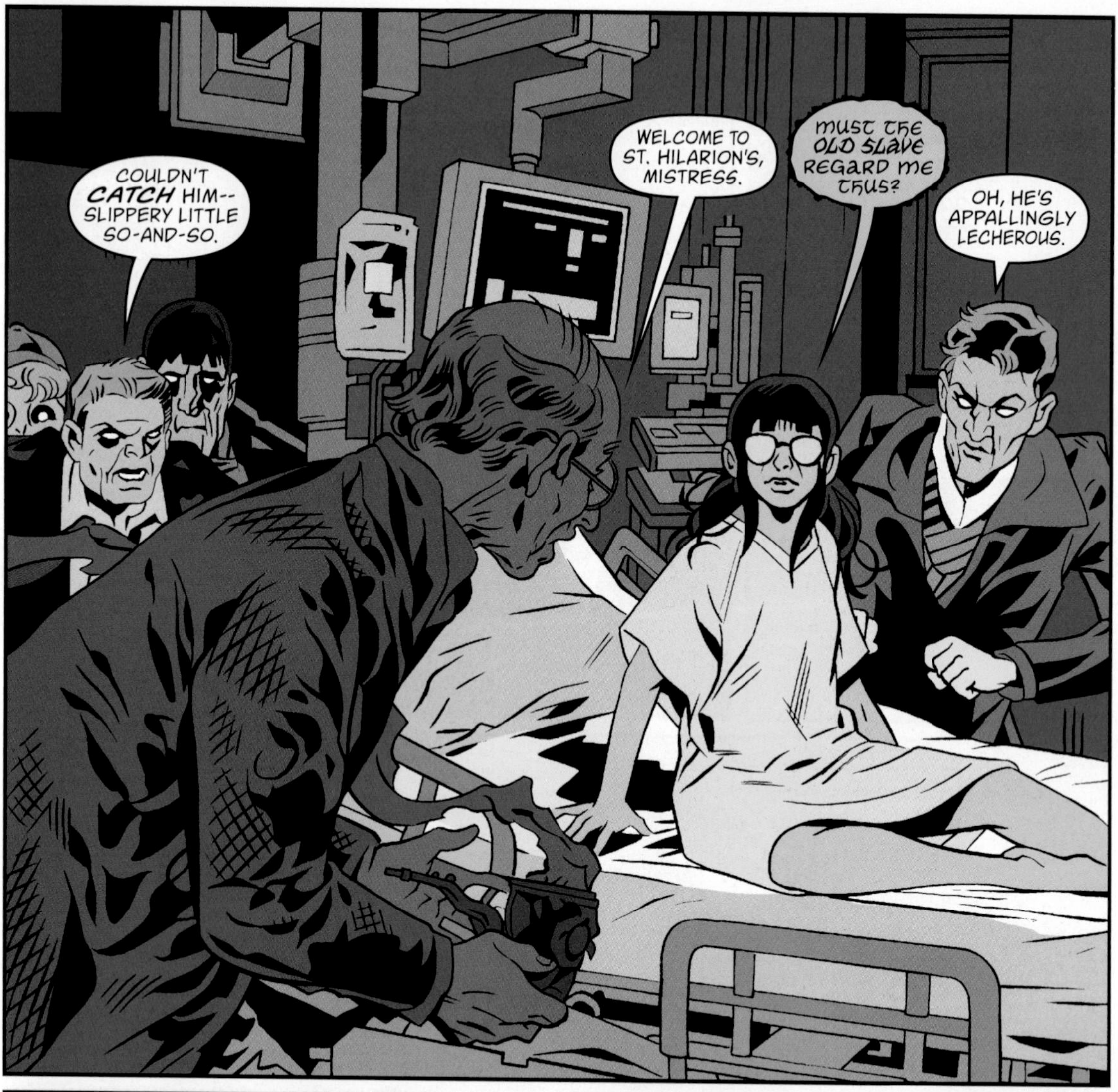
COULDN'T CATCH HIM-- SLIPPERY LITTLE SO-AND-SO.
WELCOME TO ST. HILARION'S, MISTRESS.
MUST THE OLD SLAVE REGARD ME THUS?
OH, HE'S APPALLINGLY LECHEROUS.

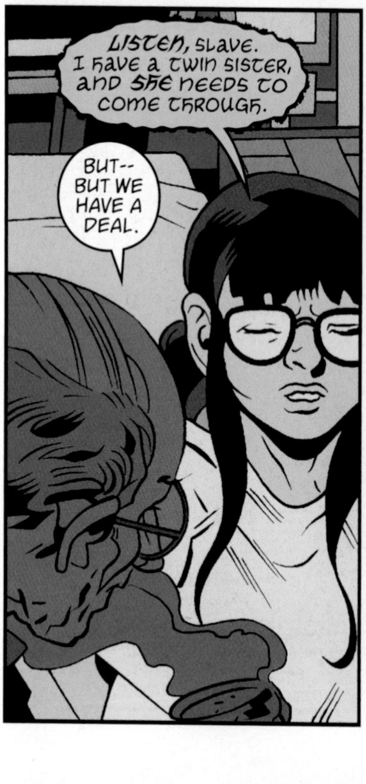
LISTEN, SLAVE. I HAVE A TWIN SISTER, AND SHE NEEDS TO COME THROUGH.
BUT-- BUT WE HAVE A DEAL.

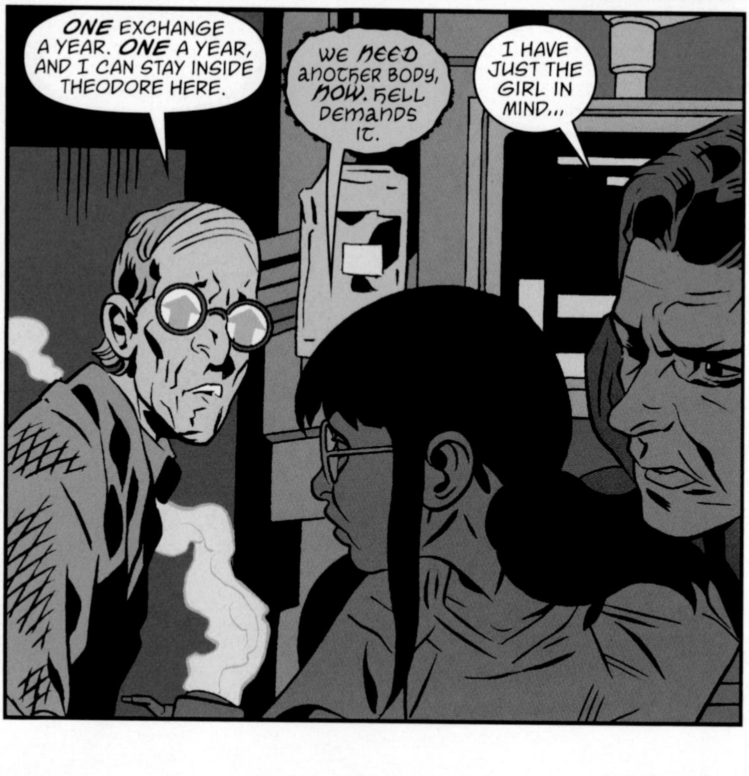
ONE EXCHANGE A YEAR. ONE A YEAR, AND I CAN STAY INSIDE THEODORE HERE.
WE NEED ANOTHER BODY, NOW. HELL DEMANDS IT.
I HAVE JUST THE GIRL IN MIND...

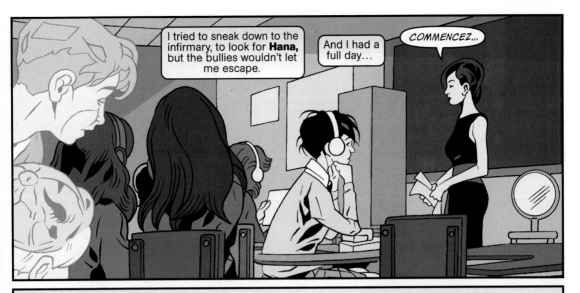

I tried to sneak down to the infirmary, to look for **Hana**, but the bullies wouldn't let me escape.

And I had a full day…

COMMENCEZ…

St. Hilarion's TIMETABLE FOR CRYSTAL PALACE SURNAME VON HOVERKRAFT

8am - French	12am - Theology	3pm - Greek	7pm - Homework
9am - Double Geography	1pm - Lunch	4pm - Hockey	10pm - Lights Out
11am - Meditation	2pm - Latin	6pm - Dinner	

My dad had a penchant for French au pairs, so I'd learned all this stuff while playing with dollies.

JE ME SUIS COUCHE: I GO TO BED.

JE ME SUIS COUCHE.

JE M'IMAGINAIS: I IMAGINE MYSELF.

All through the reflexive verbs I was worrying about **Hana**.

SE LEVER, S'IL VOUS PLAIT.

EXCITING NEWS, CHILDREN. WE HAVE SECURED FUNDING FOR ANOTHER FRENCH EXCHANGE THIS YEAR.

AND ALL OF YOU ARE ELIGIBLE.

EVEN OUR NEWEST GIRL.

NOTHING TO DO WITH HER BEING FAMOUS…

SIR, HOW IS HANA WATANABE?

STILL A LITTLE FRAGILE, I'M AFRAID.

I WILL GO AND CHECK ON HER NOW.

It wasn't until the evening that I was able to sneak away.

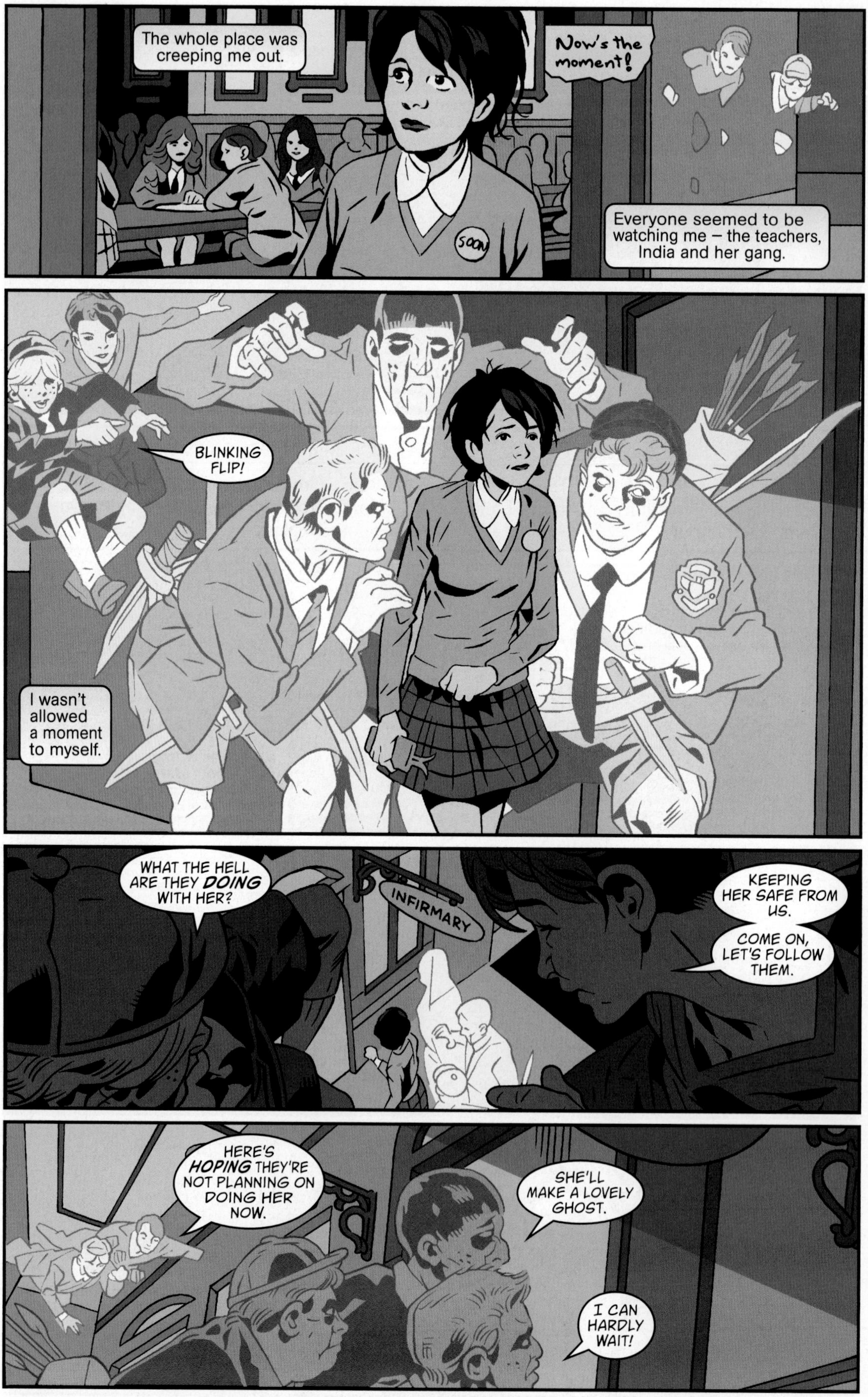
The whole place was creeping me out.
Now's the moment!
SOON
Everyone seemed to be watching me – the teachers, India and her gang.
BLINKING FLIP!
I wasn't allowed a moment to myself.
WHAT THE HELL ARE THEY DOING WITH HER?
INFIRMARY
KEEPING HER SAFE FROM US.
COME ON, LET'S FOLLOW THEM.
HERE'S HOPING THEY'RE NOT PLANNING ON DOING HER NOW.
SHE'LL MAKE A LOVELY GHOST.
I CAN HARDLY WAIT!

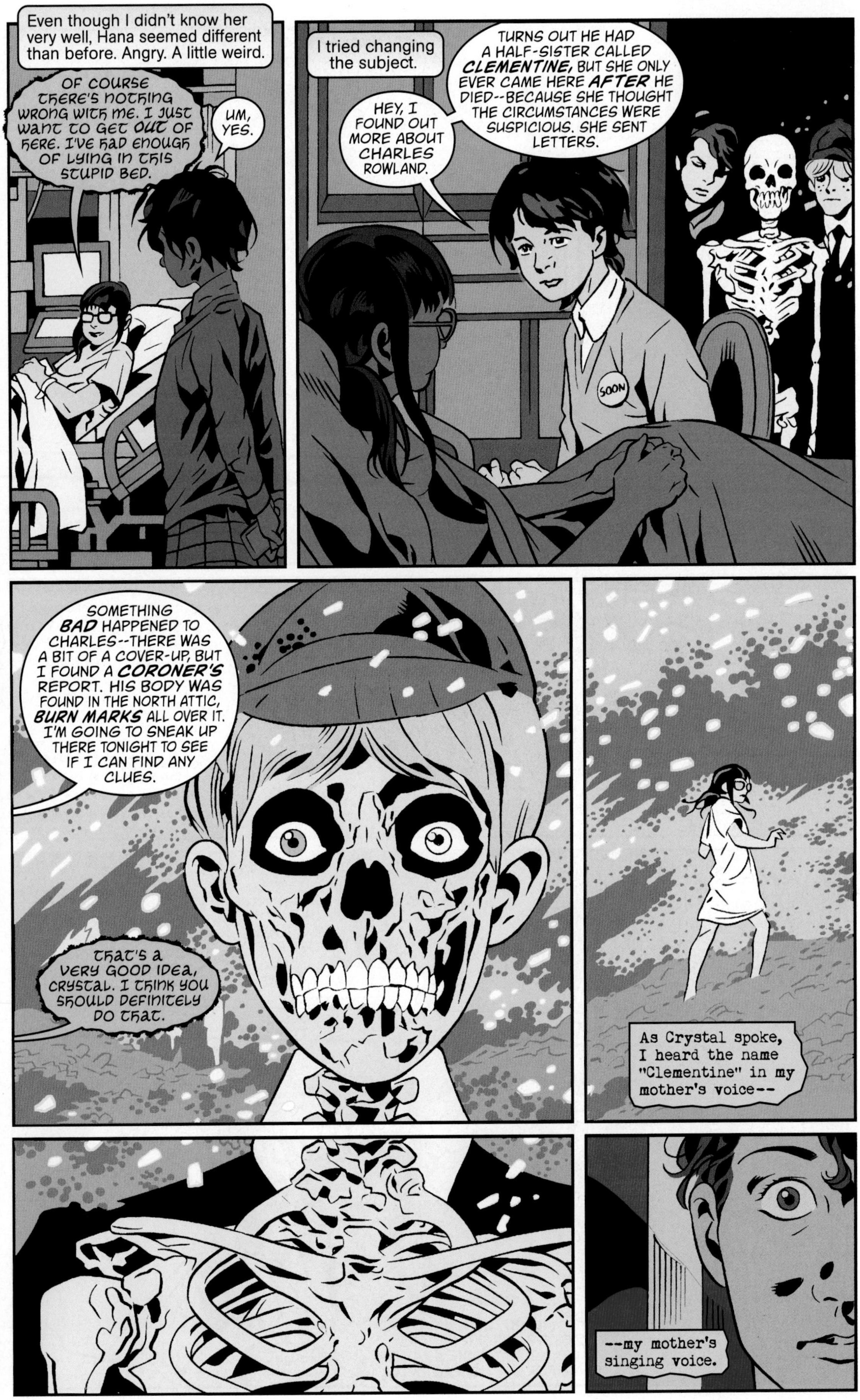
Even though I didn't know her very well, Hana seemed different than before. Angry. A little weird.
OF COURSE THERE'S NOTHING WRONG WITH ME. I JUST WANT TO GET OUT OF HERE. I'VE HAD ENOUGH OF LYING IN THIS STUPID BED.
UM, YES.
I tried changing the subject.
HEY, I FOUND OUT MORE ABOUT CHARLES ROWLAND.
TURNS OUT HE HAD A HALF-SISTER CALLED CLEMENTINE, BUT SHE ONLY EVER CAME HERE AFTER HE DIED--BECAUSE SHE THOUGHT THE CIRCUMSTANCES WERE SUSPICIOUS. SHE SENT LETTERS.
SOON
SOMETHING BAD HAPPENED TO CHARLES--THERE WAS A BIT OF A COVER-UP, BUT I FOUND A CORONER'S REPORT. HIS BODY WAS FOUND IN THE NORTH ATTIC, BURN MARKS ALL OVER IT. I'M GOING TO SNEAK UP THERE TONIGHT TO SEE IF I CAN FIND ANY CLUES.
THAT'S A VERY GOOD IDEA, CRYSTAL. I THINK YOU SHOULD DEFINITELY DO THAT.
As Crystal spoke, I heard the name "Clementine" in my mother's voice--
--my mother's singing voice.

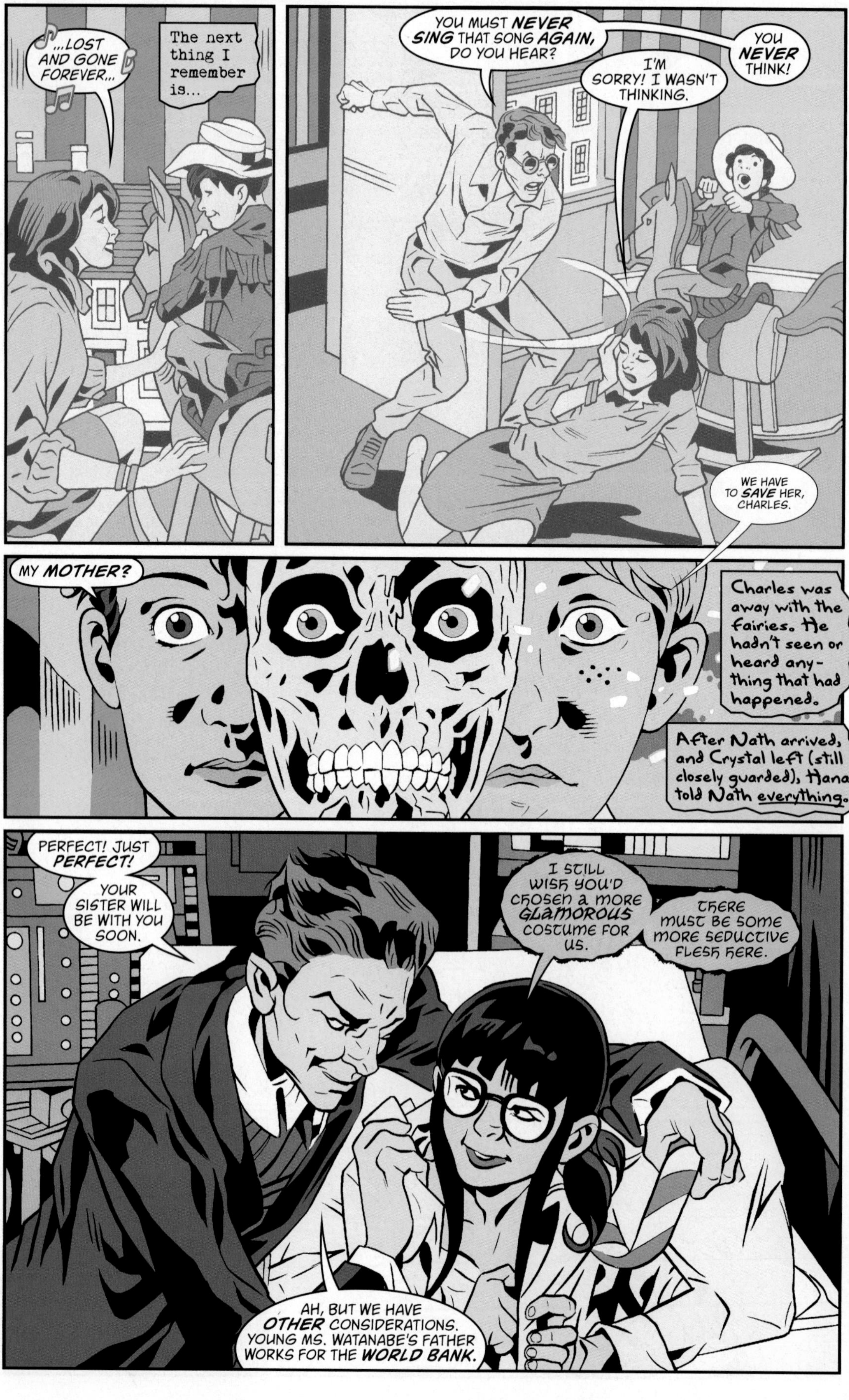

...LOST AND GONE FOREVER...
The next thing I remember is...
YOU MUST NEVER SING THAT SONG AGAIN, DO YOU HEAR?
YOU NEVER THINK!
I'M SORRY! I WASN'T THINKING.
WE HAVE TO SAVE HER, CHARLES.
MY MOTHER?
Charles was away with the fairies. He hadn't seen or heard anything that had happened.
After Nath arrived, and Crystal left (still closely guarded), Hana told Nath everything.
PERFECT! JUST PERFECT!
YOUR SISTER WILL BE WITH YOU SOON.
I STILL WISH YOU'D CHOSEN A MORE GLAMOROUS COSTUME FOR US.
THERE MUST BE SOME MORE SEDUCTIVE FLESH HERE.
AH, BUT WE HAVE OTHER CONSIDERATIONS. YOUNG MS. WATANABE'S FATHER WORKS FOR THE WORLD BANK.

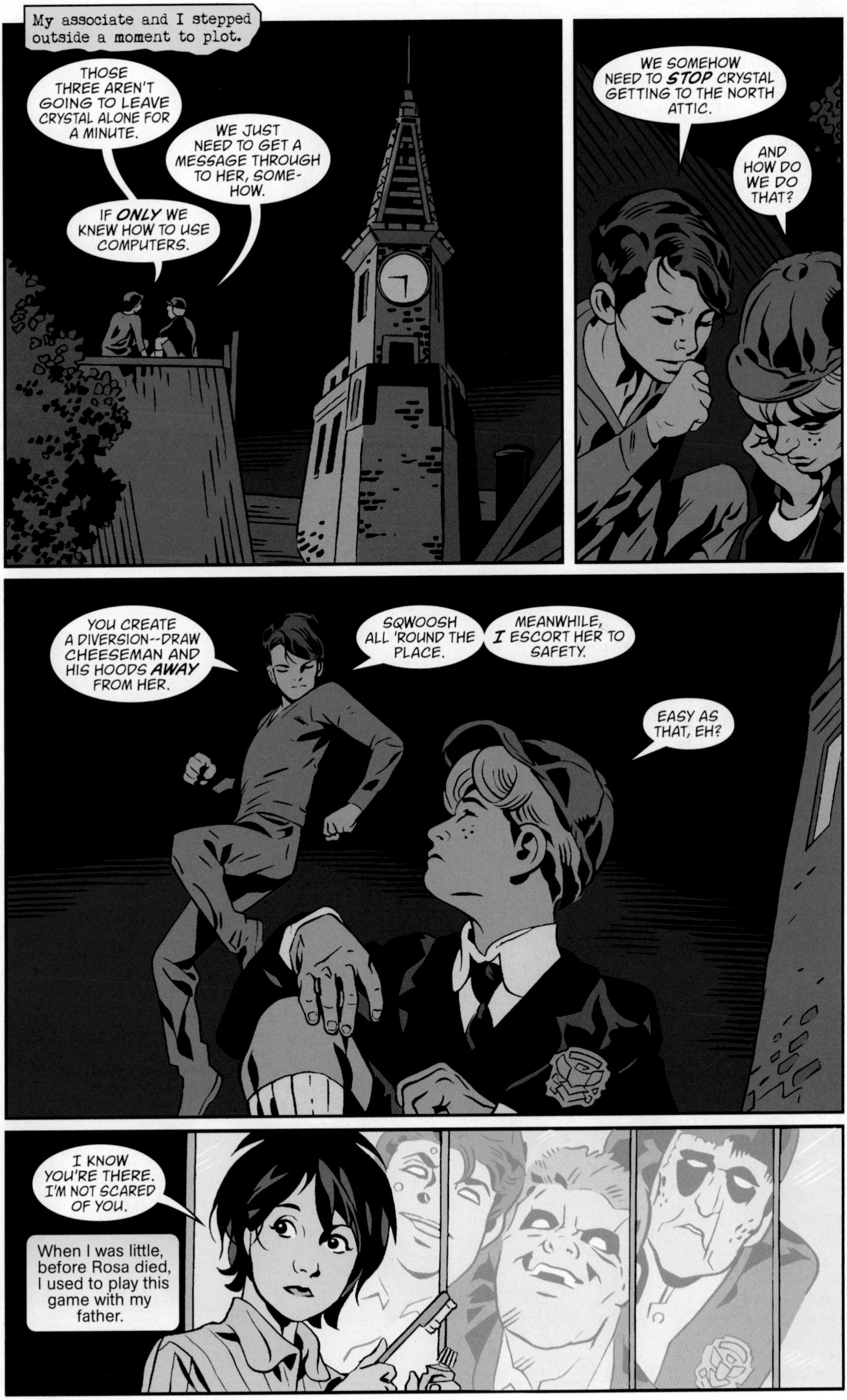
My associate and I stepped outside a moment to plot.
THOSE THREE AREN'T GOING TO LEAVE CRYSTAL ALONE FOR A MINUTE.
WE JUST NEED TO GET A MESSAGE THROUGH TO HER, SOME-HOW.
IF *ONLY* WE KNEW HOW TO USE COMPUTERS.
WE SOMEHOW NEED TO *STOP* CRYSTAL GETTING TO THE NORTH ATTIC.
AND HOW DO WE DO THAT?
YOU CREATE A DIVERSION--DRAW CHEESEMAN AND HIS HOODS *AWAY* FROM HER.
SQWOOSH ALL 'ROUND THE PLACE.
MEANWHILE, *I* ESCORT HER TO SAFETY.
EASY AS THAT, EH?
I KNOW YOU'RE THERE. I'M NOT SCARED OF YOU.
When I was little, before Rosa died, I used to play this game with my father.

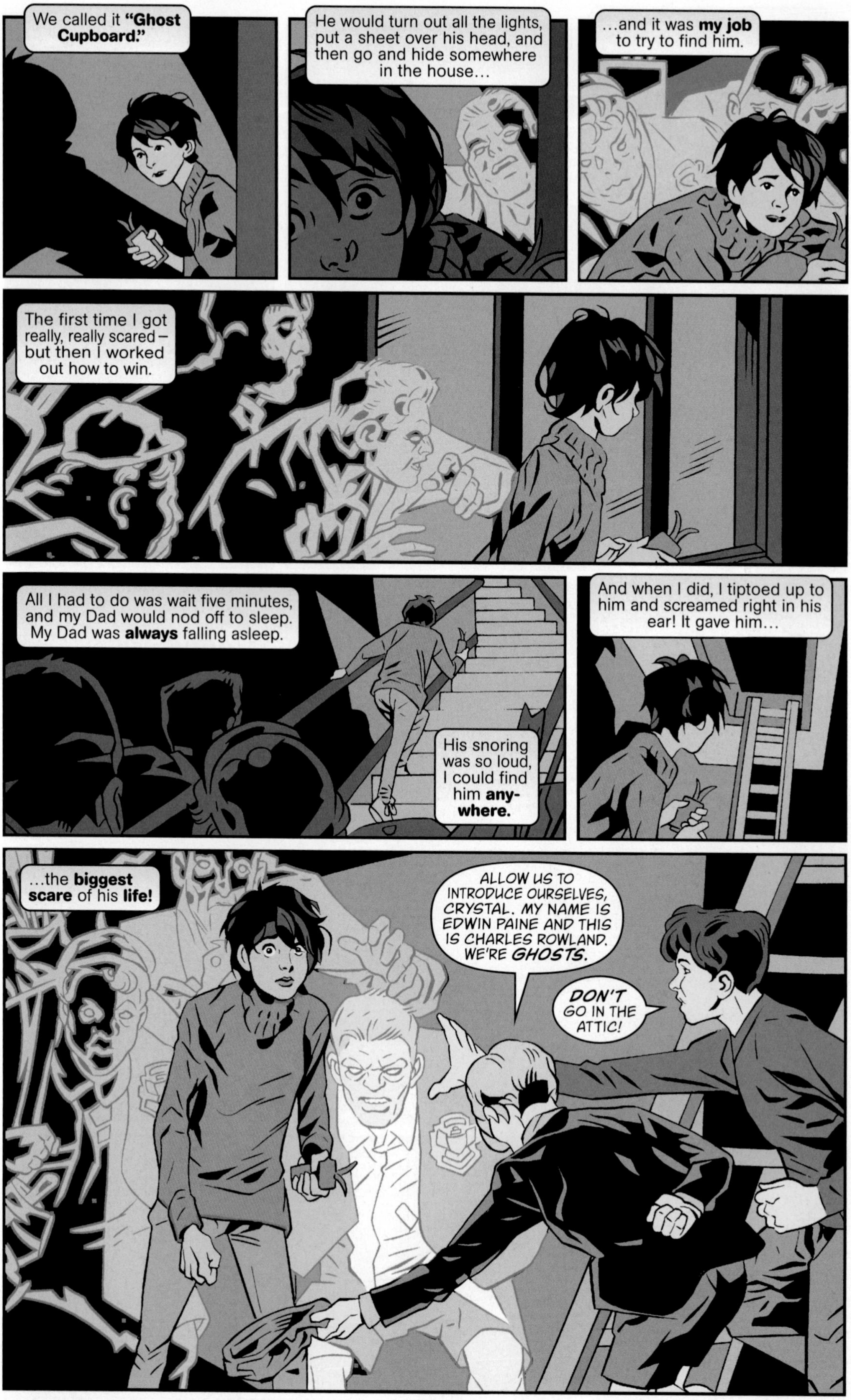

We called it **"Ghost Cupboard."**
He would turn out all the lights, put a sheet over his head, and then go and hide somewhere in the house...
...and it was **my job** to try to find him.
The first time I got really, really scared – but then I worked out how to win.
All I had to do was wait five minutes, and my Dad would nod off to sleep. My Dad was **always** falling asleep.
His snoring was so loud, I could find him **any-where.**
And when I did, I tiptoed up to him and screamed right in his ear! It gave him...
...the **biggest scare** of his **life!**
ALLOW US TO INTRODUCE OURSELVES, CRYSTAL. MY NAME IS EDWIN PAINE AND THIS IS CHARLES ROWLAND. WE'RE ***GHOSTS.***
DON'T GO IN THE ATTIC!

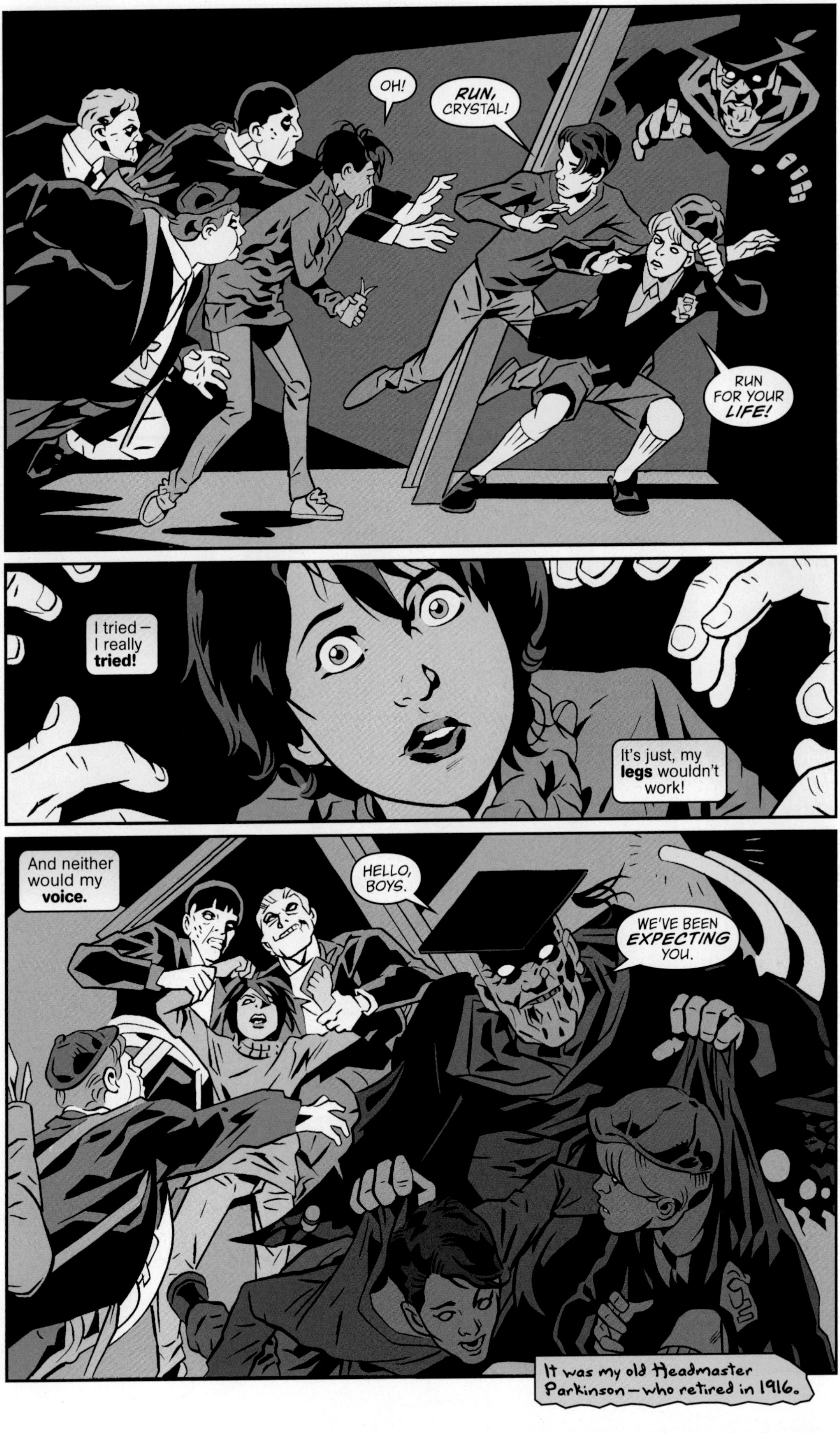
OH!
RUN, CRYSTAL!
RUN FOR YOUR LIFE!
I tried— I really tried!
It's just, my legs wouldn't work!
And neither would my voice.
HELLO, BOYS.
WE'VE BEEN EXPECTING YOU.
It was my old Headmaster Parkinson—who retired in 1916.

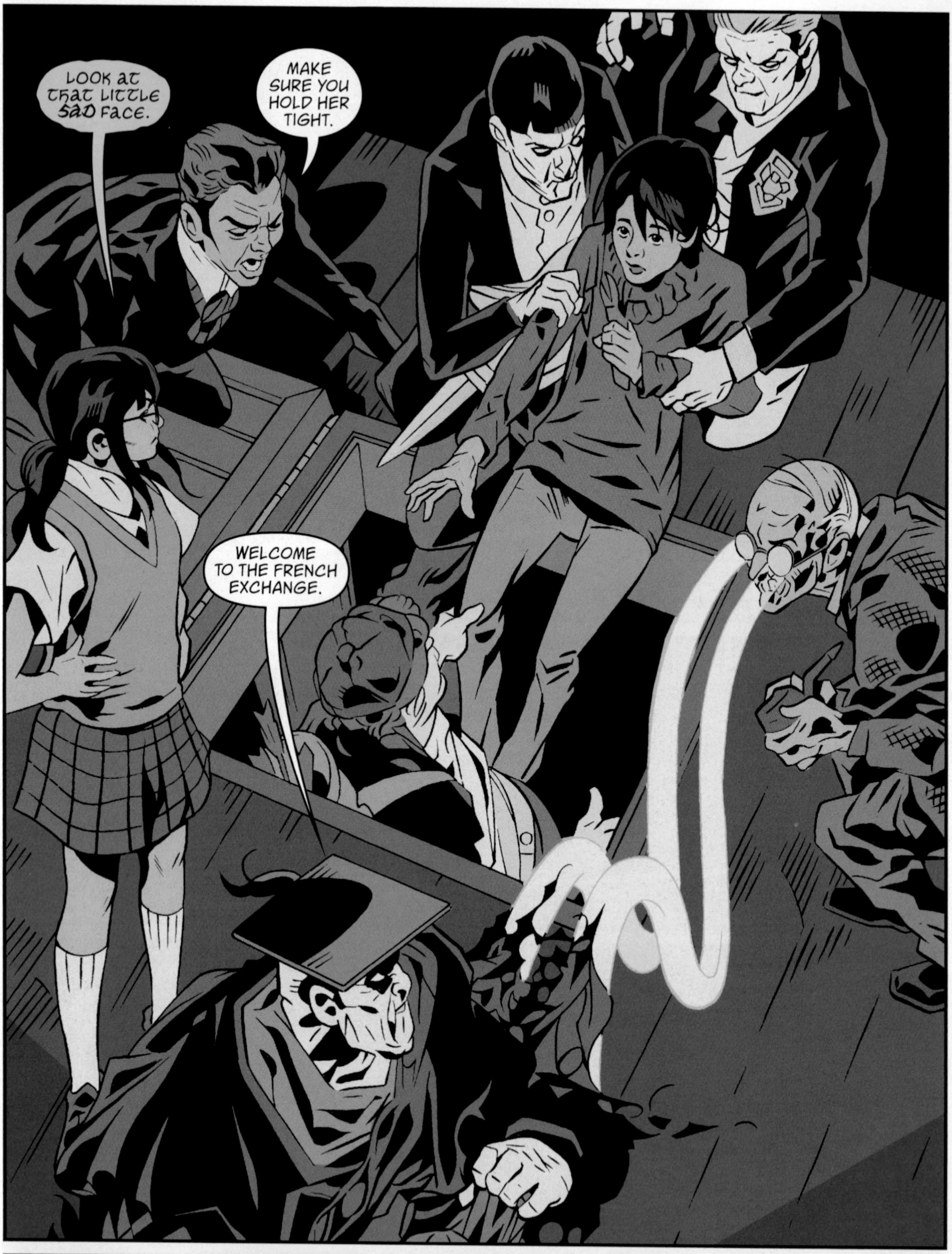
LOOK AT THAT LITTLE SAD FACE.
MAKE SURE YOU HOLD HER TIGHT.
WELCOME TO THE FRENCH EXCHANGE.

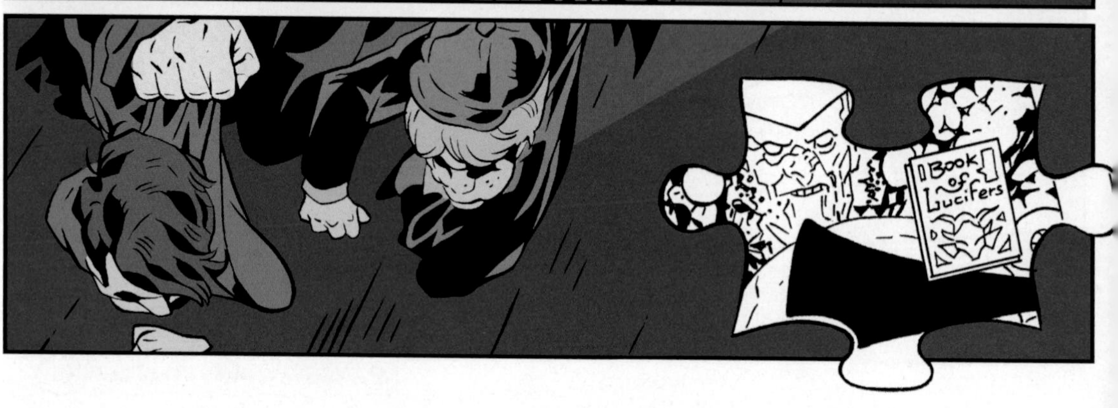
Book of Lucifers

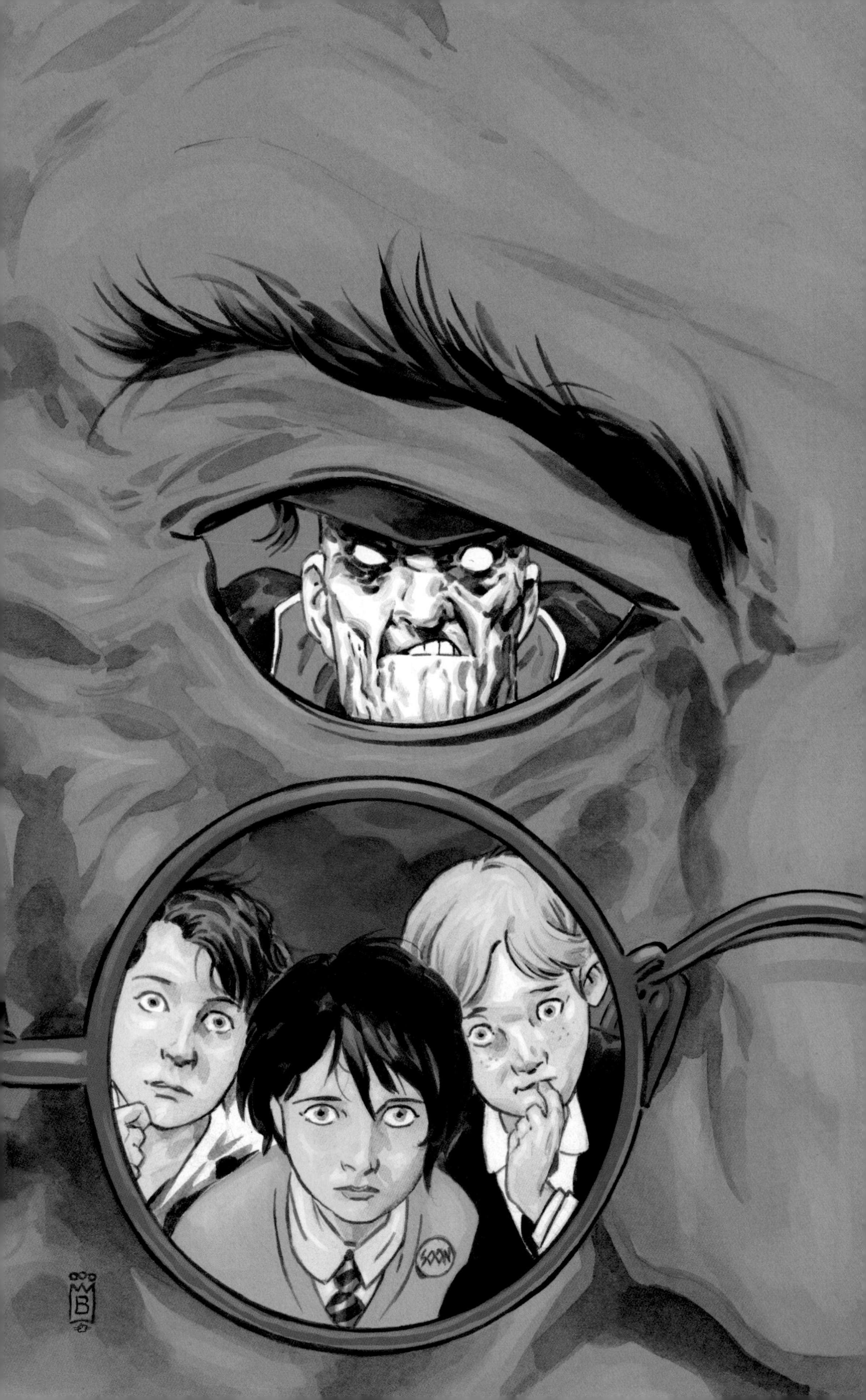
SOON

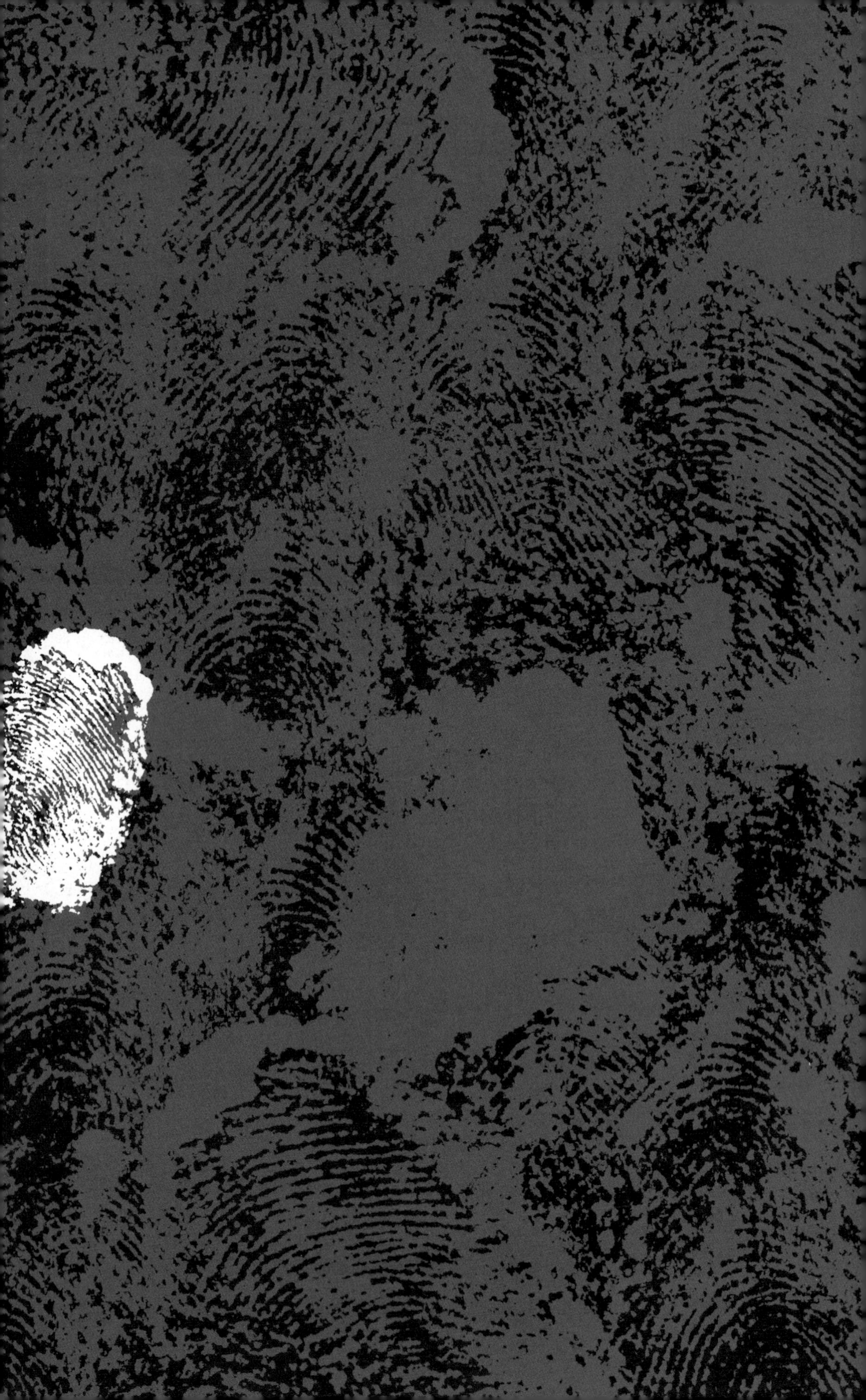

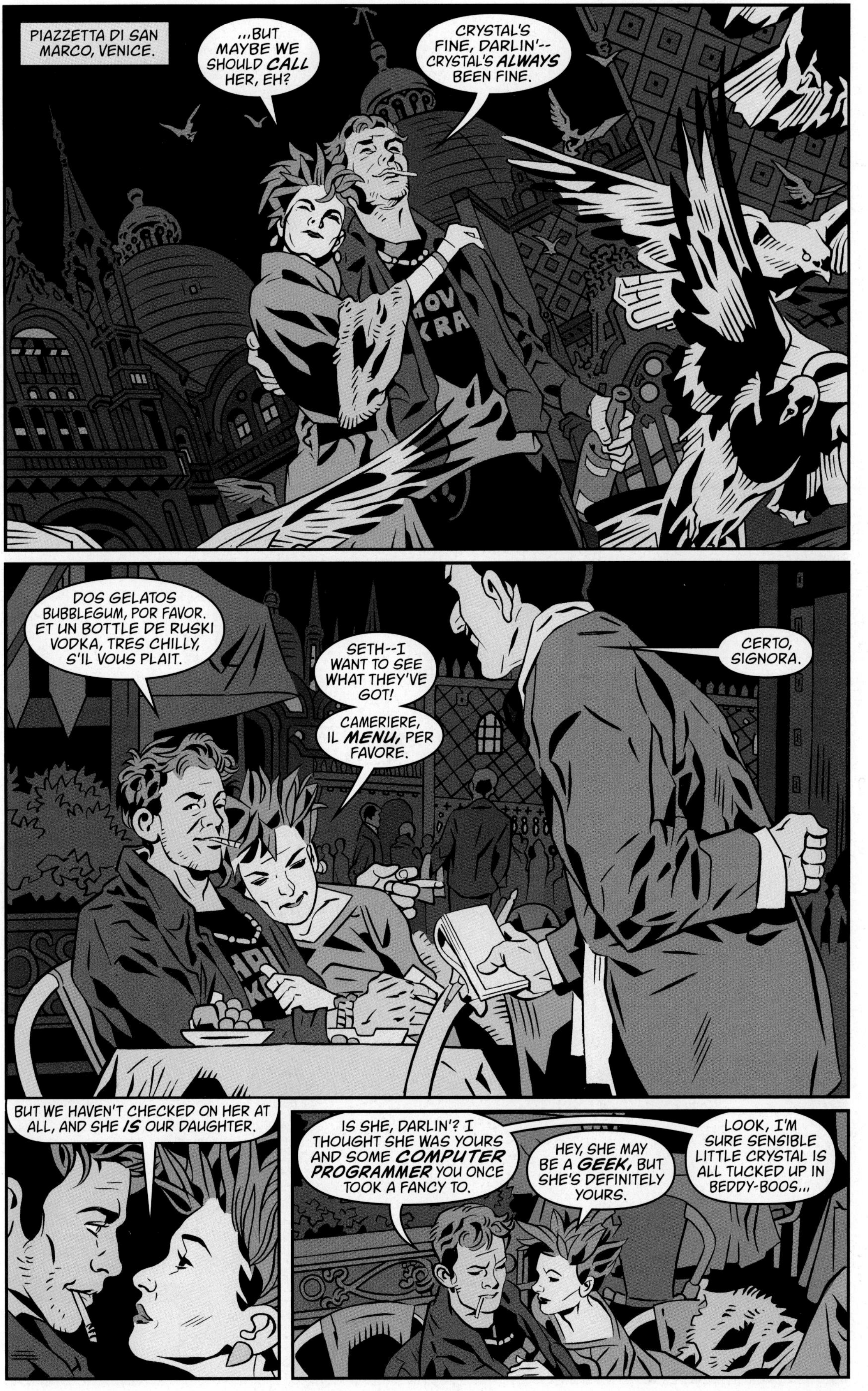

PIAZZETTA DI SAN MARCO, VENICE.
...BUT MAYBE WE SHOULD CALL HER, EH?
CRYSTAL'S FINE, DARLIN'-- CRYSTAL'S ALWAYS BEEN FINE.
DOS GELATOS BUBBLEGUM, POR FAVOR. ET UN BOTTLE DE RUSKI VODKA, TRES CHILLY, S'IL VOUS PLAIT.
SETH--I WANT TO SEE WHAT THEY'VE GOT!
CAMERIERE, IL MENU, PER FAVORE.
CERTO, SIGNORA.
BUT WE HAVEN'T CHECKED ON HER AT ALL, AND SHE IS OUR DAUGHTER.
IS SHE, DARLIN'? I THOUGHT SHE WAS YOURS AND SOME COMPUTER PROGRAMMER YOU ONCE TOOK A FANCY TO.
HEY, SHE MAY BE A GEEK, BUT SHE'S DEFINITELY YOURS.
LOOK, I'M SURE SENSIBLE LITTLE CRYSTAL IS ALL TUCKED UP IN BEDDY-BOOS...

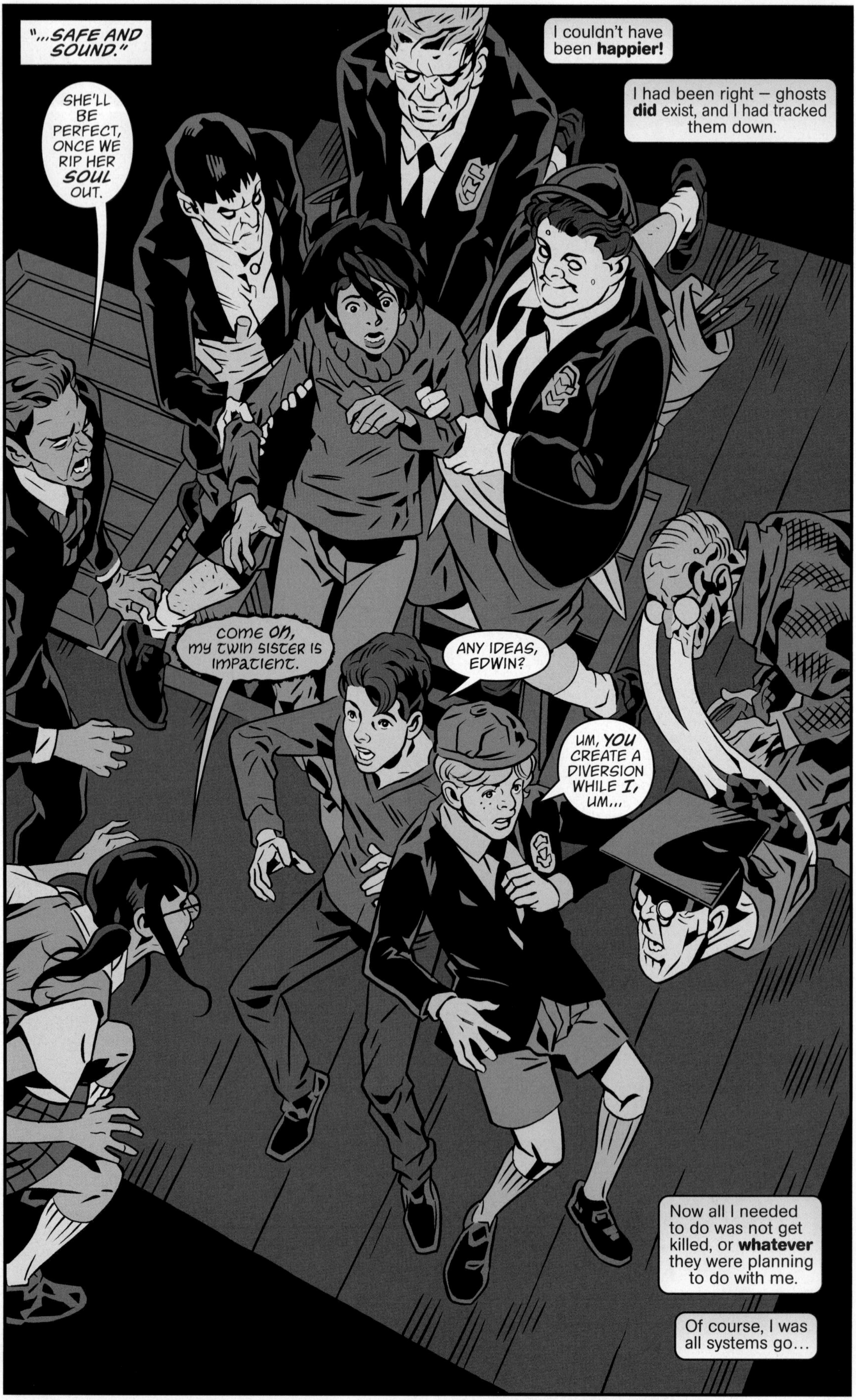
"...SAFE AND SOUND."
I couldn't have been **happier!**
I had been right — ghosts **did** exist, and I had tracked them down.
SHE'LL BE PERFECT, ONCE WE RIP HER SOUL OUT.
COME ON, MY TWIN SISTER IS IMPATIENT.
ANY IDEAS, EDWIN?
UM, YOU CREATE A DIVERSION WHILE I, UM...
Now all I needed to do was not get killed, or **whatever** they were planning to do with me.
Of course, I was all systems go...

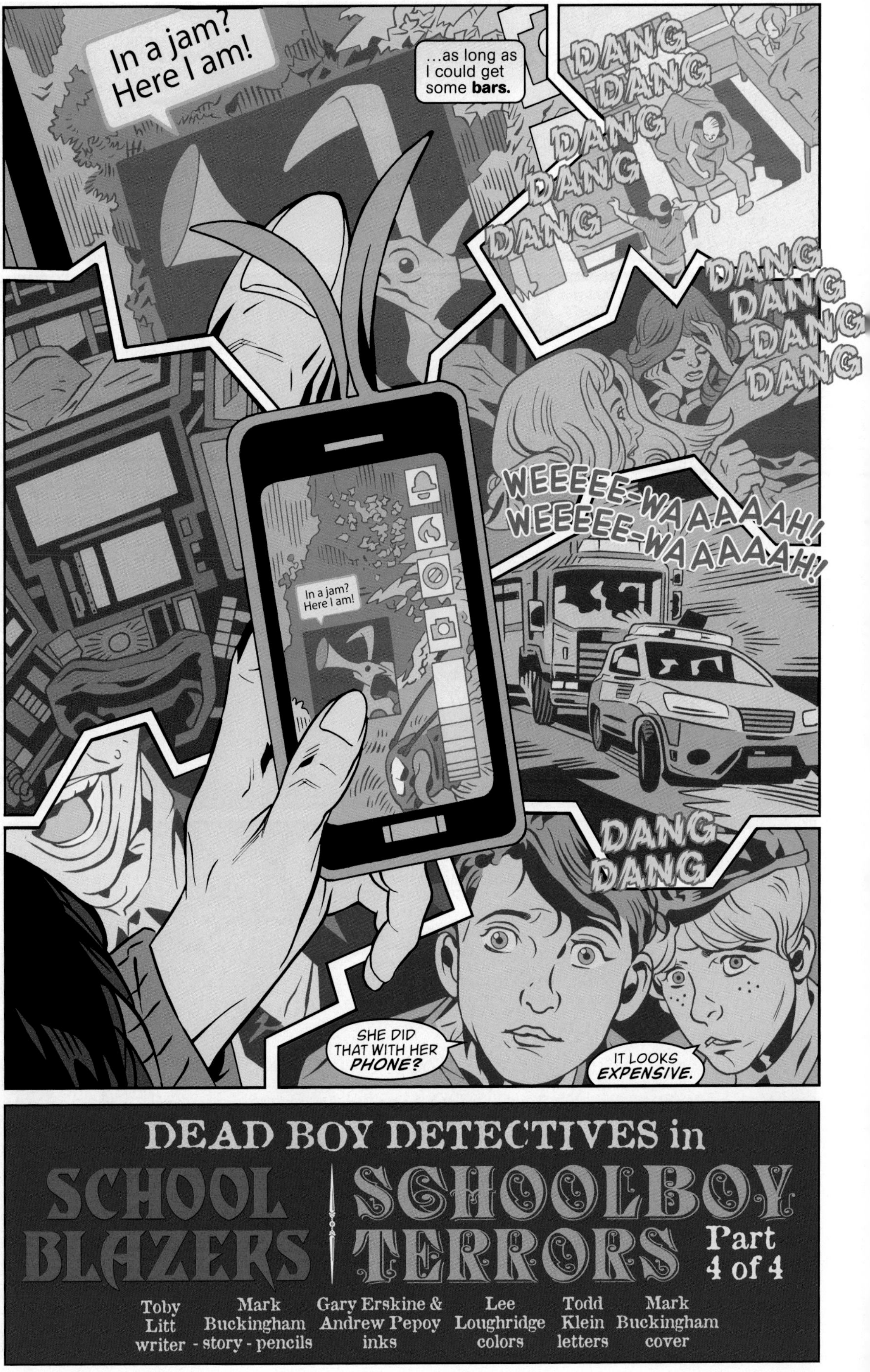

In a jam? Here I am!
...as long as I could get some **bars.**
DANG
DANG
DANG
DANG
DANG
DANG
DANG
DANG
DANG
WEEEEE-WAAAAAH!
WEEEEE-WAAAAAH!
In a jam? Here I am!
DANG
DANG
SHE DID THAT WITH HER *PHONE?*
IT LOOKS *EXPENSIVE.*

DEAD BOY DETECTIVES in

SCHOOL BLAZERS | SCHOOLBOY TERRORS

Part 4 of 4

Toby Litt writer
Mark Buckingham - story - pencils
Gary Erskine & Andrew Pepoy inks
Lee Loughridge colors
Todd Klein letters
Mark Buckingham cover

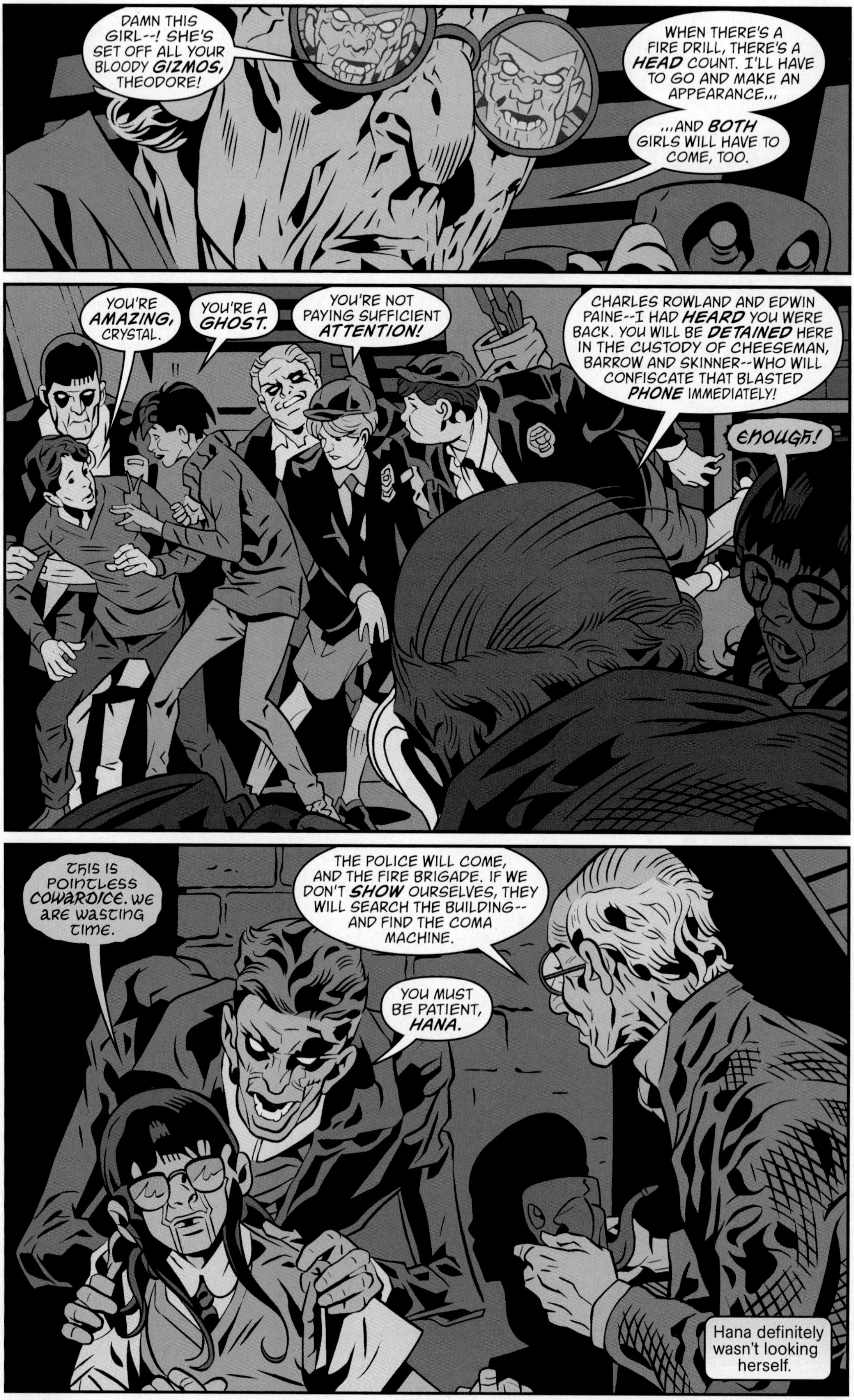
DAMN THIS GIRL--! SHE'S SET OFF ALL YOUR BLOODY GIZMOS, THEODORE!
WHEN THERE'S A FIRE DRILL, THERE'S A HEAD COUNT. I'LL HAVE TO GO AND MAKE AN APPEARANCE...
...AND BOTH GIRLS WILL HAVE TO COME, TOO.
YOU'RE AMAZING, CRYSTAL.
YOU'RE A GHOST.
YOU'RE NOT PAYING SUFFICIENT ATTENTION!
CHARLES ROWLAND AND EDWIN PAINE--I HAD HEARD YOU WERE BACK. YOU WILL BE DETAINED HERE IN THE CUSTODY OF CHEESEMAN, BARROW AND SKINNER--WHO WILL CONFISCATE THAT BLASTED PHONE IMMEDIATELY!
ENOUGH!
THIS IS POINTLESS COWARDICE. WE ARE WASTING TIME.
THE POLICE WILL COME, AND THE FIRE BRIGADE. IF WE DON'T SHOW OURSELVES, THEY WILL SEARCH THE BUILDING--AND FIND THE COMA MACHINE.
YOU MUST BE PATIENT, HANA.
Hana definitely wasn't looking herself.

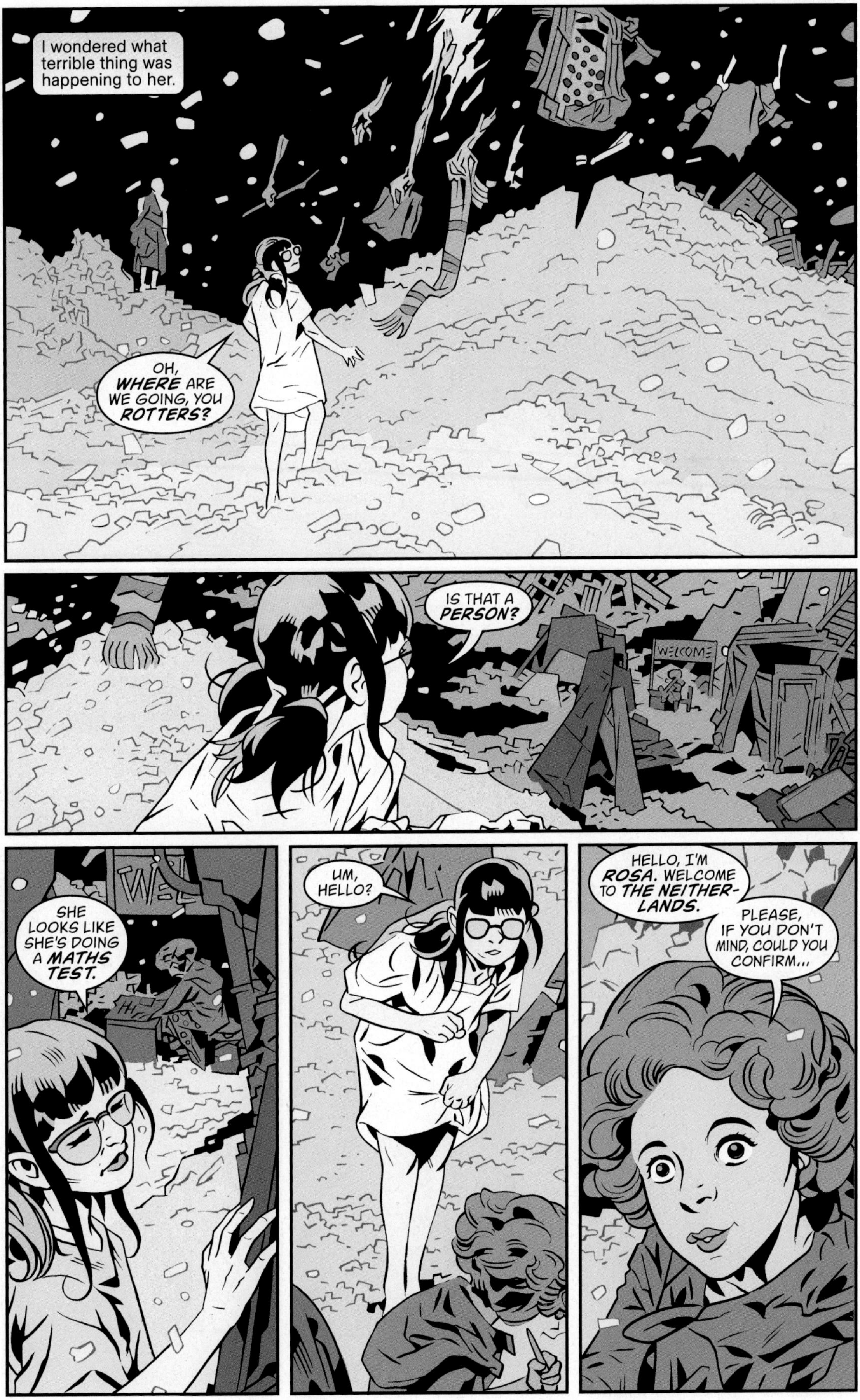
I wondered what terrible thing was happening to her.
OH, WHERE ARE WE GOING, YOU ROTTERS?
IS THAT A PERSON?
WELCOME
SHE LOOKS LIKE SHE'S DOING A MATHS TEST.
UM, HELLO?
HELLO, I'M ROSA. WELCOME TO THE NEITHER-LANDS.
PLEASE, IF YOU DON'T MIND, COULD YOU CONFIRM...

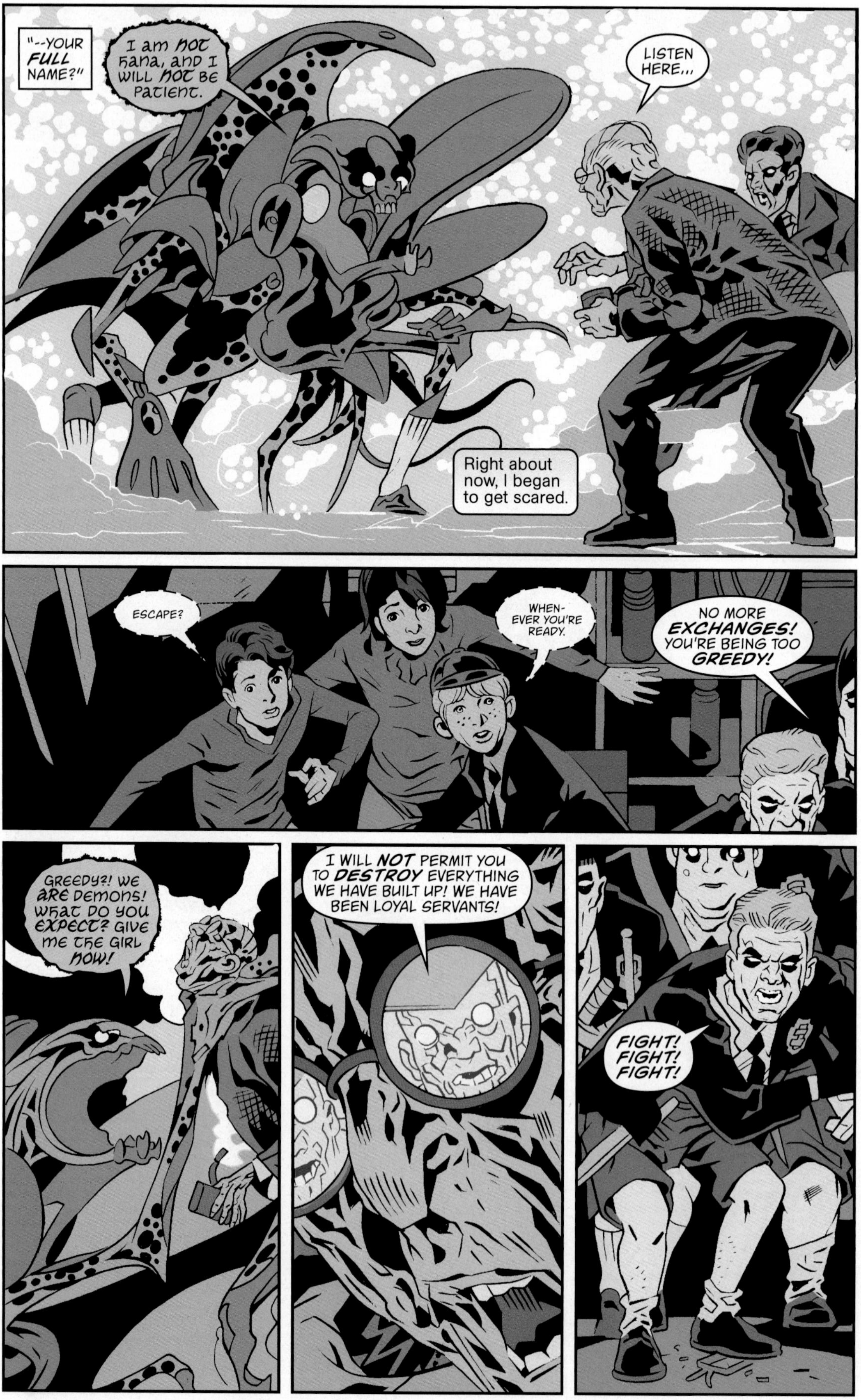
"--YOUR FULL NAME?"
I am NOT Hana, and I will NOT be patient.
LISTEN HERE...
Right about now, I began to get scared.
ESCAPE?
WHEN-EVER YOU'RE READY.
NO MORE EXCHANGES! YOU'RE BEING TOO GREEDY!
GREEDY?! WE ARE DEMONS! WHAT DO YOU EXPECT? GIVE ME THE GIRL NOW!
I WILL NOT PERMIT YOU TO DESTROY EVERYTHING WE HAVE BUILT UP! WE HAVE BEEN LOYAL SERVANTS!
FIGHT! FIGHT! FIGHT!

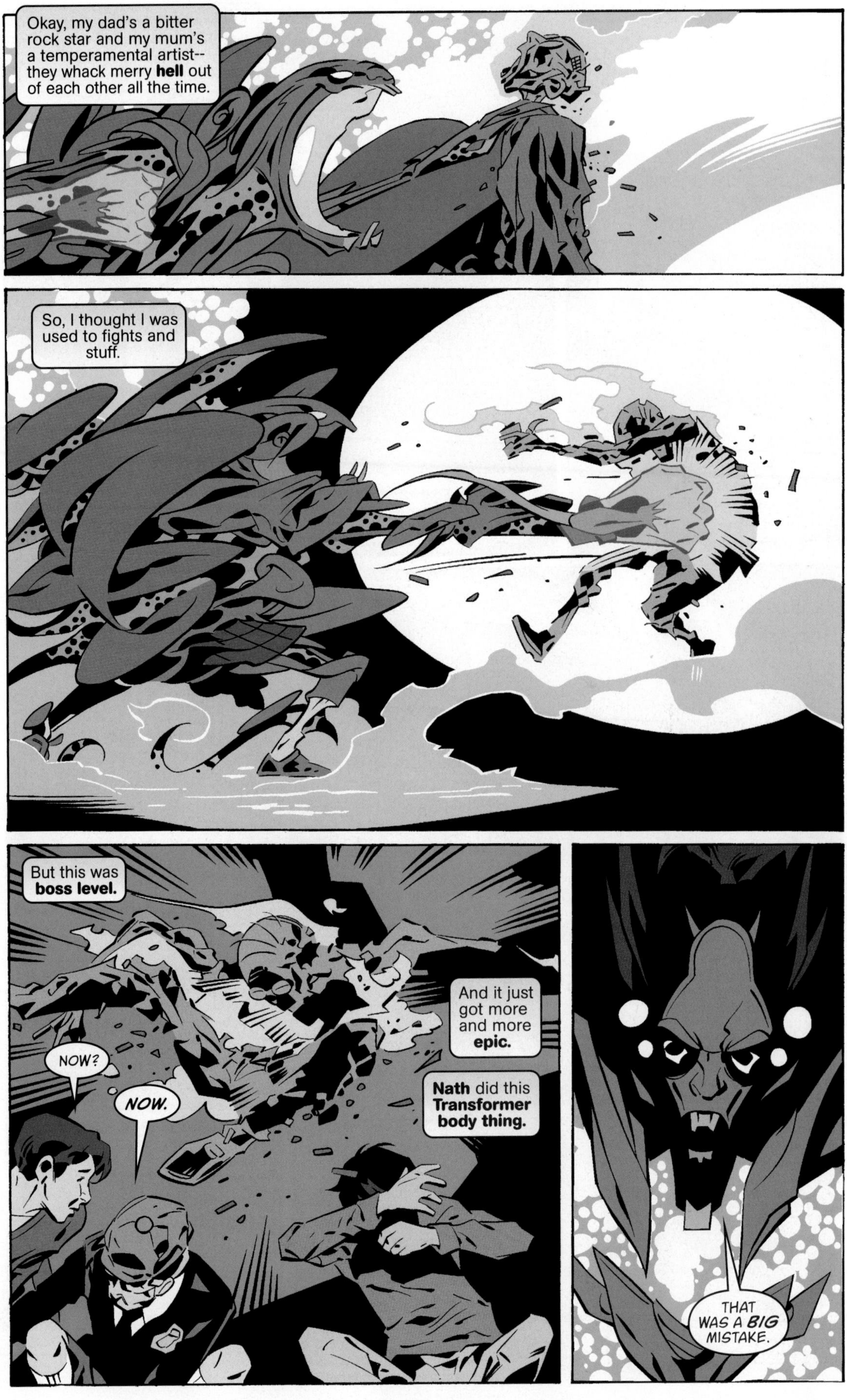
Okay, my dad's a bitter rock star and my mum's a temperamental artist-- they whack merry **hell** out of each other all the time.
So, I thought I was used to fights and stuff.
But this was **boss level.**
And it just got more and more **epic.**
NOW?
NOW.
Nath did this **Transformer body thing.**
THAT WAS A ***BIG*** MISTAKE.

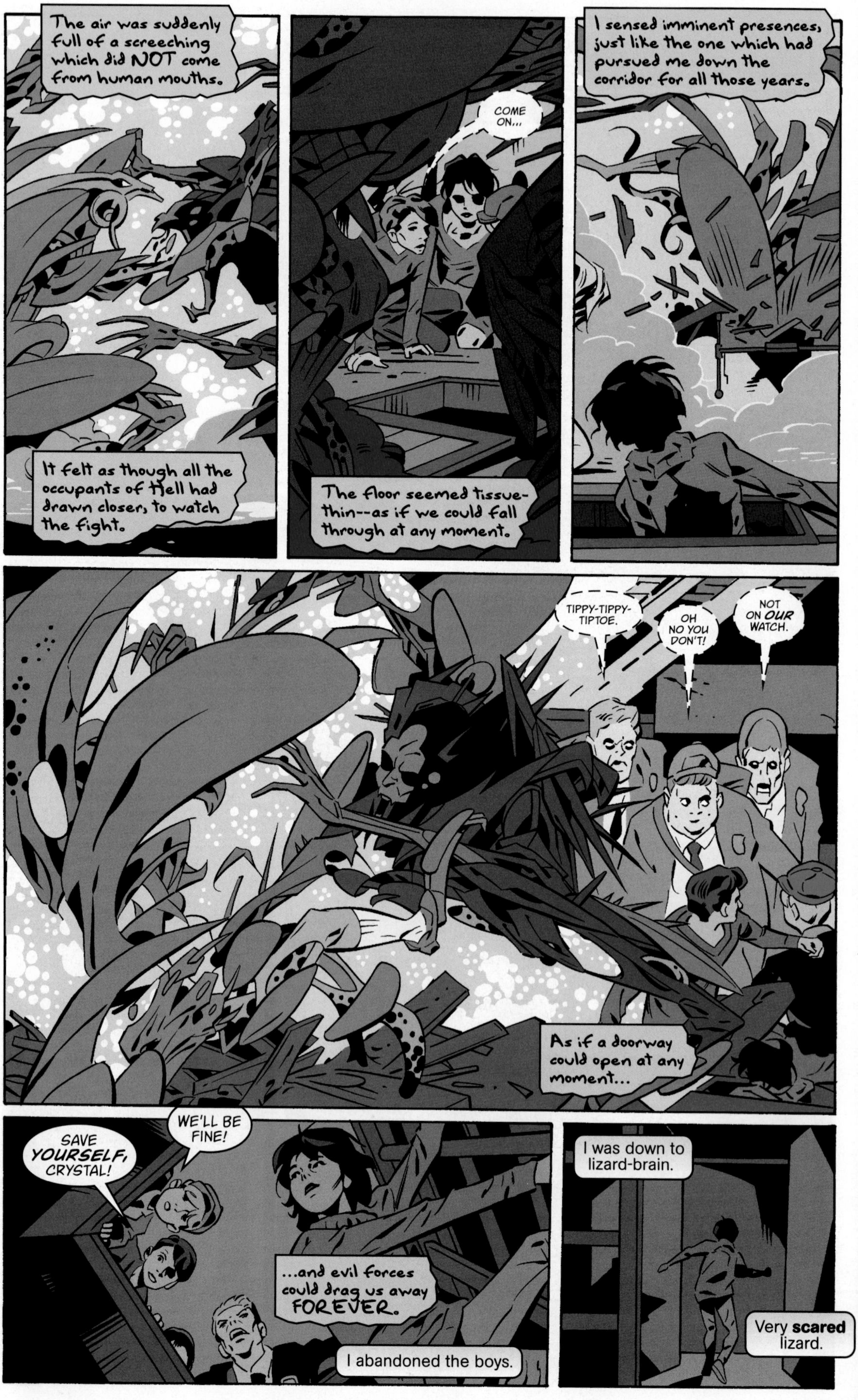

The air was suddenly full of a screeching which did NOT come from human mouths.
It felt as though all the occupants of Hell had drawn closer, to watch the fight.
COME ON...
The floor seemed tissue-thin--as if we could fall through at any moment.
I sensed imminent presences, just like the one which had pursued me down the corridor for all those years.
TIPPY-TIPPY-TIPTOE.
OH NO YOU DON'T!
NOT ON OUR WATCH.
As if a doorway could open at any moment...
SAVE YOURSELF, CRYSTAL!
WE'LL BE FINE!
...and evil forces could drag us away FOREVER.
I abandoned the boys.
I was down to lizard-brain.
Very scared lizard.

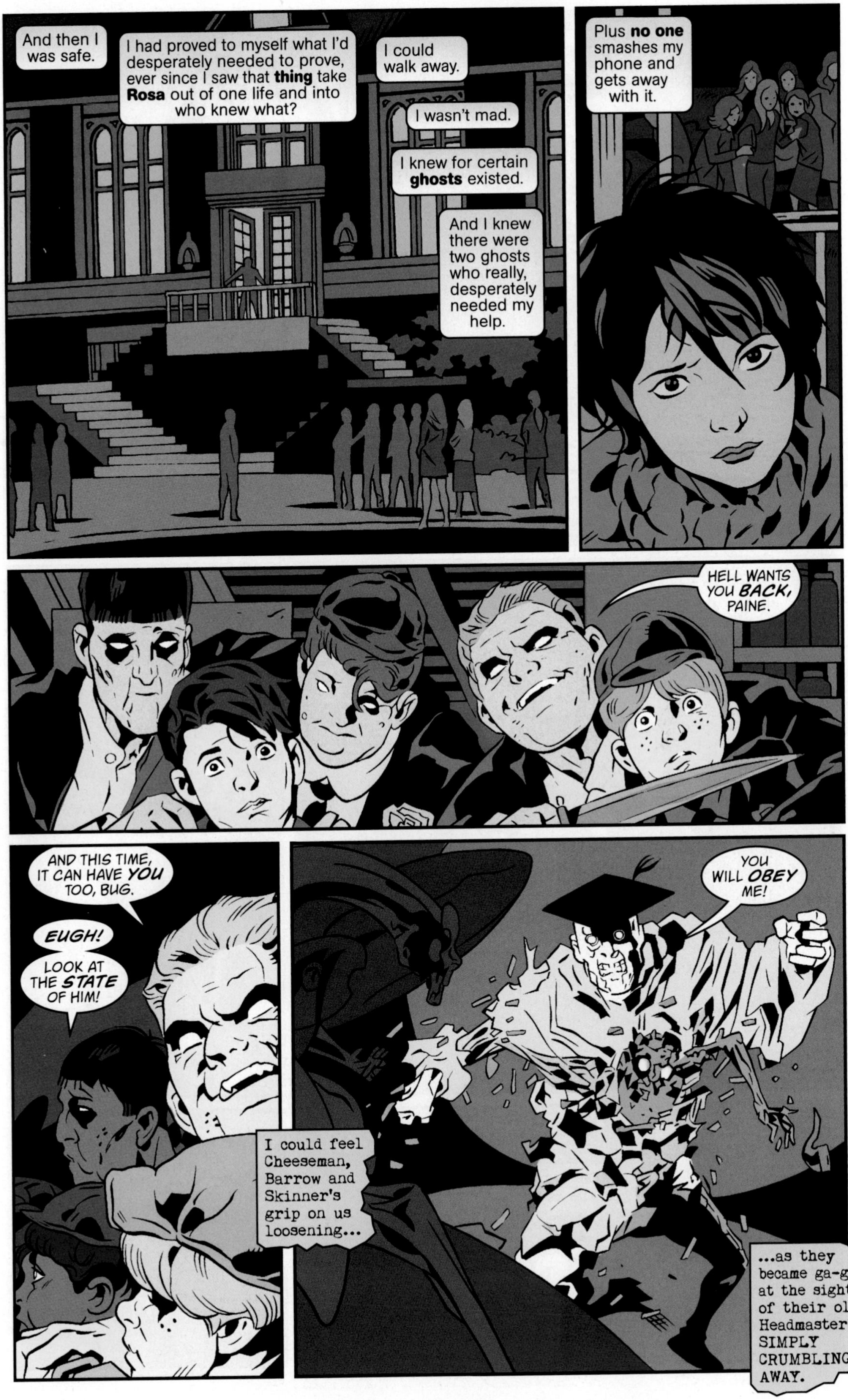
And then I was safe.
I had proved to myself what I'd desperately needed to prove, ever since I saw that **thing** take **Rosa** out of one life and into who knew what?
I could walk away.
I wasn't mad.
I knew for certain **ghosts** existed.
And I knew there were two ghosts who really, desperately needed my help.
Plus **no one** smashes my phone and gets away with it.
HELL WANTS YOU *BACK*, PAINE.
AND THIS TIME, IT CAN HAVE *YOU* TOO, BUG.
EUGH!
LOOK AT THE *STATE* OF HIM!
YOU WILL *OBEY* ME!
I could feel Cheeseman, Barrow and Skinner's grip on us loosening...
...as they became ga-ga at the sight of their old Headmaster SIMPLY CRUMBLING AWAY.

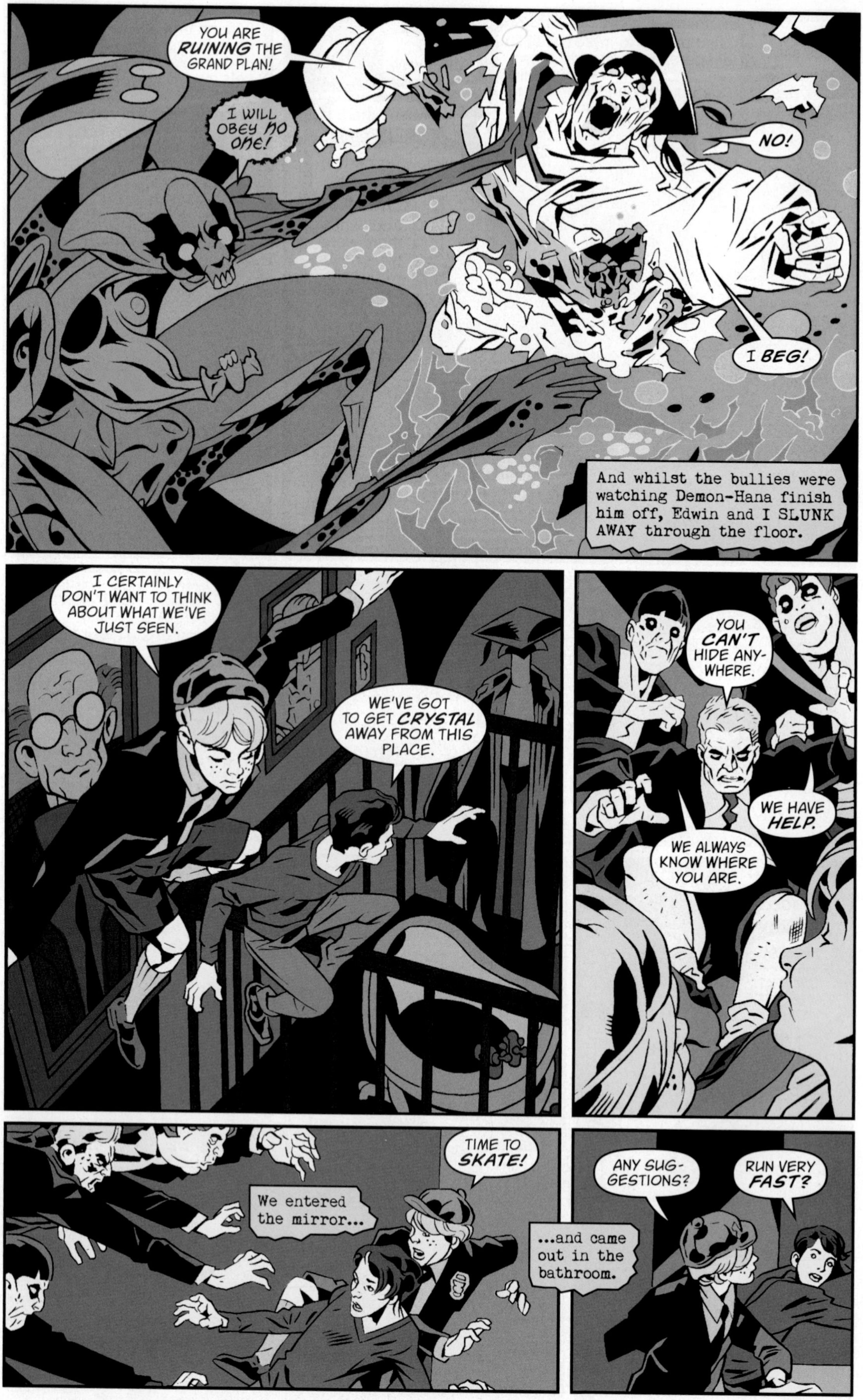

YOU ARE RUINING THE GRAND PLAN!
I WILL OBEY NO ONE!
NO!
I BEG!
And whilst the bullies were watching Demon-Hana finish him off, Edwin and I SLUNK AWAY through the floor.
I CERTAINLY DON'T WANT TO THINK ABOUT WHAT WE'VE JUST SEEN.
WE'VE GOT TO GET CRYSTAL AWAY FROM THIS PLACE.
YOU CAN'T HIDE ANY-WHERE.
WE HAVE HELP.
WE ALWAYS KNOW WHERE YOU ARE.
TIME TO SKATE!
We entered the mirror...
...and came out in the bathroom.
ANY SUG-GESTIONS?
RUN VERY FAST?

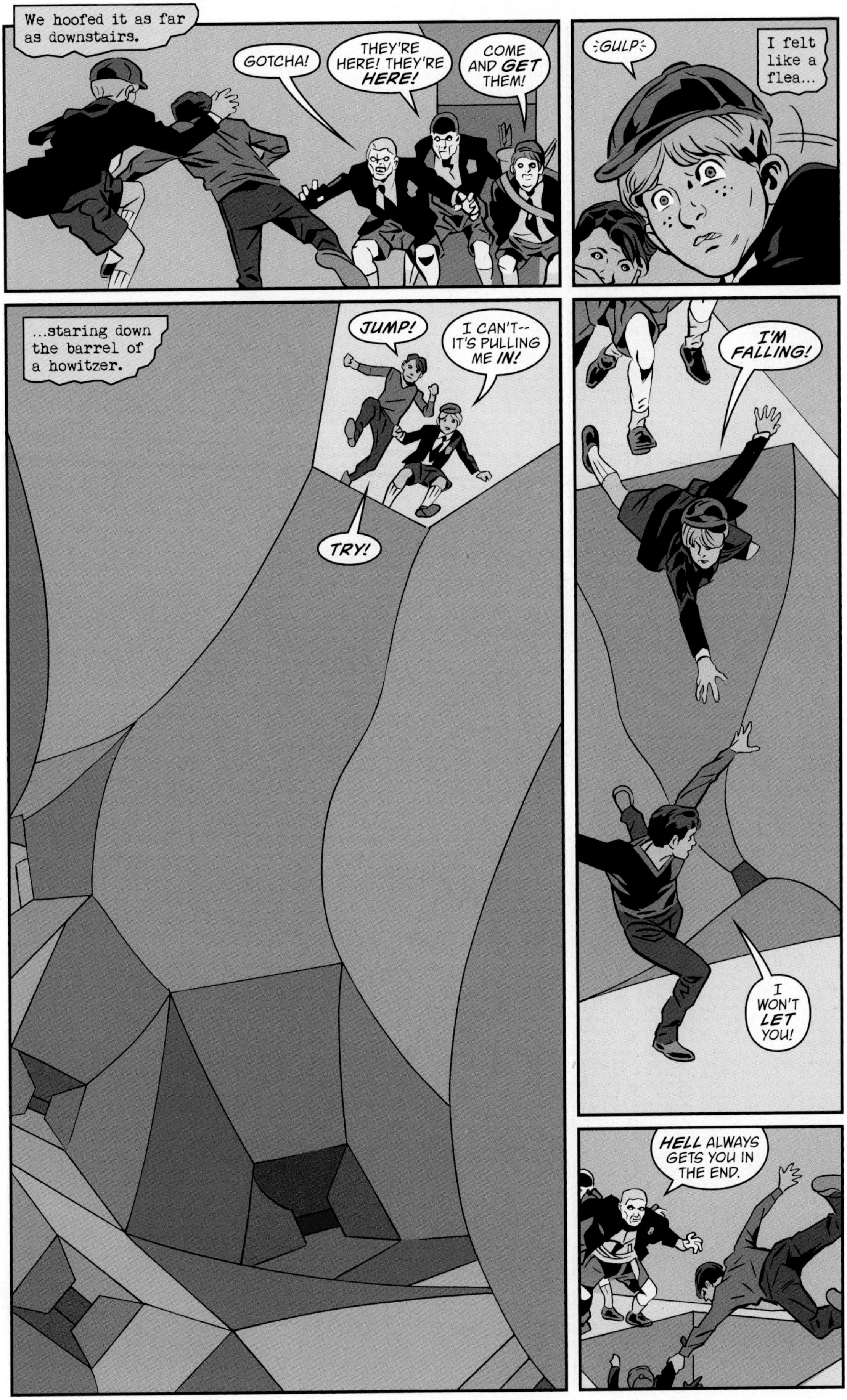
We hoofed it as far as downstairs.
GOTCHA!
THEY'RE HERE! THEY'RE HERE!
COME AND GET THEM!
GULP
I felt like a flea...
...staring down the barrel of a howitzer.
JUMP!
I CAN'T-- IT'S PULLING ME IN!
TRY!
I'M FALLING!
I WON'T LET YOU!
HELL ALWAYS GETS YOU IN THE END.

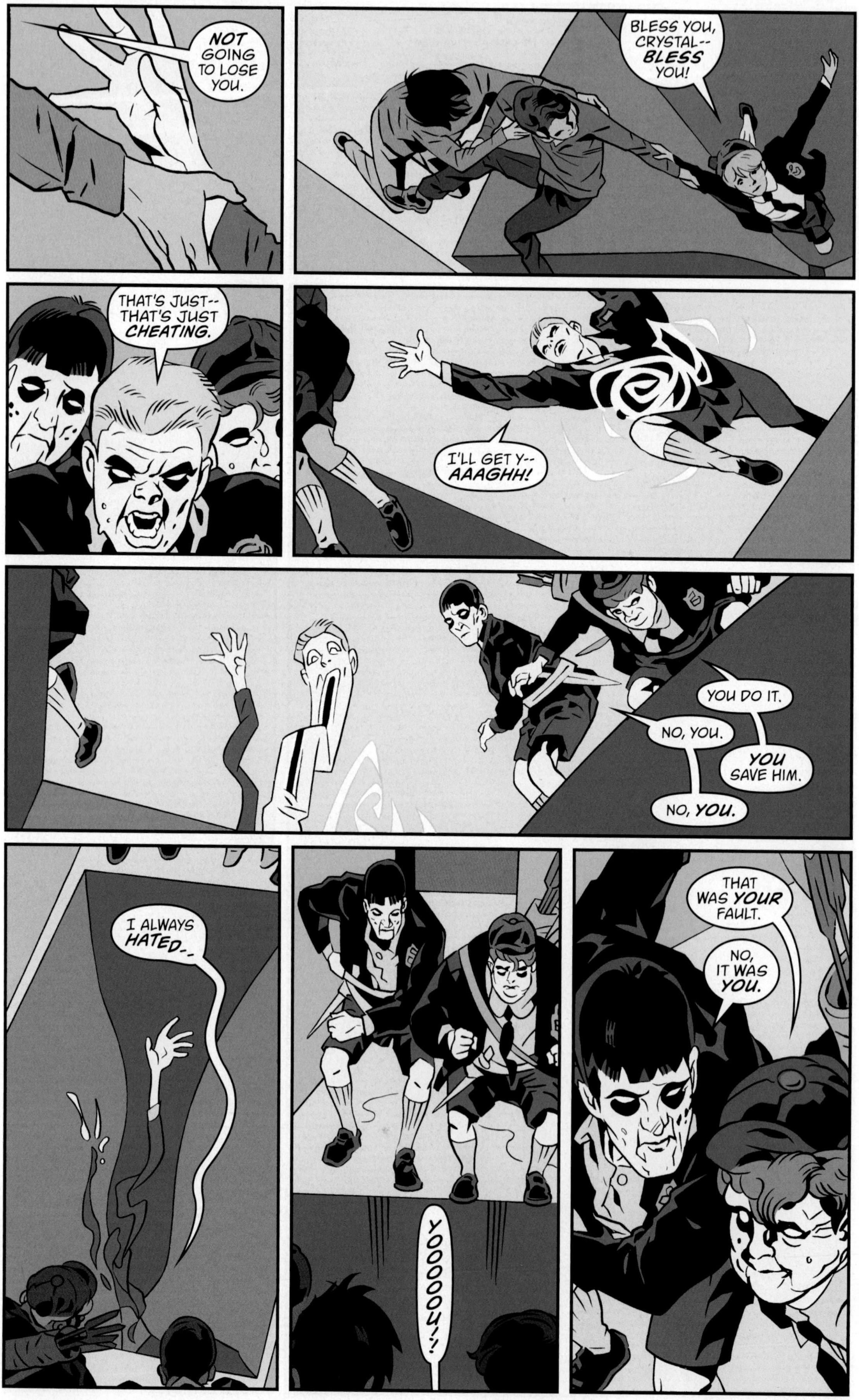

NOT GOING TO LOSE YOU.
BLESS YOU, CRYSTAL-- BLESS YOU!
THAT'S JUST-- THAT'S JUST CHEATING.
I'LL GET Y-- AAAGHH!
YOU DO IT.
NO, YOU.
YOU SAVE HIM.
NO, YOU.
I ALWAYS HATED--
YOOOOOU?!
THAT WAS YOUR FAULT.
NO, IT WAS YOU.

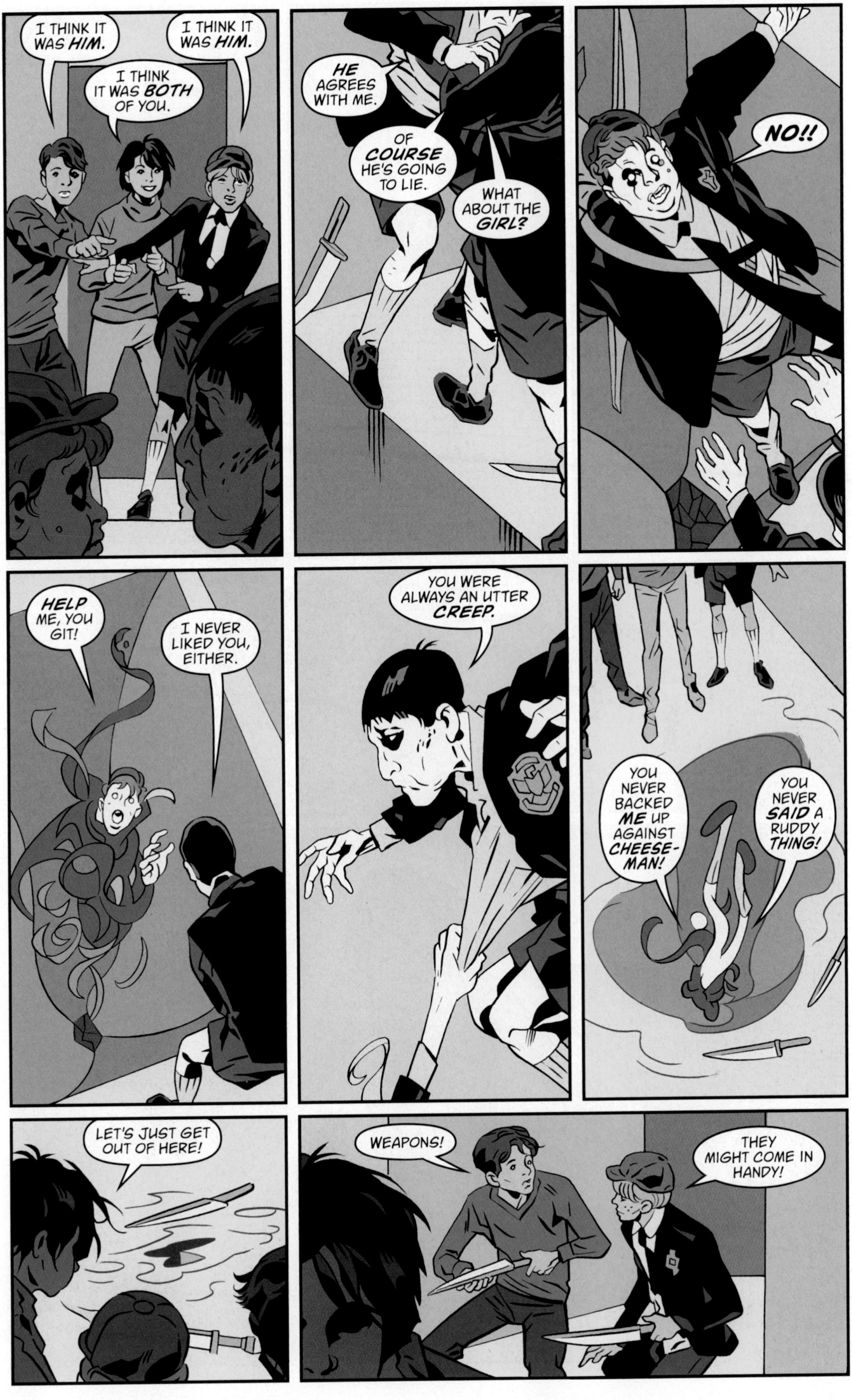

I THINK IT WAS HIM.
I THINK IT WAS BOTH OF YOU.
I THINK IT WAS HIM.
HE AGREES WITH ME.
OF COURSE HE'S GOING TO LIE.
WHAT ABOUT THE GIRL?
NO!!
HELP ME, YOU GIT!
I NEVER LIKED YOU, EITHER.
YOU WERE ALWAYS AN UTTER CREEP.
YOU NEVER BACKED ME UP AGAINST CHEESE-MAN!
YOU NEVER SAID A RUDDY THING!
LET'S JUST GET OUT OF HERE!
WEAPONS!
THEY MIGHT COME IN HANDY!

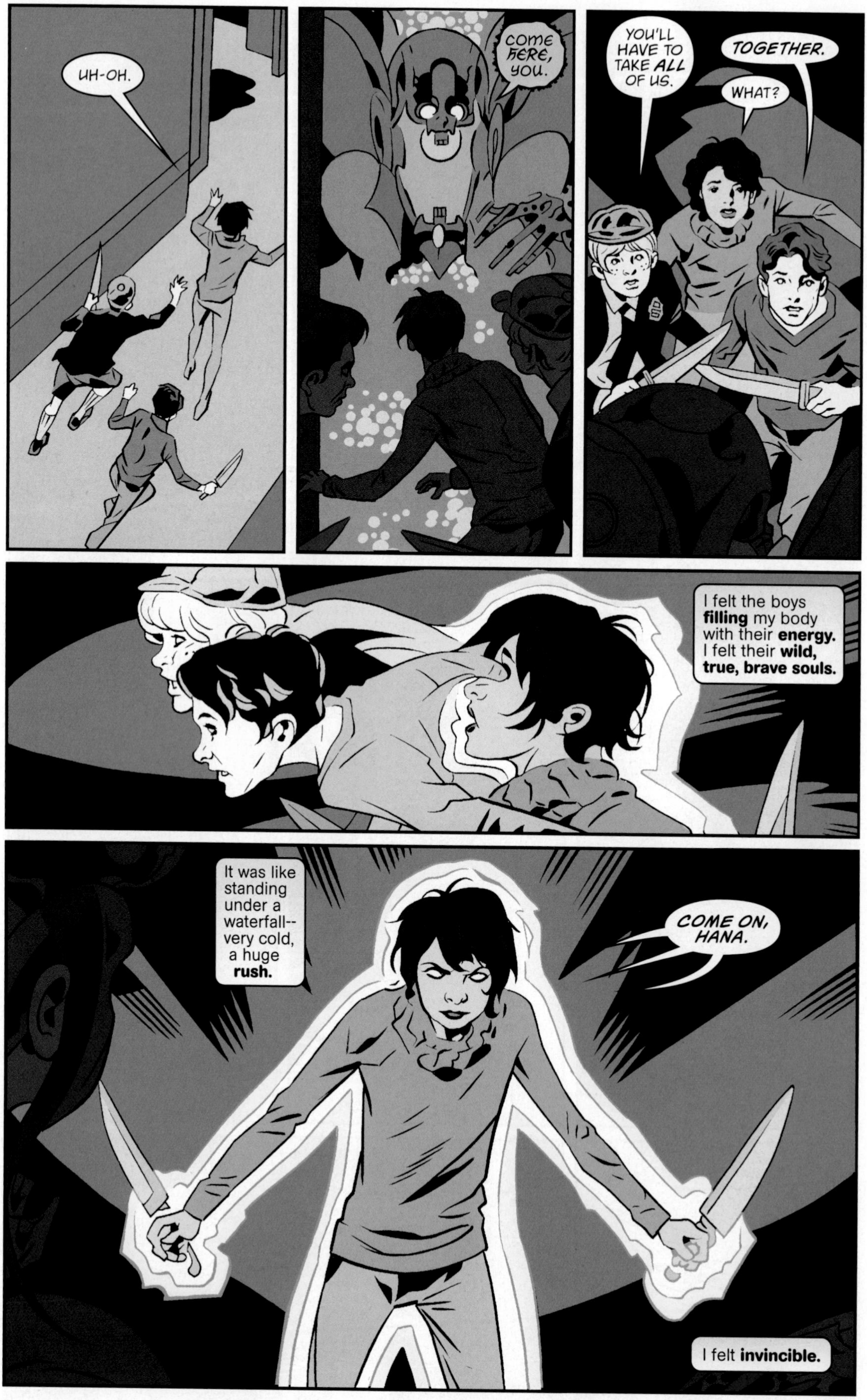
UH-OH.
COME HERE, YOU.
YOU'LL HAVE TO TAKE ALL OF US.
TOGETHER.
WHAT?
I felt the boys filling my body with their energy. I felt their wild, true, brave souls.
It was like standing under a waterfall-- very cold, a huge rush.
COME ON, HANA.
I felt invincible.

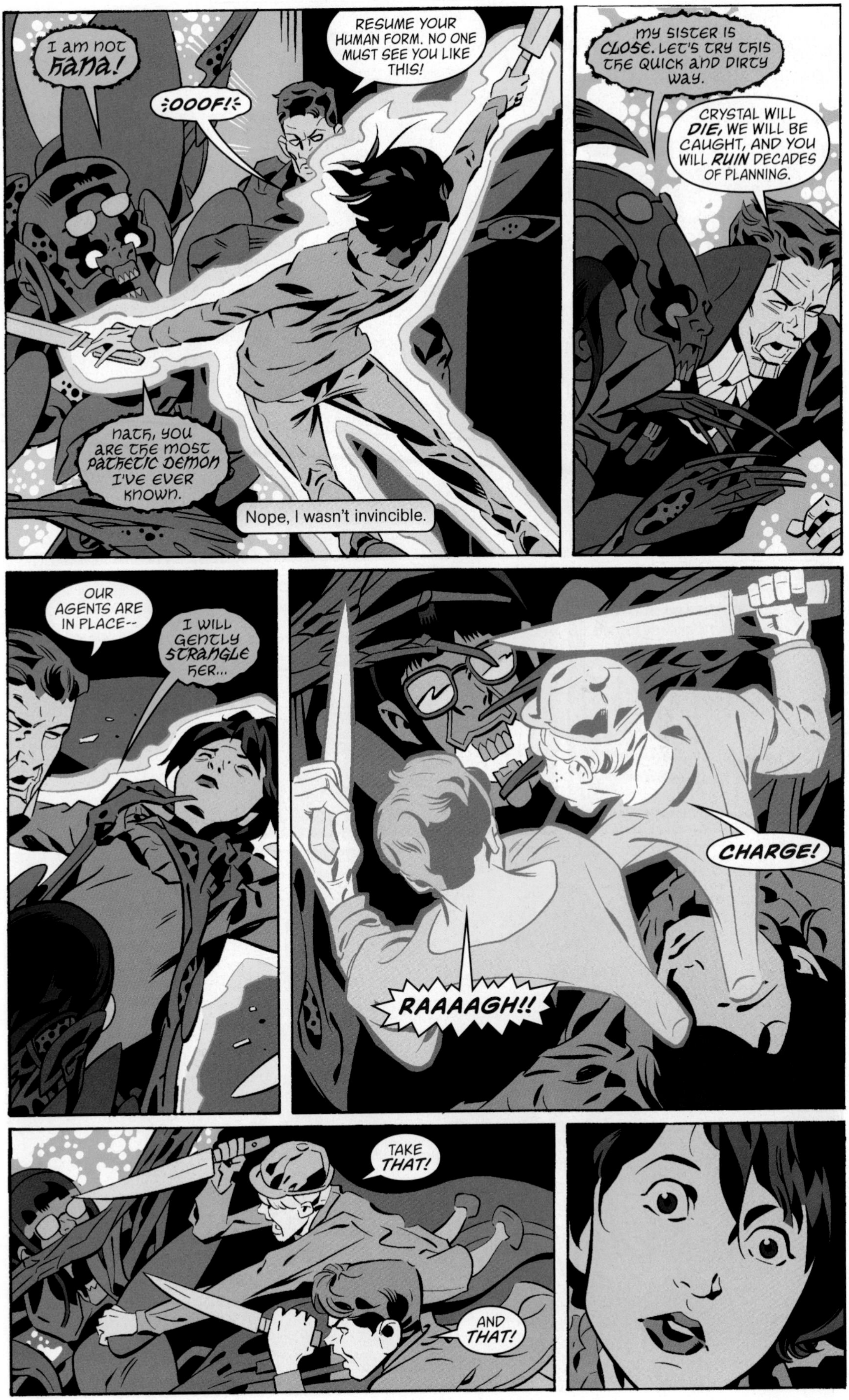

I am not Hana!
RESUME YOUR HUMAN FORM. NO ONE MUST SEE YOU LIKE THIS!
OOOF!
Nath, you are the most PATHETIC DEMON I'VE EVER known.
Nope, I wasn't invincible.
my sister is CLOSE. Let's try this the quick and dirty way.
CRYSTAL WILL DIE, WE WILL BE CAUGHT, AND YOU WILL RUIN DECADES OF PLANNING.
OUR AGENTS ARE IN PLACE--
I will gently strangle her...
CHARGE!
RAAAAGH!!
TAKE THAT!
AND THAT!

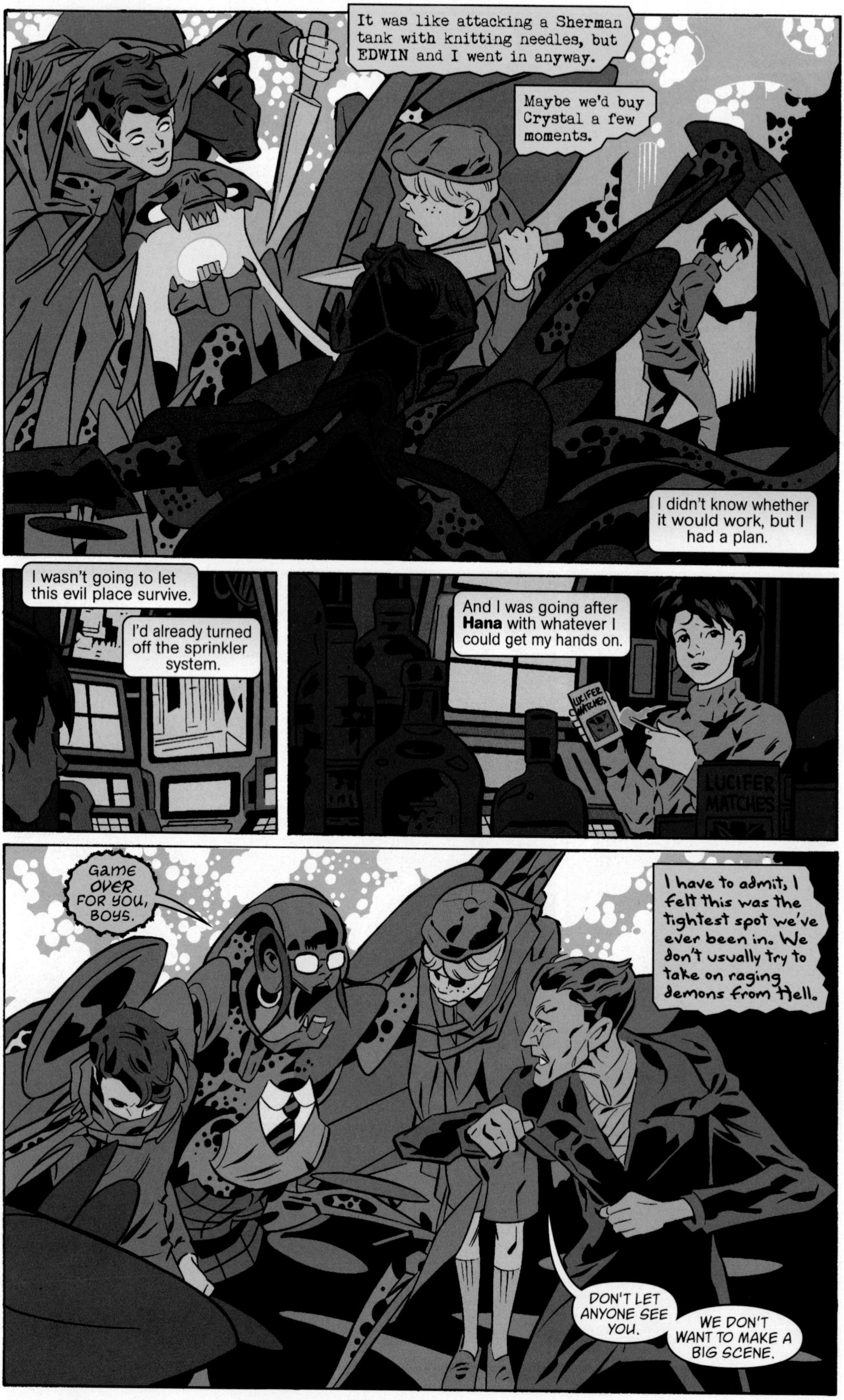
It was like attacking a Sherman tank with knitting needles, but EDWIN and I went in anyway.
Maybe we'd buy Crystal a few moments.
I didn't know whether it would work, but I had a plan.
I wasn't going to let this evil place survive.
I'd already turned off the sprinkler system.
And I was going after Hana with whatever I could get my hands on.
LUCIFER MATCHES
LUCIFER MATCHES
GAME OVER FOR YOU, BOYS.
I have to admit, I felt this was the tightest spot we've ever been in. We don't usually try to take on raging demons from Hell.
DON'T LET ANYONE SEE YOU.
WE DON'T WANT TO MAKE A BIG SCENE.

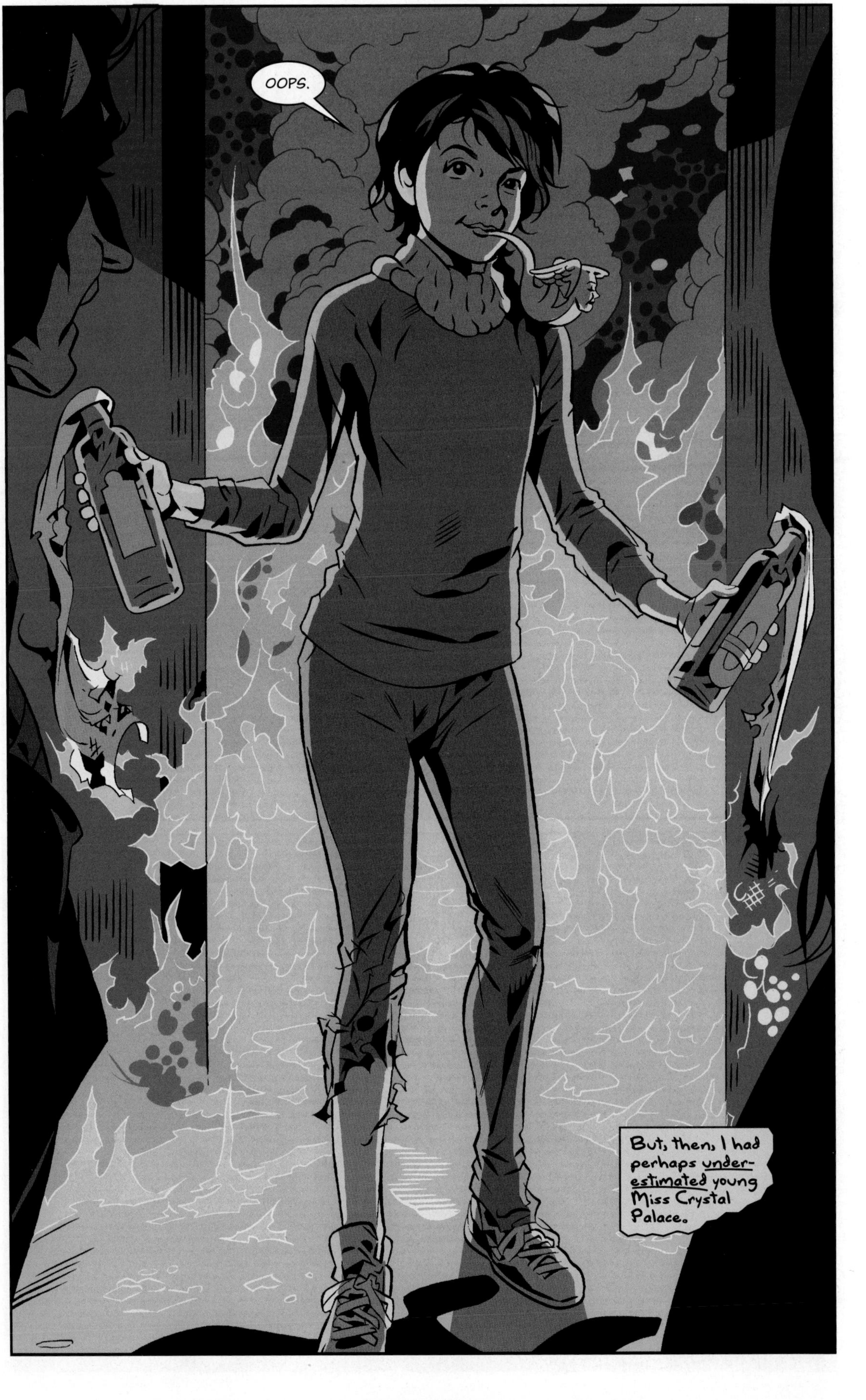
OOPS.
But, then, I had perhaps under-estimated young Miss Crystal Palace.

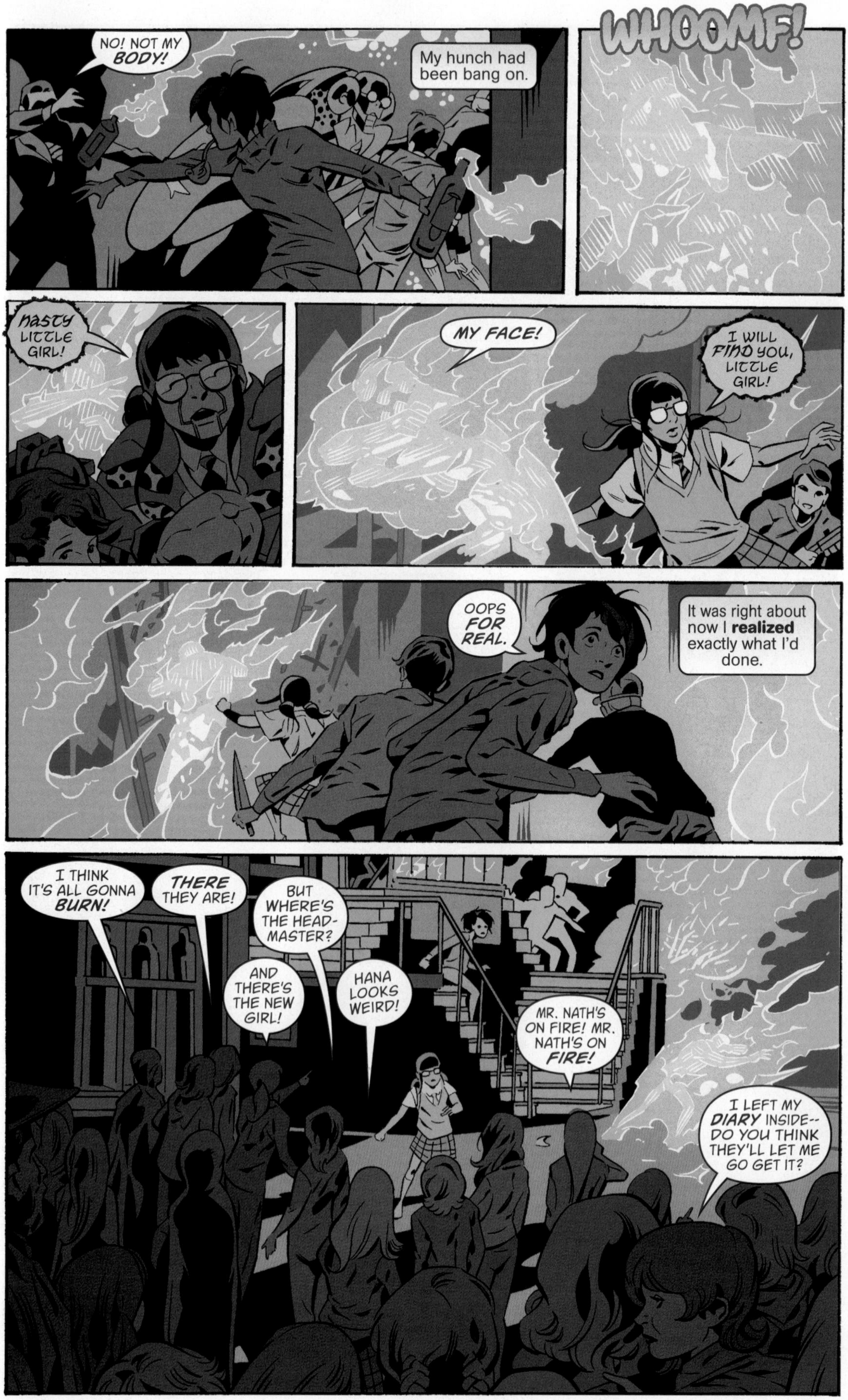
NO! NOT MY BODY!
My hunch had been bang on.
WHOOMF!
nasty little girl!
MY FACE!
I WILL FIND YOU, LITTLE GIRL!
OOPS FOR REAL.
It was right about now I **realized** exactly what I'd done.
I THINK IT'S ALL GONNA BURN!
THERE THEY ARE!
BUT WHERE'S THE HEAD-MASTER?
AND THERE'S THE NEW GIRL!
HANA LOOKS WEIRD!
MR. NATH'S ON FIRE! MR. NATH'S ON FIRE!
I LEFT MY DIARY INSIDE-- DO YOU THINK THEY'LL LET ME GO GET IT?

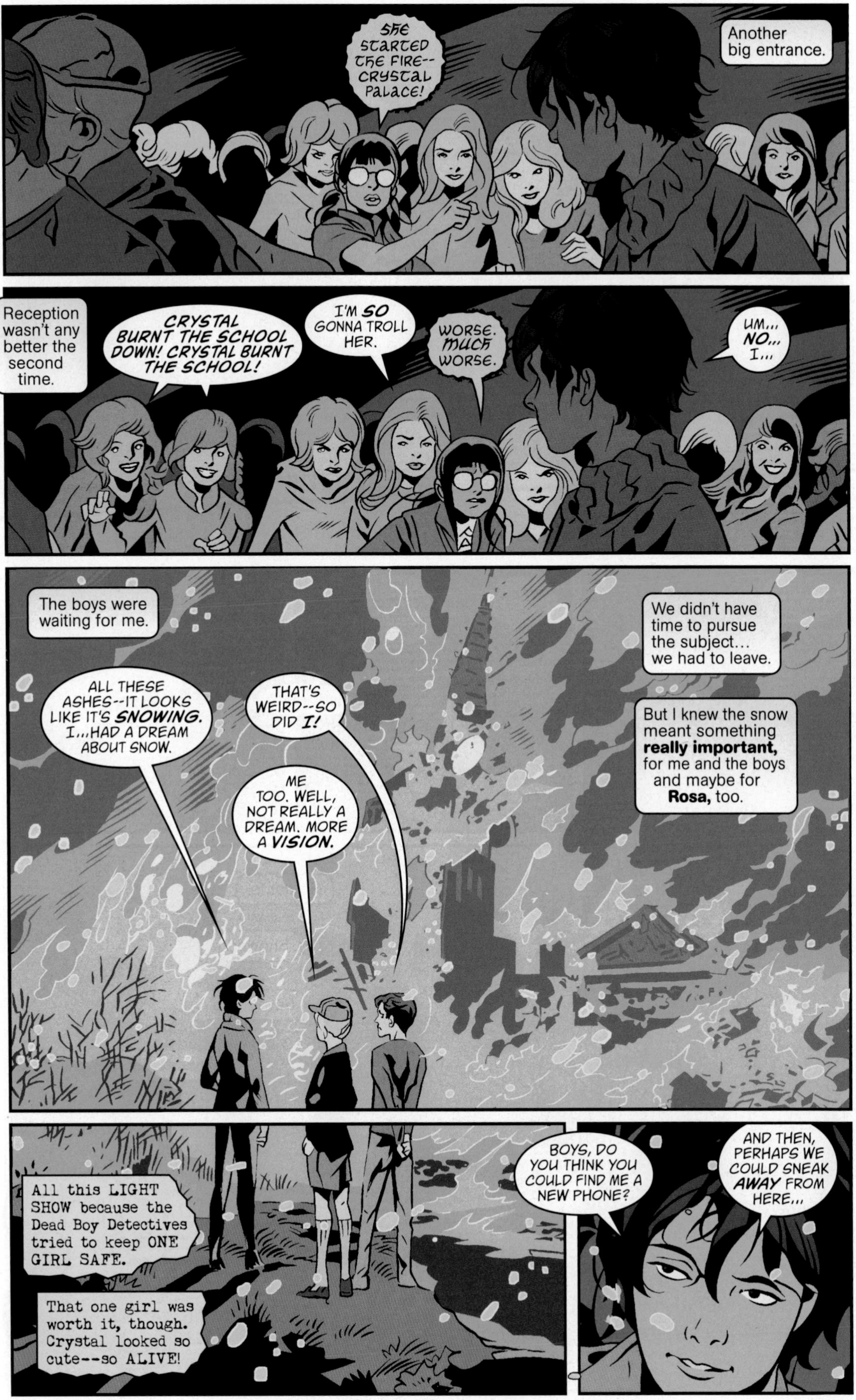
SHE STARTED THE FIRE-- CRYSTAL PALACE!
Another big entrance.
Reception wasn't any better the second time.
CRYSTAL BURNT THE SCHOOL DOWN! CRYSTAL BURNT THE SCHOOL!
I'M SO GONNA TROLL HER.
WORSE. MUCH WORSE.
UM... NO... I...
The boys were waiting for me.
ALL THESE ASHES--IT LOOKS LIKE IT'S SNOWING. I...HAD A DREAM ABOUT SNOW.
THAT'S WEIRD--SO DID I!
ME TOO. WELL, NOT REALLY A DREAM. MORE A VISION.
We didn't have time to pursue the subject... we had to leave.
But I knew the snow meant something really important, for me and the boys and maybe for Rosa, too.
All this LIGHT SHOW because the Dead Boy Detectives tried to keep ONE GIRL SAFE.
That one girl was worth it, though. Crystal looked so cute--so ALIVE!
BOYS, DO YOU THINK YOU COULD FIND ME A NEW PHONE?
AND THEN, PERHAPS WE COULD SNEAK AWAY FROM HERE...

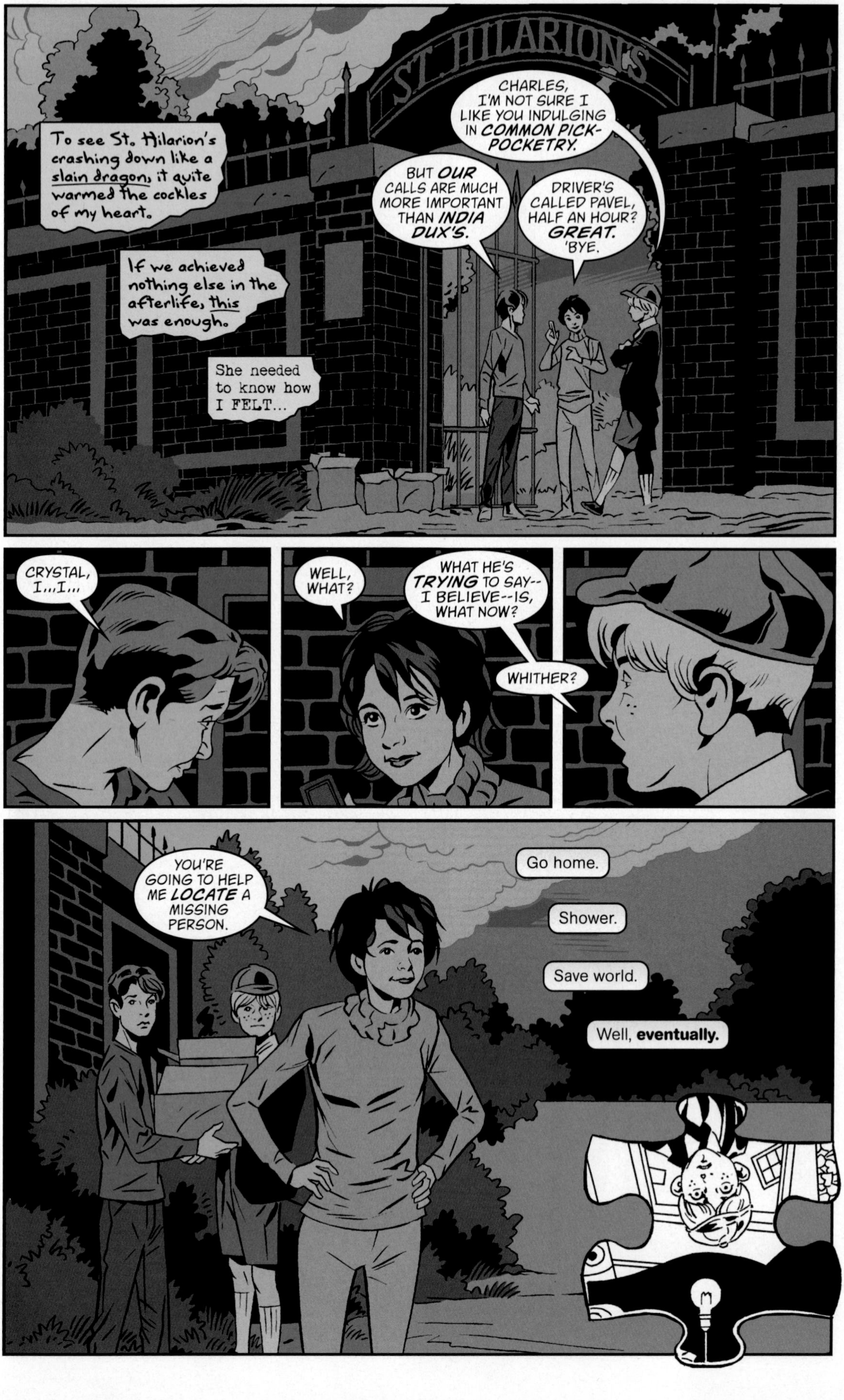

ST. HILARION'S
To see St. Hilarion's crashing down like a slain dragon, it quite warmed the cockles of my heart.
If we achieved nothing else in the afterlife, this was enough.
She needed to know how I FELT...
CHARLES, I'M NOT SURE I LIKE YOU INDULGING IN COMMON PICK-POCKETRY.
BUT OUR CALLS ARE MUCH MORE IMPORTANT THAN INDIA DUX'S.
DRIVER'S CALLED PAVEL, HALF AN HOUR? GREAT. 'BYE.
CRYSTAL, I...I...
WELL, WHAT?
WHAT HE'S TRYING TO SAY-- I BELIEVE--IS, WHAT NOW?
WHITHER?
YOU'RE GOING TO HELP ME LOCATE A MISSING PERSON.
Go home.
Shower.
Save world.
Well, eventually.

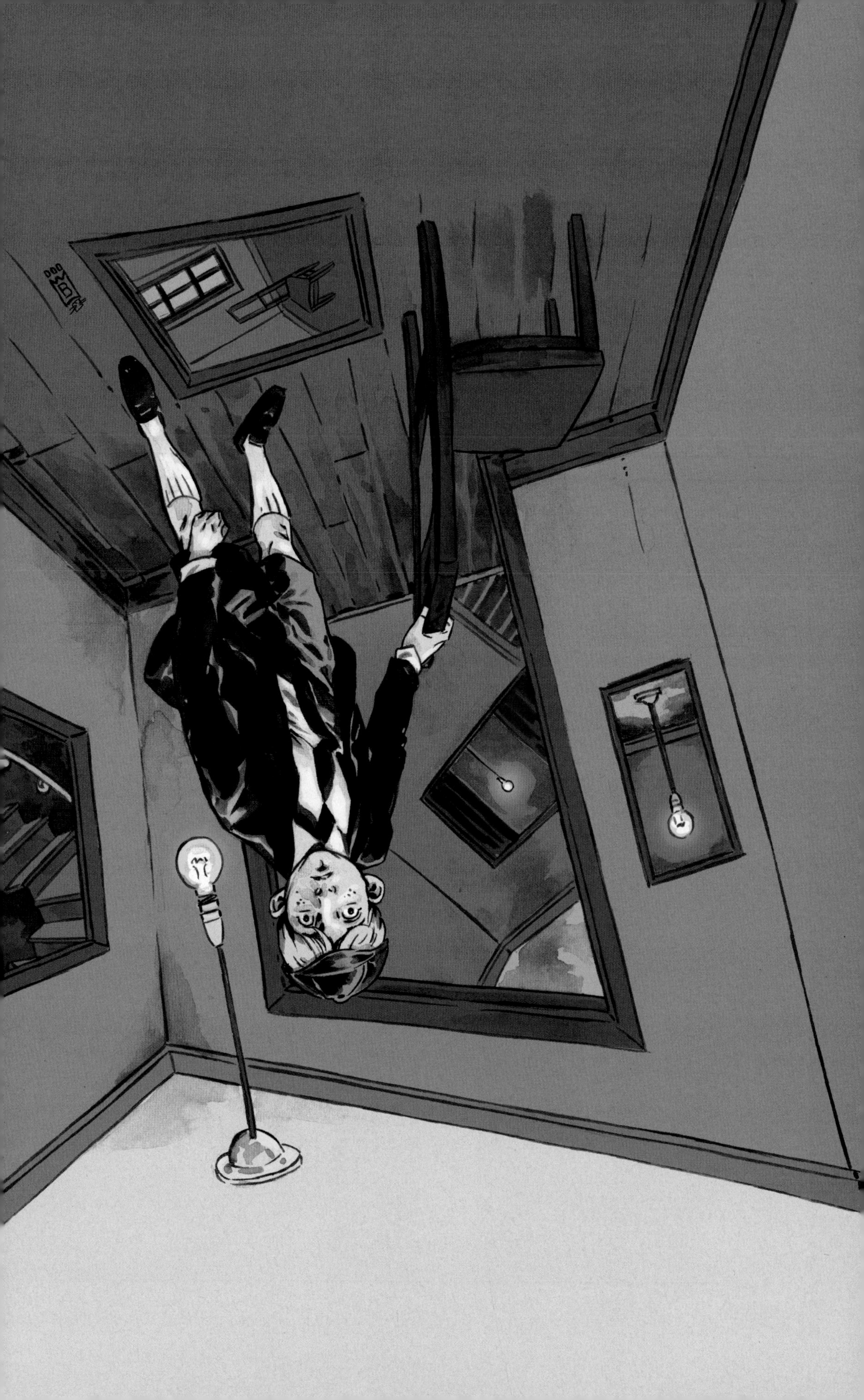

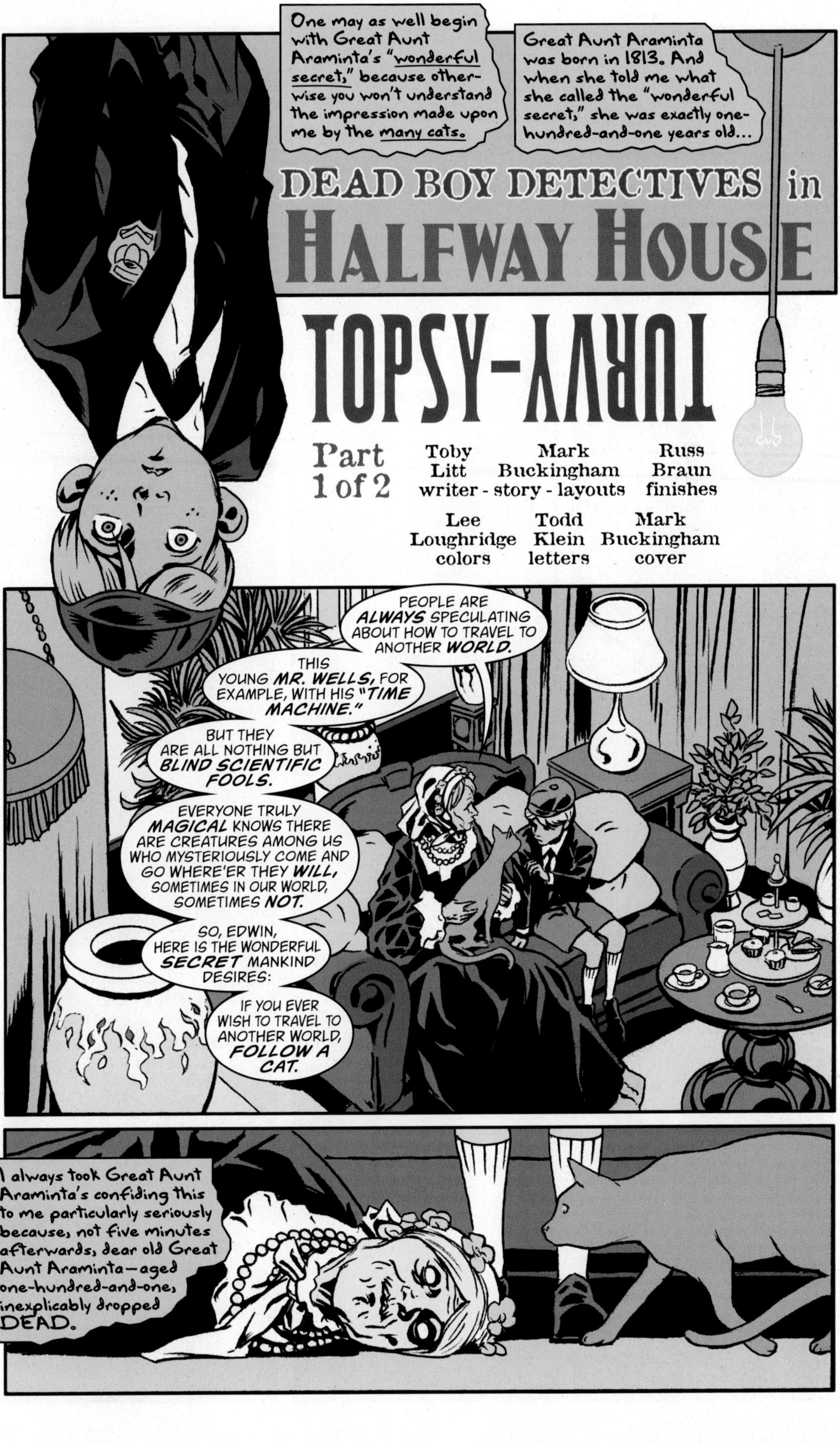
One may as well begin with Great Aunt Araminta's "wonderful secret," because otherwise you won't understand the impression made upon me by the many cats.
Great Aunt Araminta was born in 1813. And when she told me what she called the "wonderful secret," she was exactly one-hundred-and-one years old...
DEAD BOY DETECTIVES in
HALFWAY HOUSE
TOPSY-TURVY
Part 1 of 2
Toby Litt writer - story - layouts
Mark Buckingham writer - story - layouts
Russ Braun finishes
Lee Loughridge colors
Todd Klein letters
Mark Buckingham cover
PEOPLE ARE ALWAYS SPECULATING ABOUT HOW TO TRAVEL TO ANOTHER WORLD.
THIS YOUNG MR. WELLS, FOR EXAMPLE, WITH HIS "TIME MACHINE."
BUT THEY ARE ALL NOTHING BUT BLIND SCIENTIFIC FOOLS.
EVERYONE TRULY MAGICAL KNOWS THERE ARE CREATURES AMONG US WHO MYSTERIOUSLY COME AND GO WHERE'ER THEY WILL, SOMETIMES IN OUR WORLD, SOMETIMES NOT.
SO, EDWIN, HERE IS THE WONDERFUL SECRET MANKIND DESIRES:
IF YOU EVER WISH TO TRAVEL TO ANOTHER WORLD, FOLLOW A CAT.
I always took Great Aunt Araminta's confiding this to me particularly seriously because, not five minutes afterwards, dear old Great Aunt Araminta—aged one-hundred-and-one, inexplicably dropped DEAD.

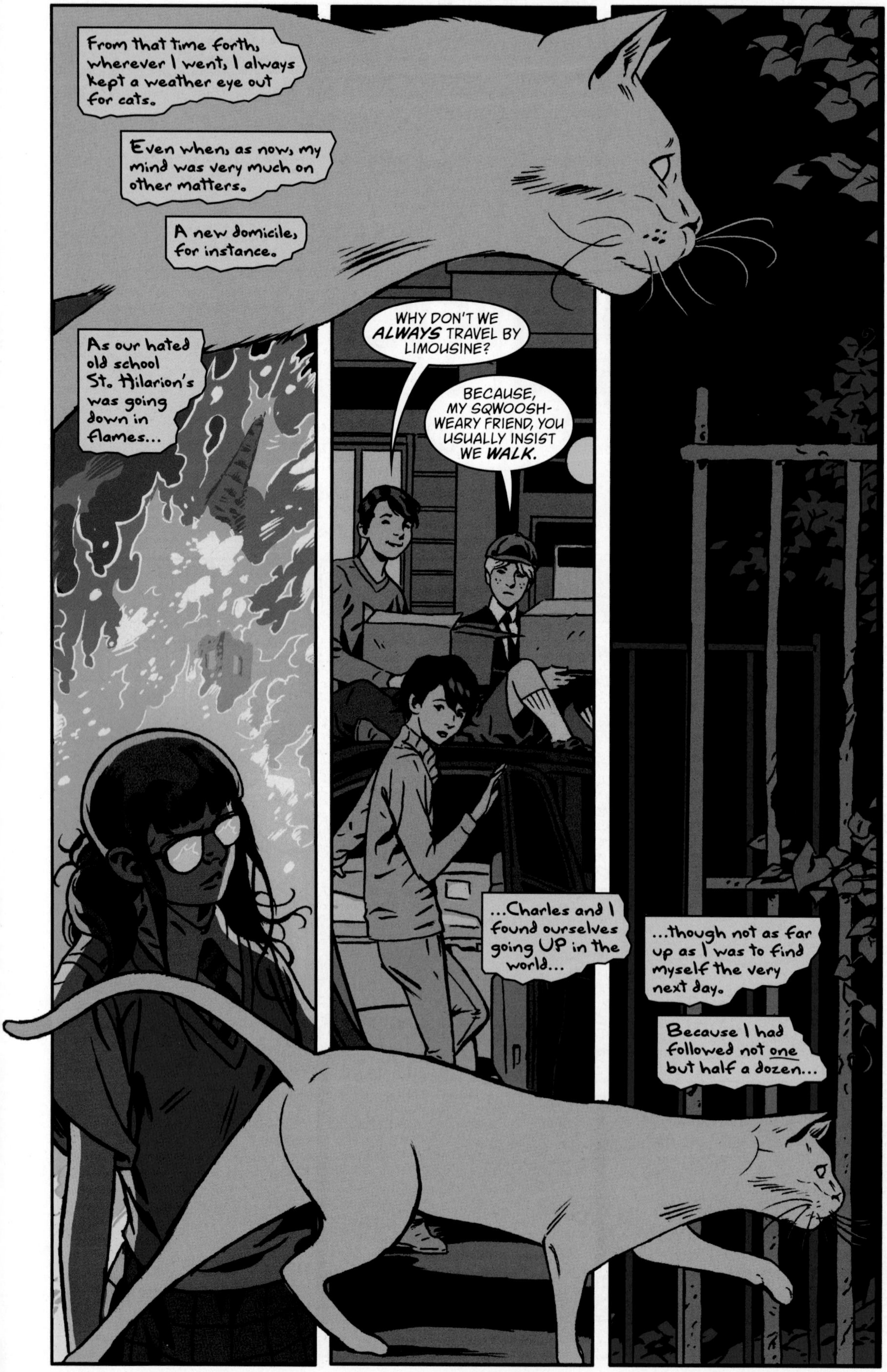
From that time forth, wherever I went, I always kept a weather eye out for cats.
Even when, as now, my mind was very much on other matters.
A new domicile, for instance.
As our hated old school St. Hilarion's was going down in flames...
WHY DON'T WE ALWAYS TRAVEL BY LIMOUSINE?
BECAUSE, MY SQWOOSH-WEARY FRIEND, YOU USUALLY INSIST WE WALK.
...Charles and I found ourselves going UP in the world...
...though not as far up as I was to find myself the very next day.
Because I had followed not one but half a dozen...

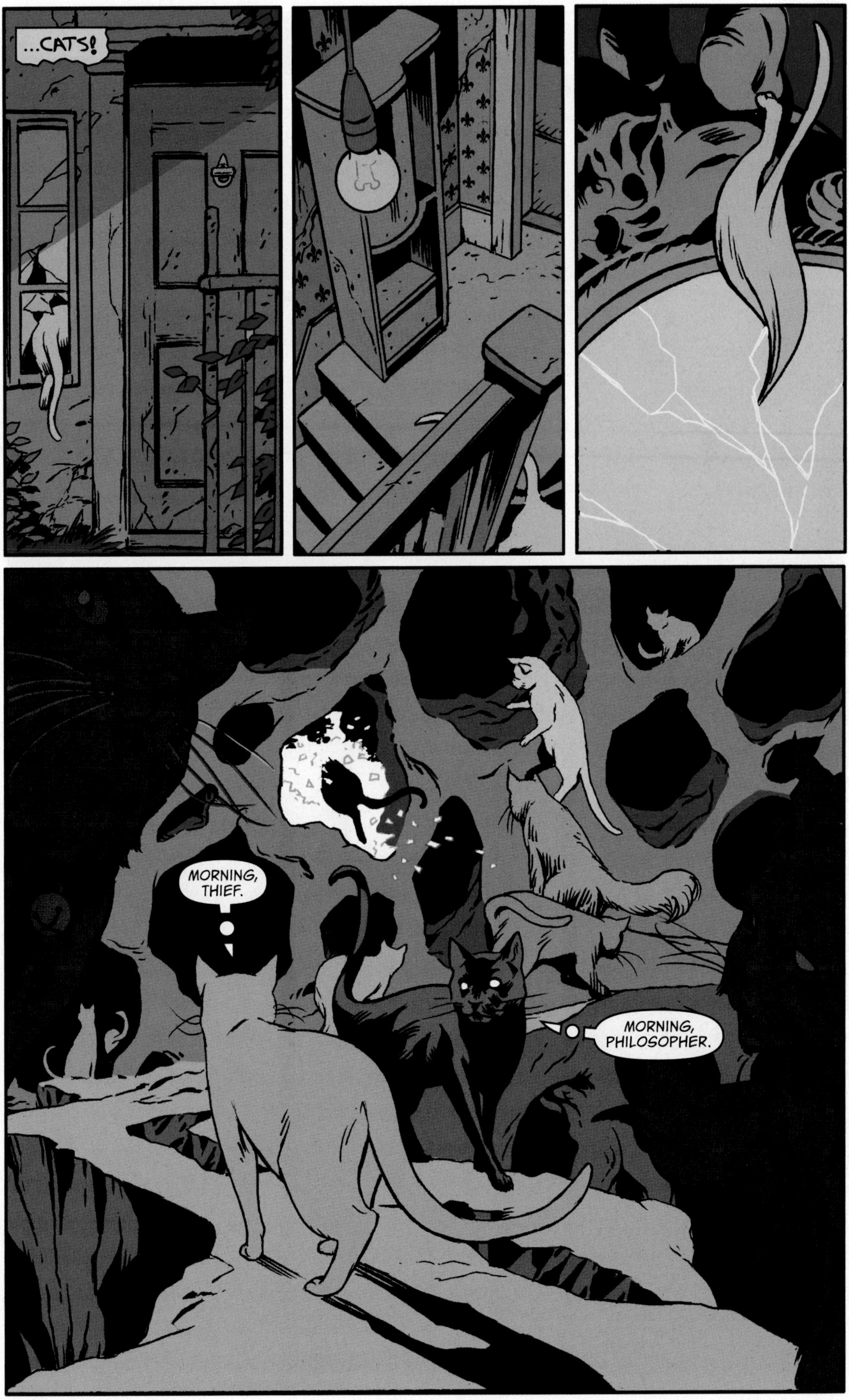
...CATS!
MORNING, THIEF.
MORNING, PHILOSOPHER.

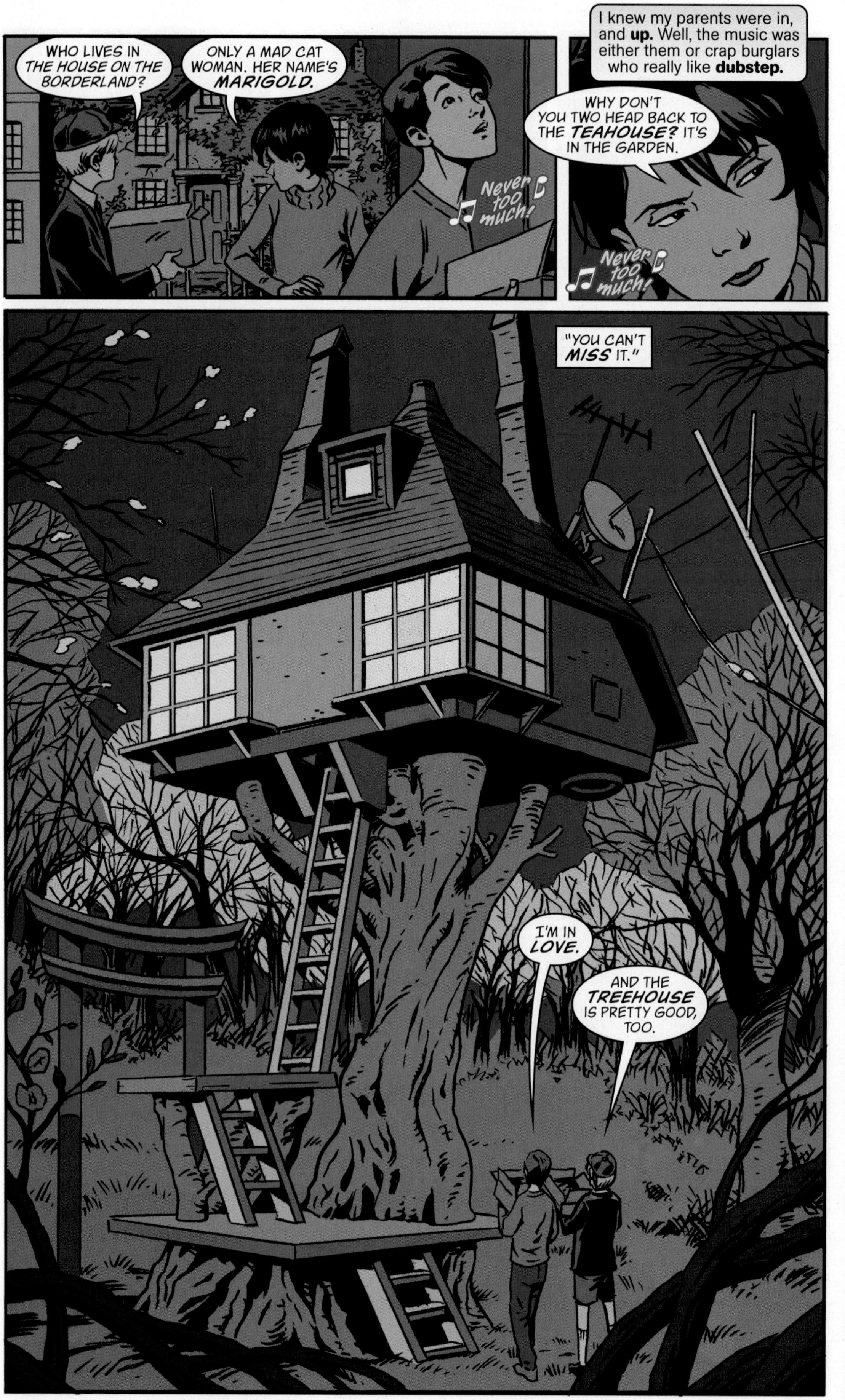

WHO LIVES IN THE HOUSE ON THE BORDERLAND?
ONLY A MAD CAT WOMAN. HER NAME'S MARIGOLD.
Never too much!
I knew my parents were in, and up. Well, the music was either them or crap burglars who really like dubstep.
WHY DON'T YOU TWO HEAD BACK TO THE TEAHOUSE? IT'S IN THE GARDEN.
Never too much!
"YOU CAN'T MISS IT."
I'M IN LOVE.
AND THE TREEHOUSE IS PRETTY GOOD, TOO.

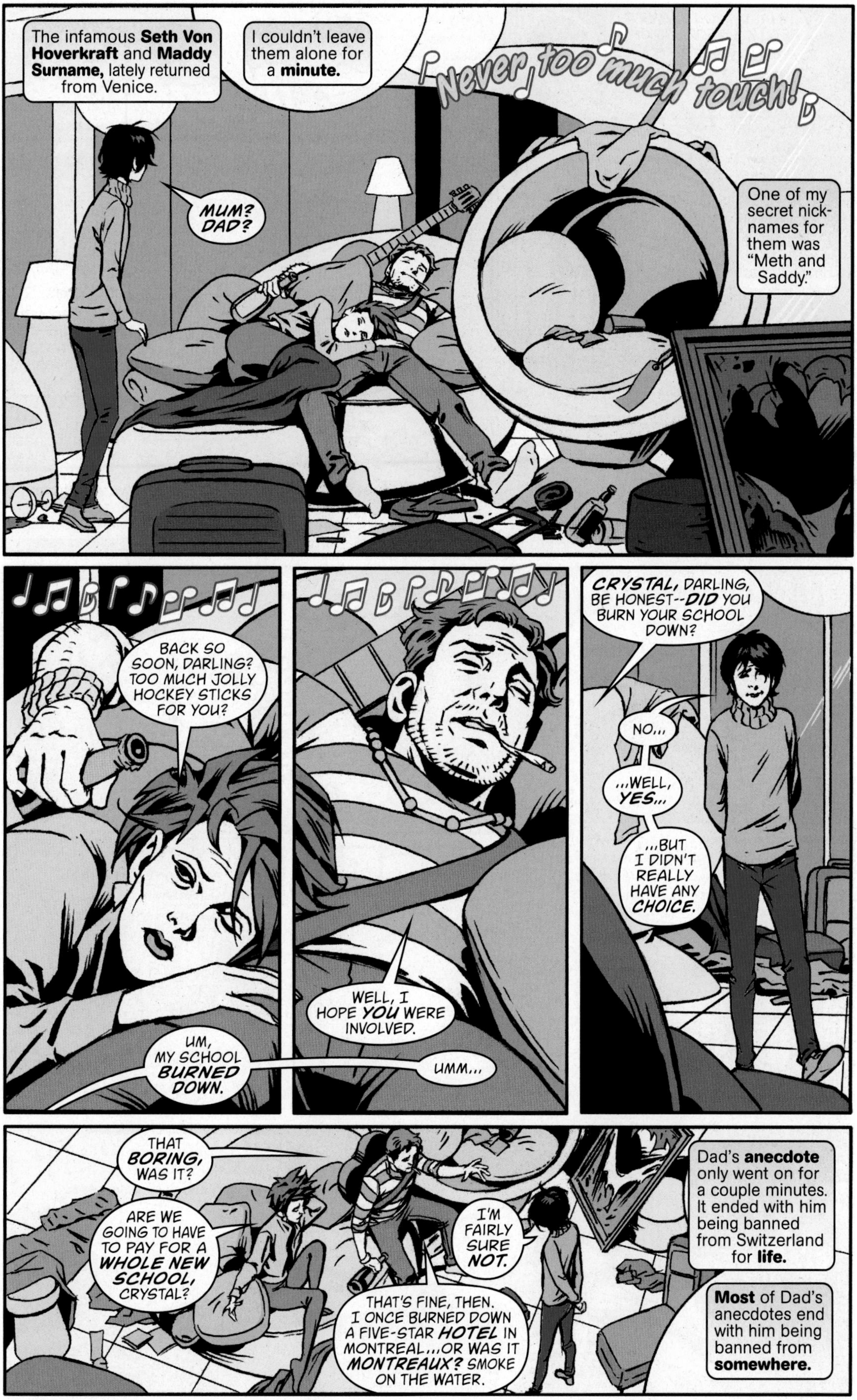
The infamous **Seth Von Hoverkraft** and **Maddy Surname,** lately returned from Venice.
I couldn't leave them alone for a **minute.**
Never too much touch!
MUM? DAD?
One of my secret nick-names for them was "Meth and Saddy."
BACK SO SOON, DARLING? TOO MUCH JOLLY HOCKEY STICKS FOR YOU?
UM, MY SCHOOL ***BURNED DOWN.***
WELL, I HOPE ***YOU*** WERE INVOLVED.
UMM...
CRYSTAL, DARLING, BE HONEST--***DID*** YOU BURN YOUR SCHOOL DOWN?
NO...
...WELL, ***YES...***
...BUT I DIDN'T REALLY HAVE ANY ***CHOICE.***
THAT ***BORING,*** WAS IT?
ARE WE GOING TO HAVE TO PAY FOR A ***WHOLE NEW SCHOOL,*** CRYSTAL?
I'M FAIRLY SURE ***NOT.***
THAT'S FINE, THEN. I ONCE BURNED DOWN A FIVE-STAR ***HOTEL*** IN MONTREAL...OR WAS IT ***MONTREAUX?*** SMOKE ON THE WATER.
Dad's **anecdote** only went on for a couple minutes. It ended with him being banned from Switzerland for **life.**
Most of Dad's anecdotes end with him being banned from **somewhere.**

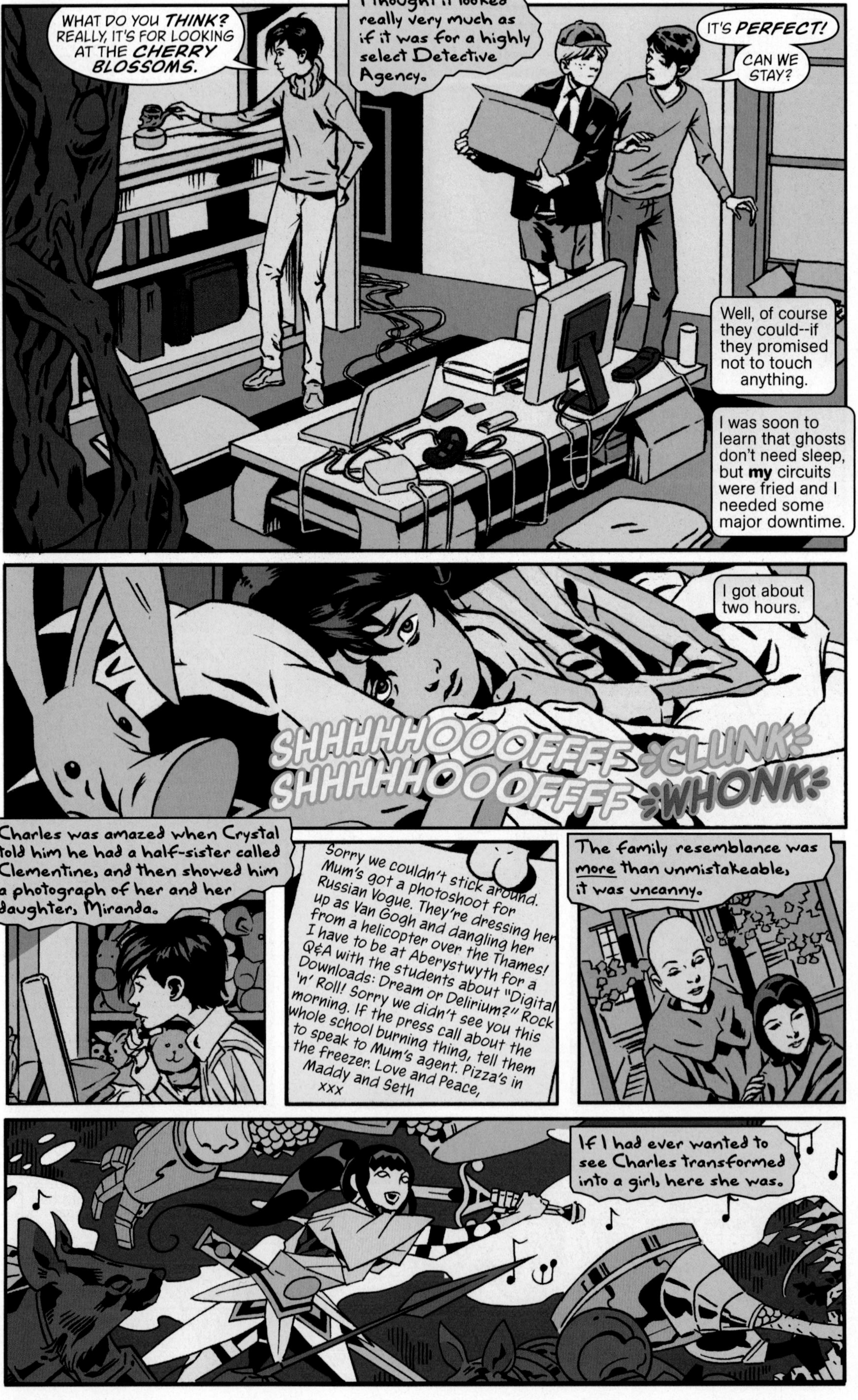

WHAT DO YOU THINK? REALLY, IT'S FOR LOOKING AT THE CHERRY BLOSSOMS.
I thought it looked really very much as if it was for a highly select Detective Agency.
IT'S PERFECT!
CAN WE STAY?
Well, of course they could--if they promised not to touch anything.
I was soon to learn that ghosts don't need sleep, but my circuits were fried and I needed some major downtime.
I got about two hours.
SHHHHHOOOOFFFF
SHHHHHOOOOFFFF
CLUNK
WHONK
Charles was amazed when Crystal told him he had a half-sister called Clementine, and then showed him a photograph of her and her daughter, Miranda.
Sorry we couldn't stick around. Mum's got a photoshoot for Russian Vogue. They're dressing her up as Van Gogh and dangling her from a helicopter over the Thames! I have to be at Aberystwyth for a Q&A with the students about "Digital Downloads: Dream or Delirium?" Rock 'n' Roll! Sorry we didn't see you this morning. If the press call about the whole school burning thing, tell them to speak to Mum's agent. Pizza's in the freezer. Love and Peace, Maddy and Seth xxx
The family resemblance was more than unmistakeable, it was uncanny.
If I had ever wanted to see Charles transformed into a girl, here she was.

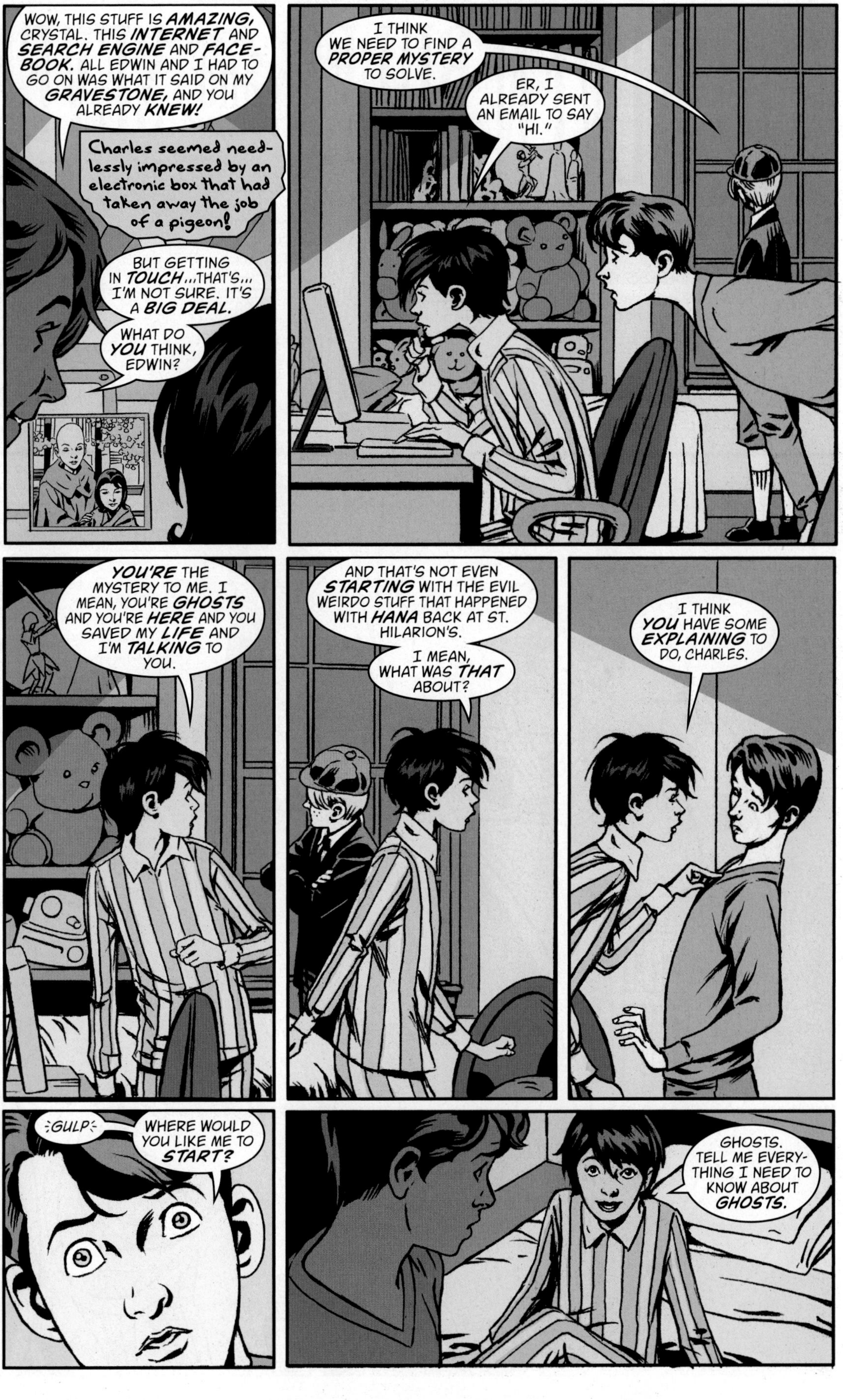
WOW, THIS STUFF IS AMAZING, CRYSTAL. THIS INTERNET AND SEARCH ENGINE AND FACE-BOOK. ALL EDWIN AND I HAD TO GO ON WAS WHAT IT SAID ON MY GRAVESTONE, AND YOU ALREADY KNEW!
Charles seemed needlessly impressed by an electronic box that had taken away the job of a pigeon!
BUT GETTING IN TOUCH...THAT'S... I'M NOT SURE. IT'S A BIG DEAL.
WHAT DO YOU THINK, EDWIN?
I THINK WE NEED TO FIND A PROPER MYSTERY TO SOLVE.
ER, I ALREADY SENT AN EMAIL TO SAY "HI."
YOU'RE THE MYSTERY TO ME. I MEAN, YOU'RE GHOSTS AND YOU'RE HERE AND YOU SAVED MY LIFE AND I'M TALKING TO YOU.
AND THAT'S NOT EVEN STARTING WITH THE EVIL WEIRDO STUFF THAT HAPPENED WITH HANA BACK AT ST. HILARION'S.
I MEAN, WHAT WAS THAT ABOUT?
I THINK YOU HAVE SOME EXPLAINING TO DO, CHARLES.
GULP
WHERE WOULD YOU LIKE ME TO START?
GHOSTS. TELL ME EVERYTHING I NEED TO KNOW ABOUT GHOSTS.

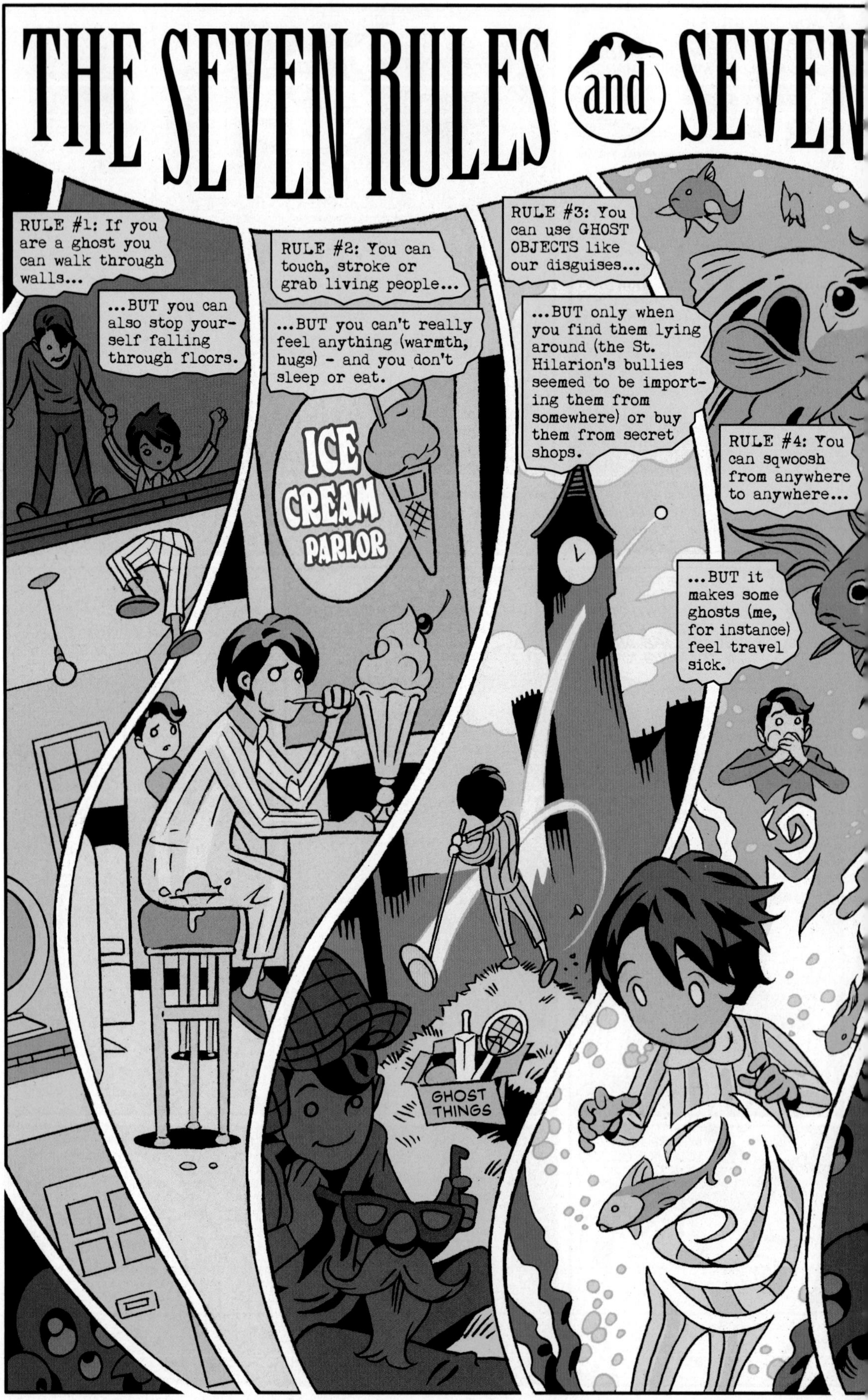
THE SEVEN RULES and SEVEN
RULE #1: If you are a ghost you can walk through walls...
...BUT you can also stop yourself falling through floors.
RULE #2: You can touch, stroke or grab living people...
...BUT you can't really feel anything (warmth, hugs) - and you don't sleep or eat.
ICE CREAM PARLOR
RULE #3: You can use GHOST OBJECTS like our disguises...
...BUT only when you find them lying around (the St. Hilarion's bullies seemed to be importing them from somewhere) or buy them from secret shops.
GHOST THINGS
RULE #4: You can sqwoosh from anywhere to anywhere...
...BUT it makes some ghosts (me, for instance) feel travel sick.

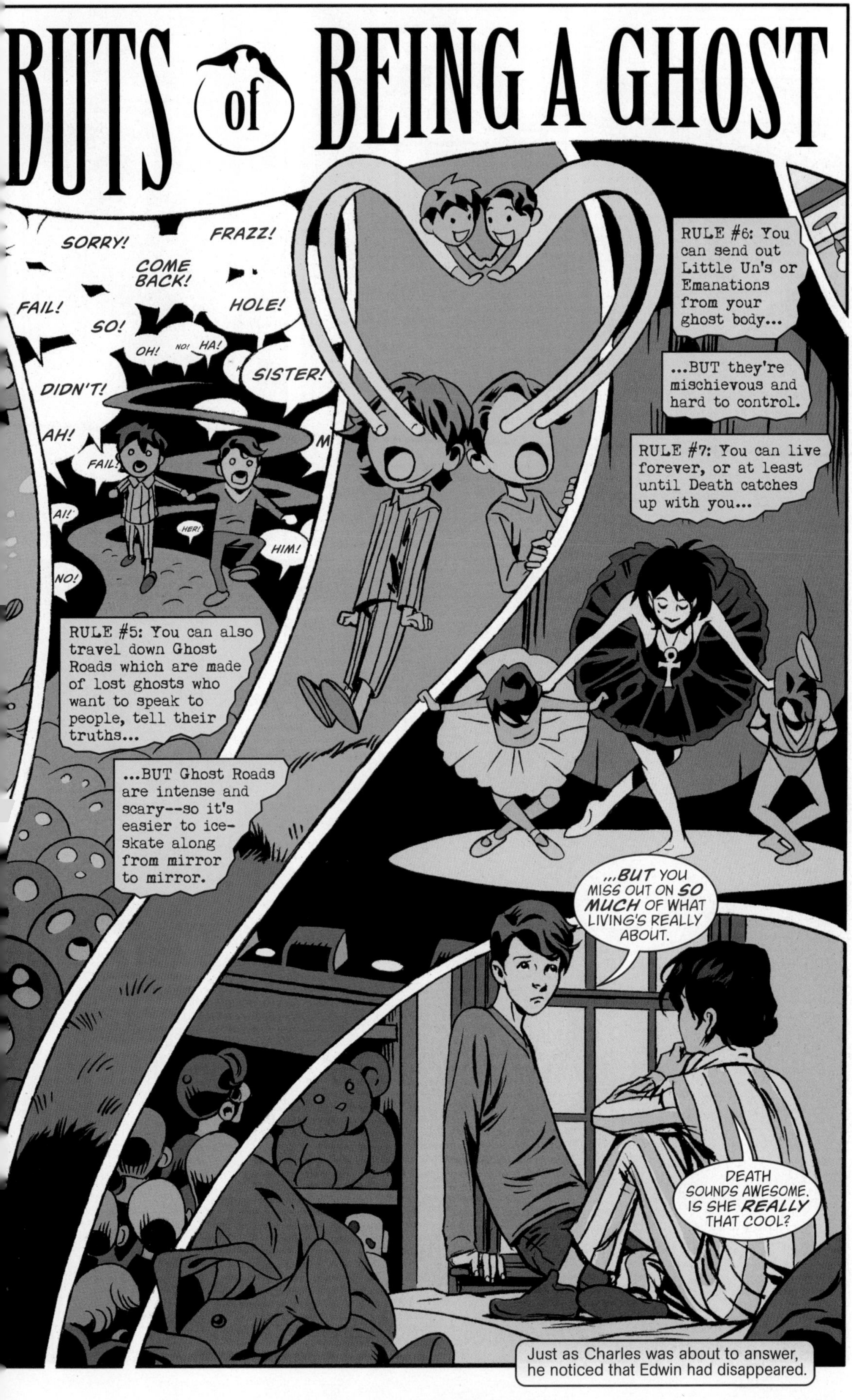
BUTS of BEING A GHOST
SORRY!
FRAZZ!
COME BACK!
FAIL!
SO!
HOLE!
OH!
NO!
HA!
SISTER!
DIDN'T!
AH!
FAIL!
AI!
HER!
HIM!
NO!
RULE #5: You can also travel down Ghost Roads which are made of lost ghosts who want to speak to people, tell their truths...
...BUT Ghost Roads are intense and scary--so it's easier to ice-skate along from mirror to mirror.
RULE #6: You can send out Little Un's or Emanations from your ghost body...
...BUT they're mischievous and hard to control.
RULE #7: You can live forever, or at least until Death catches up with you...
...BUT YOU MISS OUT ON SO MUCH OF WHAT LIVING'S REALLY ABOUT.
DEATH SOUNDS AWESOME. IS SHE REALLY THAT COOL?
Just as Charles was about to answer, he noticed that Edwin had disappeared.

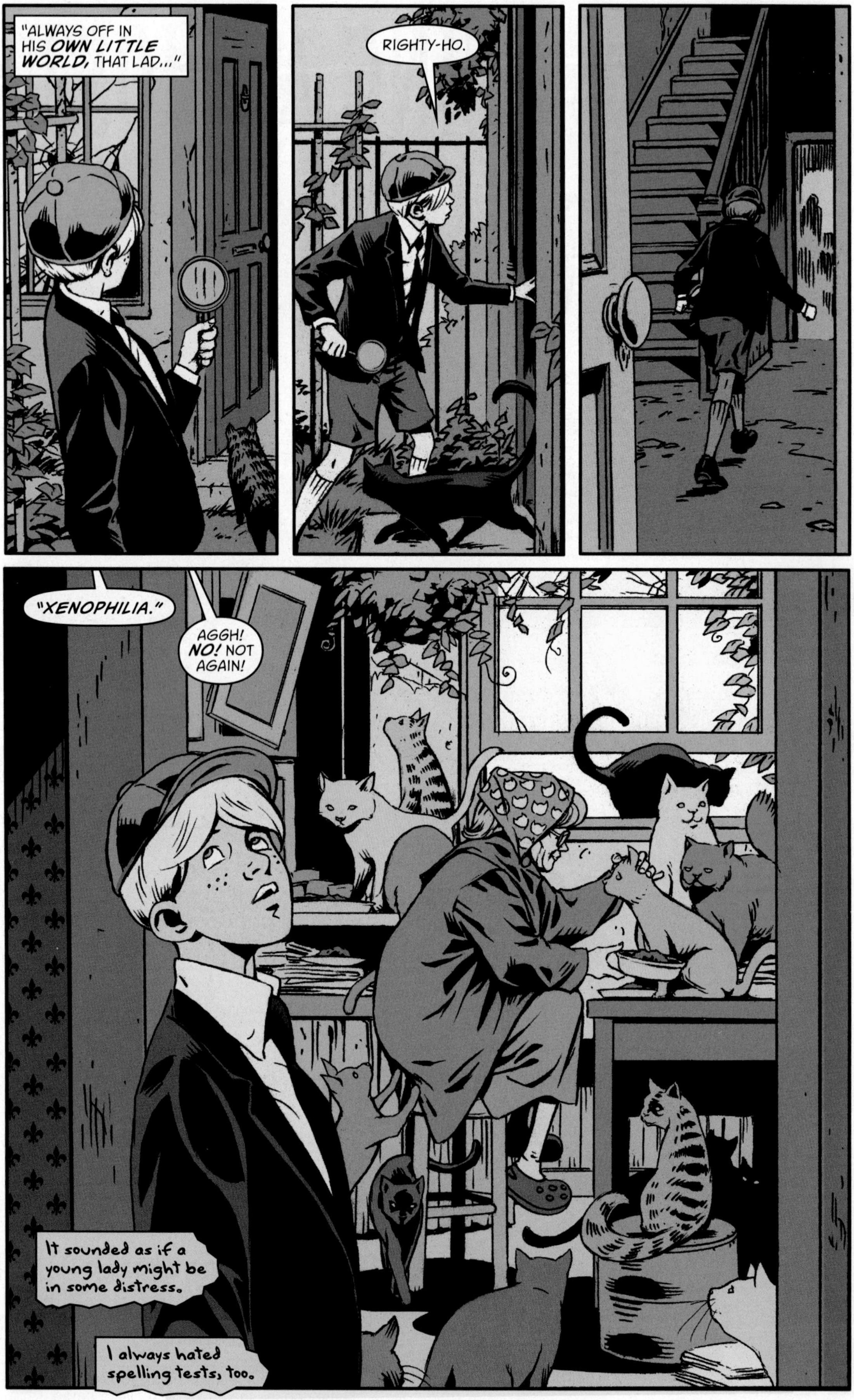
"ALWAYS OFF IN HIS OWN LITTLE WORLD, THAT LAD..."
RIGHTY-HO.
"XENOPHILIA."
AGGH! NO! NOT AGAIN!
It sounded as if a young lady might be in some distress.
I always hated spelling tests, too.

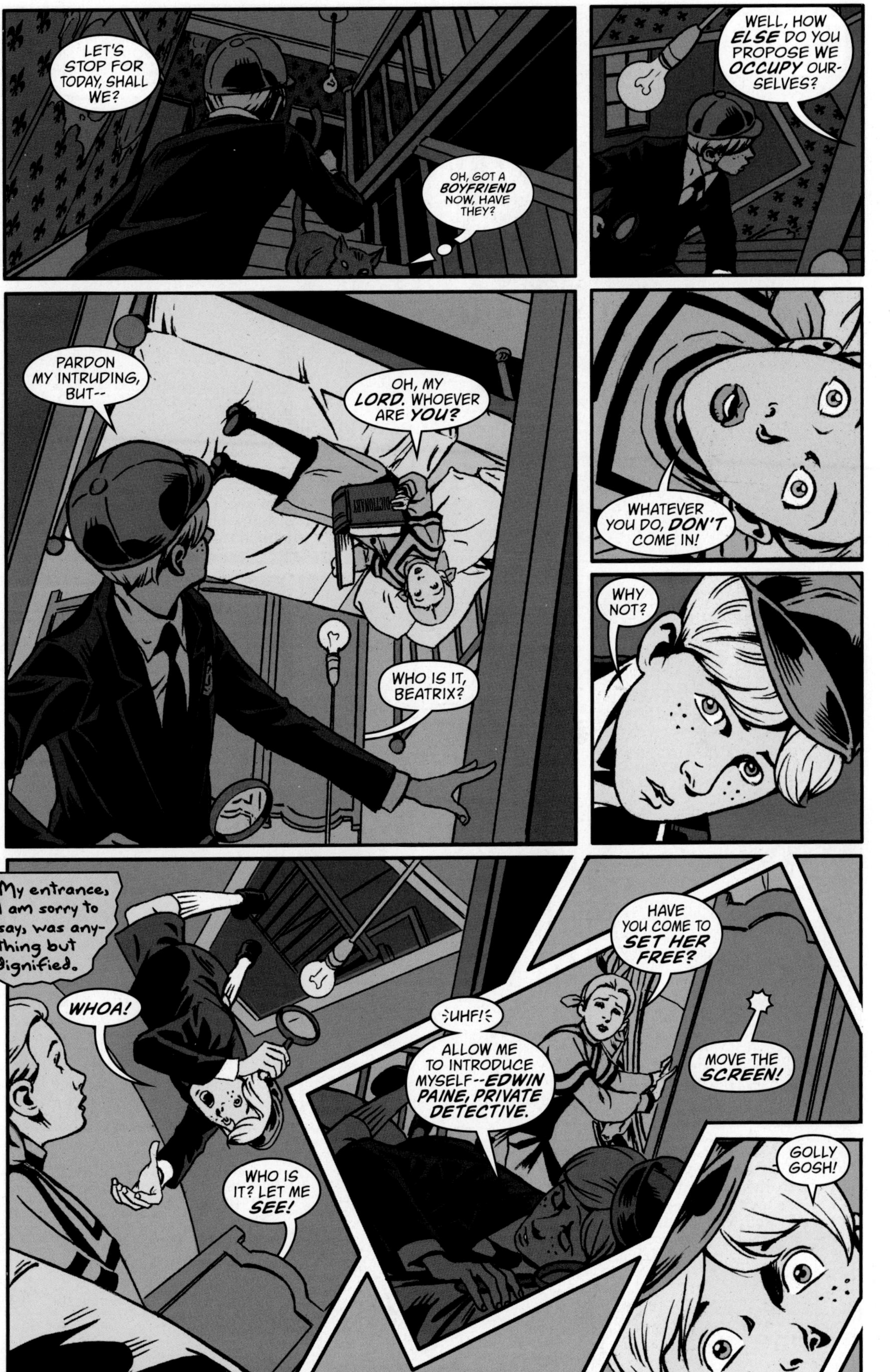
LET'S STOP FOR TODAY, SHALL WE?
OH, GOT A BOYFRIEND NOW, HAVE THEY?
WELL, HOW ELSE DO YOU PROPOSE WE OCCUPY OUR-SELVES?
PARDON MY INTRUDING, BUT--
OH, MY LORD. WHOEVER ARE YOU?
DICTIONARY
WHO IS IT, BEATRIX?
WHATEVER YOU DO, DON'T COME IN!
WHY NOT?
My entrance, I am sorry to say, was any-thing but dignified.
WHOA!
WHO IS IT? LET ME SEE!
UHF!
ALLOW ME TO INTRODUCE MYSELF--EDWIN PAINE, PRIVATE DETECTIVE.
HAVE YOU COME TO SET HER FREE?
MOVE THE SCREEN!
GOLLY GOSH!

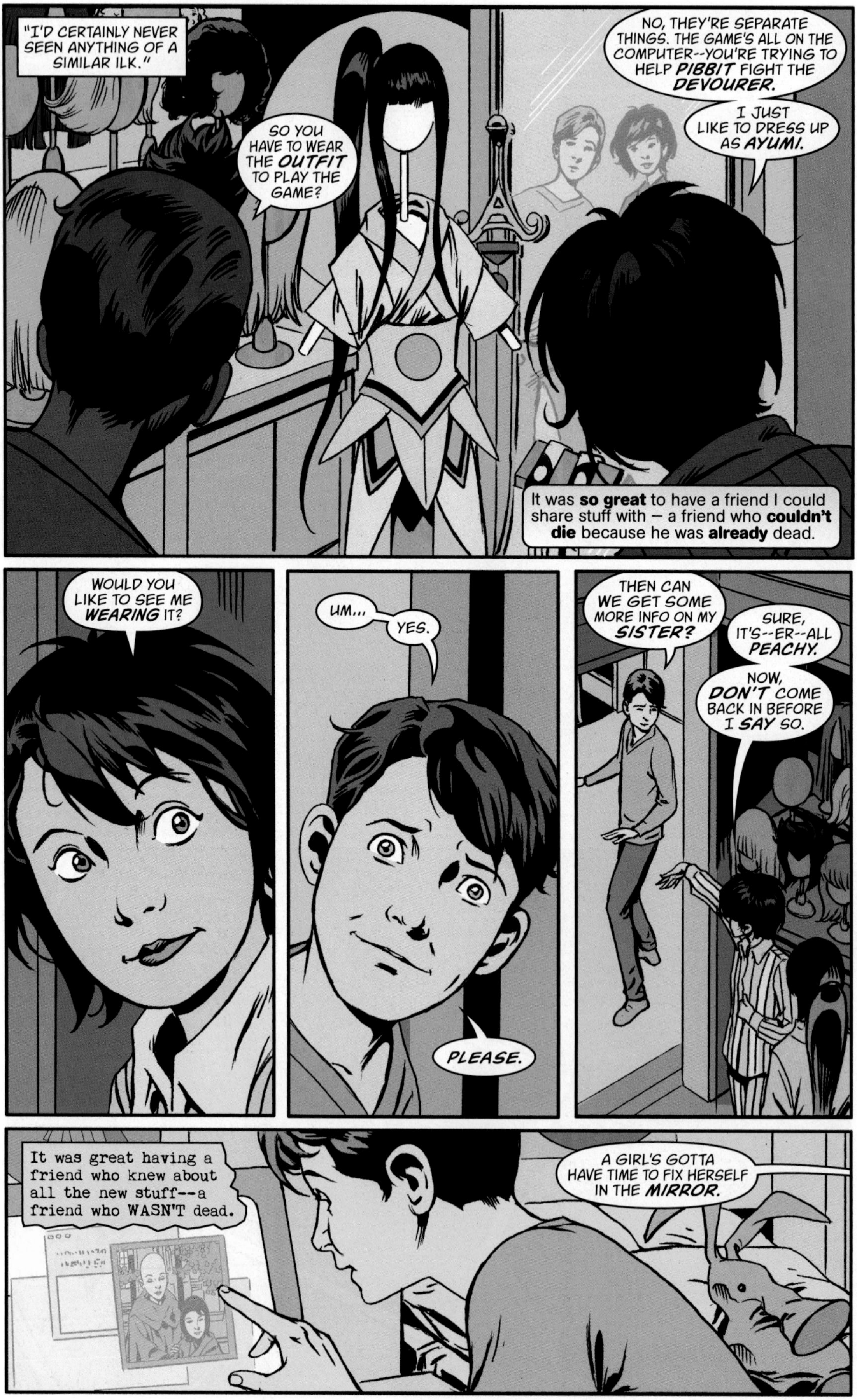
"I'D CERTAINLY NEVER SEEN ANYTHING OF A SIMILAR ILK."
SO YOU HAVE TO WEAR THE OUTFIT TO PLAY THE GAME?
NO, THEY'RE SEPARATE THINGS. THE GAME'S ALL ON THE COMPUTER--YOU'RE TRYING TO HELP PIBBIT FIGHT THE DEVOURER.
I JUST LIKE TO DRESS UP AS AYUMI.
It was so great to have a friend I could share stuff with – a friend who couldn't die because he was already dead.
WOULD YOU LIKE TO SEE ME WEARING IT?
UM...
YES.
PLEASE.
THEN CAN WE GET SOME MORE INFO ON MY SISTER?
SURE, IT'S--ER--ALL PEACHY.
NOW, DON'T COME BACK IN BEFORE I SAY SO.
It was great having a friend who knew about all the new stuff--a friend who WASN'T dead.
A GIRL'S GOTTA HAVE TIME TO FIX HERSELF IN THE MIRROR.

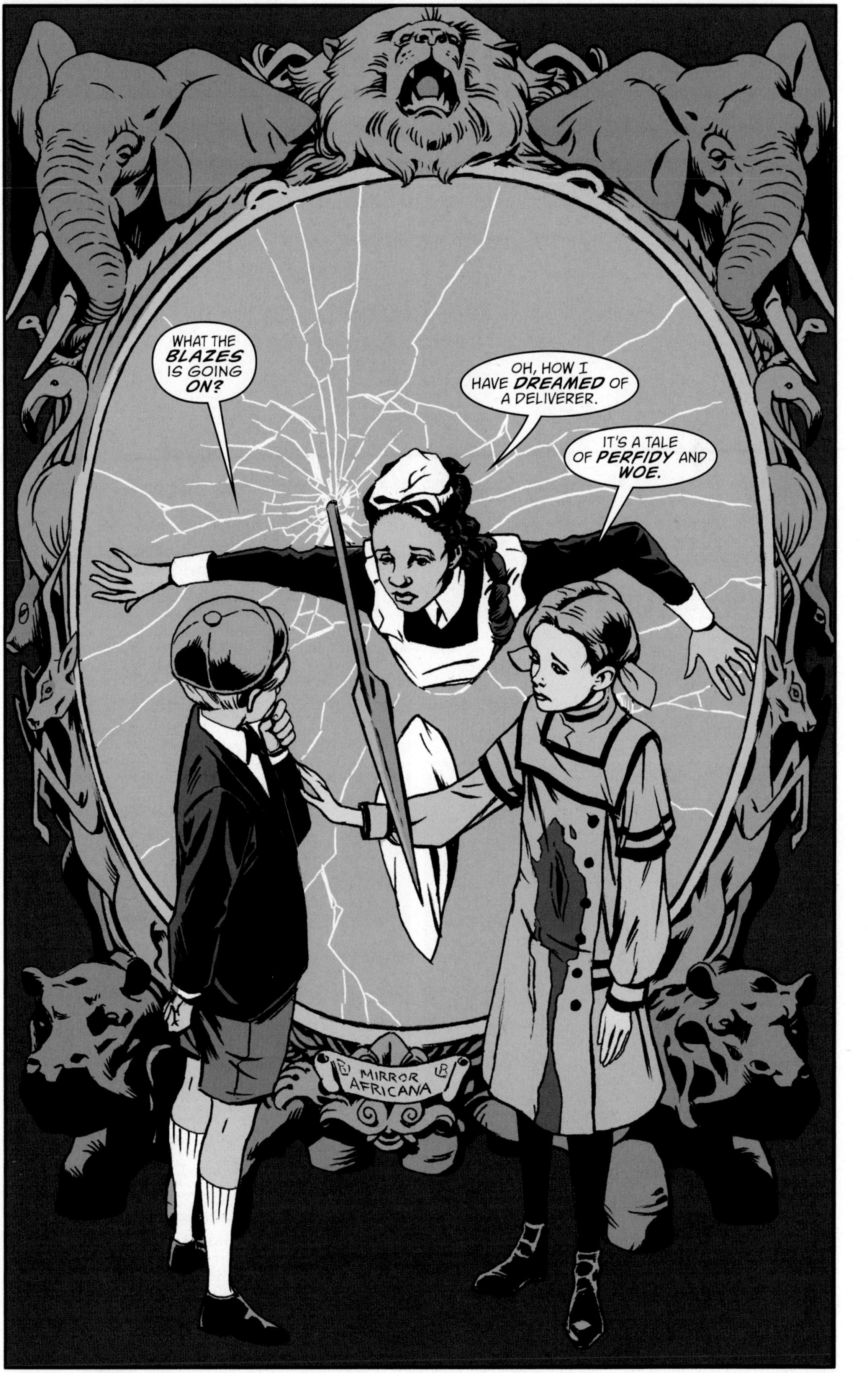
WHAT THE BLAZES IS GOING ON?
OH, HOW I HAVE DREAMED OF A DELIVERER.
IT'S A TALE OF PERFIDY AND WOE.
MIRROR AFRICANA

The Dark Mirror of Africa

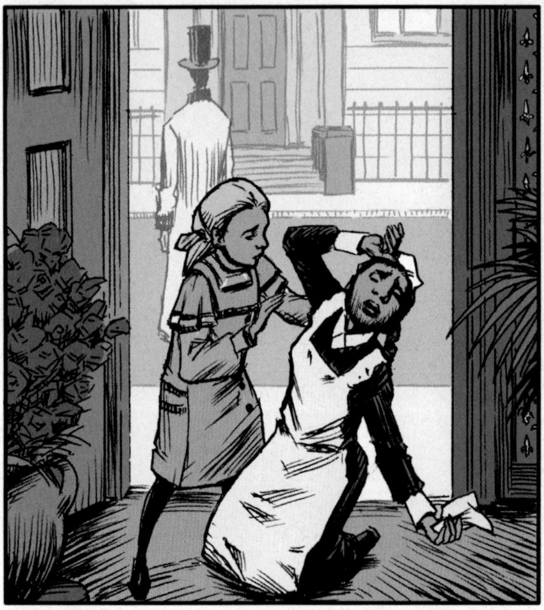

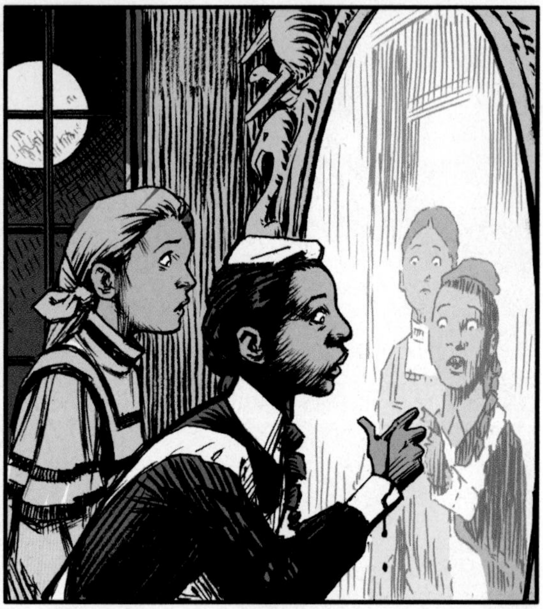

LADY BEATRIX and her loyal maid, PERSEPHONE, very much desire to visit what is commonly known as "The Dark Continent" — specifically, to visit PERSEPHONE'S GRANDFATHER whom they had recently heard was sadly dying of consumption. Yet when BEATRIX asked for permission for them to travel, her parents — quite understandably — refused to allow them that liberty.

BEATRIX'S father, LORD QUARLES, was a renowned adventurer who had brought the mysterious "Mirror Africana" back with him from a previous sub-Saharan expedition. BEATRIX and PERSEPHONE had heard rumours that the "Mirror Africana" was possessed of magical powers — that, on receipt of a blood offering, it could transport a body to "The Dark Continent" in a twinkling. One night, the two foolish girls decided to test the unlikely truth of this.

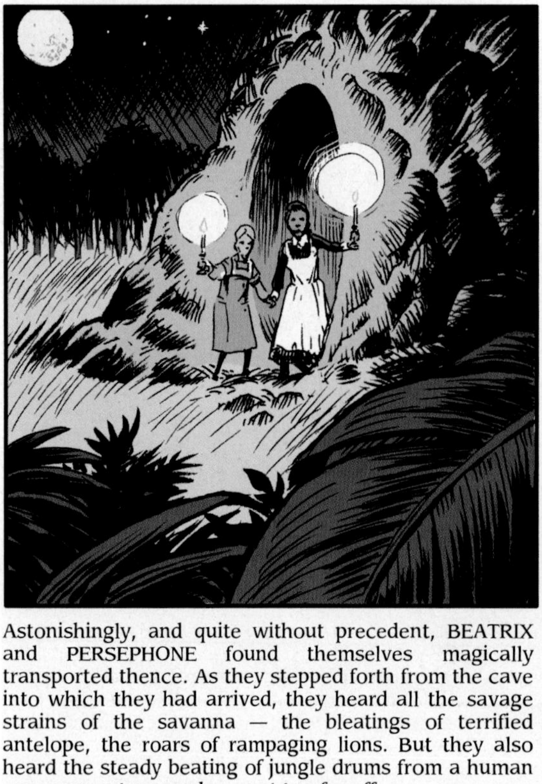

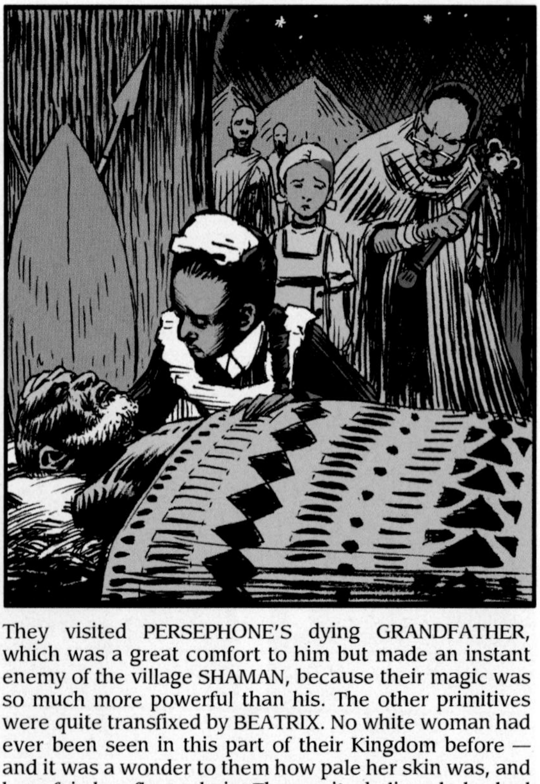

Astonishingly, and quite without precedent, BEATRIX and PERSEPHONE found themselves magically transported thence. As they stepped forth from the cave into which they had arrived, they heard all the savage strains of the savanna — the bleatings of terrified antelope, the roars of rampaging lions. But they also heard the steady beating of jungle drums from a human encampment somewhere not too far off.

They visited PERSEPHONE'S dying GRANDFATHER, which was a great comfort to him but made an instant enemy of the village SHAMAN, because their magic was so much more powerful than his. The other primitives were quite transfixed by BEATRIX. No white woman had ever been seen in this part of their Kingdom before — and it was a wonder to them how pale her skin was, and how fair her flaxen hair. They quite believed she had fallen from the sun.

The Dark Mirror of Africa

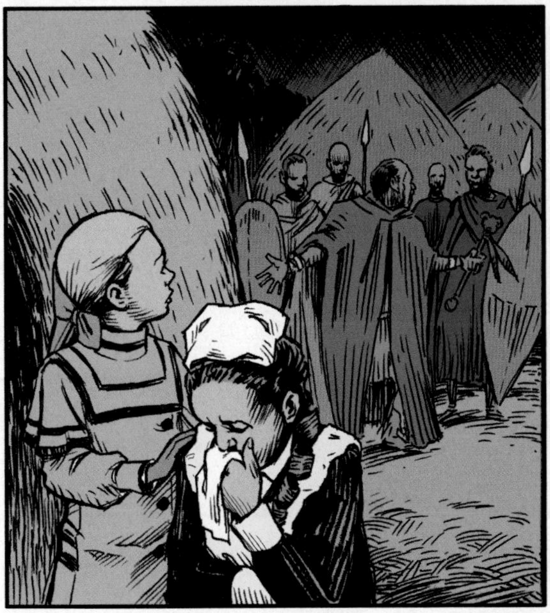

As soon as PERSEPHONE'S GRANDFATHER expired, which was not long after PERSEPHONE arrived, the SHAMAN began a whispering campaign against BEATRIX and the grieving PERSEPHONE. He claimed they were witches who had brought death with them, and if they were not swiftly dealt with, who knew which of the villagers would be the next to suffer?

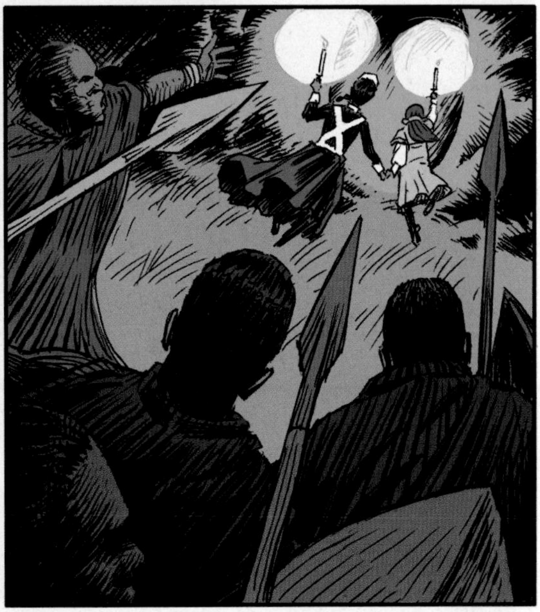

That moonlit night, BEATRIX and PERSEPHONE — forewarned by friendly natives — fled from the village back towards the cave whence they had emerged. They had not long departed when the two girls realized they were being tracked by a horde of Zulus led by the SHAMAN who had spread such virulent calumny regarding them. With every step, their spear-wielding pursuers gained upon BEATRIX and PERSEPHONE!

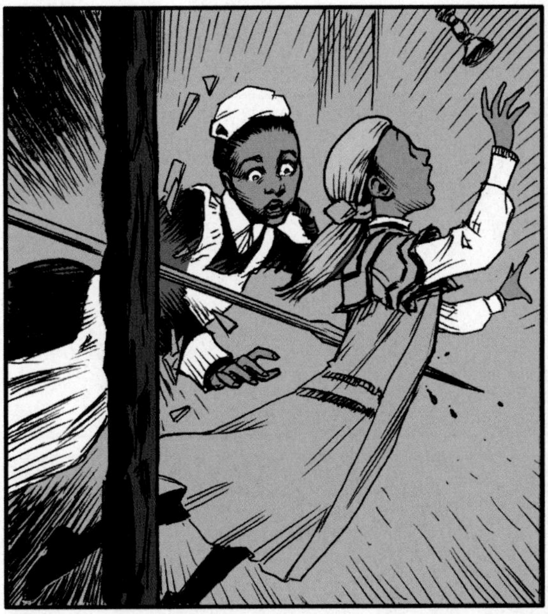

BEATRIX managed to pass completely back through the looking-glass, but a spear that was hurled at just that moment shattered the mirror — with the double effect of wounding poor, doomed BEATRIX fatally in the abdomen and trapping tragic PERSEPHONE exactly as she can be found today. These events that have been laid out before you — in all their initial unlikelihood and final horror — happened in the Year of Our Lord 1888.

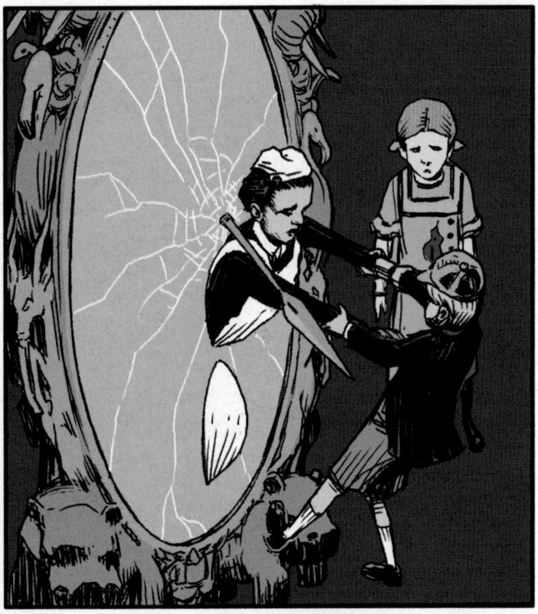

BEATRIX'S family was utterly devastated — particularly LADY QUARLES, who had the house shut up with the shattered mirror inside it, with orders that the place never be touched. Since that day, BEATRIX has tried everything she can think of to release her dear companion PERSEPHONE, but nothing has succeeded.

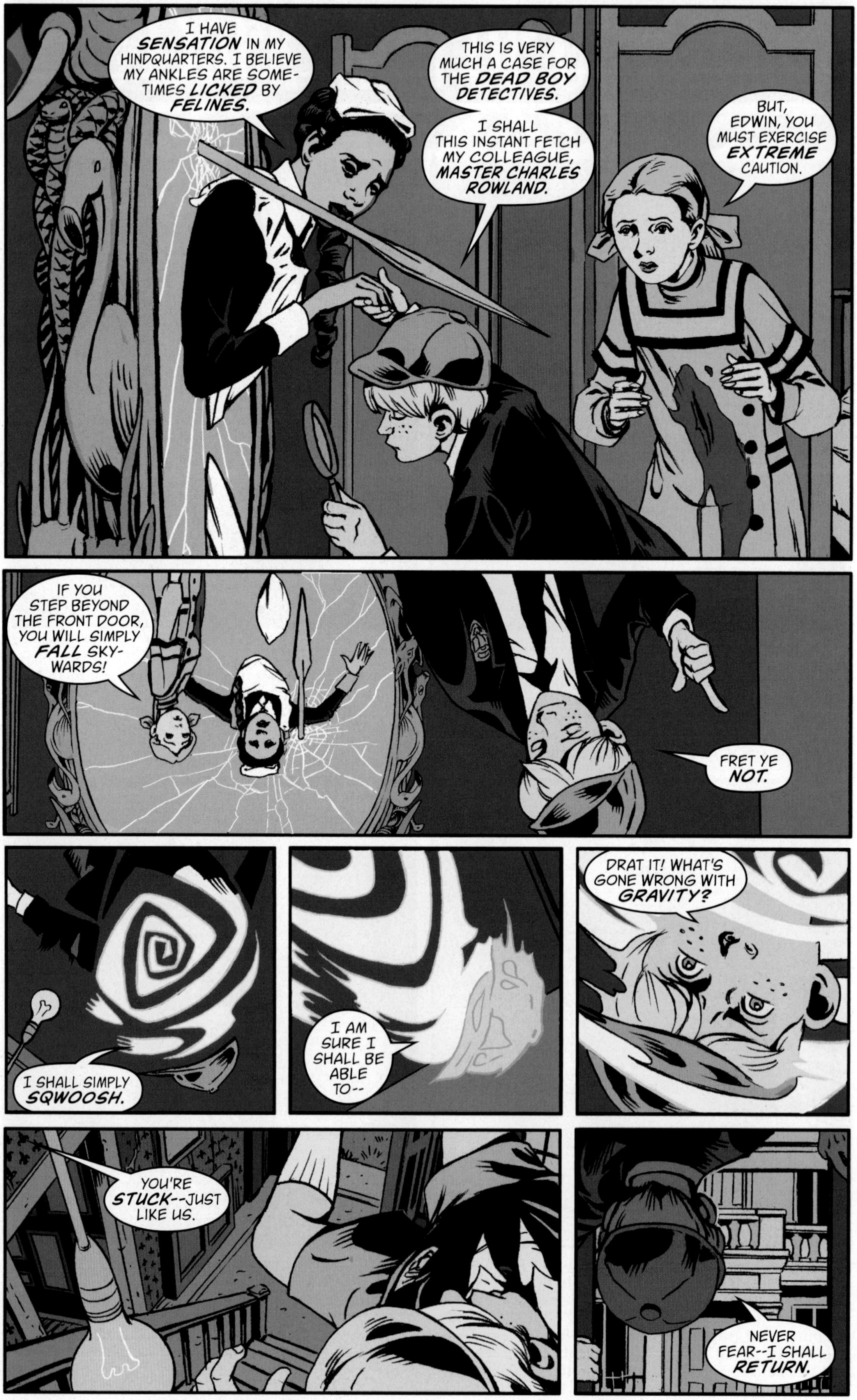
I HAVE SENSATION IN MY HINDQUARTERS. I BELIEVE MY ANKLES ARE SOME-TIMES LICKED BY FELINES.
THIS IS VERY MUCH A CASE FOR THE DEAD BOY DETECTIVES.
I SHALL THIS INSTANT FETCH MY COLLEAGUE, MASTER CHARLES ROWLAND.
BUT, EDWIN, YOU MUST EXERCISE EXTREME CAUTION.
IF YOU STEP BEYOND THE FRONT DOOR, YOU WILL SIMPLY FALL SKY-WARDS!
FRET YE NOT.
I SHALL SIMPLY SQWOOSH.
I AM SURE I SHALL BE ABLE TO--
DRAT IT! WHAT'S GONE WRONG WITH GRAVITY?
YOU'RE STUCK--JUST LIKE US.
NEVER FEAR--I SHALL RETURN.

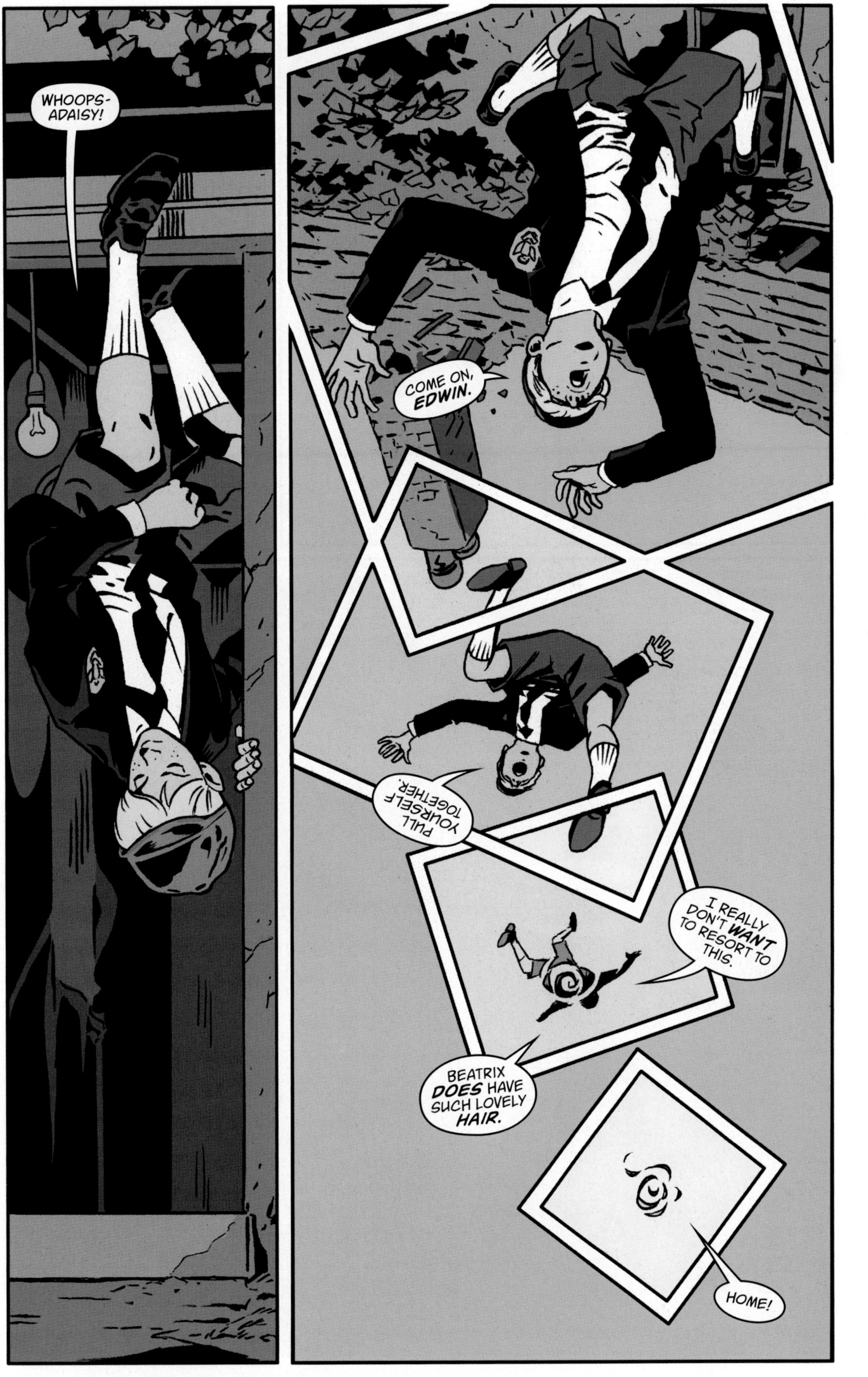
WHOOPS-ADAISY!
COME ON, EDWIN.
PULL YOURSELF TOGETHER.
I REALLY DON'T WANT TO RESORT TO THIS.
BEATRIX DOES HAVE SUCH LOVELY HAIR.
HOME!

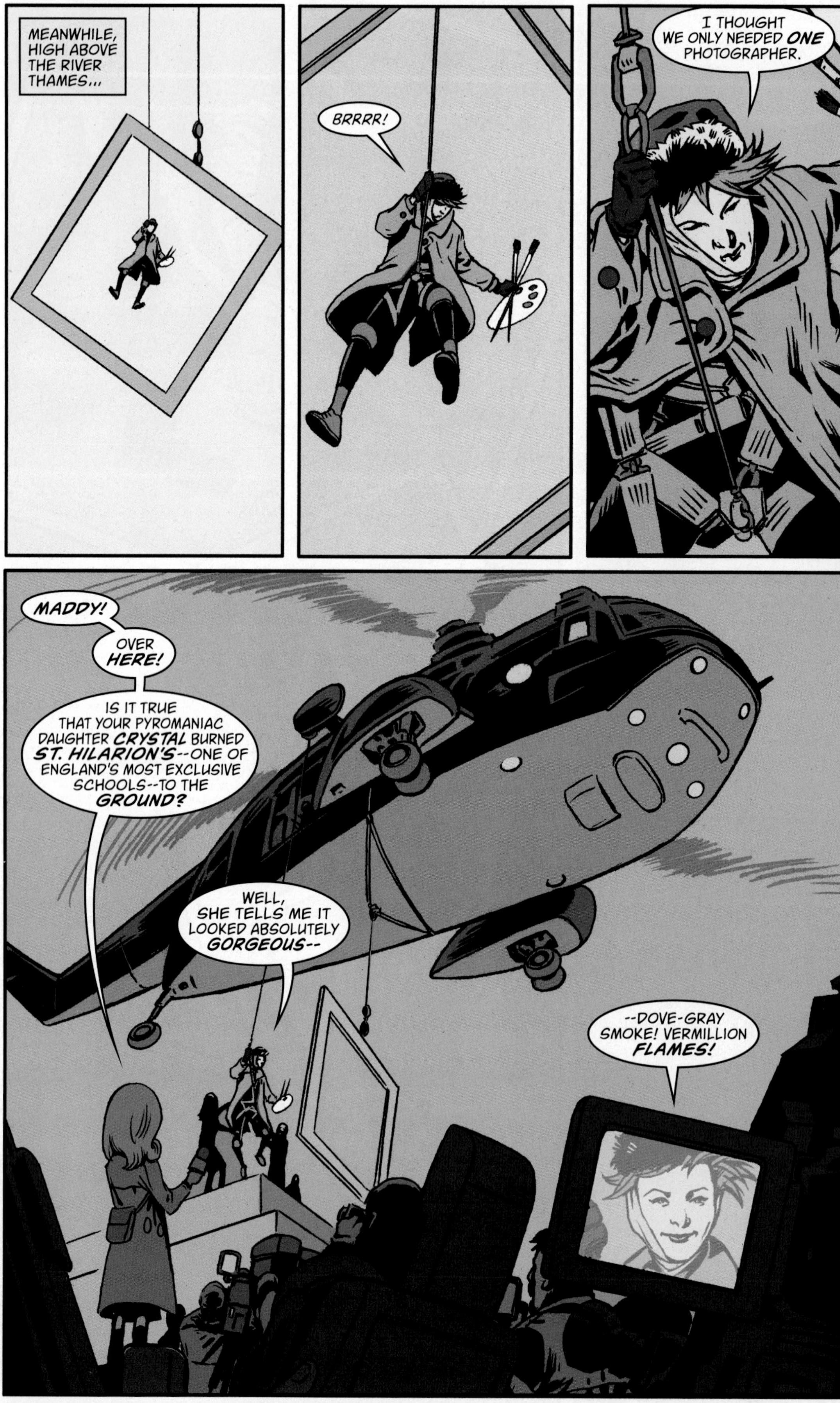
MEANWHILE, HIGH ABOVE THE RIVER THAMES...
BRRRR!
I THOUGHT WE ONLY NEEDED ***ONE*** PHOTOGRAPHER.
MADDY!
OVER ***HERE!***
IS IT TRUE THAT YOUR PYROMANIAC DAUGHTER ***CRYSTAL*** BURNED ***ST. HILARION'S***--ONE OF ENGLAND'S MOST EXCLUSIVE SCHOOLS--TO THE ***GROUND?***
WELL, SHE TELLS ME IT LOOKED ABSOLUTELY ***GORGEOUS--***
--DOVE-GRAY SMOKE! VERMILLION ***FLAMES!***

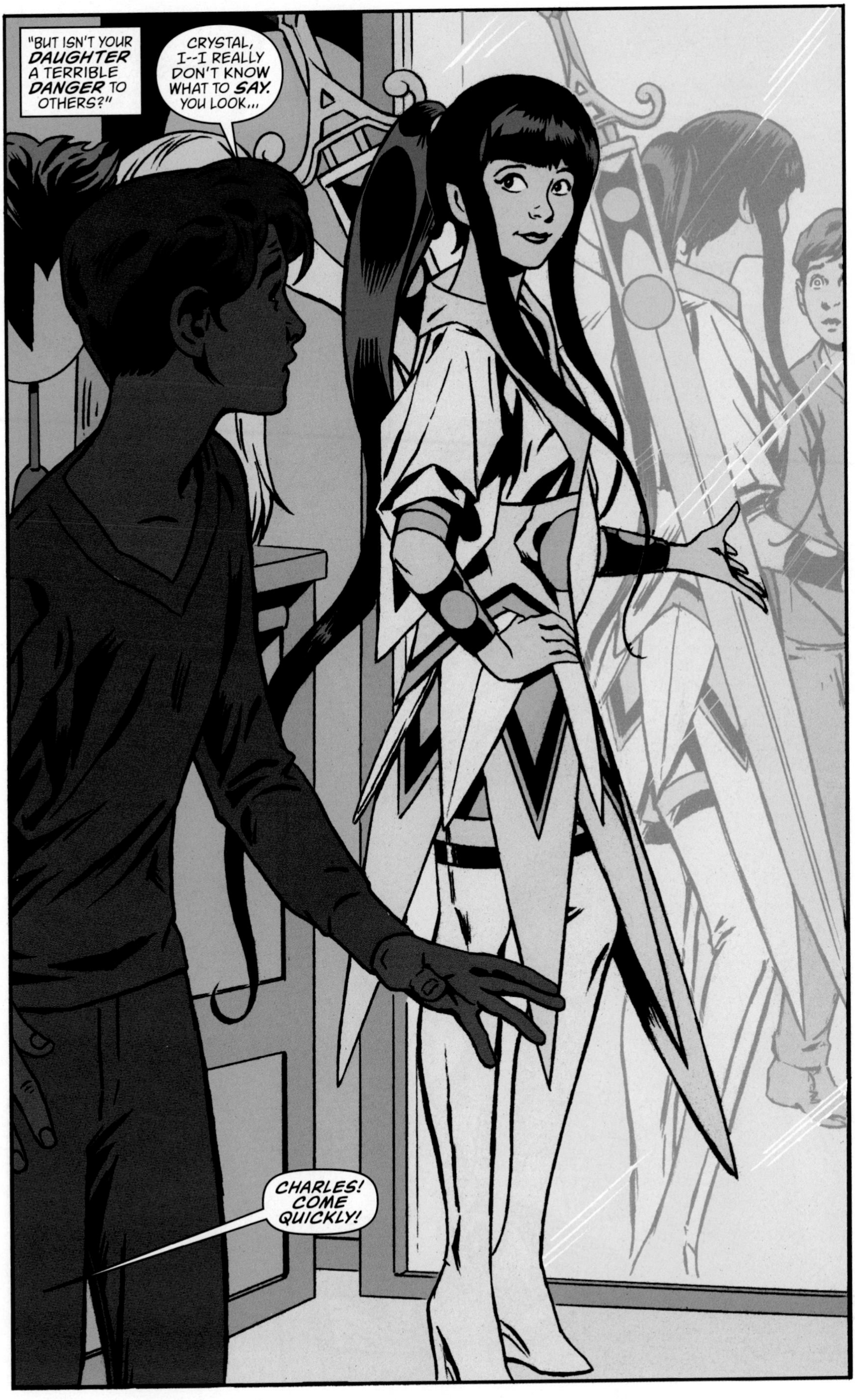
"BUT ISN'T YOUR DAUGHTER A TERRIBLE DANGER TO OTHERS?"
CRYSTAL, I--I REALLY DON'T KNOW WHAT TO SAY. YOU LOOK...
CHARLES! COME QUICKLY!

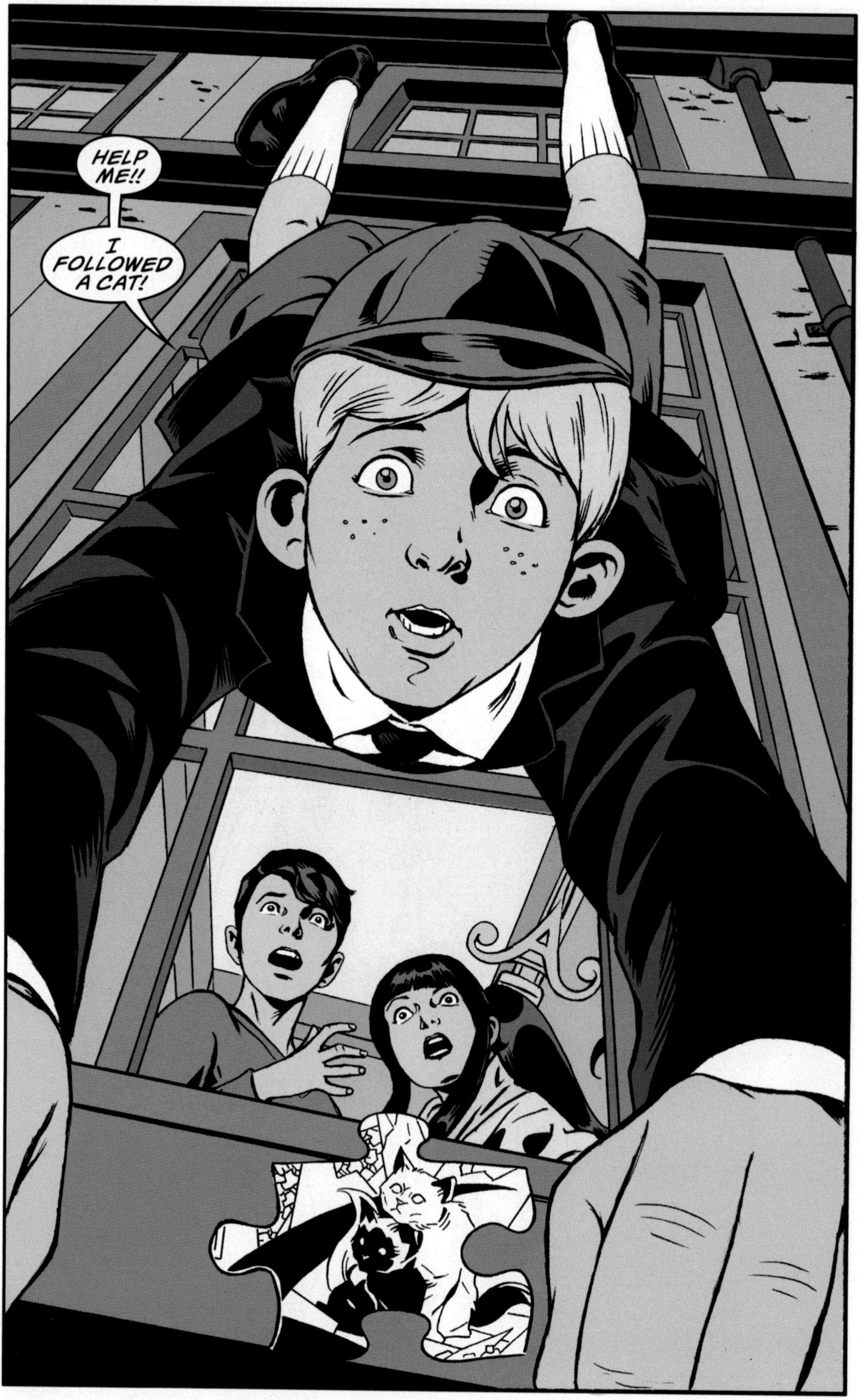
HELP ME!!
I FOLLOWED A CAT!

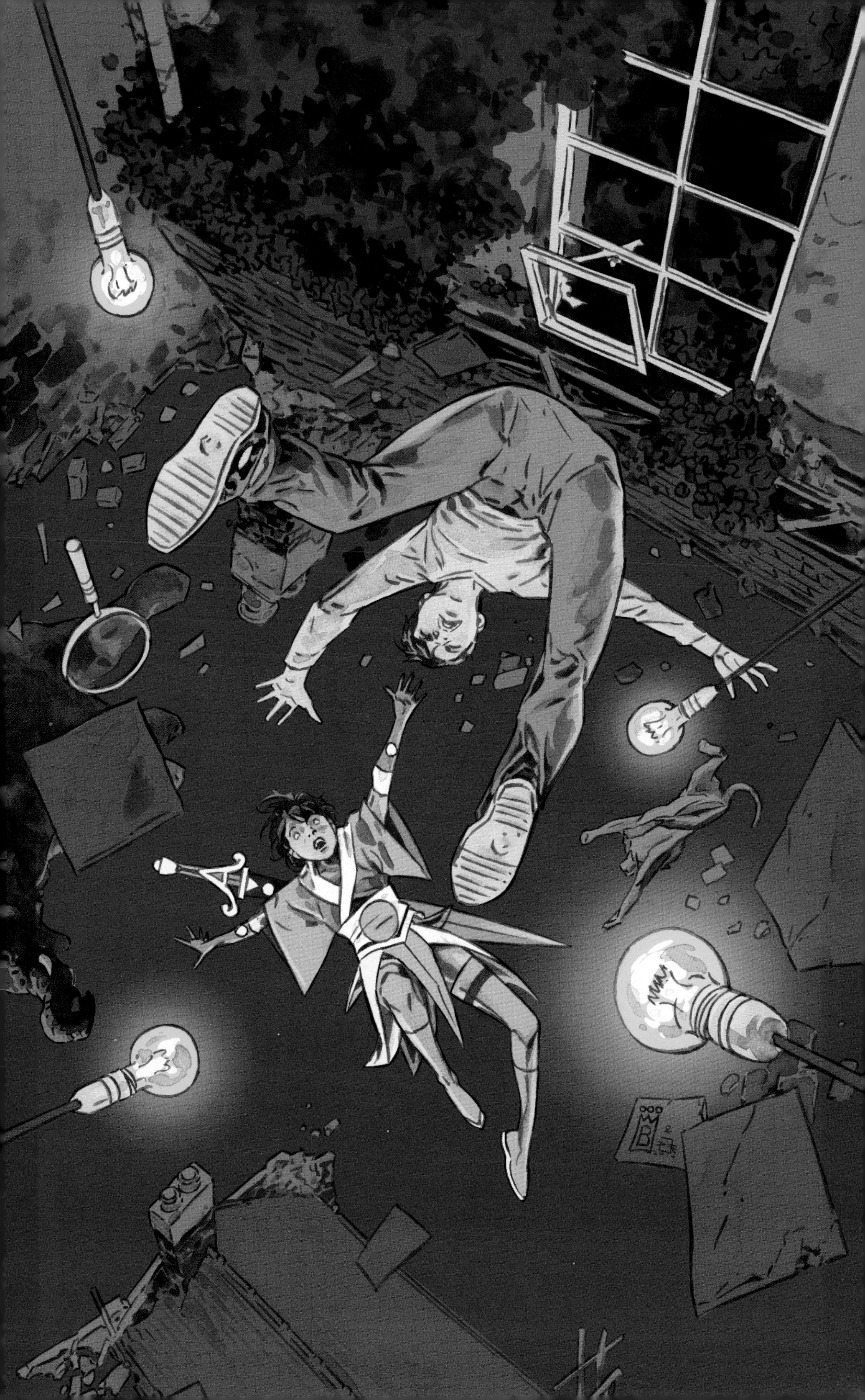

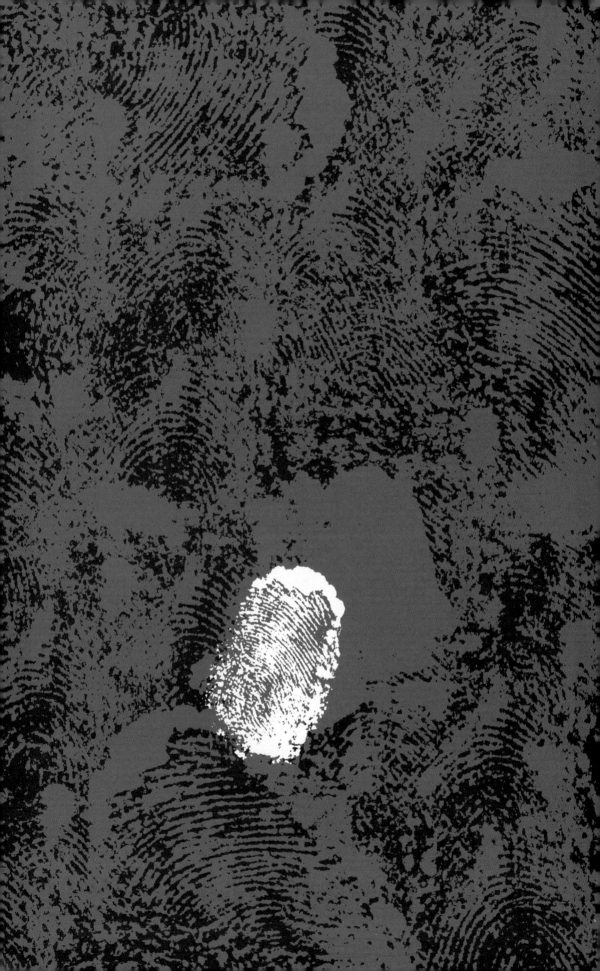

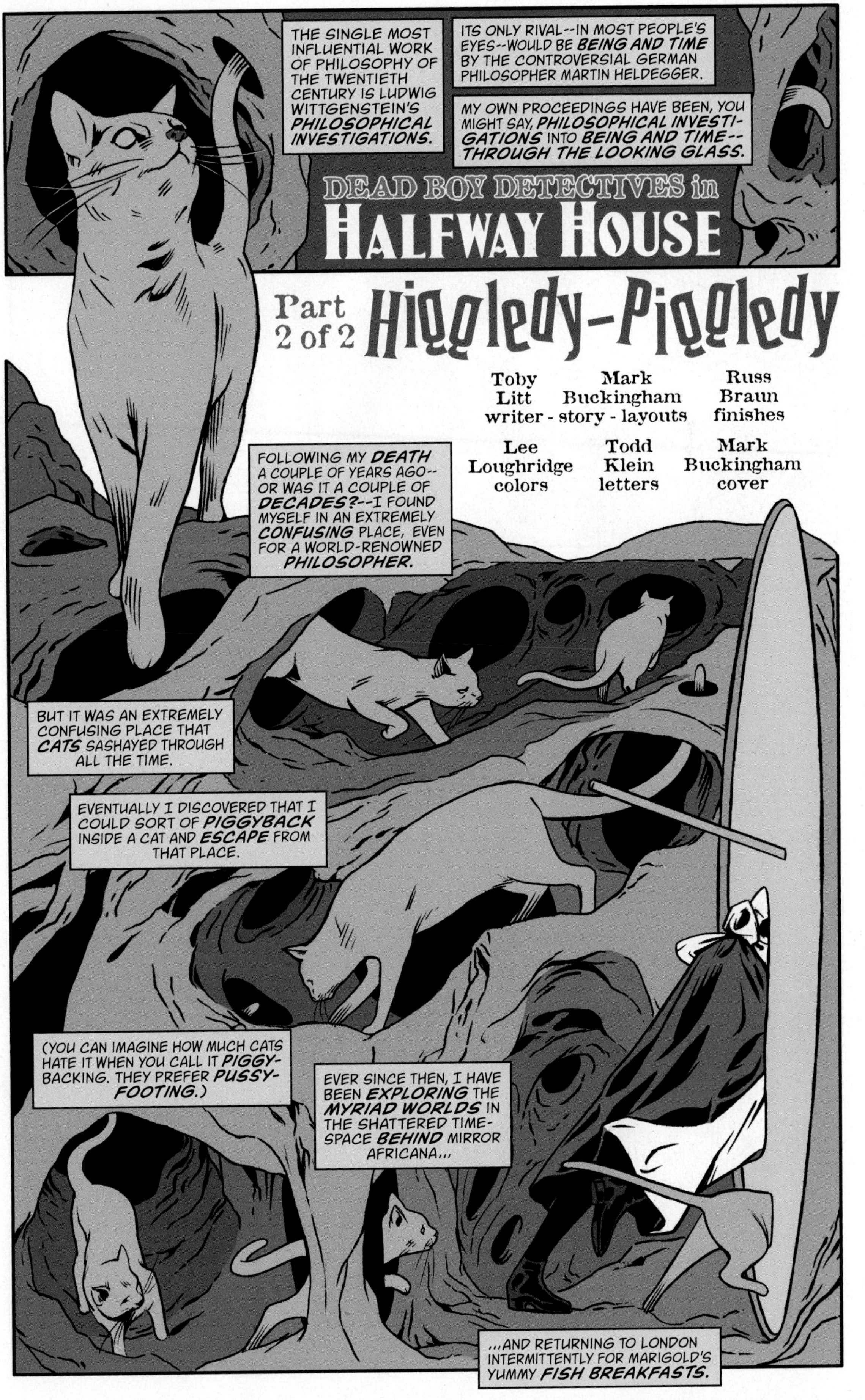
THE SINGLE MOST INFLUENTIAL WORK OF PHILOSOPHY OF THE TWENTIETH CENTURY IS LUDWIG WITTGENSTEIN'S PHILOSOPHICAL INVESTIGATIONS.
ITS ONLY RIVAL--IN MOST PEOPLE'S EYES--WOULD BE BEING AND TIME BY THE CONTROVERSIAL GERMAN PHILOSOPHER MARTIN HELDEGGER.
MY OWN PROCEEDINGS HAVE BEEN, YOU MIGHT SAY, PHILOSOPHICAL INVESTIGATIONS INTO BEING AND TIME--THROUGH THE LOOKING GLASS.
DEAD BOY DETECTIVES in
HALFWAY HOUSE
Part 2 of 2 Higgledy-Piggledy
Toby Litt writer - Mark Buckingham story - layouts
Russ Braun finishes
Lee Loughridge colors
Todd Klein letters
Mark Buckingham cover
FOLLOWING MY DEATH A COUPLE OF YEARS AGO--OR WAS IT A COUPLE OF DECADES?--I FOUND MYSELF IN AN EXTREMELY CONFUSING PLACE, EVEN FOR A WORLD-RENOWNED PHILOSOPHER.
BUT IT WAS AN EXTREMELY CONFUSING PLACE THAT CATS SASHAYED THROUGH ALL THE TIME.
EVENTUALLY I DISCOVERED THAT I COULD SORT OF PIGGYBACK INSIDE A CAT AND ESCAPE FROM THAT PLACE.
(YOU CAN IMAGINE HOW MUCH CATS HATE IT WHEN YOU CALL IT PIGGY-BACKING. THEY PREFER PUSSY-FOOTING.)
EVER SINCE THEN, I HAVE BEEN EXPLORING THE MYRIAD WORLDS IN THE SHATTERED TIME-SPACE BEHIND MIRROR AFRICANA...
...AND RETURNING TO LONDON INTERMITTENTLY FOR MARIGOLD'S YUMMY FISH BREAKFASTS.

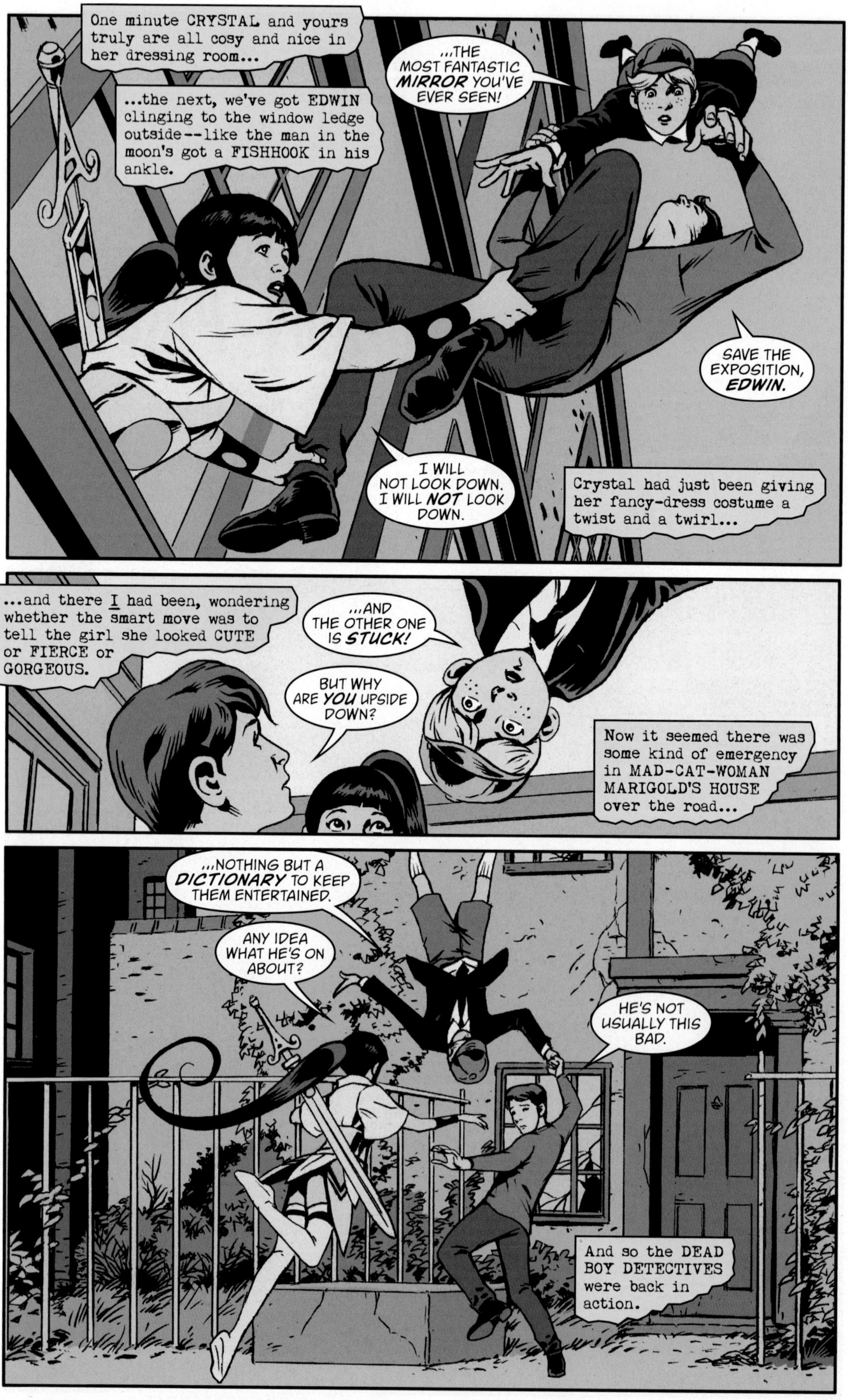

One minute CRYSTAL and yours truly are all cosy and nice in her dressing room...
...the next, we've got EDWIN clinging to the window ledge outside--like the man in the moon's got a FISHHOOK in his ankle.
...THE MOST FANTASTIC MIRROR YOU'VE EVER SEEN!
SAVE THE EXPOSITION, EDWIN.
I WILL NOT LOOK DOWN. I WILL NOT LOOK DOWN.
Crystal had just been giving her fancy-dress costume a twist and a twirl...
...and there I had been, wondering whether the smart move was to tell the girl she looked CUTE or FIERCE or GORGEOUS.
...AND THE OTHER ONE IS STUCK!
BUT WHY ARE YOU UPSIDE DOWN?
Now it seemed there was some kind of emergency in MAD-CAT-WOMAN MARIGOLD'S HOUSE over the road...
...NOTHING BUT A DICTIONARY TO KEEP THEM ENTERTAINED.
ANY IDEA WHAT HE'S ON ABOUT?
HE'S NOT USUALLY THIS BAD.
And so the DEAD BOY DETECTIVES were back in action.

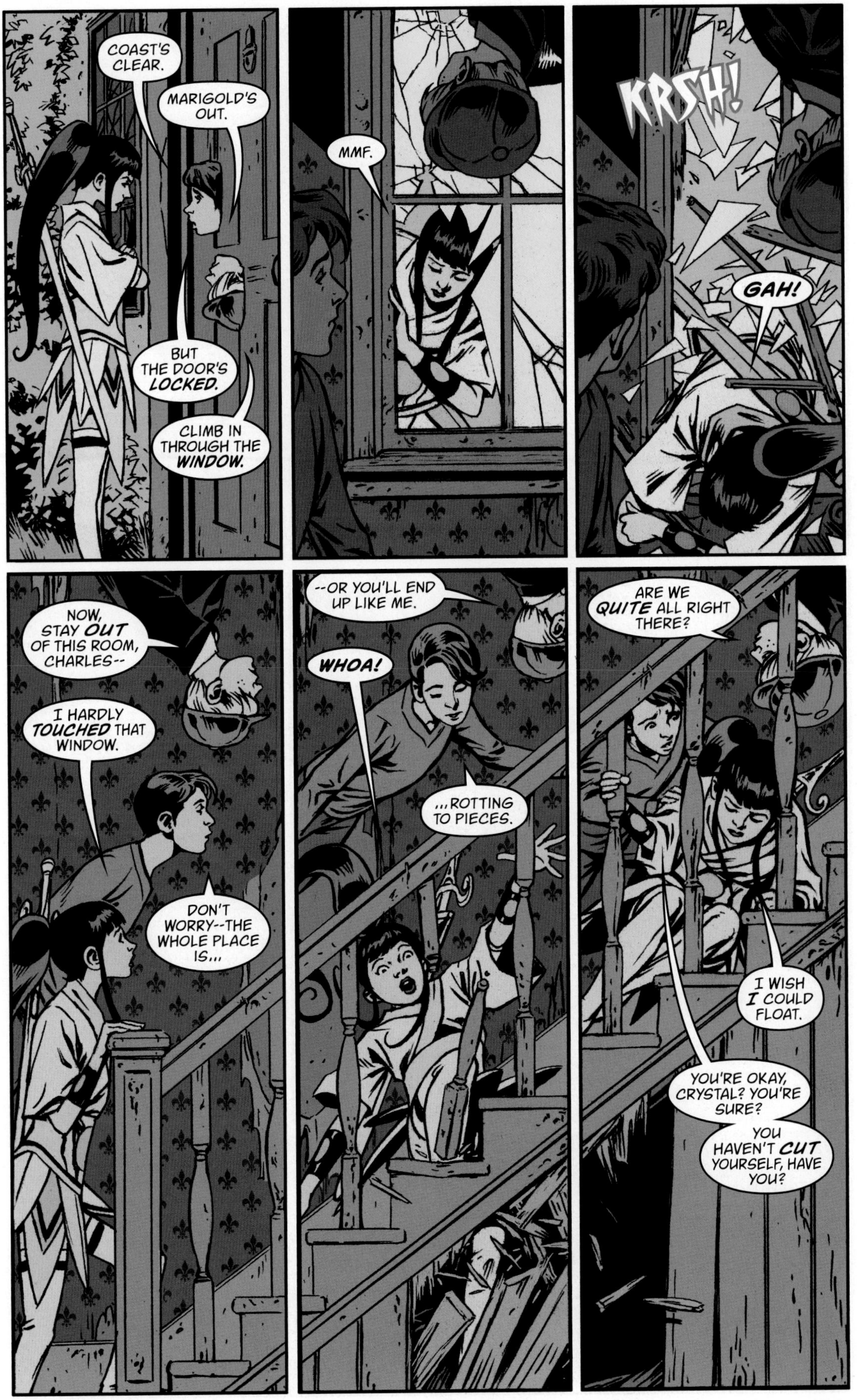
COAST'S CLEAR.
MARIGOLD'S OUT.
BUT THE DOOR'S LOCKED.
CLIMB IN THROUGH THE WINDOW.
MMF.
KRSH!
GAH!
NOW, STAY OUT OF THIS ROOM, CHARLES--
I HARDLY TOUCHED THAT WINDOW.
DON'T WORRY--THE WHOLE PLACE IS...
--OR YOU'LL END UP LIKE ME.
WHOA!
...ROTTING TO PIECES.
ARE WE QUITE ALL RIGHT THERE?
I WISH I COULD FLOAT.
YOU'RE OKAY, CRYSTAL? YOU'RE SURE?
YOU HAVEN'T CUT YOURSELF, HAVE YOU?

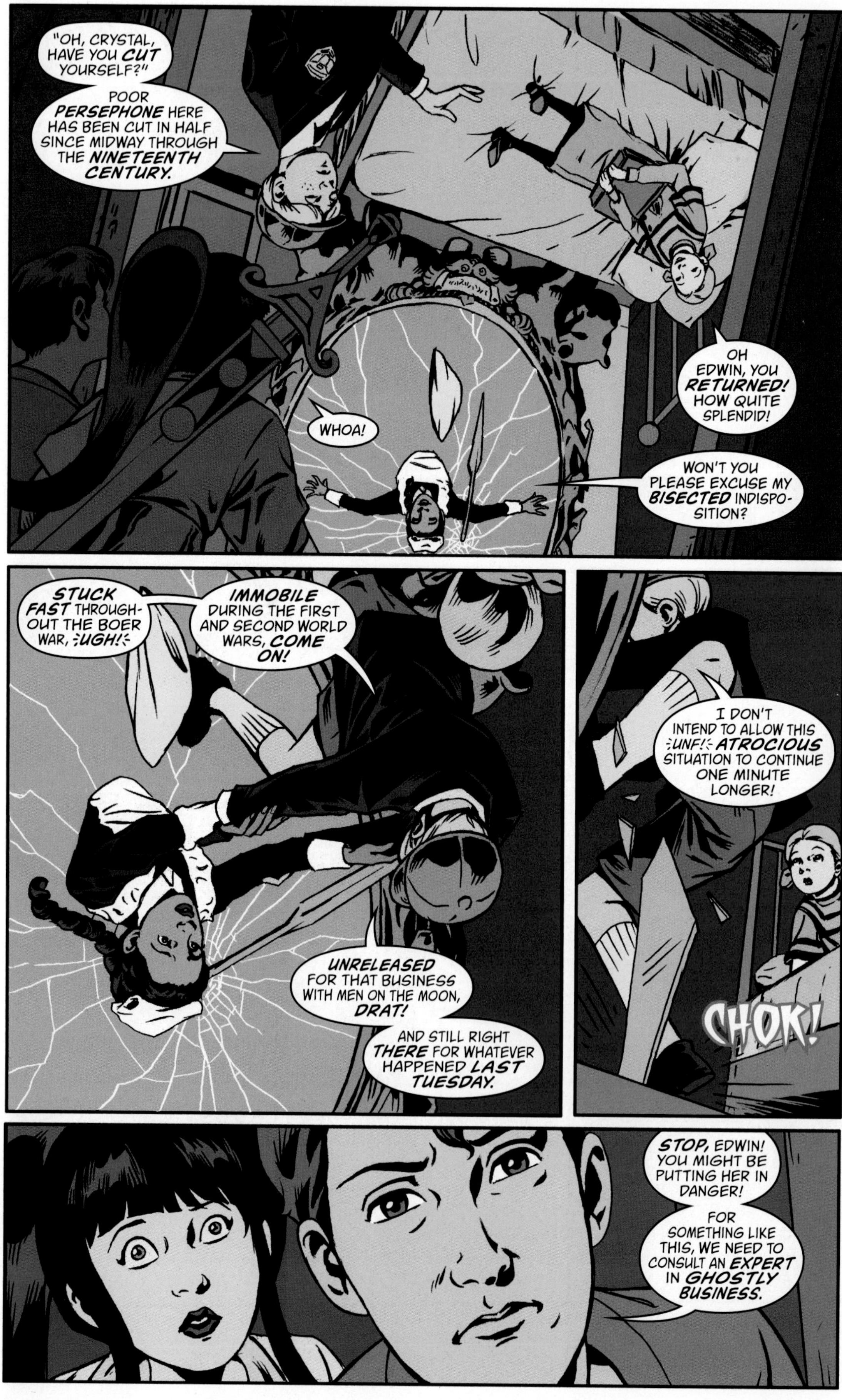
"OH, CRYSTAL, HAVE YOU CUT YOURSELF?"
POOR PERSEPHONE HERE HAS BEEN CUT IN HALF SINCE MIDWAY THROUGH THE NINETEENTH CENTURY.
OH EDWIN, YOU RETURNED! HOW QUITE SPLENDID!
WHOA!
WON'T YOU PLEASE EXCUSE MY BISECTED INDISPO-SITION?
STUCK FAST THROUGH-OUT THE BOER WAR, UGH!
IMMOBILE DURING THE FIRST AND SECOND WORLD WARS, COME ON!
UNRELEASED FOR THAT BUSINESS WITH MEN ON THE MOON, DRAT!
AND STILL RIGHT THERE FOR WHATEVER HAPPENED LAST TUESDAY.
I DON'T INTEND TO ALLOW THIS UNF! ATROCIOUS SITUATION TO CONTINUE ONE MINUTE LONGER!
CHOK!
STOP, EDWIN! YOU MIGHT BE PUTTING HER IN DANGER!
FOR SOMETHING LIKE THIS, WE NEED TO CONSULT AN EXPERT IN GHOSTLY BUSINESS.

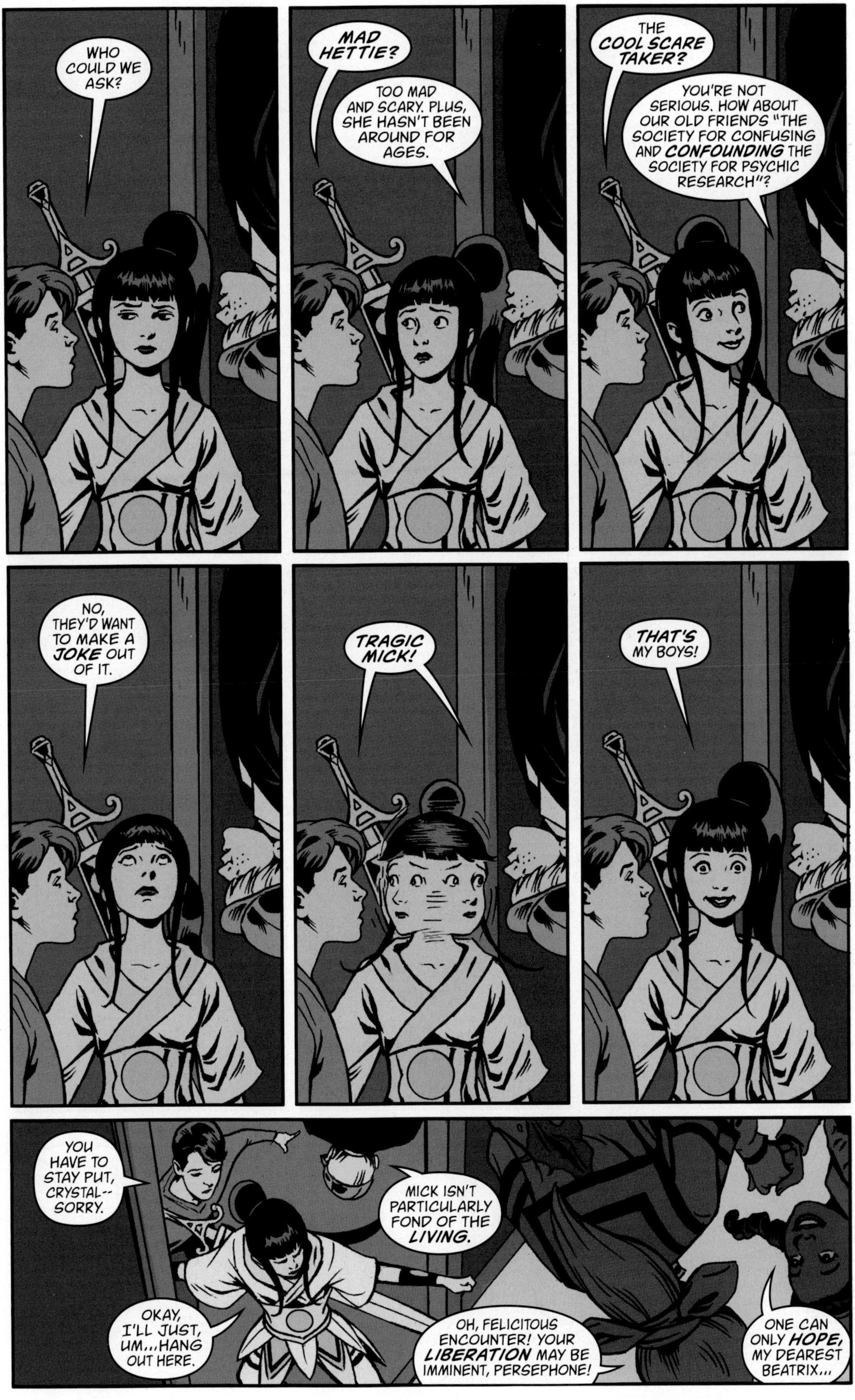
WHO COULD WE ASK?
MAD HETTIE?
TOO MAD AND SCARY. PLUS, SHE HASN'T BEEN AROUND FOR AGES.
THE COOL SCARE TAKER?
YOU'RE NOT SERIOUS. HOW ABOUT OUR OLD FRIENDS "THE SOCIETY FOR CONFUSING AND CONFOUNDING THE SOCIETY FOR PSYCHIC RESEARCH"?
NO, THEY'D WANT TO MAKE A JOKE OUT OF IT.
TRAGIC MICK!
THAT'S MY BOYS!
YOU HAVE TO STAY PUT, CRYSTAL-- SORRY.
MICK ISN'T PARTICULARLY FOND OF THE LIVING.
OKAY, I'LL JUST, UM...HANG OUT HERE.
OH, FELICITOUS ENCOUNTER! YOUR LIBERATION MAY BE IMMINENT, PERSEPHONE!
ONE CAN ONLY HOPE, MY DEAREST BEATRIX...

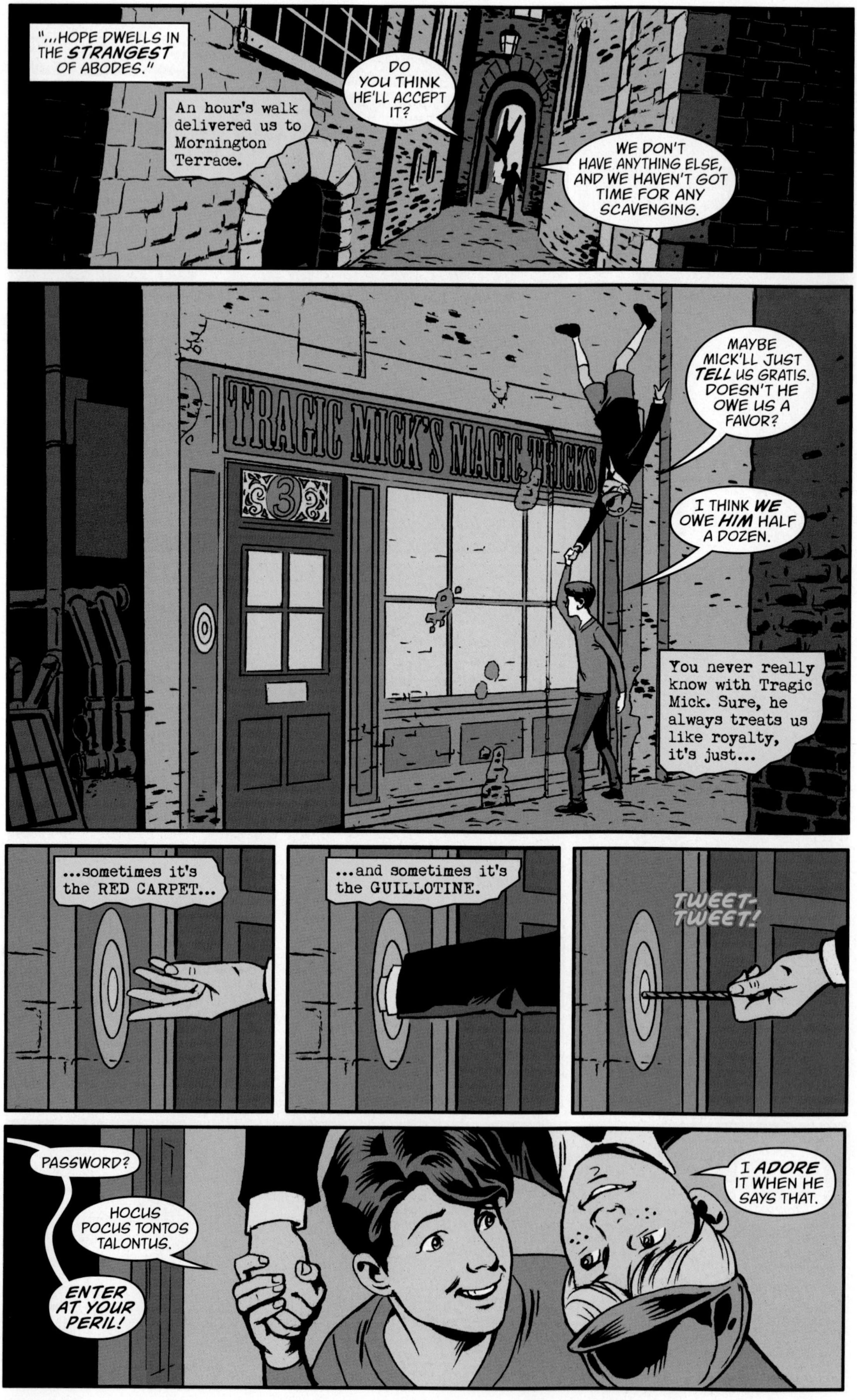
"...HOPE DWELLS IN THE STRANGEST OF ABODES."
An hour's walk delivered us to Mornington Terrace.
DO YOU THINK HE'LL ACCEPT IT?
WE DON'T HAVE ANYTHING ELSE, AND WE HAVEN'T GOT TIME FOR ANY SCAVENGING.
TRAGIC MICK'S MAGIC TRICKS
3
MAYBE MICK'LL JUST TELL US GRATIS. DOESN'T HE OWE US A FAVOR?
I THINK WE OWE HIM HALF A DOZEN.
You never really know with Tragic Mick. Sure, he always treats us like royalty, it's just...
...sometimes it's the RED CARPET...
...and sometimes it's the GUILLOTINE.
TWEET-TWEET!
PASSWORD?
HOCUS POCUS TONTOS TALONTUS.
ENTER AT YOUR PERIL!
I ADORE IT WHEN HE SAYS THAT.

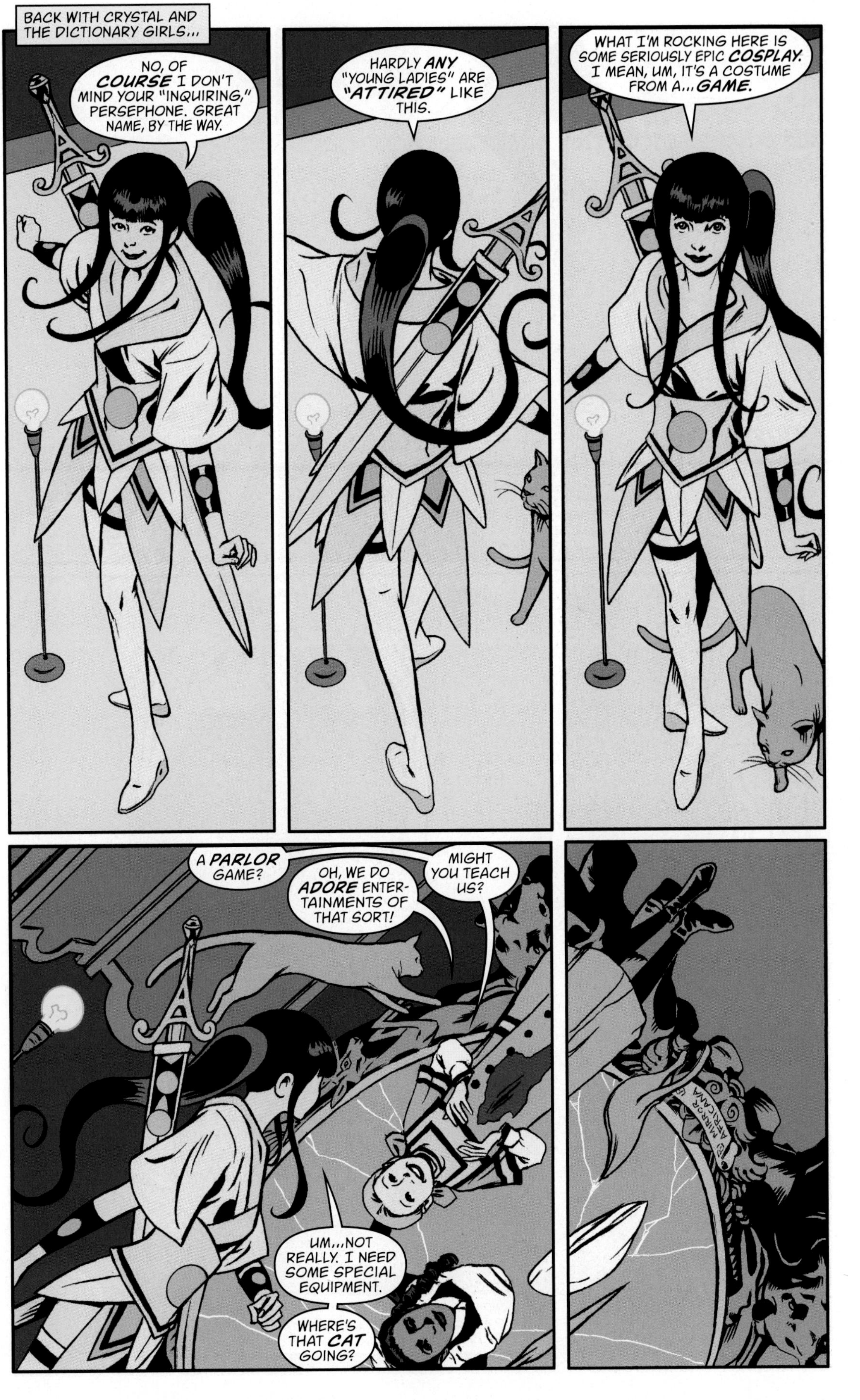
BACK WITH CRYSTAL AND THE DICTIONARY GIRLS...
NO, OF COURSE I DON'T MIND YOUR "INQUIRING," PERSEPHONE. GREAT NAME, BY THE WAY.
HARDLY ANY "YOUNG LADIES" ARE "ATTIRED" LIKE THIS.
WHAT I'M ROCKING HERE IS SOME SERIOUSLY EPIC COSPLAY. I MEAN, UM, IT'S A COSTUME FROM A... GAME.
A PARLOR GAME?
OH, WE DO ADORE ENTERTAINMENTS OF THAT SORT!
MIGHT YOU TEACH US?
UM... NOT REALLY. I NEED SOME SPECIAL EQUIPMENT.
WHERE'S THAT CAT GOING?

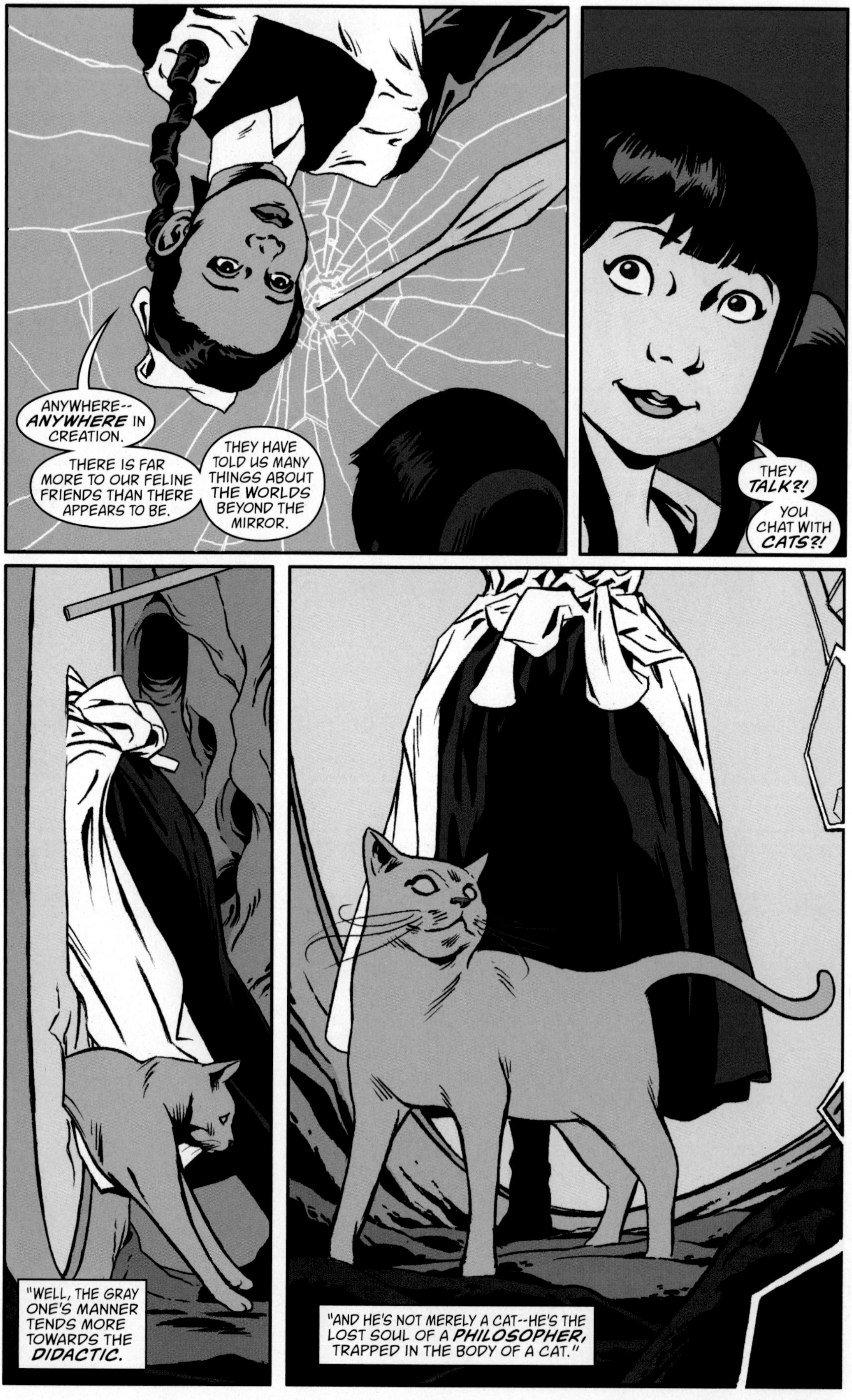

ANYWHERE-- ANYWHERE IN CREATION.
THERE IS FAR MORE TO OUR FELINE FRIENDS THAN THERE APPEARS TO BE.
THEY HAVE TOLD US MANY THINGS ABOUT THE WORLDS BEYOND THE MIRROR.
THEY TALK?!
YOU CHAT WITH CATS?!
"WELL, THE GRAY ONE'S MANNER TENDS MORE TOWARDS THE DIDACTIC.
"AND HE'S NOT MERELY A CAT--HE'S THE LOST SOUL OF A PHILOSOPHER, TRAPPED IN THE BODY OF A CAT."

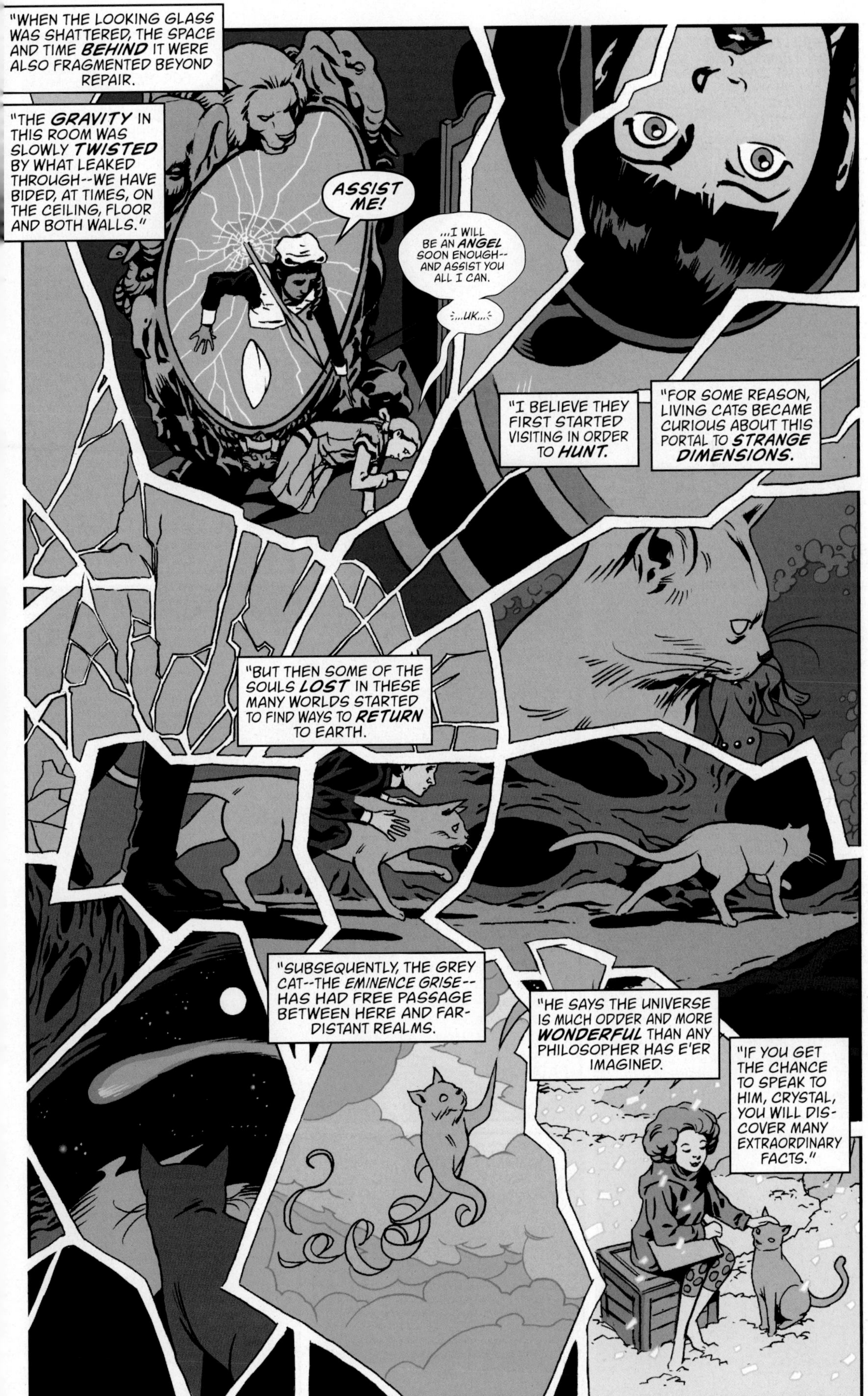
"WHEN THE LOOKING GLASS WAS SHATTERED, THE SPACE AND TIME BEHIND IT WERE ALSO FRAGMENTED BEYOND REPAIR.
"THE GRAVITY IN THIS ROOM WAS SLOWLY TWISTED BY WHAT LEAKED THROUGH--WE HAVE BIDED, AT TIMES, ON THE CEILING, FLOOR AND BOTH WALLS."
ASSIST ME!
...I WILL BE AN ANGEL SOON ENOUGH--AND ASSIST YOU ALL I CAN.
...UK...
"FOR SOME REASON, LIVING CATS BECAME CURIOUS ABOUT THIS PORTAL TO STRANGE DIMENSIONS.
"I BELIEVE THEY FIRST STARTED VISITING IN ORDER TO HUNT.
"BUT THEN SOME OF THE SOULS LOST IN THESE MANY WORLDS STARTED TO FIND WAYS TO RETURN TO EARTH.
"SUBSEQUENTLY, THE GREY CAT--THE EMINENCE GRISE--HAS HAD FREE PASSAGE BETWEEN HERE AND FAR-DISTANT REALMS.
"HE SAYS THE UNIVERSE IS MUCH ODDER AND MORE WONDERFUL THAN ANY PHILOSOPHER HAS E'ER IMAGINED.
"IF YOU GET THE CHANCE TO SPEAK TO HIM, CRYSTAL, YOU WILL DISCOVER MANY EXTRAORDINARY FACTS."

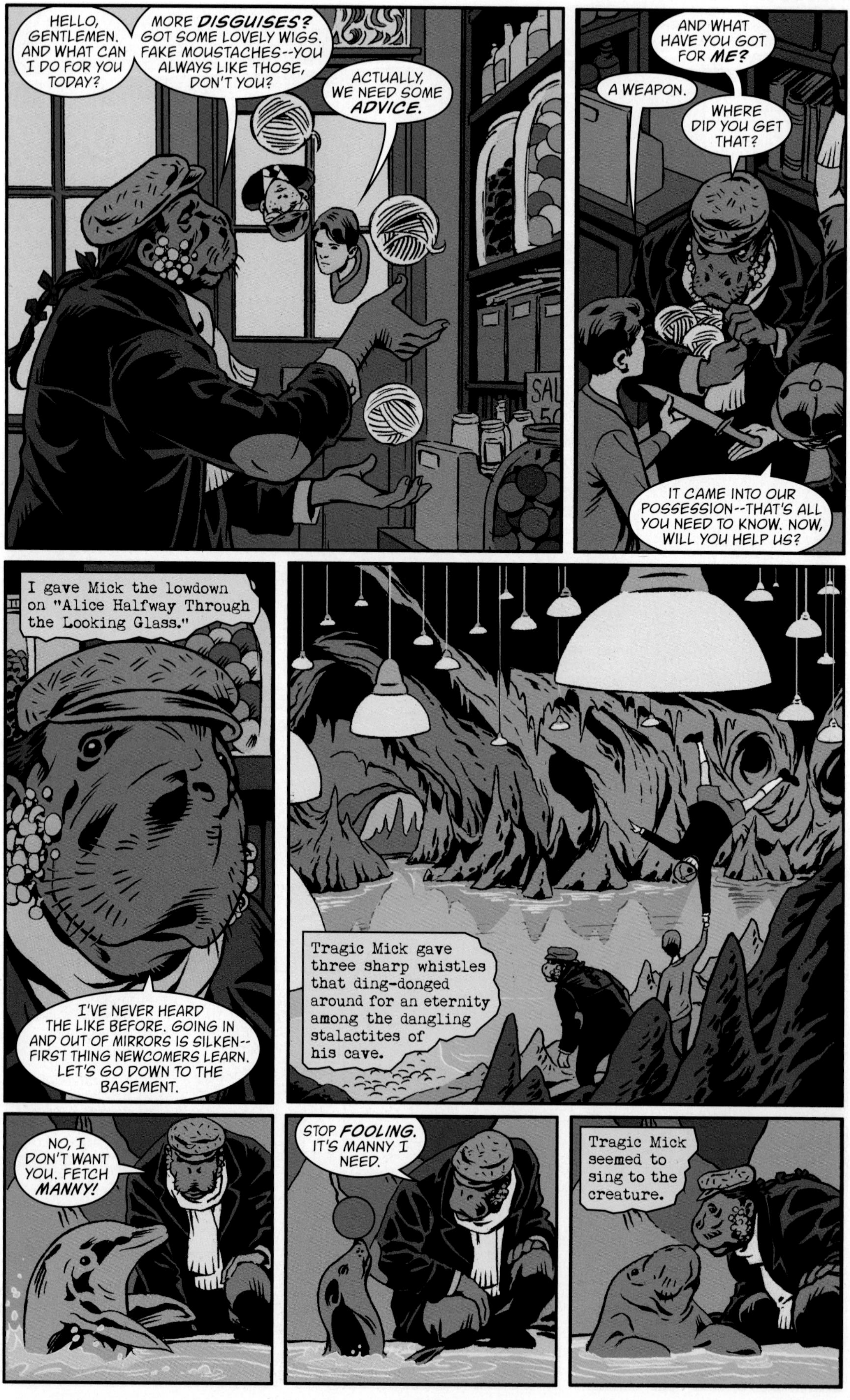
HELLO, GENTLEMEN. AND WHAT CAN I DO FOR YOU TODAY?
MORE *DISGUISES?* GOT SOME LOVELY WIGS. FAKE MOUSTACHES--YOU ALWAYS LIKE THOSE, DON'T YOU?
ACTUALLY, WE NEED SOME *ADVICE.*
AND WHAT HAVE YOU GOT FOR *ME?*
A WEAPON.
WHERE DID YOU GET THAT?
IT CAME INTO OUR POSSESSION--THAT'S ALL YOU NEED TO KNOW. NOW, WILL YOU HELP US?
I gave Mick the lowdown on "Alice Halfway Through the Looking Glass."
I'VE NEVER HEARD THE LIKE BEFORE. GOING IN AND OUT OF MIRRORS IS SILKEN--FIRST THING NEWCOMERS LEARN. LET'S GO DOWN TO THE BASEMENT.
Tragic Mick gave three sharp whistles that ding-donged around for an eternity among the dangling stalactites of his cave.
NO, I DON'T WANT YOU. FETCH *MANNY!*
STOP *FOOLING.* IT'S MANNY I NEED.
Tragic Mick seemed to sing to the creature.

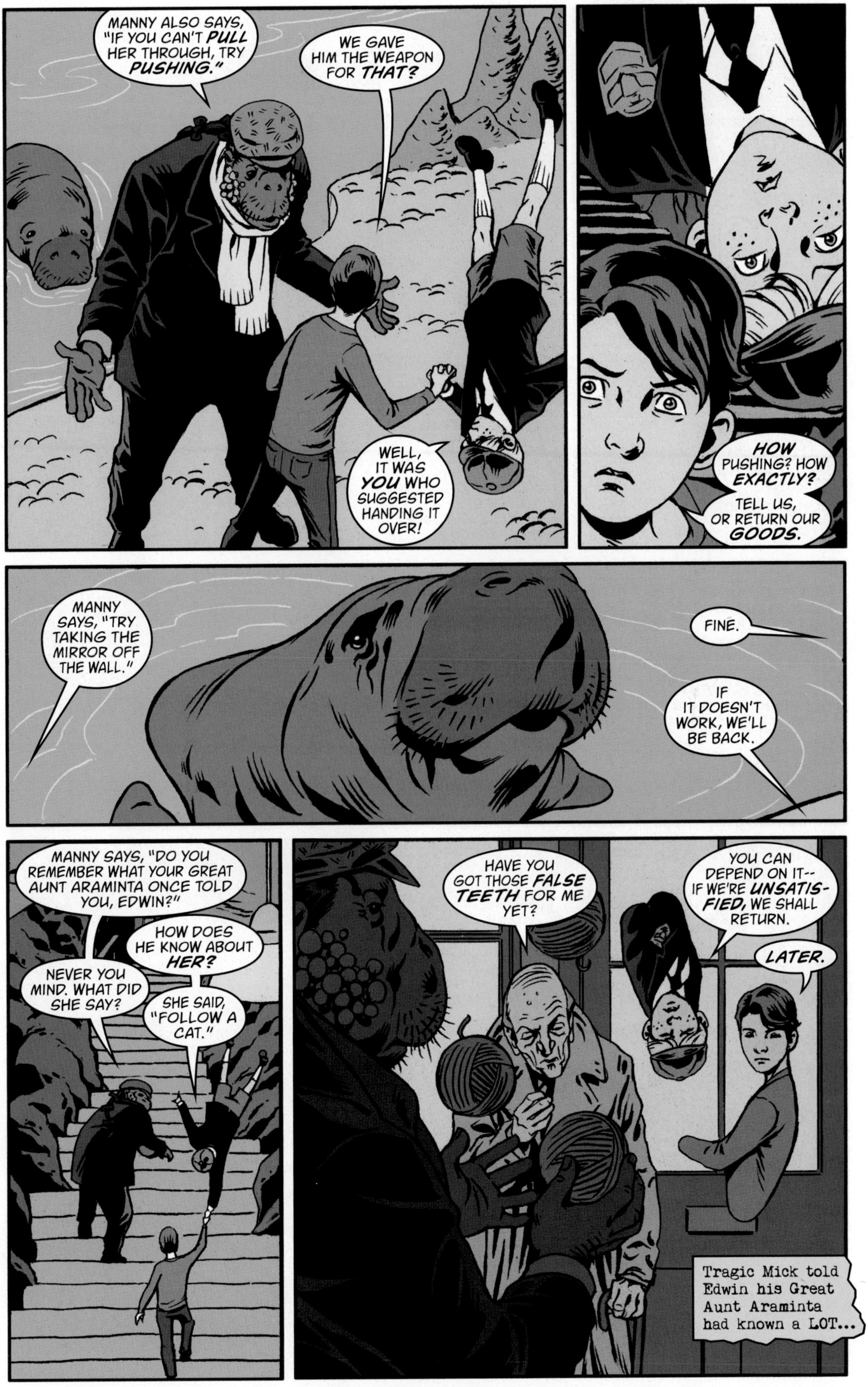
MANNY ALSO SAYS, "IF YOU CAN'T PULL HER THROUGH, TRY PUSHING."
WE GAVE HIM THE WEAPON FOR THAT?
WELL, IT WAS YOU WHO SUGGESTED HANDING IT OVER!
HOW PUSHING? HOW EXACTLY?
TELL US, OR RETURN OUR GOODS.
MANNY SAYS, "TRY TAKING THE MIRROR OFF THE WALL."
FINE.
IF IT DOESN'T WORK, WE'LL BE BACK.
MANNY SAYS, "DO YOU REMEMBER WHAT YOUR GREAT AUNT ARAMINTA ONCE TOLD YOU, EDWIN?"
HOW DOES HE KNOW ABOUT HER?
NEVER YOU MIND. WHAT DID SHE SAY?
SHE SAID, "FOLLOW A CAT."
HAVE YOU GOT THOSE FALSE TEETH FOR ME YET?
YOU CAN DEPEND ON IT-- IF WE'RE UNSATIS-FIED, WE SHALL RETURN.
LATER.
Tragic Mick told Edwin his Great Aunt Araminta had known a LOT...

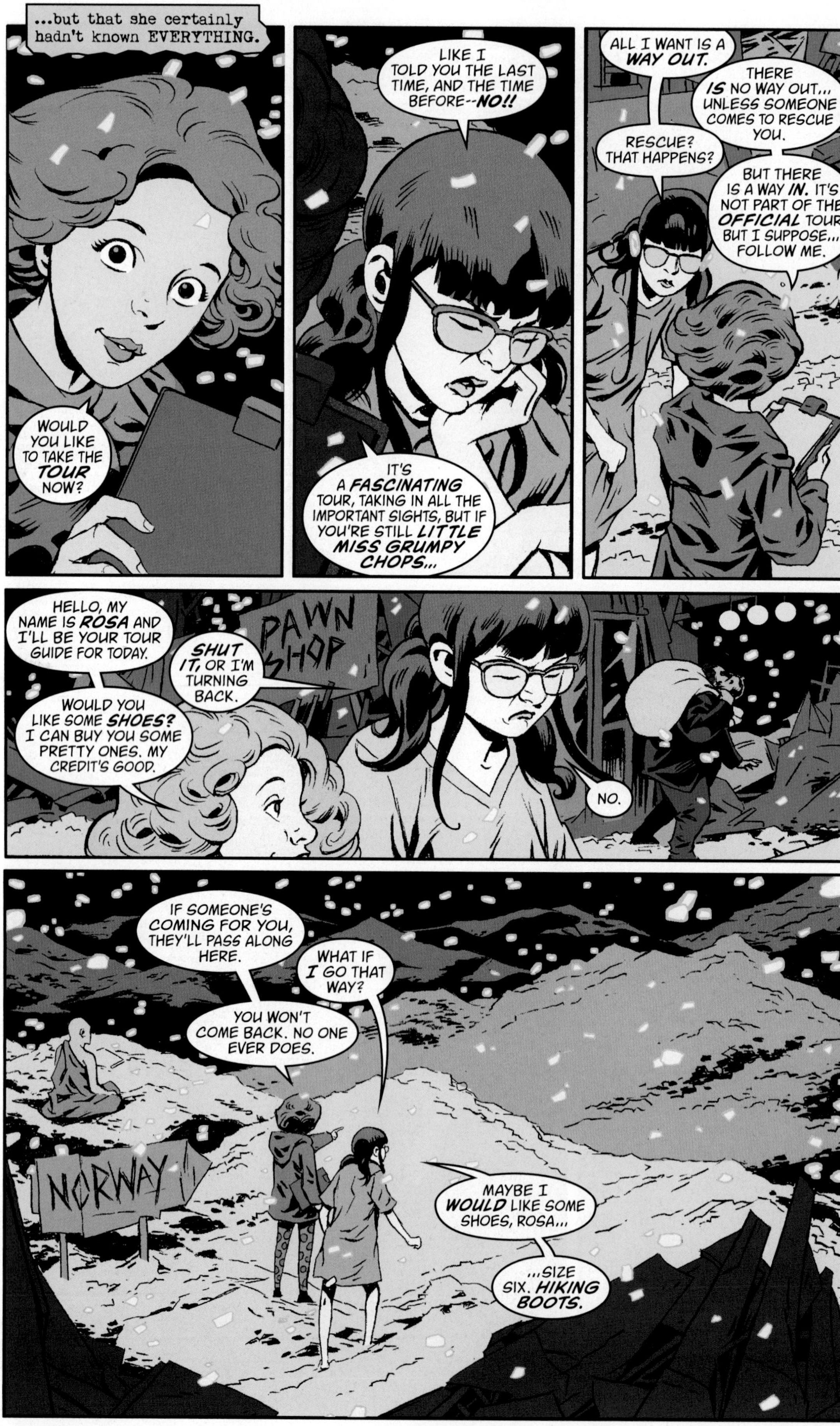
...but that she certainly hadn't known EVERYTHING.
WOULD YOU LIKE TO TAKE THE TOUR NOW?
LIKE I TOLD YOU THE LAST TIME, AND THE TIME BEFORE--NO!!
IT'S A FASCINATING TOUR, TAKING IN ALL THE IMPORTANT SIGHTS, BUT IF YOU'RE STILL LITTLE MISS GRUMPY CHOPS...
ALL I WANT IS A WAY OUT.
THERE IS NO WAY OUT... UNLESS SOMEONE COMES TO RESCUE YOU.
RESCUE? THAT HAPPENS?
BUT THERE IS A WAY IN. IT'S NOT PART OF THE OFFICIAL TOUR, BUT I SUPPOSE... FOLLOW ME.
PAWN SHOP
HELLO, MY NAME IS ROSA AND I'LL BE YOUR TOUR GUIDE FOR TODAY.
SHUT IT, OR I'M TURNING BACK.
WOULD YOU LIKE SOME SHOES? I CAN BUY YOU SOME PRETTY ONES. MY CREDIT'S GOOD.
NO.
IF SOMEONE'S COMING FOR YOU, THEY'LL PASS ALONG HERE.
WHAT IF I GO THAT WAY?
YOU WON'T COME BACK. NO ONE EVER DOES.
NORWAY
MAYBE I WOULD LIKE SOME SHOES, ROSA...
...SIZE SIX. HIKING BOOTS.

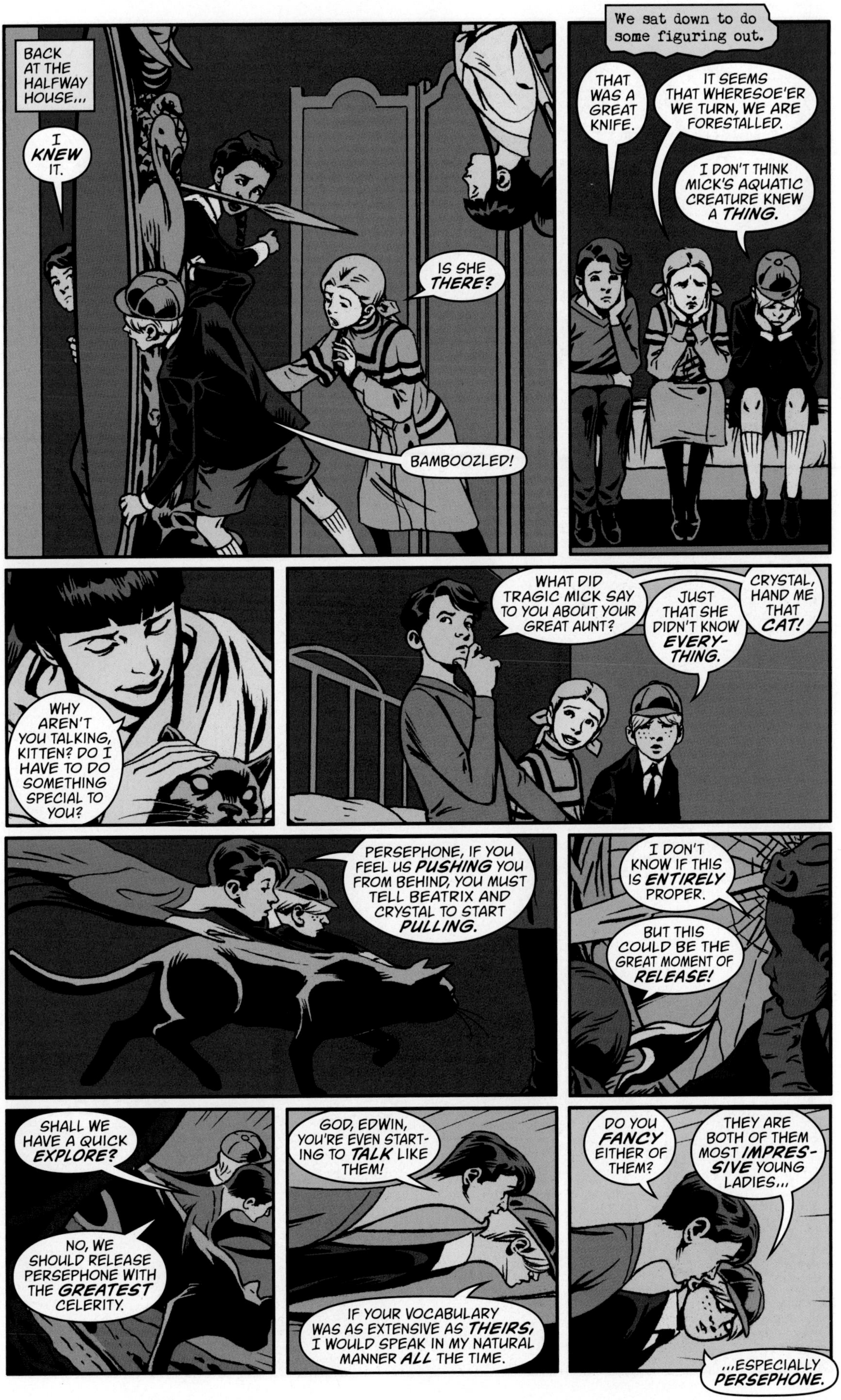

BACK AT THE HALFWAY HOUSE...
I KNEW IT.
IS SHE THERE?
BAMBOOZLED!
We sat down to do some figuring out.
THAT WAS A GREAT KNIFE.
IT SEEMS THAT WHERESOE'ER WE TURN, WE ARE FORESTALLED.
I DON'T THINK MICK'S AQUATIC CREATURE KNEW A THING.
WHY AREN'T YOU TALKING, KITTEN? DO I HAVE TO DO SOMETHING SPECIAL TO YOU?
WHAT DID TRAGIC MICK SAY TO YOU ABOUT YOUR GREAT AUNT?
JUST THAT SHE DIDN'T KNOW EVERY-THING.
CRYSTAL, HAND ME THAT CAT!
PERSEPHONE, IF YOU FEEL US PUSHING YOU FROM BEHIND, YOU MUST TELL BEATRIX AND CRYSTAL TO START PULLING.
I DON'T KNOW IF THIS IS ENTIRELY PROPER.
BUT THIS COULD BE THE GREAT MOMENT OF RELEASE!
SHALL WE HAVE A QUICK EXPLORE?
NO, WE SHOULD RELEASE PERSEPHONE WITH THE GREATEST CELERITY.
GOD, EDWIN, YOU'RE EVEN START-ING TO TALK LIKE THEM!
IF YOUR VOCABULARY WAS AS EXTENSIVE AS THEIRS, I WOULD SPEAK IN MY NATURAL MANNER ALL THE TIME.
DO YOU FANCY EITHER OF THEM?
THEY ARE BOTH OF THEM MOST IMPRES-SIVE YOUNG LADIES...
...ESPECIALLY PERSEPHONE.

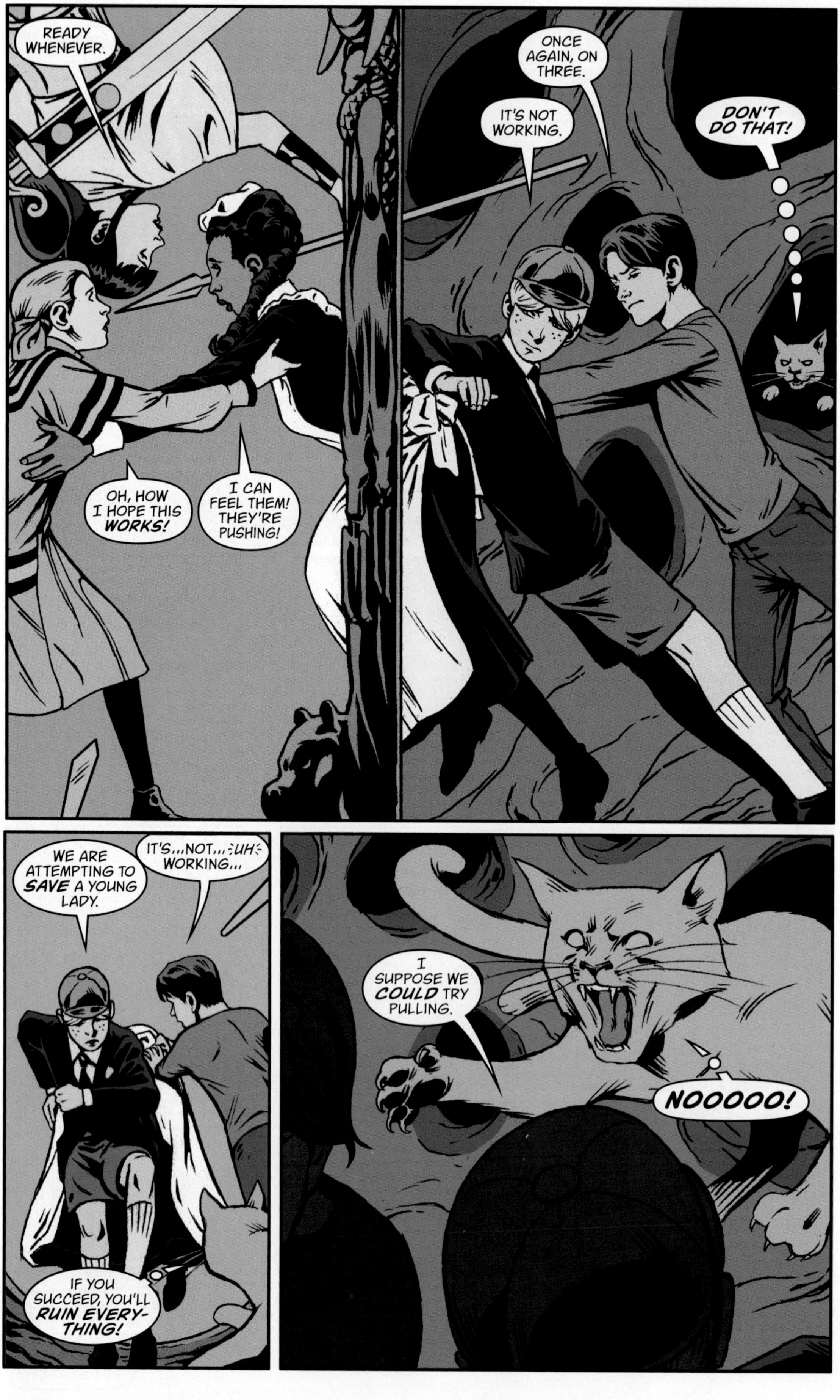
READY WHENEVER.
OH, HOW I HOPE THIS WORKS!
I CAN FEEL THEM! THEY'RE PUSHING!
ONCE AGAIN, ON THREE.
IT'S NOT WORKING.
DON'T DO THAT!
WE ARE ATTEMPTING TO SAVE A YOUNG LADY.
IT'S...NOT... UH WORKING...
IF YOU SUCCEED, YOU'LL RUIN EVERY-THING!
I SUPPOSE WE COULD TRY PULLING.
NOOOOO!

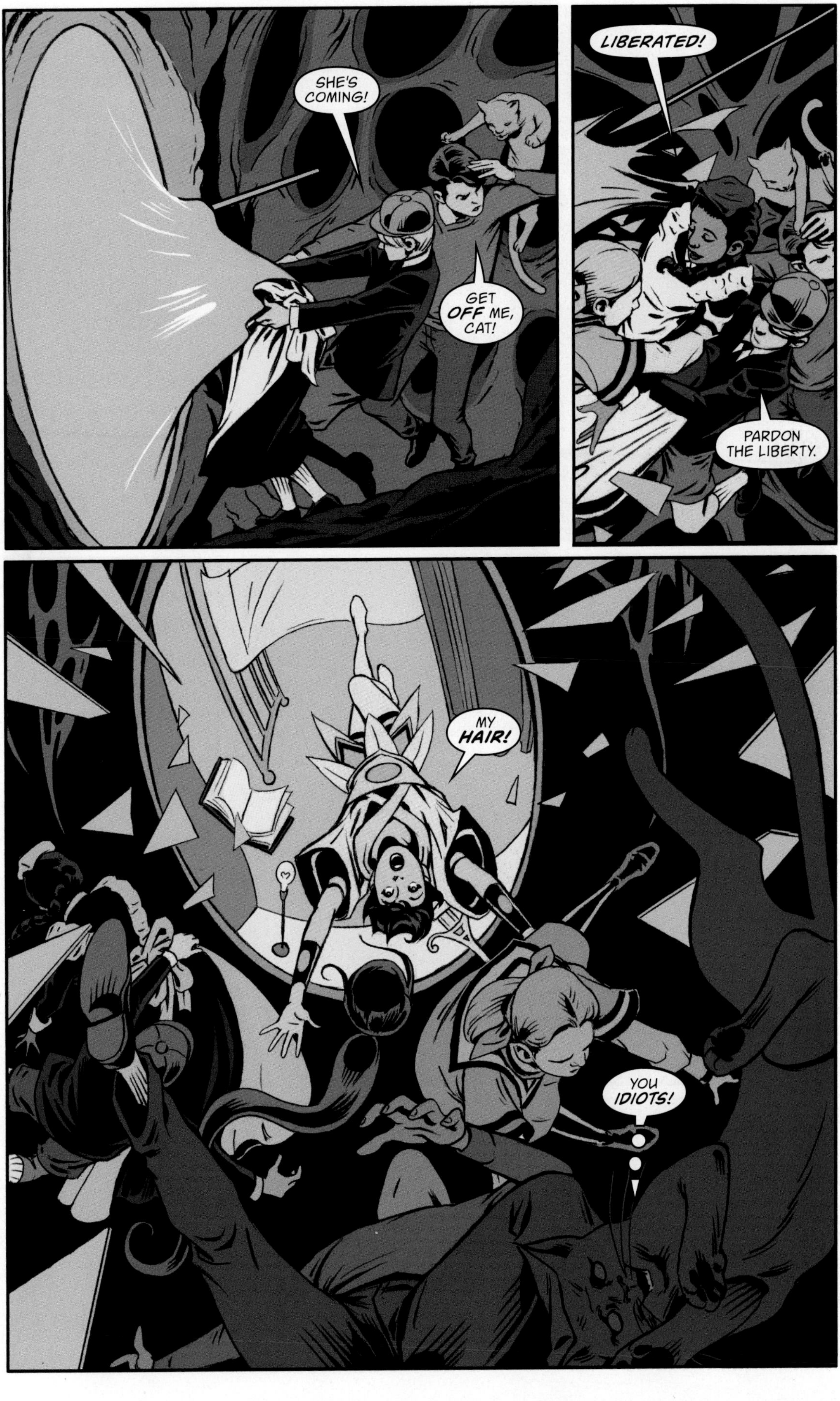
SHE'S COMING!
GET OFF ME, CAT!
LIBERATED!
PARDON THE LIBERTY.
MY HAIR!
YOU IDIOTS!

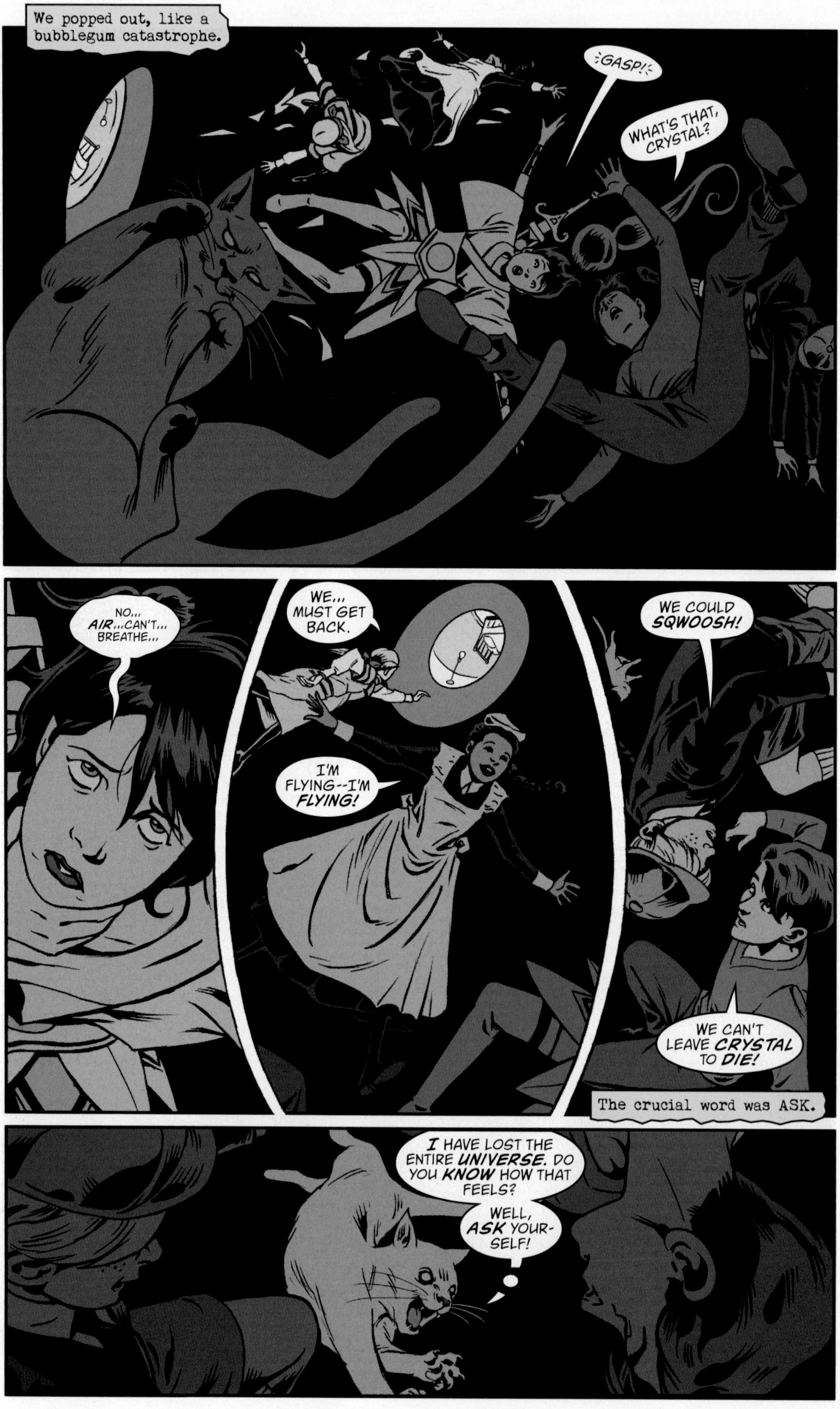
We popped out, like a bubblegum catastrophe.
GASP!
WHAT'S THAT, CRYSTAL?
NO... AIR...CAN'T... BREATHE...
WE... MUST GET BACK.
I'M FLYING--I'M FLYING!
WE COULD SQWOOSH!
WE CAN'T LEAVE CRYSTAL TO DIE!
The crucial word was ASK.
I HAVE LOST THE ENTIRE UNIVERSE. DO YOU KNOW HOW THAT FEELS?
WELL, ASK YOUR-SELF!

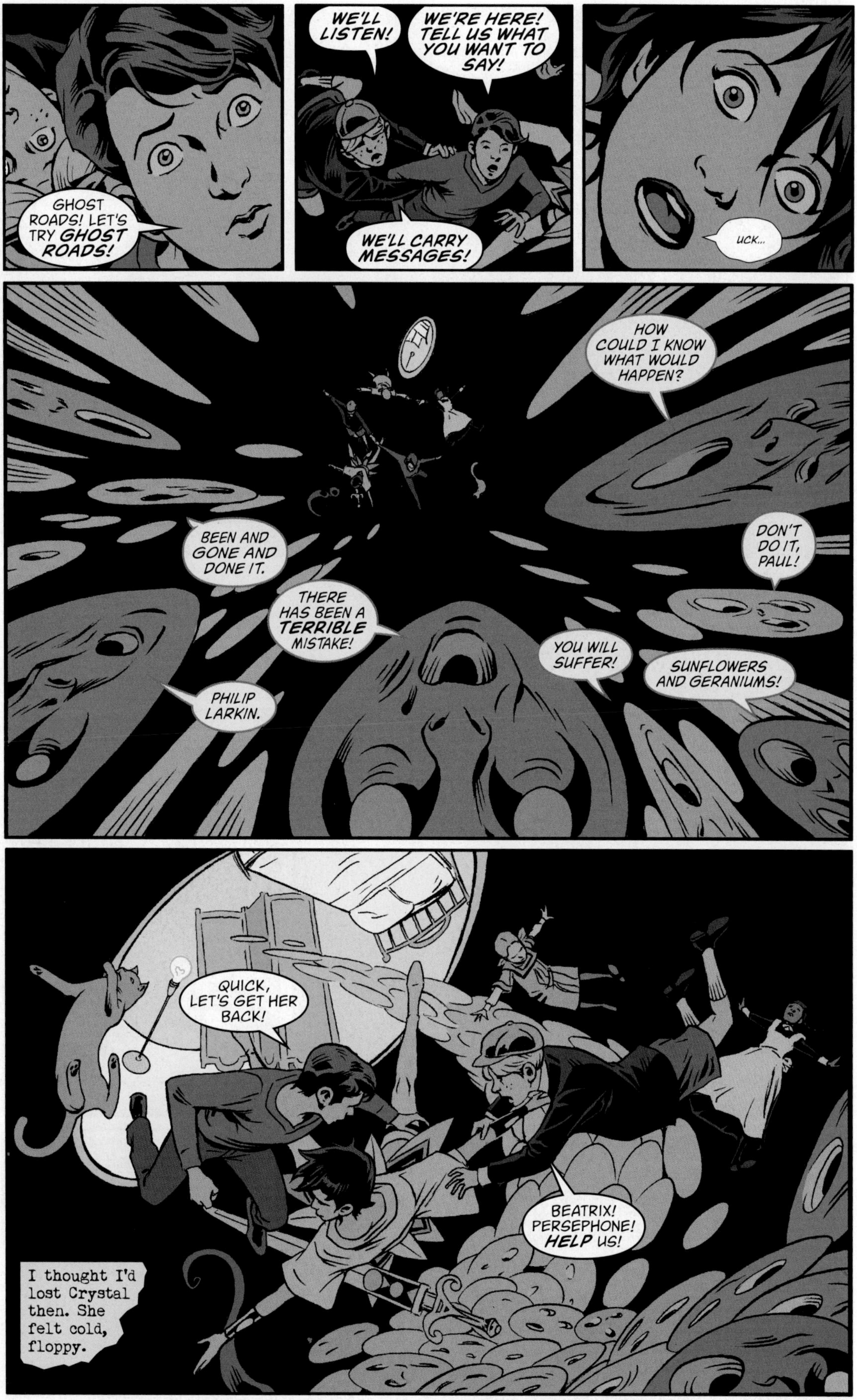
GHOST ROADS! LET'S TRY GHOST ROADS!
WE'LL LISTEN!
WE'RE HERE! TELL US WHAT YOU WANT TO SAY!
WE'LL CARRY MESSAGES!
UCK...
HOW COULD I KNOW WHAT WOULD HAPPEN?
BEEN AND GONE AND DONE IT.
DON'T DO IT, PAUL!
THERE HAS BEEN A TERRIBLE MISTAKE!
YOU WILL SUFFER!
SUNFLOWERS AND GERANIUMS!
PHILIP LARKIN.
QUICK, LET'S GET HER BACK!
BEATRIX! PERSEPHONE! HELP US!
I thought I'd lost Crystal then. She felt cold, floppy.

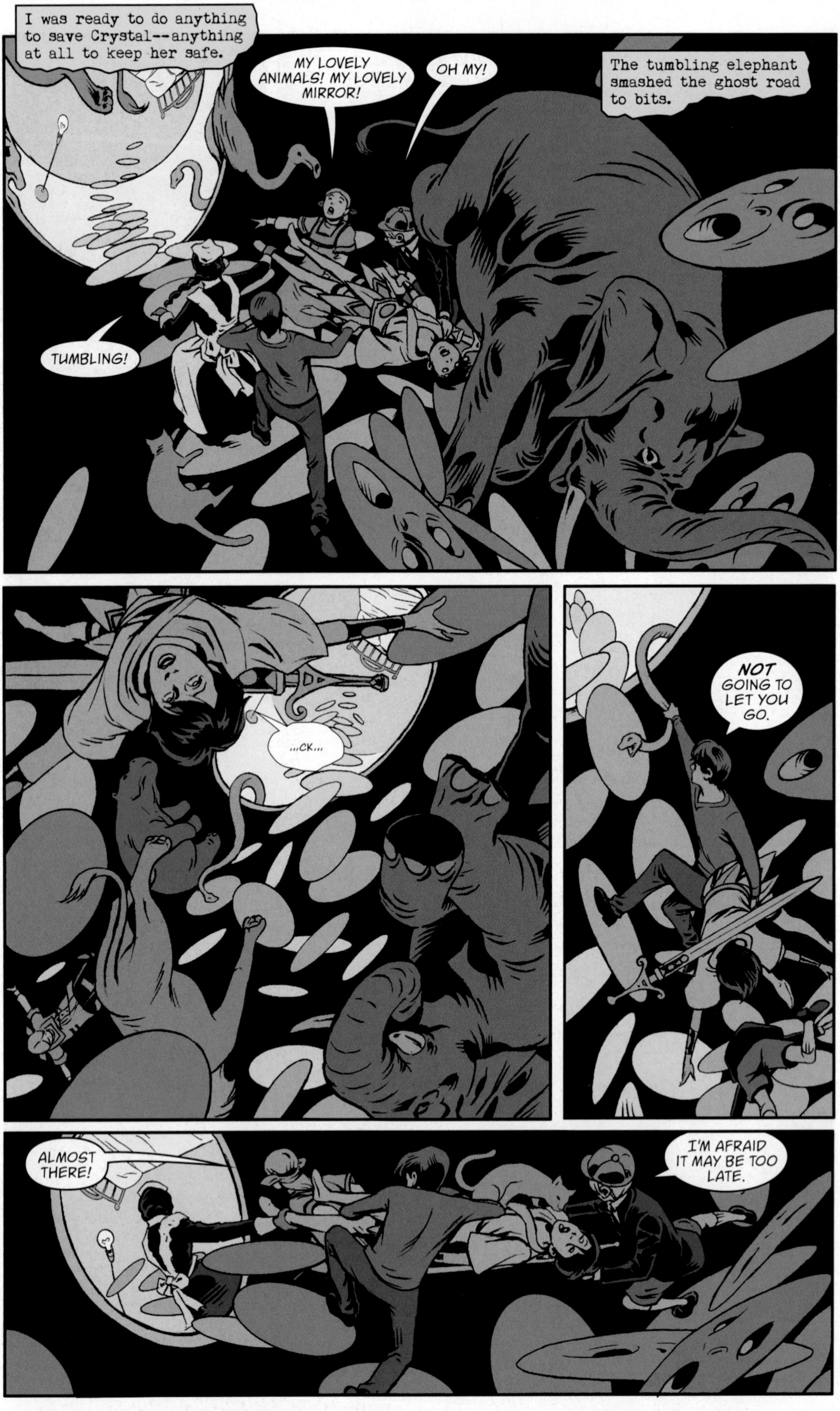
I was ready to do anything to save Crystal--anything at all to keep her safe.
MY LOVELY ANIMALS! MY LOVELY MIRROR!
OH MY!
The tumbling elephant smashed the ghost road to bits.
TUMBLING!
...CK...
NOT GOING TO LET YOU GO.
ALMOST THERE!
I'M AFRAID IT MAY BE TOO LATE.

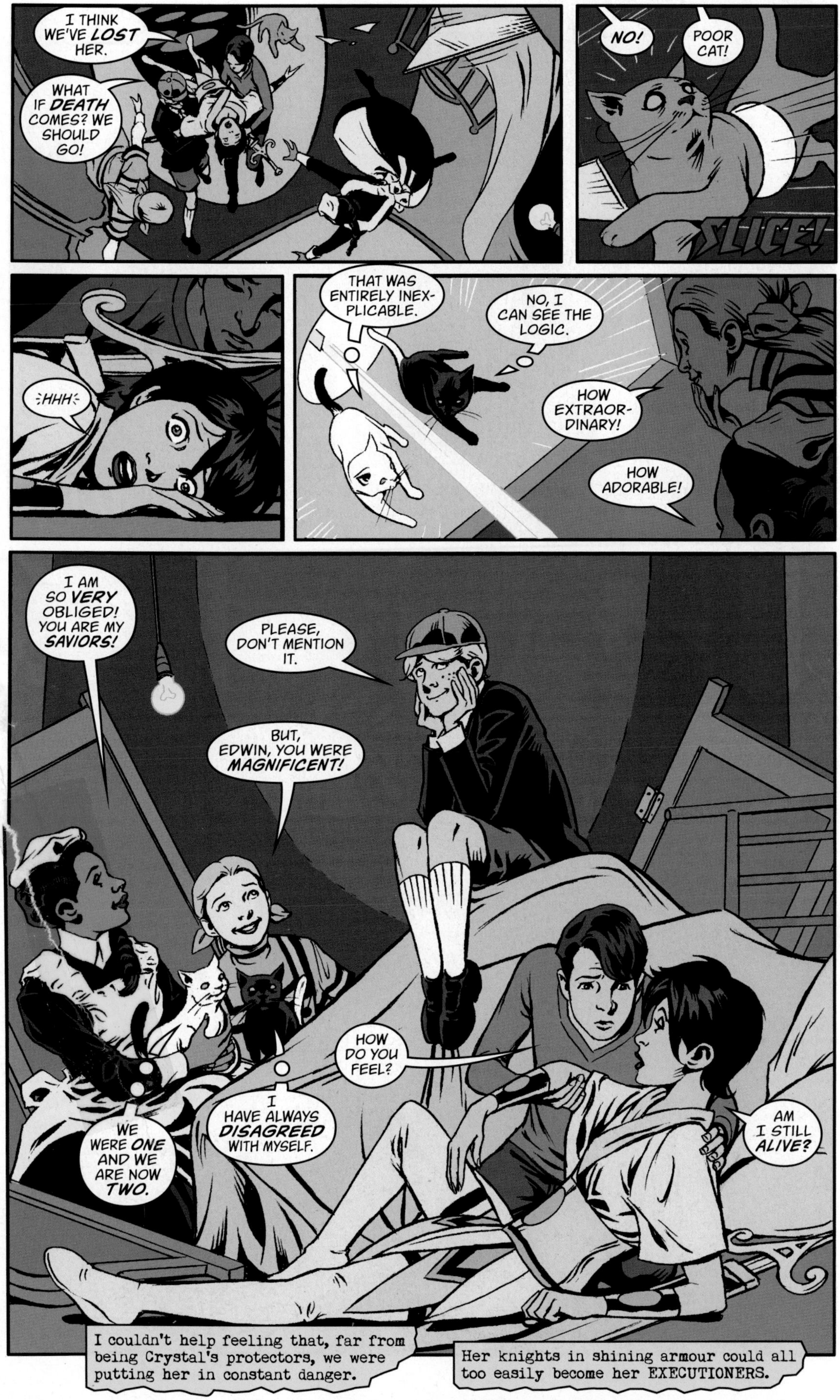
I THINK WE'VE LOST HER.
WHAT IF DEATH COMES? WE SHOULD GO!
NO!
POOR CAT!
SLICE!
HHH
THAT WAS ENTIRELY INEXPLICABLE.
NO, I CAN SEE THE LOGIC.
HOW EXTRAORDINARY!
HOW ADORABLE!
I AM SO VERY OBLIGED! YOU ARE MY SAVIORS!
PLEASE, DON'T MENTION IT.
BUT, EDWIN, YOU WERE MAGNIFICENT!
HOW DO YOU FEEL?
AM I STILL ALIVE?
WE WERE ONE AND WE ARE NOW TWO.
I HAVE ALWAYS DISAGREED WITH MYSELF.
I couldn't help feeling that, far from being Crystal's protectors, we were putting her in constant danger.
Her knights in shining armour could all too easily become her EXECUTIONERS.

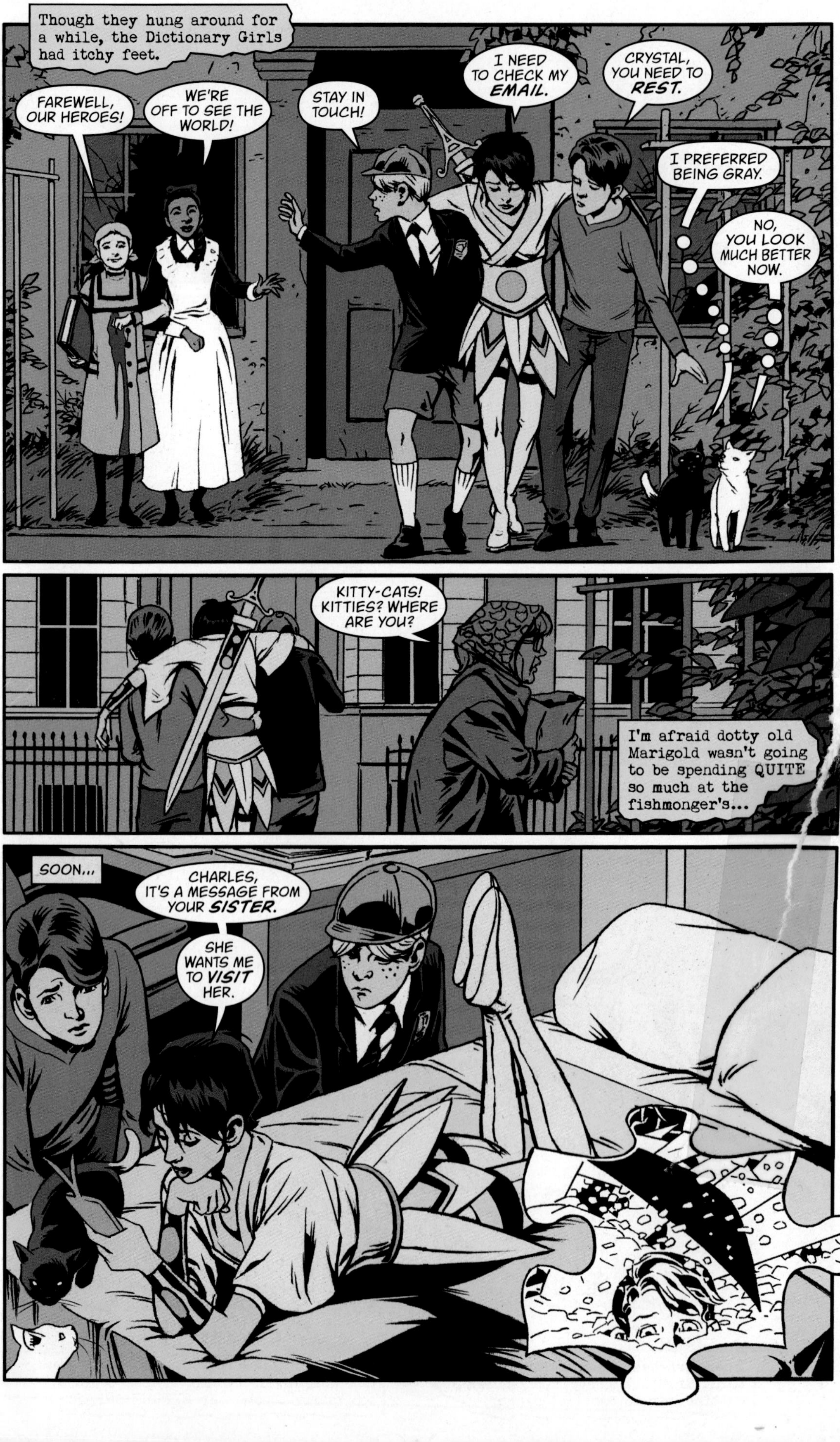

Though they hung around for a while, the Dictionary Girls had itchy feet.
FAREWELL, OUR HEROES!
WE'RE OFF TO SEE THE WORLD!
STAY IN TOUCH!
I NEED TO CHECK MY EMAIL.
CRYSTAL, YOU NEED TO REST.
I PREFERRED BEING GRAY.
NO, YOU LOOK MUCH BETTER NOW.
KITTY-CATS! KITTIES? WHERE ARE YOU?
I'm afraid dotty old Marigold wasn't going to be spending QUITE so much at the fishmonger's...
SOON...
CHARLES, IT'S A MESSAGE FROM YOUR SISTER.
SHE WANTS ME TO VISIT HER.